Trust, Organizations and the Digital Economy

Trust is a pervasive catalyst of human and business relationships that has inspired interest in researchers and practitioners alike. It has been shown to enhance engagement, communication, organizational performance, and online activities. Despite its role to cultivate cooperation, knowledge-sharing, and innovation, trust through digital means or even trust in digital media has presented new opportunities and challenges in society. Examples include wider and faster dissemination of trust-influencing messages, and richer options of digital cues that engage, disrupt, or even transform how trust is formulated. Despite that, trust helps people to live through risky and uncertain situations, and the many capabilities enabled on the digital platforms have made the formation and sustaining of trust very different compared to traditional means.

Trust in today's digital environment plays an important role and is intertwined with concepts including reliability, quality, and privacy. This book aims to bring together the theory and practice of trust in the new digital era and will present theoretical and practical foundations. Trust is not given; we must work to build it, but it is a very fragile and intangible asset once built. It is easy to destroy and challenging to rebuild.

Researchers, academics, and students in the fields of management, responsibility, and business ethics will gain knowledge on trust and related concepts, learn about the theoretical underpinnings of trust and how it sustains itself through digital dissemination, and explore empirically validated practice regarding trust and its related concepts.

Joanna Paliszkiewicz is a Professor and Director of the Management Institute at Warsaw University of Life Sciences, Poland.

Kuanchin Chen is a John W. Snyder Faculty Fellow, Professor of Computer Information Systems, and Co-director of the Center for Business Analytics at Western Michigan University, USA.

Routledge Advances in Management and Business Studies

Management Theory, Innovation, and Organisation
A Model of Managerial Competencies
Katarzyna Szczepańska-Woszczyna

Collaborative Spaces at Work
Innovation, Creativity and Relations
Edited by Fabrizio Montanari, Elisa Mattarelli and Elisa Mattarelli

Online Place Branding
The Case of Hong Kong
Phoenix Lam

Performance Drivers in the Australian Banking and Financial Industry
Ami-Lee Kelly, Ashish Malik and Philip J. Rosenberger III

Public Value and the Digital Economy
Usman W. Chohan

Management Education and Automation
Edited by Hamid H. Kazeroony and Denise Tsang

Trust, Organizations and the Digital Economy
Theory and Practice
Edited by Joanna Paliszkiewicz and Kuanchin Chen

Chinese Business and the Belt and Road Initiative
Institutional Strategies
Jerry J. Zhang

Management Control Systems, Decision-Making, and Innovation Development
The CDI Model
Dawid Szutowski

For more information about this series, please visit: www.routledge.com/Routledge-Advances-in-Management-and-Business-Studies/book-series/SE0305

Trust, Organizations and the Digital Economy

Theory and Practice

Edited by Joanna Paliszkiewicz and Kuanchin Chen

Routledge
Taylor & Francis Group
NEW YORK AND LONDON

First published 2022
by Routledge
605 Third Avenue, New York, NY 10158

and by Routledge
2 Park Square, Milton Park, Abingdon, Oxon, OX14 4RN

Routledge is an imprint of the Taylor & Francis Group, an informa business

Library of Congress Cataloging-in-Publication Data
Names: Paliszkiewicz, Joanna Olga, editor. | Chen, Kuanchin, editor.
Title: Trust, organizations and the digital economy: theory and practice/edited by Joanna Paliszkiewicz and Kuanchin Chen.
Description: 1 Edition. | New York, NY: Routledge, 2022. | Series: Routledge advances in management and business studies | Includes bibliographical references and index.
Identifiers: LCCN 2021016742 (print) | LCCN 2021016743 (ebook) | ISBN 9780367762148 (hardback) | ISBN 9780367762186 (paperback) | ISBN 9781003165965 (ebook)
Subjects: LCSH: Organizational change. | Information technology--Management. | Communication in management. | Social responsibility of business. | Employee motivation. | Trust.
Classification: LCC HD58.8 .T778 2022 (print) | LCC HD58.8 (ebook) | DDC 658.3/15--dc23
LC record available at https://lccn.loc.gov/2021016742
LC ebook record available at https://lccn.loc.gov/2021016743

ISBN: 978-0-367-76214-8 (hbk)
ISBN: 978-0-367-76218-6 (pbk)
ISBN: 978-1-003-16596-5 (ebk)

DOI: 10.4324/9781003165965

Typeset in Sabon
by MPS Limited, Dehradun

This book is dedicated to my husband Radek, daughter Natalia and friends who constantly motivate me to stay resilient and encouraged.

Joanna

To my wife Cathy and my children for your love and encouragement

KC

Contents

Tables

Figures

Editors

Joanna Paliszkiewic works as a full professor at the Warsaw University of Life Sciences (WULS—SGGW). She is the director of the Management Institute. She is also an adjunct professor at the University of Vaasa in Finland. She is well recognized in Poland and abroad for her expertise in management issues: knowledge management and trust management. She has published over 210 papers/manuscripts and is the author/co-author/editor of 13 books.

She has been a part of many scholarship endeavors in the United States, Ireland, Slovakia, Taiwan, the United Kingdom, and Hungary. She has actively participated in presenting research results at various international conferences. Currently, she serves as the deputy editor-in-chief of the *Management and Production Engineering Review*. She is an associate editor for the *Journal of Computer Information Systems, Expert Systems with Applications*, and *Intelligent Systems with Applications*. She is the vice president of the Polish Association for Production Engineering. She also serves as chair of the International Cooperation in European Business Club. She serves as the vice president of the International Association for Computer Information Systems in the United States. She is a board member of the Intellectual Capital Accreditation Association. She has successfully supervised many Ph.D. students leading them to completion of their degrees. She has also served as an external reviewer for several Ph.D. students in Poland, India, and Finland. She is actively involved in participating in the scientific committees of many international conferences. She was named the 2013 Computer Educator of the Year by IACIS.

Kuanchin Chen is a Professor of Computer Information Systems and John W. Snyder Faculty Fellow at Western Michigan University. He is a co-director of WMU's Center for Business Analytics and also an associate editor of the *Behaviour & Information Technology* journal. His research interests include electronic business, analytics, social networking, project management, privacy, security & trust, online behavioral issues, data mining, and human-computer interactions. He has published in journals, such as *Information Systems Journal, Decision Support Systems, Information &*

Management, IEEE Transactions on Systems, Man, and Cybernetics, International Journal of Information Management, Journal of Database Management, Internet Research, Communications of the Association for Information Systems, Electronic Commerce Research and Applications, Journal of Global Information Management, DATA BASE for Advances in Information Systems, IEEE Transactions on Education, Decision Sciences Journal of Innovative Education, International Journal of Medical Informatics, Journal of Computer Information Systems and many others. He has been editor, associate editor, and editorial member of several scholarly journals. Dr. Chen is also the recipient of several research and teaching awards, including awards given by scholarly journals and conferences, department, college, university, and U.S. Fulbright program. He has frequently been invited to present research talks at universities, government agencies, and other institutions.

Contributors

Agnieszka Biernat-Jarka, Warsaw University of Life Sciences, Poland

Michał Borowy, Warsaw University of Life Sciences, Poland

Joseph Rene Corbeil, The University of Texas Rio Grande Valley, USA

Maria Elena Corbeil, The University of Texas Rio Grande Valley, USA

Piroska Dobos, University Doctoral School on Safety and Security Sciences, Hungary

Grzegorz Dziczkowski, University of Economics in Katowice, Poland

Monika Gębska, Warsaw University of Life Sciences, Poland

Szymon Głowania, University of Economics in Katowice, Poland

Jerzy Gołuchowski, University of Economics in Katowice. Poland

Jeretta Horn Nord, Oklahoma State University, USA

Sławomir Jarka, Warsaw University of Life Sciences, Poland

Anna Jasiulewicz, Warsaw University of Life Sciences, Poland

Ewa Jaska, Warsaw University of Life Sciences, Poland

Anna Korombel, Czestochowa University of Technology, Poland

Barbara Kożuch, Jagiellonian University in Krakow, Poland

Olga Ławińska, Czestochowa University of Technology, Poland

Anna Losa-Jończyk, University of Economics in Katowice. Poland

Magdalena Mądra Sawicka, Warsaw University of Life Sciences, Poland

Marek Matejun, University of Lodz, Poland

Konrad Michalski, Warsaw University of Life Sciences, Poland

Daria Murawska, Warsaw University of Life Sciences, Poland

Andrzej Parzonko, Warsaw University of Life Sciences, Poland

Piotr Pietrzak, Warsaw University of Life Sciences, Poland

Wojciech Pizło, Warsaw University of Life Sciences, Poland

Marcin Ratajczak, Warsaw University of Life Sciences, Poland

Henryk Runowski, Warsaw University of Life Sciences, Poland

Ewa Stawicka, Warsaw University of Life Sciences, Poland

Piotr Sulewski, Warsaw University of Life Sciences, Poland

Katalin Takács-György, Takács-György, Óbuda University, Hungary

Josu Takala, University of Vaasa, Finland

Vesa-Jukka Vornanen, City of Kotka, Finland

Adam Wąs, Warsaw University of Life Sciences, Poland

Agnieszka Werenowska, Warsaw University of Life Sciences, Poland

Ludwik Wicki, Warsaw University of Life Sciences, Poland

Joanna Wyleżałek, Warsaw University of Life Sciences, Poland

Barbara Wyrzykowska, Warsaw University of Life Sciences, Poland

Bogna Zacny, University of Economics in Katowice, Poland

Foreword

This 21-chapter edited book by Joanna Paliszkiewicz and Kuanchin Chen is an appealing read that focuses on challenges and opportunities of trust in the digital economy that affects practitioners and academics. It also points the organizations in the right direction to understand trust for competitive advantage.

The first nine chapters contain the theoretical foundations with various topics, i.e., the meaning and interdisciplinary nature of trust, the dimensions of trust, the global politics concerning trust culture, trust in business, trust and AI, trust and virtual organizations, CSR communications, creating a framework for analysis, and trust in machine-learning systems.

The remaining 12 chapters cover issues and challenges of trust in the digital economy. These topics are diverse and are almost guaranteed to attract the readers' attention. Each chapter uniquely stands to offer insights into the topic it examines and discusses.

The book is a good read. The topics are interesting and engaging. This book offers immense insights into and knowledge about trust, organizations, and the digital economy. It can easily capture the interest of university professors, practitioners, and organizations.

Alex Koohang, PhD
Eminent Scholar and Peyton Anderson
Endowed Chair in Information Technology, Professor of Information Technology
Middle Georgia State University, USA

Foreword

Principally, I'm honored to be requested to write a foreword for this book edited by Joanna Paliszkiewicz and Kuanchin Chen.

With the stunning developments in digitalization in all spheres of life, the curiosity on understanding these novelties is rising in importance synchronously. This book is starting to a new thread to discover the concept, dimensions, and applications of trust on organizations in the digitalized economy. The concept of trust is the fundamental element in building and sustaining the relationship, social constructs, or communities. However, the developments in the information and communication technologies cause the concept of trust and its applications to reevaluate and reconceptualize.

This book presents theoretical and practical perspectives concerning how trust is built and developed in new practices such as digitalization, artificial intelligence, virtual organizations and teams, digital economy, machine-learning systems, Internet technologies, social media, and blockchain. Thus, this book serves as a great example of a future guide to help researchers and practitioners to understand the concept, roles, and functions of trust in the digitalized environment.

Fatih Çetin, PhD
Professor of Management
Niğde Ömer Halisdemir University, Turkey

Preface

Trust is an important element in business and society that has attracted researchers and practitioners from many disciplines. Trust is essential to foster cooperation, knowledge-sharing, and innovation. Trust helps people to live in a risky and uncertain situation. Increasing engagement, improving communication, and influencing organizational performance are among the benefits of trust. Trust has also been shown to influence technology adoption, online transaction, social media, and website usage decisions.

As contexts vary across how trust is built and exercised, it is not a concept that can be easily researched from a limited disciplinary lens. As we see trust being studied in different contexts, scope, and targets, readers of this book will benefit from theoretical and practical implications drawn from multiple disciplines. This book presents the main challenges and opportunities posed by trust in the digital economy in a manner relevant to both practitioners and scholars. The book is also useful for companies and organizations to leverage trust for an optimal course of action.

The purpose of this book is to bring together the theory and practice of trust, organizations, and the digital economy. The book has two parts: theoretical and practical.

The first theoretical part contains nine chapters. The purpose of **Chapter 1** is to present the meaning and interdisciplinary nature of trust in the digital economy based on a critical literature review and to propose opportunities for future research in this area. **Chapter 2** discusses research on the new dimensions of trust that are important while more and more interactions of individuals and organizations are increasingly conducted digitally. **Chapter 3** attempts to demonstrate the relationship between global politics implemented using mass media and social changes in the area of the culture of trust, taking into account the intentional actions of political actors, which have their strong connection with economic interests. **Chapter 4** presents the problem of trust in business relationships. This analysis focuses on trust in an organization and the trust-building process in teams both within and outside the organization. **Chapter 5** discusses the benefits and challenges of

AI in education, current and emerging AI applications at all educational levels and best practice resources for increasing stakeholder trust in and responsible use of AI to manage the academic enterprise and prepare learners for today and tomorrow's careers. The aim of **Chapter 6** is to identify the research gap concerning the issues relating to virtual organizations and virtual teams as well as the subject of trust as the factor moderating team performance. **Chapter 7** focuses on the role of CSR communication strategies in trust-building and consumer engagement. **Chapter 8** provides insights into the state of the art of the digital economy and digital trust. The aim of **Chapter 9** is to characterize the concept of trust in the context of artificial intelligence systems and present methods to increase the level of trust in the results of machine learning algorithms.

The second section entitled: "Trust in the Digital Economy: Issues and Challenges" contains 10 chapters. **Chapter 10** focuses on trust and modern Internet technology solutions in the banking sector. The aim is to check whether stakeholders trust modern banking solutions and which elements contribute to building trust in IoT in banking. **Chapter 11** focuses on trust as a factor influencing the willingness to pay taxes. The hypothesis that people's trust in the government as well as in the legal and judicial system has a positive effect on the willingness to pay taxes has been confirmed. **Chapter 12** presents the crucial role of trust in adapting logistics to the new condition. The main aim of the chapter is to introduce the term of trust in the context of changes in contemporary logistics taking into account current obstacles such as the COVID-19 crisis. **Chapter 13** presents the mutual trust in the city strategy implementation. The implementation of a power-free system for control preparedness process and perform joint city operations during the COVID-19 crisis is presented. **Chapter 14** focuses on determining blockchain technology's effect on the level of consumers' trust in the food production process. **Chapter 15** shows the role of digital technology in building trust in agriculture. The research results present the possibility of trust-building through the implementation of digital technologies. **Chapter 16** is entitled, "Influence of Trust Level on Insurance Decisions of Farmers. "The research aims at examining the level of farmers' trust in insurers based on previous business experiences with them. **Chapter 17** focuses on building trust and managing brand relationships with stakeholders. The results indicate that both dimensions of trust (trustworthy image and assessment of partners' reliability) play a role of a significant moderator in the process of external support exploitation in small businesses. The main aim of **Chapter 18** is to define the function and indicate possibilities of using the Internet in trust-building for the products and services offered by innovative start-ups. **Chapter 19** is entitled "Trust Building Strategy among Food Listed Companies in the Digital Economy E". investors quick information to evaluate and monitor the companies performance and keeps building trust among key stakeholders. The aim of **Chapter 20** is to identify enterprises' social media activities that earn the most trust in the brand among Gen Zers, inducing them to make purchasing decisions. **Chapter 21** describes social media as a tool for building trust and managing brand relationships with customers.

This book provides a theoretical and practical background related to trust, organizations, and the digital economy. The editors believe that the collection of chapters can be relevant to professionals, researchers, and student's needs. The authors try to diagnose the situation and show the new challenges related to trust and the digital economy.

Part I

Trust: Theoretical Foundations

1 The Meaning and Interdisciplinary Nature of Trust in the Digital Economy – Future Directions

Joanna Paliszkiewicz[1], *Jerzy Gołuchowski*[2], *and Kuanchin Chen*[3]

[1] *Warsaw University of Life Sciences*
[2] *University of Economics in Katowice*
[3] *Western Michigen University*

Introduction

Trust has long been recognized as a key catalyst for the success of many human activities. Researchers and practitioners have explored the meaning and nature of trust for decades (e.g., Mayer et al., 1995; Paliszkiewicz, 2013; Paliszkiewicz & Koohang, 2016). The role of trust in the digital economy is even more significant because communication cues that are often present in face-to-face interactions are minimal or even nonexistent in the virtual world. Trust is essential in building employee commitment (Eikeland, 2015; Lewicka & Krot, 2015), loyalty (Costigan et al., 1998), communication and knowledge exchange (Malhotra & Murnighan, 2002; Young & Daniel, 2003; Tyler, 2003; Li et al., 2010; Hakanen & Soudunsaari, 2012; Bencsik & Juhasz, 2020), effective implementation of strategies (Doney et al., 1998), learning (Koole, 2020), and organizational performance (Paliszkiewicz et al., 2014; Paliszkiewicz et al., 2015; Koohang et al., 2017).

The aim of this chapter is to present the meaning and interdisciplinary nature of trust in the digital economy based on a critical literature review and propose opportunities for future research in this area. In this chapter, the definitions of trust and future research are presented, drawing findings from disciplines such as psychology, sociology, economy, management, and information systems (e-commerce, virtual communities, artificial intelligence, and security policy). The chapter concludes with the limitations of the study and general future directions.

DOI: 10.4324/9781003165965-1

The Definition and Future Directions of Trust in Different Disciplines

Psychology

In psychology research, trust is related to personality and how that personality functions in human interactions. For example, trust is described by Rotter (1967) as an expectancy, belief, or feeling that is deeply rooted in personality and has its origins in an individual's early psychosocial development. Personality psychologists such as Wrightsman (1966) have viewed trust as a personality trait that reflects the general expectancies of others' trustworthiness. This form of trust relates to a person's innate nature that characterizes the person's propensity to trust, which is empirically verified as an antecedent of trust (Liao et al., 2011).

According to Gibb (1978), trust is very close to love and instinctive. People differ in terms of how much and when they are willing to trust (Das & Teng, 2004). Yakovleva et al. (2010) defined trust as a dyadic construct in which one party's behavior influences the other party's perceptions and actions. More research is needed concerning personality and propensity to trust, especially to technology and artificial intelligence (AI). As AI increasingly performs the tasks that were once performed by humans, fear of being replaced by AI lingers. However, opportunities abound for both humans and AI to contribute what they excel at doing in a symbiosis way. Despite this goal-oriented perspective that centers on both parties' benefits, it also takes the proper psychological processes and personality traits to build successful collaboration. Further research should explore how trust is developed in this symbiosis or other human–AI relationships.

Sociology

Sociologists described trust as a part of the social structure and base for any relationship (e.g., Garfinkel, 1967; Granoveter, 1985; Shapiro, 1987). Work by Fukuyama (1995), Lincoln (1990), and Fisman and Khanna (1999) suggests that approaches to trust are related to national and social culture. Sztompka (1999) described trust as the expectation that other people, groups, or institutions with whom we interact will act in ways conducive to our well-being. Shapiro (1987, p. 626) defines trust as "a social relationship in which principals [...] invest resources, authority or responsibility in another to act on their behalf for some uncertain future return". Rousseau et al. (1998) defined social trust as the willingness to accept the vulnerability to others' actions based on positive expectations regarding those others' intentions and/or behavior. Differences in trust can be specific to a country or culture (Zaheer & Zaheer, 2006). Although cross-cultural studies on trust have been popular (Bond & Forgas, 1984; Zhang & Bond, 1993), trust also varies across other levels of human societies (country, society, culture, region, religion, and organization). The interwoven relationships across multiple of these levels still require further investigations. Trust is particularly relevant in the digital era because collaborations are performed across one or more of these societal levels. This kind of research is essential to drive successful international business relations and enhance collaborations between people and various organizations.

Economics

Trust is also of interest in economics. For example, Anderson and Naurus (1990) defined trust as a firm's belief that another firm will perform actions resulting in positive outcomes for both firms and not take unexpected actions that would result in negative consequences. Sako (1992) considered trust to be a state of mind, an expectation held by one trading partner about another who will behave or respond in a predictable and mutually acceptable manner. According to Ganesan (1994), trust is the willingness to rely on an exchange partner in whom one has confidence. James (2002) described trust as an expectation that people will not be exploited by others, which exists when there are no strong incentives for people to behave opportunistically. According to Bromiley and Cummings (1992), trust reduces transaction costs. The literature review confirmed that trust substantially affects economic growth, and it is a necessary factor for economic development (Zak & Knack, 2001).

Trust in economics is often a calculated trust that factors risk into the trust equations, predicts another actor's behavior or expectations, and maximizes benefits for involved parties. Further study is needed in this calculative trust, perceived risk, and prognosis of people's behavior in a virtual environment.

Management Science

Trust is an essential concept in management (Grudzewski et al., 2007), including trust and team performance (Lin et al., 2016), collaboration (Leung et al., 2013), integration (Morita & Burns, 2014), communication and knowledge management (McAllister, 1995;Lewis & Weigert, 1985), and leadership (Koohang et al., 2017). In management, trust is conceptualized as an individual's state of mind. Mayer et al. (1995, p. 712) characterized trust as "the willingness of a party to be vulnerable to the actions of another party based on the expectation that the other party will perform a particular action important to the trustor". Paliszkiewicz (2013) defined trust as the belief and optimistic expectation that another party will act in such a way that it is beneficial to the trusting party and will act reliably and behave or respond in a predictable and mutually acceptable manner.

In management, further studies are needed to explain the factors influencing trust-building in organizations and between employees, especially in the virtual environment. It would be interesting to evaluate how and why trust changes over time. Research is also needed to expand on the dark side of trust and trust breaches. Future research can examine the main effects as well as mediators and moderators of organizational trust.

Information Systems Research

Trust in information systems research has been shown in different domains, such as e-commerce (Papadopoulou et al., 2003; Liao et al., 2011; Xiao et al., 2016), virtual communities (Leimeister et al., 2006), artificial intelligence (Chen et al., 2008; Liou et al., 2016), and security policy (Koohang et al., 2020).

Trust in E-commerce

In e-commerce, trust is recognized as the bedrock for customer retention (Papadopoulou et al., 2003) that affects a consumer's intention to transact and share information (Liao et al., 2011). It is even more critical in electronic transactions than in the traditional market (Xiao et al., 2016). Trust in e-commerce concerns more about the transactional process and the parties involved (Kassim & Abdullah, 2008). Pavlou (2003, p. 106) described trust in e-commerce as "a belief that allows consumers to willingly become vulnerable to Web retailers after having taken the retailers' characteristics into consideration".

Understanding how trust is built and maintained dominates research in e-commerce because the switching cost for consumers to switch among different e-stores is low (Xiao et al., 2016). According to the aforementioned study, reputation, communication, familiarity, information quality, security, privacy, ease of use, and usefulness are often factors affecting trust for inexperienced buyers. In contrast, better support for service quality and system quality are the two most important factors that influence trust for experienced buyers (Kim et al., 2004; Chang & Chen, 2008; Jairak 2014; Ajzen 2002). Trust is essential for e-business's success not only in attracting new customers but also in retaining them (Mouriuchi & Takahashi, 2016).

Several ideas for future research can be suggested in this area. It would be interesting to evaluate how and why trust levels change over time. For example, how long do previous service encounters play a role in trust-building? How does trust vary across product or service life cycles? A final area for future research relates to a systematic approach to understanding customer perceptions and attitudes in virtual environments in different cultures.

Trust in Virtual Communities

The virtual community is comprised of members who share an interest, repeatedly interact, generate shared resources, develop governance policies, demonstrate reciprocity, and share cultural norms (Preece, 2000). Turban et al. (2006, p. 737) defined a virtual community as "a group of people with similar interests who interact with one another using the Internet". It is easier to create a website to satisfy consumer needs, but it takes a concerted effort to cultivate mutual trust in a virtual environment. Trust is the core element in social interactions as it influences the degrees and forms of interaction in cyberspace (Chen et al., 2008). Trust increases as members in a virtual community perform in accordance with social and behavioral norms. (Liou et al., 2016). Two kinds of trust are present in virtual societies: cognitive and affective trust (Lewis & Weigert, 1985; McAllister, 1995). Cognitive trust is based on the reliability and credibility of members in a community (Johnson & Grayson, 2005), whereas affective trust is based on care and concern (Corritore et al., 2003). Trust decreases the uncertainty in a virtual environment and enhances information sharing (Chai & Kim, 2010; Wu & Sukoco, 2010). Future research should examine the dynamics of trust and distrust, including research addressing how different cultures meet and interact and how diverse communities learn to trust each other.

Trust and Artificial Intelligence

AI has changed the attitude to human–technology relationships. Gillath et al. (2021) suggest that the way humans treat each other is potentially similar to how they interact with or think about AI. AI is the simulation of human intelligence processes by computer systems. These processes include learning (the acquisition of information and rules for using the information), reasoning (using rules to reach approximate or definite conclusions), and self-correction. The research on trust in nonhumans (i.e., autonomous machines, robots, and AIs) also focuses on the cognitive route to trust (e.g., Stormont, 2008; Hancock et al., 2011; Akash et al., 2017) and affective factors (Gillath et al. 2021). Affective trust is based on a sense of security people gain from emotional bonds with others (Lewis & Weigert, 1985; Johnson & Grayson, 2005). Cognitive trust is related to people's willingness and ability to rely on others (Rempel et al., 1985). These so-called "others" could be AI applications ranging from narrowed or weak AI (e.g., voice commanded systems and GPS) to broad or strong AI (e.g., companion robots).

It is the societal norm that people tend to expect few or no errors from human experts (Jiang et al., 2004; Akash et al., 2017). The same expectation is also extended to nonhuman machines. Therefore, trust in AI could decrease when errors occur (Dzindolet et al., 2002). AI that shows anthropomorphism (such as companion robots and intelligent pets) engenders more trust (Waytz et al., 2014; Crandall et al., 2018), but those with aggressive-looking systems hinder trust (Siau & Wang, 2018). In a different study, Sarkar et al. (2017) found that people high on extraversion perceived interactions with robots as more positive. Mou and Xu (2017) have demonstrated that people showed more openness, agreeableness, extroversion, conscientiousness, and self-disclosure when interacting with humans than interacting with AI. Conversely, past negative experiences were shown to be associated with decreased trust in AI (Dikmen & Burns, 2017), in a fashion similar to trust in automation (Hengstler et al., 2016; Dikmen & Burns, 2017). Negative attitudes toward technology were also found to predict low trust in AI (self-driving taxis; Tussyadiah et al., 2017)

Despite that AI brings productivity, performance, and effectiveness while reducing stress and risks (e.g., Thau et al., 2007), fear of AI replacing jobs has long been part of the game. Signs of job loss due to automation and intelligent systems began when the industry started using such systems. However, new opportunities are also created for a symbiotic relationship between humans and AI. Further studies are needed to explain how to build and rebuild trust in AI systems and the role of trust in such human-AI symbiosis.

Trust and Security Policy

Trust is also related to information security. Information security policy is defined as the "... aggregate of directives, regulations, rules, and practices that prescribes how an organization manages, protects, and distributes information" (Nieles, 2017, p. 26). Trustworthy security implements in organizations reduce resistance to security mechanisms' deployment (Sasse et al., 2007; Keval & Sasse, 2010; Toh & Srinivas, 2012).

Trust has other different meanings taking under consideration hard and soft security. In hard security, trust is implied in the security mechanism itself. Trust in soft security is related to the mechanism of controlling access (Hexmoor et al., 2006). A higher level of trust in technology is linked to a better quality of security decisions made by employees (Kirschenbaum et al., 2012). Individuals' perceptions about technology's security also increase their trust in technology (Ajzen, 2002; Taherdoost et al., 2011).

Conclusion

In this chapter, approaches to trust and possible future research directions were presented, drawing findings from disciplines, including psychology, sociology, management, economy, and information system research (e-commerce, virtual communities, artificial intelligence, and security policy).

Summarizing the presented reflection on the nature of trust, we can find that trust in the digital economy is regarded as:

- An individual feature from the viewpoint of personality theories,
- The belief in the positive intentions, attitudes, and behavior of others,
- An attitude of the trustor about the trustee,
- An intention of the trustee to act in the trustor's interests, and
- A feeling that the trustee is benevolent.

The presented study has some limitations. By restricting literature review to the ProQuest and Google Scholar, Google books databases, this publication may not have allowed a complete coverage of all empirical studies across different fields. Still, it was possible to observe the main trends of research.

The review of empirical studies has brought several possible research directions. Besides, the authors also see the general areas that need more or even deeper attention to shed light on how trust plays in the digital economy. Examples of these areas include long-term tracking of trust changes, comparative studies including multiple societal levels, and how emerging technologies engender trust. Methodological improvements in measuring (e.g., mix-method approaches), monitoring (e.g., functional MRI), and tracking (e.g., long-term behavior-tracking) trust will likely lead to new insights.

References

Ajzen, I. (2002). Perceived behavioral control, self-efficacy, locus of control, and the theory of planned behavior. *Journal of Applied Social Psychology*, *32*, 665–668.

Akash, K., Hu, W., Reid, T., & Jain, N. (2017). Dynamic modeling of trust in human-machine interactions. *American Control Conference*. Seattle, WA, 1542–1548.

Anderson, J. C., & Naurus, J. (1990). A model of distributor firm and manufacturer firm working partnerships. *Journal of Marketing*, *54*, 42–58.

Bencsik, A., & Juhasz, T. (2020). Impacts of informal knowledge sharing (workplace gossip) on organisational trust. *Economics and Sociology*, *13*(1), 249–270.

Bond, M. H., & Forgas, J. P. (1984). Linking person perception to behavior intention across cultures: The role of cultural collectivism. *Journal of Cross-Cultural Psychology*, *15*(3), 337–352.

Bromiley, P., & Cummings, L. L. (1992). *Transaction costs in organizations with trust*. Working paper, No. 28. University of Minnesota, Strategic Management Research Center, Minneapolis.

Chai, S., & Kim, M. (2010). What makes bloggers share knowledge? An investigation on the role of trust. *International Journal of Information Management*, *30*(5), 408–415.

Chang, H. H., & Chen, S. W. (2008). The impact of online store environment cues on purchase intention: Trust and perceived risk as a mediator. *Online Information Review*, *32*(6), 818–841.

Chen, Y., Wu, J., & Chung, Y. (2008). Cultural impact on trust: A comparison of virtual communities in china, Hong Kong, and Taiwan. *Journal of Global Information Technology Management*, *11*(1), 28–48.

Corritore, C. L., Kracher, B., & Wiedenbeck, S. (2003). On-line trust: Concepts, evolving themes, a model. *International Journal of Human-Computer Studies*, *58*(6), 737–758.

Costigan, R. D., Ilter, S. S., & Berman, J. J. (1998). A multi-dimensional study of trust in organizations. *Journal of Managerial Issues*, *10*, 303–317.

Crandall, J. W., Oudah, M., Tennom, Ishowo-Oloko, F., Abdallah, S., Bonnefon, J. F., Cebrian, M., Shariff, A., Goodrich, M. A., & Rahwan, I. (2018). Cooperating with machines. *Nature Communications*, *9*, 1–12. https://www.nature.com/articles/s41467-017-02597-8.pdf.

Das, T. K., & Teng, B. S. (2004). The risk-based view of trust: A conceptual framework. *Journal of Business and Psychology*, *19*(1), 85–116.

Dikmen, M., & Burns, C. M. (2017). Trust in autonomous vehicles: The case of Tesla autopilot and summon. In *2017 IEEE International Conference on Systems, Man, and Cybernetics (SMC)*.

Doney, P. M., Cannon, J. P., & Mullen, M. R. (1998). Understanding the influence of national culture on the development of trust. *Academy of Management Review*, *23*(3), 601–620.

Dzindolet, M. T., Pierce, L. G., Beck, H. P., & Dawe, L. A. (2002). The perceived utility of human and automated aids in a visual detection task. *Human Factors*, *44*, 79–94.

Eikeland, T. B. (2015). Emergent trust and work life relationships: How to approach the relational moment of trust. *Nordic Journal of Working Life Studies*, *5*(3), 59–77.

Fisman, R., & Khanna, T. (1999). Is trust a historical residue? Information flows and trust levels. *Journal of Economic Behavior Organization*, *38*(1), 79–92.

Fukuyama, F. (1995). Trust: The social virtues and the creation of prosperity. New York, NY: Free Press.

Ganesan, S. (1994). Determinant of long-term orientation in buyer-seller relationships. *Journal of Marketing*, *58*(April), 1–19.

Garfinkel, H. (1967). *Studies in ethnomethodology*. Englewood Cliffs, NJ: Prentice-Hall.

Gibb, J. R. (1978). *Trust, a new view of personal and organizational development*. Los Angeles, CA: Guild of Tutors Press, International College.

Gillath, O., Ai, T., Branicky, M. S., Keshmir, S., Davison, R. B., & Spaulding, R. (2021). Attachment and trust in artificial intelligence. *Computers in Human Behavior*, *115*. https://doi.org/10.1016/j.chb.2020.106607.

Granoveter, M. (1985). Economic action and social structure. *American Journal of Sociology*, *91*(3), 481–510.

Grudzewski, W. M., Hejduk, I. K., Sankowska, A., & Wańtuchowicz, M. (2007). *Zarządzanie zaufaniem w organizacjach wirtualnych* [Trust management in virtual organization]. Warsaw, PL: Difin.

Hakanen, M., & Soudunsaari, A. (2012). Building trust in high-performing teams. *Technology Innovation Management Review*, *2*(6), 38–41.

Hancock, P. A., Billings, D. R., Schaefer, K. E., Chen, J. Y., De Visser, E. J., & Parasuraman, R. (2011). A meta-analysis of factors affecting trust in human-robot interaction. *Human Factors*, *53*, 517–527.

Hengstler, M., Enkel, E., & Duelli, S. (2016). Applied artificial intelligence and trust-the case of autonomous vehicles and medical assistance devices. *Technological Forecasting and Social Change*, *105*, 105–120.

Hexmoor, H., Wilson, S., & Bhattaram, S. (2006). A theoretical inter-organizational trust-based security model. *The Knowledge Engineering Review*, *21*(2), 127–161.

Jairak, R., Praneetpolgrang, P., & Chirawichitchai, N. (2014). A roadmap for establishing trust management strategy in E-commerce services using quality-based assessment. *International Journal of Information Engineering and Electronic Business*, *6*(5), 1–9.

James, H. S. (2002). The trust paradox: A survey of economic inquiries into the nature of trust and trustworthiness. *Journal of Economic Behavior & Organization*, *47*, 291–307.

Jiang, X., Khasawneh, M. T., Master, R., Bowling, S. R., Gramopadhye, A. K., Melloy, B. J., & Grimes, L. (2004). Measurement of human trust in a hybrid inspection system based on signal detection theory measures. *International Journal of Industrial Ergonomics*, *34*, 407–419.

Johnson, D., & Grayson, K. (2005). Cognitive and affective trust in service relationships. *Journal of Business Research*, *58*(4), 500–507.

Kassim, N. M., & Abdullah, N. A. (2008). Customer loyalty in e-commerce settings: An empirical study. *Electronic Markets*, *18*(3), 275–290.

Keval, H. U., & Sasse, M. A. (2010). Not the usual suspects: A study of factors reducing the effectiveness of CCTV. *Security Journal*, *23*(2), 134–154.

Kim, H. W., Xu, Y., & Koh, J. (2004). A comparison of online trust building factors between potential customers and repeat customers. *Journal of the Association for Information Systems*, *5*(10), 392–420.

Kirschenbaum, A., Mariani, M., Van Gulijk, C., Lubasz, S., Rapoport, C., & Andriessen, H. (2012). Airport security: An ethnographic study. *Journal of Air Transport Management*, *18*(1), 68–73.

Koohang, A., Nowak, A., Paliszkiewicz, J., & Horn Nord, J. (2020). Information security policy compliance: Leadership, trust, role values, and awareness. *Journal of Computer Information Systems*, *60*(1), 1–8.

Koohang, A., Paliszkiewicz, J., & Gołuchowski, J. (2017). The impact of leadership on trust, knowledge management, and organizational performance: A research model. *Industrial Management & Data Systems*, *117*(3), 521–537.

Koole, B. (2020). Trusting to learn and learning to trust. A framework for analyzing the interactions of trust and learning in arrangements dedicated to instigating social change. *Technological Forecasting & Social Change*, *161*, 1–9.

Leimeister, J. M., Sidiras, P., & Krcmar, H. (2006). Exploring success factors of virtual communities: The perspectives of members and operators. *Journal of Organizational Computing & Electronic Commerce*, *16*(3/4), 279–300.

Leung, W. O., Liang, X., Priem, R., & Shaffer, M. (2013). Top management team trust, behavioral integration and the performance of international joint ventures. *Journal of Asia Business Studies*, *7*(2), 99–122.

Lewicka, D., & Krot, K. (2015). The model of HRM-trust-commitment relationships. *Industrial Management & Data Systems*, *115*(8), 1457–1480.
Lewis, D. J., & Weigert, A. (1985). Trust as a social reality. *Social Forces*, *63*(4), 967–985.
Li, J. J., Poppo, L., & Zhou, K. Z. (2010). Relational mechanisms, formal contracts, and local knowledge acquisition by international subsidiaries. *Strategic Management Journal*, *31*(4), 349–370.
Liao, C., Liu, C. C., & Chen, K. (2011). Examining the impact of privacy, trust and risk perceptions beyond monetary transactions: An integrated model. *Electronic Commerce Research and Applications*, *10*(6), 702–715.
Lin, H. L., Trang, T. D. H., & Yu-sheng, L. (2016). CEO transformational leadership and firm performance: A moderated mediation model of TMT trust climate and environmental dynamism. *Asia Pacific Journal of Management*, *33*(4), 981–1008.
Lincoln, J. R. (1990). Japanese organization and organization theory. *Research in Organizational Behavior*, *12*, 255–295.
Liou, D., Chih, W., Hsu, L., & Huang, C. (2016). Investigating information sharing behavior: The mediating roles of the desire to share information in virtual communities. *Information Systems and eBusiness Management*, *14*(2), 187–216.
Malhotra, D., & Murnighan, J. K. (2002). The effects of contracts on interpersonal trust. *Administrative Science Quarterly*, *47*(3), 534–559.
Mayer, R. C., Davis, J. H., & Schoorman, F. D. (1995). An integrative model of organizational trust. *Academy of Management Review*, *20*(3), 709–734.
McAllister, D. J. (1995). Affect and cognition based trust as foundations for interpersonal cooperation in organizations. *Academy of Management Journal*, *38*(1), 24–59.
Morita, P. P., & Burns, C. M. (2014). Trust tokens in team development. *Team Performance Management*, *20*(1/2), 39–64.
Mou, Y., & Xu, K. (2017). The media inequality: Comparing the initial human-human and human-AI social interactions. *Computers in Human Behavior*, *72*, 432–440.
Mouriuchi, E., & Takahashi, I. (2016). Satisfaction trust and loyalty of repeat online consumer within the Japanese online supermarket trade. *Australasian Marketing Journal*, *24*(2), 146–156.
Nieles, M., Dempsey, K., & Pillitteri, V. (2017). An introduction to information security. NIST Special Publication 800-12 Revision 1. Retrieved from website: https://nvlpubs.nist.gov/nistpubs/SpecialPublications/NIST.SP.800–12r1.pdf.
Paliszkiewicz, J. (2013). *Zaufanie w zarządzaniu*, [Trust in management]. Warszawa, PL: Wydawnictwo Naukowe PWN.
Paliszkiewicz, J., Gołuchowski, J., & Koohang, A. (2015). Leadership, trust, and knowledge management in relation to organizational performance: Developing an instrument. *Online Journal of Applied Knowledge Management*, *3*(2), 19–35.
Paliszkiewicz, J., & Koohang, A. (2016). *Social media and trust: A multinational study of university students*. Santa Rosa, CA: Informing Science Press.
Paliszkiewicz, J., Koohang, A., & Horn Nord, J. (2014). Management trust, organizational trust, and organizational performance: Empirical validation of an instrument. *Online Journal of Applied Knowledge Management*, *2*(1), 28–39.

Papadopoulou, P., Kanellis, P., & Martakos, D. (2003). Designing electronic commerce environments on trust-building principles. *Systèmes d'Information Et Management*, *8*(3), 55–74.

Pavlou, P. A. (2003). Consumer acceptance of electronic commerce: Integrating trust and risk with the technology acceptance model. *International Journal of Electronic Commerce*, *7*(3), 101–134.

Preece, J. (2000). *Online communities: Designing usability, supporting sociability*. Chichester, UK: John Wiley & Sons.

Rempel, J. K., Holmes, J. G., & Zanna, M. P. (1985). Trust in close relationships. *Journal of Personality and Social Psychology*, *49*, 95–112.

Rotter, J. B. (1967). A new scale of the measurement of interpersonal trust. *Journal of Personality*, *35*, 651–665.

Rousseau, D. M., Sitkin, S. B., Burt, R. S., & Camerer, C. (1998). Not so different after all: A cross-discipline view of trust. *Academy of Management Review*, *23*, 393–404.

Sako, M. (1992). *Prices, quality and trust, inter-firm relations*. Cambridge, UK: Britain & Japan: Cambridge University Press.

Sarkar, S., Araiza-Illan, D., & Eder, K. (2017). *Effects of faults, experience, and personality on trust in a robot Co-worker*. Retrieved from website: https://arxiv.org/abs/1703.02335.

Sasse, A., Ashenden, D., Lawrence, D., Coles-Kemp, L., Fléchais, I., & Kearney,P. (2007). *Human factors working group white paper: Human vulnerabilities in security systems knowledge transfer networks*. London, GB: University College London.

Shapiro, S. P. (1987). The social control of impersonal trust. *American Journal of Sociology*, *93*(3), 623–658.

Siau, K., & Wang, W. (2018). Trusting artificial intelligence in healthcare. In *24th Americas Conference on Information Systems* (New Orleans).

Stormont, D. P. (2008). Analyzing human trust of autonomous systems in hazardous environments. In *Proc. of the human implications of human-robot interaction workshop at AAAI* (pp. 27–32) Retrieved from website: https://www.aaai.org/Papers/Workshops/2008/WS-08-05/WS08-05-006.pdf.

Sztompka, P. (1999). *Trust: A sociological theory*. Cambridge, UK: Cambridge University Press.

Taherdoost, H., Sahibuddin, S., Namayandeh, M., & Jalaliyoon, N. (2011). Propose an educational plan for computer ethics and information security. *Procedia – Social and Behavioral Science*, *28*, 815–819.

Thau, S., Crossley, C., Bennett, R. J., & Sczesny, S. (2007). The relationship between trust, attachment, and antisocial work behaviors. *Human Relations*, *60*, 1155–1179.

Toh, S., & Srinivas, E. (2012). Perceptions of task cohesiveness and organizational support increase trust and information sharing between host country nationals and expatriate coworkers in Oman. *Journal of World Business*, *47*(4), 696–705.

Turban, E., King, D., Viehland, D., & Lee, J. (2006). *Electronic commerce: A managerial perspective*. Upper Saddle River, NJ: Pearson Education Inc.

Tussyadiah, I. P., Zach, F. J., & Wang, J. (2017). Attitudes toward autonomous on demand mobility system: The case of self-driving taxi. In R. Schegg &

B. Stangl (Eds.), *Information and Communication Technologies in Tourism 2017*. Cham, CH: Springer. https://doi.org/10.1007/978-3-319-51168-9_54.

Tyler, T. R. (2003). Trust within organisations. *Personnel Review*, *32*(5), 556–568.

Waytz, A., Heafner, J., & Epley, N. (2014). The mind in the machine: Anthropomorphism increases trust in an autonomous vehicle. *Journal of Experimental Social Psychology*, *52*, 113–117.

Wrightsman, L. S. (1966). Personality and attitudinal correlates of trusting and trustworthy behaviors in a two-person game. *Journal of Personality and Social Psychology*, *4*, 328–332.

Wu, W. Y., & Sukoco, B. M. (2010). Why should I share? Examining consumers' motives and trust on knowledge sharing. *Journal of Computer Information Systems*, *50*(4), 11–19.

Xiao, L., Guo, Z., D'Ambra, J., & Fu, B. (2016). Building loyalty in e-commerce. *Program*, *50*(4), 431–461.

Yakovleva, M., Reilly, R. R., & Werko, R. (2010). Why do we trust? Moving beyond individual to dyadic perceptions. *Journal of Applied Psychology*, *95*(1), 79–91.

Young, L., & Daniel, K. (2003). Affectual trust in the workplace. *International Journal of Human Resource Management*, *14*(1), 139–155.

Zaheer, S., & Zaheer, A. (2006). Trust across borders. *Journal of International Business Studies*, *37*(1), 21–29.

Zak, P. J., & Knack, S. (2001). Trust and growth. *The Economic Journal*, *111*(470), 295–321.

Zhang, J. X., & Bond, M. H. (1993). Target-based interpersonal trust: Cross-cultural comparison and its cognitive model. *Acta Psychologia Sinica*, *25*(2), 164–172.

2 The Dimensions of Trust in the Digital Era

Barbara Kożuch
Jagiellonian University in Kraków

Introduction

Without trust, people would have been paralyzed by inaction (Hawley, 2012). This known truth prompts more and more interest in this issue.

Trust is one of the phenomena that many researchers have studied for years; however, its characteristics are still not sufficiently recognized. One of the effective ways to know trust properties is to examine its dimensions. Given the new circumstances in which current and future organizations will operate, new dimensions of trust must be sought. This exploration is based on an analysis of existing concepts of the general trust, chosen types of trust, and typologies of trust dimensions and proposes the digital trust model. It will allow us to understand better the specificity of trust and its importance in the digital era.

The aim of the chapter is to present the dimensions of trust. The chapter is organized as follows: dimensions of trust are addressed followed by an extensive review and analysis of trust literature. Based on this analysis, the simplified model of digital trust is presented.

Understanding the Nature of Trust

Although much research has been done, there is no generally recognized systemic conceptual apparatus for this research area. First of all, it concerns the concepts of trust and trustworthiness.

Following deep reasoning based on reviewed literature (Colquitt et al., 2007), there are different views of trust understanding. For example, trust is recognized as:

- A behavioral intention,
- Choosing, judging, or preferring – an internal action,
- A synonym for trustworthiness,
- A facet of inherited personality,
- A synonym for cooperation or risk-taking.

DOI: 10.4324/9781003165965-2

For example, some authors like Mayer et al. (1995) or Gabarro (1978) claim that trustworthiness with its elements is the antecedent of trust, but according to Morgan and Hunt (1994), antecedents of trust are shared values, communication, and opportunistic behavior. Furthermore, while Mayer et al. distinguished three trustworthiness elements: ability, benevolence, and integrity, Gabarro (1978) notices two elements: competence and character. Moreover, Mayer et al. argue that risk and cooperation cannot be equated with trust. Their observation seems accurate.

In contrast, it can be assumed that trust and trustworthiness are, to some extent, the same as the latter includes the aspects of trust within which it is analyzed. In other words, elements of trustworthiness are the essential elements of trust. Therefore, the interchangeable use of these terms can be considered justified.

The analysis of exemplary definitions (Table 2.1) indicates a similarity in understanding trust. Any possible differences relate to a broader or narrower formulation of the definition or a slightly different distribution of accents. Generally, one can say that a trustee – as the party whom someone trusts, is believed to act to someone's benefit, or at least does not act against him or her being reliable and behaving foreseeably, and also in accordance with the commonly accepted rules (Paliszkiewicz, 2013). In other words, trust is usually described as the trustor's expectancy that will be treated with fairness and will not be harmed by the trustee.

Focusing on dimensions of trust (or facets, pillars, factors, features, drivers, and others) makes understanding this multifaceted notion easier. It allows researchers and practitioners to understand better the specificity of trust and its importance in managing organizations in the digital era.

Such reflections confirm several research considerations that trust is a complex construct (Sztompka, 2007; Llewellyn et al., 2013) and is still not fully recognized. Hence, some types of trust can be distinguished, that is, basic or general trust, simple, blind, or authentic one (Kożuch, 2014, 2014a)

When considering the nature of trust, it is essential to emphasize its fragility. This conclusion often concerns the rapid loss of trust, while it takes a lot of time and effort to build it (Mattila & Seppälä, 2016; Gaehtgens & Allan, 2017).

However, recent months show the opposite situation: an increase instead of the loss of trust. The Edelman Barometer (2020) reported that in May 2020, trust in the government was 65%, while in December 2019, it was 54%, that is, the increase of 11 percentage points. As Bishop points out, in 2011, The Edelman Trust Barometer reported a jump in trusting government from 27% to 48% following the 9/11 attacks, only for it to fall the following year. Both examples may indicate a specific understanding of trust as an expression of hope than of conviction. The author suspects that it is probably a "big bubble of trust" and rightly

Table 2.1 Chosen Definitions of the General Trust

Authors	*Definitions: Trust Is Understood as ...*
Coleman (1990, p. 99)	rational decision to accept a bet
Giddens (1990, p. 34)	confidence in the reliability of a person or system, regarding a given set of outcomes or events, where that confidence expresses a faith in the probity or love of another, or in the correctness of abstract principles (technical knowledge)
Putman (1995, p. 285)	facilitating coordination of activities
Fukuyama (1995, p. 26)	expecting community members to behave honestly and cooperatively, based on commonly recognized standards
Earl and Cvetkovich (1995, p. 38)	an optimization strategy aimed at adapting to a complex social environment with more opportunities
Seligman (1997, p. 43)	belief in the goodwill of the other party taken in conditions of the ambiguity of its intentions and calculations
Sztompka (1999, p. 25).	a bet made about future contingent actions of others
Lin (2001, p. 147)	anticipating or expecting a partner to take into account their partner's interests in the exchange
Kożuch (2014a, pp. 42–43)	the expectation of the trustee that the other party will treat them fairly and will not be harmed by them
Krot and Lewicka (2016, p. 22)	a set of specific expectations toward a partner, consent to remain in a relationship of interdependence or dependence
Kotow (2018, p. 13)	the assumption that a particular turn of events will occur that will achieve the expected result

Source: Own development based on the field literature.

states that “At some point, (...) the public will begin to feel that the external threat is being tamed, if not yet defeated. Its focus will start to turn inward again. (...) Political rancor will return to normal levels, and trust in government will likely fall” (Bishop, 2020). Up to a point, these assumptions are confirmed by the opinion polls results on the 9-month COVID-19 pandemic in Poland. In March 2020, this support was 42%, and in June, when public opinion positively assessed the way of dealing with the pandemic, it was 44%. In November, when it became clear that the government was not coping with the pandemic, only 30% of respondents gave a positive opinion. Although a month later, positive ratings were 33%, it can be assumed that confidence in the government will decline in the face of further difficulties (KOMUNIKAT, 2020).

From the perspective of discussions held, it is reasonable to say that at the core of trust's nature is the emphasis placed on incomplete information about the future trustor's expectations that the trustee will not act to his or her detriment. Furthermore, it is difficult to build and sustain trust, and at the same time, it is easy to destroy it.

Trust in the Digital Era

The importance and role of trust in the contemporary world adapt to the socio-economic changes that shape our environment and ourselves. According to Sztompka (2007, pp. 45–53), the main changes in our world embrace such observations:

1. Contemporary people more and more often choose orientation toward the future and see their subjectivity. It means a shift from societies where fate was the benchmark to societies based on human subjectivity.
2. Interdependencies are intensifying, not only on a societal scale but also globally, as the COVID-19 pandemic has hardly proven. These interdependencies strengthen the importance of trust in the credibility of those we cooperate with, resulting in conditions of increasing unpredictability of their future behavior.
3. The development of societies manifests itself, among other things, in increasing possibilities, which means that predicting which option will be chosen may be burdened with increasing errors.
4. The complexity of the environment increases, making the environment less transparent and incomprehensible for the participants of social, organizational, and technical processes.
5. Innovation and advanced technological changes also increase the anonymity of those on whom society's well-being depends, thus also increase the importance of indirect links. For example, it is difficult to directly contact the producers of items that satisfy societies' needs, and recently the direct contact with those who distribute goods has become increasingly limited.
6. Mass migrations and numerous long journeys cause changes in the immediate environment, such as in the workplace or at rest. This environment is becoming more and more full of strangers and unfamiliar, and thereby challenging to deal with.
7. Huge civilization and technical achievements have their dark side. They are the source of unfavorable phenomena, such as disasters (construction, industrial) or changes in the natural environment leading to changes in the climate faced by contemporary people.

All these aspects increase uncertainty and create a demand for trust as a resource that allows facing the challenges of the modern world and the concepts and theories of trust, including the conditions for creating trust and counteracting the negative phenomena associated with it.

According to the findings of Giddens (1990, pp. 33–35), the essential circumstance in which a need for trust arises is not the lack of driving force but the lack of complete information. Trust is associated with reliability in the face of random events, regardless of whether they relate to people's actions or the functioning systems. This author points out that work performance is connected with direct connections in modern economies, that is, facework commitments on the one hand, and indirect connections (i.e., faceless commitment) on the other. The former concern relationships of trust maintained or expressed in social connections were established while staying in the same work environment; indirect connections lead to the belief that symbolic signs are natural (e.g., "Q" as high quality). The same refers to expert systems, that is, in other words, the efficiency of abstract systems. It, in turn, leads to the conclusion that a feature of present-day institutions is a deep connection with the mechanisms of trust in abstract systems, especially trust in expert systems, for example, supporting complex intellectual processes (Giddens, 1990, pp. 80–83). Trust in systems is an example of faceless commitments. In turn, trust in people involves facework commitments, in which indicators of the other's integrity are sought (Giddens, 1990, p. 87).

Contemporary societies have entered the digital age after the industrial one. In 2019, 85% of European Union citizens used the Internet, but only 58% had, at least, basic digital skills, such as communicating online, handling information, and making transactions (Digital Economy, 2020, p. 8). As Growiec (2018) claims, before the fruits of the industrial age were entirely harvested, humanity entered another technological revolution: the digital revolution that took off in 2000, when the Internet-connected computers into a truly global web. Hence, its hallmarks are personal computers, the Internet, mobile phones and industrial robots, and also advanced socio-technological systems, such as business ecosystems.

The digital era can be understood as the age in which everyday solving problems, working and running a business, and communication and establishing relationships occur, thanks to digital communication, social media interaction, e-commerce, digital business, and also e-public services. This approach's main issues consist of the following interconnected themes: people, excellence, economy, democracy, fairness, society, enforcement, international, and trust. The latter is seen as the main point of reference (SHAPING, 2020, pp. 1–2).

The current challenge is that trust in the digital age has proved difficult to understand, which raises questions about its nature and characteristics, the benefits and conditions for using it in managing organizations, and citizens' private lives. Recently, it is observed that interactions are increasingly conducted digitally and are affecting many aspects of people's lives. As a result, digital trust continues to grow in importance (DIGITAL, 2017, p. 4).

Many researchers and practitioners claim that trust and trustworthiness are more important in e-commerce because of the less-verifiable and less-controllable business environment (Gefen, 2000). It also refers to other digital interactions across contemporary societies.

Bearing in mind situations where trust is needed, building it on direct connections is easier to establish. In turn, a trust relationship founded on indirect connections is much more challenging to build.

To summing up, it can be said that thinking of trust in the digital era should take into account on the one hand, the nature of trust and, on the other, the specificity of digital trust, which is built on its general nature.

Dimensions of Digital Trust

Recently, there is a growing interest in the specificity of trust in the digital age; however, more research is done by practitioners than by scientists. Digital trust seems to be a topical issue in present and future management sciences and organization research. Focusing on dimensions of trust (or facets, pillars, factors, features, drivers, and others) allows us to understand this multifaceted notion better. It allows researchers and practitioners to understand better the specificity of trust and its importance in managing organizations in the digital era.

"Trust in the digital era" can be replaced with the term "digital trust". Although the former formulation is more comprehensive than the latter, people are still in direct contact in the digital era, but the widespread use of high technology is essential for developing the economy and society as a whole. What fundamentally distinguishes pre-digital trust from digital trust is trusting not only in people whom we know and abstract systems but also – and perhaps most importantly – in technical and technological systems. Therefore, digital trust can be called extended traditional trust appropriate to the digital age.

Some definitions of digital trust can be found on consulting companies' websites and in a relatively smaller number of scientific studies. One of them is the definition proposed by Gaehtgens and Allan (2017). They rightly stated that "digital trust is an evolution of traditional trust models to cover the additional requirements of digital business by deriving levels of measurable confidence to make risk-based decisions" (p. 1).

Business Insider Intelligence developed another definition in 2020. Trust is described in it as the confidence people have that a platform will protect their information and provide a safe environment for them to create and engage with content (DIGITAL, 2020, p. 3). In turn, *Insider Intelligence's* five-dimensions typology model of digital trust can be found. The model consists of: (1) security, (2) legitimacy, (3) trustworthy community, (4) bitter Ad experience, and (5) good Ad relevance. The first three identified dimensions had the most impact in the United States for social users' trust (p. 5).

Other kinds of digital trust dimensions were distinguished when the main criterion was approaching technical and technological systems. It allows us to look at various aspects of trust in fully and partially digital contexts. While analyzing trust models, such dimensions of trust in the digital era were indicated:

- Assurance understood as an ability to ensure that the service has been designed, developed, and maintained based on formalized and rigorous controls and standards;
- Accountability that means building and auditing the system of the identifiability and traceability, which helps users determine with whom it is interacting, and also determining legal, operational, and technical responsibility concerning that;
- Benevolence reads as the service provider's willingness and motivation to add value at the users' request and without expecting a reward;
- Competence and ability explained as the level of knowledge and skills helping in distinguishing between better and worse digital services;
- Integrity shows that all assets such as hardware, software, and data can be accessed or modified only by authorized parties;
- The predictability that refers to the consistency of actions and work results that can reduce existing uncertainty and risk;
- Privacy understood as a guarantee of prevention of obtaining and using important information by unauthorized entities in unenforceable ways;
- Reputation described as the value of end-users perception based on their observations or past experiences and explored by partners future behavior;
- Security is defined as providing protection and control of the most valuable assets (White Paper, 2017, p. 78).

Some authors claim that specific dimensions (drivers) of digital trust are safety, security, reliability, privacy, and data ethics (Marcial & Launer, 2019, p. 1). Other research shows that environment, experience, attitudes, and behavior are the identified drivers of digital trust (DIGITAL, 2017). Likewise, it is the concept of digital trust by Gartner Inc. They assert that digital trust is created by all entities participating in digital business and binds people, things, and organizations together in what is reflected in the distinguished eight dimensions of digital trust. There are as follows: ability, willingness, truthfulness, ethics, security, safety, reliability, and privacy (DIGITAL, 2017, p. 4).

The analysis of exemplary typologies of trust dimensions shows some similarity in developing trust sets of aspects within which the dimensions are analyzed. In many cases, different words for the same or very similar phenomena are used.

The presented material and findings based on it show three approaches to understand trust in the digital era. One presents the focus on traditional trust although it is not adapted to the specificity of digital interactions, that is, Sztompka (2007), and others understand digital trust fully in the digital context, which means that some concepts are focused only on digital business relationships based on trust, that is, The Digital Evolution Index 2017. Another approach is relatively moderate, as within it, pre-digital trust, that is, traditional trust, is also taken into account (Gaehtgens & Allan, 2017).

The latter approach seems to be most promising. The focus on the narrower approach ignores the fact that digital connections also exist in people's private lives, that is, when they study (Paliszkiewicz & Koohang, 2016). People in organizations are not only employees but also human beings who create informal relationships alongside formal ones.

Provided discussion on the dimensions of trust shows a conceptual difficulty with studying digital trust.

The analyses show that Mayer et al.'s (1995) concept dominates the literature on the subject. It continues to evolve, specifying dimensions of trust or proposing similar terms. However, they are within the analyzed model's dimensions as proposed by many researchers' constructs that are similar to ability, benevolence, and integrity. Therefore, the model based on these factors of perceived trustworthiness can be the basis of developing an integrative model of digital trust.

First of all, it consists of a set of capabilities of individuals, groups, or organizations allowing to build and/or use highly advanced devices, systems, and procedures ensuring the effectiveness of digital interactions.

The effectiveness, that embraces reliability, accountability, assurance, security, safety, predictability, and privacy, is gained due to personal or organizational competencies like providing an environment in which one can talk and act without fear of repercussion; managing in a predictable and deliberate way; operating with transparency; placing confidence in co-workers, staff members, and clients; giving proper credit to others; following through on agreed-upon actions and treating sensitive or confidential information appropriately (UNITED, p. 52); and also heighten technological awareness.

Secondly, benevolence, or willingness, in the proposed model includes the positive orientation perceived by the trustor as of the online user reflected in such attitudes (Gefen, 2000, p. 42): readiness and motivation to assist who is digitally connected to; demonstrating good intentions toward whom is digitally interconnected; and putting customers' interests before own benefits.

Cultural competencies also create benevolence as a dimension of trust in the digital era because digital connectivity binds people over the world. Among them are: awareness of cultural differences between people, understanding other cultures, engaging and integrating cultural

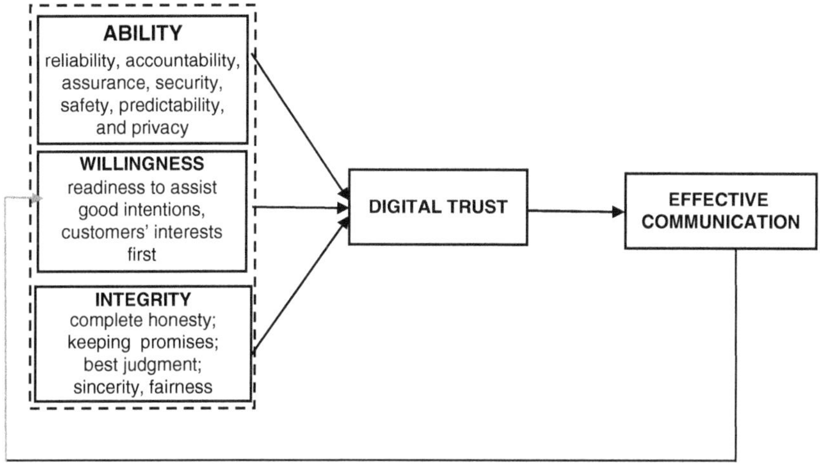

Figure 2.1 The simplified model of digital trust. Source: Own development based on the cited literature.

awareness, knowledge, and sensitivity in every digital connection (Rice & Mathews, 2012, p. 25).

Into benevolence can be included also trust disposition since positive orientation, disinterestedness, and inherited trust are the main bases of trust disposition. Although one has to agree with the researchers who believe that trust disposition, or trust propensity, affects the other three dimensions, the most significant convergence is noticeable in the case of benevolence.

Thirdly, integrity, or adherence to sound moral and ethical principles (Colquitt et al., 2007, p. 913), generally is referred to as loyalty, openness, caring, or supportiveness (Mayer et al., 1995). This dimension is created by ethical behaviors related to digital interactions like (Gefen, 2000, p. 42): signaling complete honesty; keeping promises; offering best judgment; and also, being sincere and fair.

The proposed integrative model of digital trust (Figure 2.1) is an attempt to combine the features of general trust and digital trust. It employes the analyzed dimensions of trust. It is a simplified version as it does not cover the interdependence of trust with risk-taking and producing a good performance. The proposed set of dimensions creates digital perceived trustworthiness. Since research on trust in the digital era is a new field, there is no scientific evidence of its characteristics and interdependencies yet.

In the model, effective communication is understood as an immediate outcome of emerging or strengthened trust that is the most purposeful factor of meeting the expectations of digital users.

Conclusion

The importance of continuing research on trust in the digitally connected world is following from a certain level of trust that exists in each digital business initiative, relationship, and exchange. This chapter discusses issues of understanding and then building trust in the digital era. The provided analyses shows that ability, accountability, security, and transparency are more highlighted trust dimensions. They can be found in most cited publications (including similar constructs). The proposed model of digital trust with an intermediate outcome needs to be developed in further research. For example, this model's development could include digital trust challenges such as legal and regulatory compliance, vendors' immaturity, loss of control, and limited transparency. The mentioned arguments prove that overlapping dimensions of traditional and new, that is, digital trust, is a promising way to build the integrative model of digital trust.

References

Bishop, M. (2020). *Beyond the great trust bubble*. Retrieved from website: https://www.edelman.com/research/beyond-the-great-trust-bubble.

Coleman, J. S. (1990). *Foundations of social theory*. Cambridge, MA: Harvard University Press.

Colquitt, J. A., Scott, B. A., & LePine, J. A. (2007). Trust, trustworthiness, and trust propensity: A meta-analytic test of their unique relationships with risk taking and job performance. *Journal of Applied Psychology*, *92*(4), 909–927.

DIGITAL. (2017). The Digital Evolution Index 2017. Retrieved from https://newsroom.mastercard.com/wp-content/uploads/2017/07/Mastercard_DigitalTrust_PDFPrint_FINAL_AG.pdf.

DIGITAL. (2020). The 2020 Digital Trust Report Preview. *Business* Insider. Retrieved from https://www.businessinsider.com/intelligence/digital-trust-enterprise-report-preview?IR=T.

Digital Economy. (2020). Digital Economy and Society Index (DESI). Retrieved from https://ec.europa.eu/digital-single-market/en/news/digital-economy-and-society-index-desi-2020.

Earl, T. C., & Cvetkovich, G. T. (1995). Social trust: Toward a cosmopolitan society. Westport. Connecticut: Praeger.

Edelman Barometer. (2020). *Spring update: Trust and the COVID-19 pandemic*. Retrieved from https://www.edelman.com/research/trust-2020-spring-update.

Fukuyama, F. (1995). *Trust: The social virtues and the creation of prosperity*. New York, NY: Free Press.

Gabarro, J. J. (1978). The development of trust, influence, and expectations. In A. G. Atho, & J. J. Gabarro (Eds.), *Interpersonal behaviors: Communication and understanding in relationships* (pp. 290–303). Englewood Cliffs, NJ: Prentice Hall.

Gaehtgens F., & Allan A. (2017). Digital trust — Redefining trust for the digital era: A Gartner trend insight report. Retrieved from https://www.gartner.com/en/doc/3735817-digital-trust-redefining-trust-for-the-digital-era-a-gartner-trend-insight-report.

Gefen, D. (2000). *Reflections on the dimensions of trust and trustworthiness among online consumers*. ACM SIGMIS Database: the DATABASE for Advances in Information Systems Retrieved from website: 10.1145/569905.569910.

Giddens, A. (1990). *The consequences of modernity*. Stanford, CA: Stanford University Press.

Growiec, J. (2018). The digital era, viewed from a perspective of millennia of economic growth. SGH KAE Working Papers Series Number: 2018/034.

Hawley, K. (2012). *Trust. A very short introduction*. Oxford, GB: Oxford University Press.

KOMUNIKAT. (2020). Stosunek do rządu w pierwszych dekadzie grudnia 2020 [Attitude towards the government in the first decade of December 2020]. *Komunikat z Badań, 164*/2020. CBOS.

Kotow, S. (2018). Matematyka zaufania *[Mathematics of trust]*. Warszawa: Institute of Behavioral Design & Sebastian Kotow.

Kożuch, B. (2014). Organizacyjna perspektywa zaufania publicznego. Zarys koncepcji *[An outline of organizational perspective of public trust]. Przedsiębiorczość i Zarządzanie, 11*(3), 41–51.

Kożuch, B. (2014a). Organisational perspective on public trust. In B. Kożuch, & Z. Dobrowolski (Eds.), *Creating public trust, an organisational perspective* (pp. 13–27). Frankfurt am Main: Peterlang.

Krot, K., & D. Lewicka, D. (2016). *Zaufanie w organizacji innowacyjnej* [Trust in an innovative organization]. Warsaw, PL: Wydawnictwo C.H. Beck.

Lin, N. (2001). *Social capital: A theory of social structure and actions*. Cambridge, GB: Cambridge University Press.

Llewellyn, S., Brooks, S., & Mahon, A. (2013). *Trust and confidence in government and public services*. New York, NY: Routledge.

Marcial, D. E., & Launer, M. A. (2019). Towards the measurement of digital trust in the workplace: A proposed framework. *International Journal of Scientific Engineering Science, 3*(12), 2456–7361.

Mattila, J., & Seppälä, T. (2016). Digital trust, platforms, and policy. ETLA Brief No 42. Retrieved from http://pub.etla.fi/ETLA-Muistio-Brief-42, 1–2.

Mayer, R. C., Davis, J. H., & Schoorman, F.D. (1995). An integrative model of organizational trust. *The Academy of Management Review, 20*(3), 709–734.

Morgan, R. M., & Hunt, S. D. (1994). The commitment-trust theory of relationship marketing. *Journal of Marketing, 58*(3) 20–38.

Paliszkiewicz, J. (2013). *Zaufanie w zarządzaniu* [Trust in management]. Warszawa, PL: Wydawnictwo Naukowe PWN.

Paliszkiewicz, J., & Koohang, A. (2016). *Social media and trust: A multinational study of university students*. Santa Rosa, FL: Informing Science Press.

Putman, R. D. (1995). *Demokracja w działaniu: Tradycje obywatelskie we współczesnych Włoszech* [Making democracy work: Civic traditions in modern Italy]. Kraków 1995, Znak.

Rice, M. F., & Mathews, A. L. (2012). A new kind of public service professional: Possessing cultural competency awareness, knowledge, and skill. In K. A. Norman-Major, & S. T. Gooden (Eds.), *Cultural competency for public administrators*. Armonk, NE: M. E. Sharpe.

Seligman, A. B. (1997). *The problem of trust*. Princeton, NJ: Princeton University Press.

SHAPING. (2020). *Shaping Europe's digital future*. European Commission. Brussels, 19.2.2020. COM (2020) 67 final.
Sztompka, P. (1999). *Trust: A sociological theory*. Cambridge, GB: Cambridge University Press.
Sztompka, P. (2007). Zaufanie. Fundament społeczeństwa [Trust. The foundation of society]. Kraków, PL: Znak.
UNITED. (2020). United Nations competencies for the future. Retrieved from https://careers.un.org/lbw/attachments/competencies_booklet_en.pdf.
White Paper. (2017). Digital trust. For smart ICT. Version 3. September. Retrieved from https://portail-qualite.public.lu/dam-assets/publications/confiance-numerique/white-paper-digital-trust-september-2017.pdf.

3 Influence of Political Strategies on Culture of Social Trust

Joanna Wyleżałek
Warsaw University of Life Sciences

Introduction

The rapid development of telecommunication technologies and the mass movement of people in space are the basis for the diffusion of culture, while influencing changes in the area of axionormative systems of entire societies. However, these are not the only processes that influence identity changes and change of attitudes toward the surrounding social reality. Equally important, and perhaps most important due to the range of influence, seems to be the mechanisms of power, which, realizing themselves in the global dimension through mass media, influence local social activities and people's attitudes toward social institutions and toward each other.

The aim of the article is to attempt to demonstrate the relationship between global policies implemented with the use of mass media and social changes in the area of culture of trust, taking into account the intentional actions of political actors, which have a strong connection with economic interests.

Alongside the momentous, natural from the perspective of functionaries, social processes that are leading to a diverse and increasingly complex global society (Spencer, 1876), the political influence of global players who have the resources strong enough to create social development according to economic needs is becoming increasingly transparent (Stiglitz, 2002). The realization of the economic interests of certain social groups is to "justify" the use of mechanisms of social influence, which are reflected in cultural wars, that is, in the struggle for domination in the axionormative space. It means that cultural changes are increasingly influenced by competing ideologies and political visions. For them, culture is a tool in the political struggle for the domination of certain values, for example, multicultural, right-wing, left-wing, conservative, and ethnonationalist. Contemporary cultural wars are not only a struggle for definition, but also rather a global conflict aimed at dominating real politics (Burszta, 2013, p. 8).

Jan Zielonka (Ralf Dahrendorf's Professorial Fellow) in his book *Counter-revolution, Liberal Europe in retreat* claims that it is nowadays

DOI: 10.4324/9781003165965-3

noticeable that the political rhythm of our times is determined by the battle between two dangerous forces: *"undemocratic liberalism"* on the one hand and *"illiberal democracy"* on the other (Zielonka, 2018). These dangerous forces, the source of which is to be found in global concepts of world development, increasingly dominate European politics, influencing local social changes and the fate of citizens.

The article concentrates on the crack in the worldview of Polish society outlining local politics against the background of global political games. Referring to the data found, the level of social trust in Poland is presented and the role of mass media in preserving social divisions is indicated. The article is based on the assumption that in the modern world, it is political interests that shape culture, thus defining humanity (Eagleton, 2012).

Global Visions of World Development and Social Divisions

The starting point for the analysis of activities in the public sphere, including the conditions of local politics that condition the dynamics of the culture of trust should, according to the author, be different variants of the global society "images of the global order" that we encounter in social consciousness and that politicians try to implement in practice, depending on the geopolitical situation of the state, their own particular interests or loyalty, or other "behind-the-scenes" conditions.

The options of "global order" provide different visions of the world. The first of these is the model of mutually separated communities, which in its hierarchical version appears in fundamentalist religious orientations, among others in Islam, which postulate the rebirth of its own communities in a pure, ideal shape (*Global Gemeinschaft I*). The idea of a human consensus around certain common values and ideals is carried by the idea of a universal church in Catholicism, and in the secular dimension by peace movements or the human rights movement (*Global Gemeinschaft II*). In both of these variants, the postulated character dominates, while social practice indicates the realization of further variants of the global order. The third option concerns the coexistence of sovereign, independent nation-states bound together by strong mutual cooperative ties in the economic, political, and cultural fields. This model is internally differentiated: the egalitarian version sees the participating states as equal partners engaged in mutually beneficial cooperation. The hierarchical version recognizes the existence of a leading power or powers which, without interfering in the internal affairs of other countries, take on the duty to maintain the world order (*Global Gesellschaft I*). The extreme concept, however, envisages the disappearance of nation-states and first regional, then global unification under the aegis of a common political organization or supranational world government (*Global Gesellschaft II*) (Robertson, 1992, pp. 61–84).

The fundamental difference of these options results in significant differences in the scope of the policy pursued by the supporters of each concept. It is irrational, from the perspective of the policy of an economically weak or developing country, to fit into the logic of a hierarchical model of independent states or a model of "*unified globalization*", because these options are assumed to cause less participation in the global decision-making processes of economically weaker partners. The decisive factor in the implementation of a particular model is, therefore, economic strength. The economically strong global players will aim primarily at the unification model because they can guarantee themselves a privileged position in it. However, this applies not only to the richest countries in the world but also to global players whose capital is transnational. The important factor differentiating the economic position turns out to be the strategies adopted by local elites – politicians, businessmen, and managers who are co-opted by foreign capital, becoming executors of the interests of foreign corporations, with which they have their own life chances. The "comprador" elites in the alliance with foreign capital strengthen subordination (Frank, 1969). Maintaining an economic distance between the richest social groups, having a great deal of capital, and the rest of the society is a part of a political game, the principles of which perpetuate social divisions. The existence of an economically distant poor class both ensures the multiplication of profits and excludes a sharp increase in market competition.

The actions of the elites that fit into concrete visions of the global order thus become the basis for political practices that are implemented through the mass media and specific political parties. This results in a more and more often noticed ambiguous approach to the function of political parties in contemporary social life. Liberal views that political parties, together with pressure groups and other interest groups, are engaged in power struggles, representing various socio-economic groups are increasingly being replaced by the view that some groups dominating the economic area have mastered the political decision-making process (Marcuse, 1991). In extreme views, the importance of political parties can be read as marginal, since economic power is held by the ruling class (Hardt & Negri, 2000). Parliamentary politics in this configuration of events becomes a strategy that distracts attention from the real sources of political power, which should be seen in the global decisions of powerful economic players.

The sources of the disappearance of the culture of trust, social divisions, and cultural wars are therefore likely to be sought in the conflicting interests of, on the one hand, the richest global players and, on the other hand, national societies aimed at strengthening the state economy in order to negotiate a position on the international arena.

As a result, modern politics is increasingly taking the form of *"undemocratic liberalism"*, which is likely to be a tool for a unified vision of the world and an *"illiberal democracy"*, but which is becoming not a very successful antidote to the backstage mechanisms of global politics, ideologically in line with the efforts to strengthen national economies.

The functional problem in the aforementioned division is not a different vision of the world but its completely dichotomous, irreconcilable character. Although, on the axiological plane, the search for common planes of understanding seems, to some extent, possible, the idea itself, the source of different political strategies, is irreconcilable. After all, it is not possible to realize a unified vision of the world and to preserve strong nation-states at the same time (Wyleżałek, 2020).

This conflict is reflected in the growing internal contradictions both in the policy area of the European Union and in the policy area of the Member States, in which the activities of political parties fit into the unification of national strategies, and certain mass media promote different visions of the world order depending on the political preferences of the sponsor or the owner of commercial stations, and in the case of state media depending on the ideology adopted by the ruling party. Of course, social divisions, distrust in the institutions of public life, and people's distrust in each other are direct consequences of the clash of these different visions of the world promoted by the mass media in the digital age.

Decrease in the Culture of Trust as a Result of Political Strategies

Assuming the existence of links between global politics and the dichotomy of world views created by mass media, it is difficult to ignore the impact of it on the decline of the culture of trust and the deepening of social divisions.

For the purposes of this article, an example of a crack in the worldview of the Polish society is given, but it should be borne in mind that in most countries of the Old Continent, there are increasingly visible social divisions, which are politically conditioned.

It was assumed that the political conflict in Poland is divided into politicians representing the interests of the supporters of the vision of *"unified globalization"*, which is expressed in a more or less transparent way by the political actions called *"undemocratic liberalism"*, and the supporters of strengthening the national economy and the state through *"illiberal democracy"*. It was also assumed that these strategies represent two coalitions in the Polish political arena, by analogy: The Civic Coalition and the United Right, which promote certain values related to the accepted concepts of the world order and are expressed by private and public mass media.

To illustrate the axiological conflict, the focus was on the divisions built around the concept of the family, the understanding of the right to life and freedom, the attitude to the Catholic faith, and the history of the nation.

Liberalization of social life in the axiological dimension, including the expansive promotion of sexual minorities, has been attributed to the policy of global unification (*Global Gesellschaft II*) associated with *"undemocratic liberalism"*, while strengthening the traditional family or opposing the liberalization of social life in the axiological dimension has been attributed to the policy of strengthening the nation-state (*Global Gesellschaft I*) associated with *"non-liberal democracy"*.

Similarly, it was assumed that, among other things, different attitudes toward the Catholic faith and the institution of the church itself, or a different interpretation and approach to the history of one's own nation can be interpreted. The marginal share of Catholic content and the promotion of the history of one's own nation was combined with the policy of global unification (*Global Gesellschaft II*) that is *"undemocratic liberalism"*, while the strengthening of Christian values and the promotion of national history were attributed to the policy of strengthening the nation-state (*Global Gesellschaft I*) nowadays associated with *"non-liberal democracy"*.

It was also indicated, on the basis of the content provided, which media built a narrative promoting a particular worldview (Table 3.1).

Of course, the media message stirs up social emotions leading to divisions, which are then reinforced by social media that allow you to objectivize your beliefs in the sense of being in line with "what others think". Building social divisions, on the other hand, does not foster the emergence and consolidation of a culture of trust that, while fully functional from the perspective of the open systems to which the social system belongs (Bertallanfy, 1968), maybe nonfunctional from the perspective of pursuing the economic interests of global players and certain political parties or social movements funded by rich businessmen. In other words, the absence of a generalized culture of trust in social life, and thus, the existence of social divisions facilitates political games.

Social trust is usually examined in three dimensions: vertical ones – public, that is, with regard to different types of institutions, and two horizontal ones – private and generalized (CBOS, 2020).

A characteristic feature of Poland is a low level of two dimensions of trust: generalized trust in other people and trust in institutions of public life – although a slight increase can be observed in these dimensions over the last year (CBOS, 2020).

The Social Opinion Research Center created a synthetic trust index expressing a generalized attitude in social relations. It takes into account appropriately coded and aggregated declarations of shared beliefs in terms of adopting a trusting versus a mistrustful attitude in social

Table 3.1 Assumed Links Between the Visions of the Global Order, Local Politics, and the Media

Global Order	*Reflection in Political Activities: Polish Party Coalitions and Affiliation of tHeir Parties to European Groups*	*Promoted Values (Choice)*	*Selected Media for the Creation of a Specific Political Worldview*
Global Gesellschaft II • The disappearance of nation-states (including national culture) • Regional and then global unification under the aegis of a common political organization • The creation of a supranational world government	***"illiberal democracy"*** (United Right: Law and Justice – Alliance of European Conservatives and Reformists, Solidarity Poland – Movement for the Europe of Freedom and Democracy)	• Strengthening the traditional family • Opposition to the liberalization of social life in an axiological dimension • Concentration around Christian and national values	Polish Television (public media, president of the board a former politician associated with the United Right), TV Trwam (founder and director: Roman Catholic clergyman), TV Republic (editor-in-chief: right-wing journalist and investigative journalist), Polish Radio (public media: director and editor-in-chief, historical reporter), Radio Maryja (founder and director: Roman Catholic clergyman)
Global Gesellschaft II • The disappearance of nation-states (including national culture) • Regional and then global unification under the aegis of a common political organization • The creation of a supranational world government	***"undemocratic liberalism"*** (Civic Coalition: Civic Platform – European People's Party, Green Party – European Green Party)	• Promotion of sexual minorities • Liberalization of social life in the axiological dimension • Moving away from traditional Christian ethics and national values or instrumentalization of these values	TVN Group (acquired by Discovery; owned by an American businessman), RMF Group (owned by the German Bauer Media Group, owned by a German billionaire), Radio Zet belonging to Eurozet (acquired by Agora, co-owner: American millionaire)

Source: Own research.

relations. This index takes values from –3 (very high distrust) to +3 (very high trust). The results of the research conducted on a representative group of respondents in Poland in the subsequent years in which the research was conducted are as follows: 2006: –0.98, 2008: –0.62, 2010: –0.66, 2012: –0.64, 2014: –0.79, 2016: –0.72, 2018: –0.89, and 2020: –0.66.

In the case of trust in the public sphere, CBOS presents, in the following years, institutions asking respondents about trust. In the following years, the confidence in specific institutions varies depending on the socio-political situation. However, on the basis of a synthetic indicator of trust in the public sphere, it was estimated that, in 2020, an average Pole trusts, on average, every second institution presented in the survey. In the case of mass media, included in the list, the lack of trust has been consistently prevailing for several years (CBOS, 2020, 2018).

Although the lack of a generalized culture of trust in Poland after the political transformation could be explained historically, both by referring to the distant, partitional, and to the recent history associated with several decades of domination of the communist system in Poland, more than 30 years after the political transformation, it is difficult to still refer to the same conditions, especially since, according to Inglehart, vertical trust changes as a result of new experiences relatively quickly and in a predictable way (Inglehart, 1997). Meanwhile, generalized trust in social relations and trust in the institutions of public life in Poland is still low, so Poles have not had the experience to build that trust. According to the author, the search for the sources of the lack of culture of trust in Poland and beyond as well as the growing social divisions should be placed in the orbit of global influences unquestionably connected with economic interests.

The strength of these influences, on the other hand, depends on the number of recipients of media messages that promote a particular political viewpoint.

The Political Background of Social Divisions in a Local Perspective

In order to illustrate the axiological conflict connected, as assumed, with global politics, two events organized every year in Poland were emphasized: Equality Marches promoting sexual minorities and Marches for Life and Family, the participants of which represent the traditional Catholic worldview.

The Equality Marches, organized by the Foundation for Voluntary Service for Equality, took place in 2019 primarily in cities managed by presidents associated with the Civic Coalition identified with "*undemocratic liberalism*" and the unified world order (*Global Gesellschaft II*) (The Equality Marches, 2019). Some of the city presidents, who belong to liberal parties, even took patronage of this event. The media that foster and promote the Equality Marches are the mass media associated with global economic players, mainly TVN taken over by Discovery.

In the case of organizing Marches for Life and Family, there is no clear connection between the organization of the event and the sympathies or party affiliation of the city presidents (March for Life and Family, 2020). However, the marches were coordinated by certain institutions, mainly by the Foundation Centre for Life and Family, the president of which is a politician from the United Right. The Foundation is supported by Catholic circles and media, such as Polonia Christiana, Gość Niedzielny (The Sunday Guest), TV Trwam, Radio Maryja, and the right-wing circles identified with *"non-liberal democracy"* and the policy of strengthening nation-states (*Global Gesellschaft I*). Most of the media supporting the Marches for Life and Family are public and Catholic.

If the assumptions made are valid, it must also be assumed that the promotion of an extremely different worldview by mass media is not accidental. The owners or co-owners of commercial media management companies in Poland are usually world billionaires, in the interest of whom it is to maintain their economic advantage. From the perspective of the logic of social systems, it is possible in the situation of the existence of weak nation-states. Strengthening of the unification model is, therefore, done by weakening the axiological basis of the nation-states, which, in turn, prevents economic development and creates the necessity of dependence on the world's tycoons. Baumann writes on this subject as follows:

> Global finance, commerce and the information industry depend on political fragmentation due to freedom of movement and unhindered freedom to pursue their own goals. It can be said that all of them are interested in the existence of weak states (...) Having the gates wide open and saying goodbye to an independent economic policy is a basic and meekly fulfilled condition for receiving financial assistance. Weak states are exactly what the New World Order, which suspiciously often appears to be disorderly, needs to ensure its survival and reproduction. (Bauman, 2000, p. 82)

On the other hand, the ruthless closure to processional social changes causes very deep social divisions and perpetuates social distrust in institutions and generalized distrust in other people.

The promotion of a vision of the global order through excessive liberalization or radicalization of social life influences consciousness changes and the ones in the attitudes of citizens who are most often not aware of the conditions of the social processes taking place. Social division, on the other hand, becomes a facilitating effect of political games because it concentrates citizens around leaders and makes it impossible to develop a social consensus that could lead to the end of disputes and thus, to a decrease in support for each grouping representing a dichotomous worldview.

The struggle is for power and influence, and people are experiencing increasing structural violence, of which they are either unaware or unable to identify origins. Rob Nixon writes about slow structural violence as follows: "*by structural slow violence I mean violence that appears gradually and out of sight, violence with a delayed potential for destruction that is scattered across time and space, violence that is gradually overwhelming, which is usually not even perceived as violence.*" (Nixon, 2011, p. 2). In the case of structural violence, both the question of responsibility and the victim are blurred because the victim does not need to be aware of the processes to which they are subjected and, until a certain moment, of their consequences.

Conclusions

Taking into account the logic of social systems based on team games (Crozier & Friedberg, 1982), it is important to note that in order to maintain power and influence, at least to some extent, an apparent social consensus must be maintained, which is served by the actions inherent in the exercise of power. Among the basic strategies, the researchers of the issues include the definition of issues that can become a part of public debate and the elimination of topics, the public visibility of which could harm the interests of specific groups (Bachrach & Baratz, 1962, p. 641). It is also the creation of social desires or fears, which bring tangible economic effects in the form of income of large enterprises and constitute the basis for the functioning of consumer societies (Lukes, 1974, p. 23).

The consequences of the mechanisms of social influence applied more and more efficiently, with the use of mass media, are the social influence mechanisms that are becoming more and more strongly marked by social differences in the worldview, perpetuating or creating mutual mistrust.

To sum up the considerations in the article, it should be noted that:

1. The current social and political situation of countries is influenced by global policies related to the models of global society adopted by political players.
2. Depending on the economic strength of the state and the interests of the political elite, two options are adopted in practice: the unification model (*Global Gesellschaft II*) and the strategy for strengthening nation-states (*Global Gesellschaft I*).
3. The functional problem in the aforementioned division is its irreconcilable character because it is impossible to realize a unified vision of the world and to preserve strong nation-states at the same time.

4. The struggle between global projects takes place mainly in an axiological dimension and the mass nature of cultural wars is connected with the role of mass media that support and promote a specific worldview.
5. The consequence of the global policy is mistrust of institutions and generalized mistrust of other people (in Poland, it has remained unchanged since 2006, when the first systematic research on social trust was conducted).
6. Lack of generalized trust is associated with increasing structural violence that affects the quality of life of entire societies.

Discovering the sources of social divisions should nowadays be based on knowledge about different options of global policy, which determine the lack of cohesion in international politics, and thus political divisions within countries, making factual dialogue between often–only-apparent opponents impossible. Building social awareness based on factual scientific social knowledge is therefore becoming the most important task in today's social reality, and having a sociological imagination is invariably the most desirable competence on the basis of which to create a social project that breaks all divisions and dichotomies. It is, therefore, essential that the teaching of social knowledge becomes a common practice, and that sociology establishes itself as an important scientific discipline.

References

Bachrach, P., & Baratz, M. S. (1962). Decisions and nondecisions: An analytical framework. *The American Political Science Review*, 57(3), 632–642.

Bauman, Z. (2000). *Globalizacja [Globalization]*. Warszawa, PL: Państwowy Instytut Wydawniczy.

Bertallanfy, L. (1968). *General system theory. Foundations, development, applications*. New York, NY: George Braziller.

Burszta, W. (2013). *Kotwice pewności. Wojny kulturowe z popnacjonalizmem w tle [Confidence anchors. Cultural wars with post-nationalism in the background]*. Warszawa, PL: Wydawnictwo Iskry.

CBOS. (2018). O nieufności i zaufaniu [About distrust and trust]. Komunikat z badań 35/2018. Retrieved from https://www.cbos.pl/SPISKOM.POL/2018/K_035_18.PDF.

CBOS (2020). Zaufanie społeczne [Social trust]. Komunikat z badań nr 43/2020. Retrieved from: https://www.cbos.pl/SPISKOM.POL/2020/K_043_20.PDF.

Crozier, F., & Friedberg, E. (1982). Człowiek i system. Ograniczenia działania zespołowego [Man and system. Limitations of teamwork]. Warszawa, PL: Państwowe Wydawnictwo Ekonomiczne.

Eagleton, T. (2012). *Po co nam kultura? [Why do we need culture?]*. Warszawa, PL: Wydawnictwo Literackie MUZA SA.

Frank, A. G. (1969). *Latin America: Underdevelopment of revolution*. New York, NY: Monthly Review Press.

Hardt, M., & Negri, A. (2000). *Empire*. Cambridge, GB: Harvard University Press.

Inglehart, R. (1997). *Modernization and postmodernization. Cultural, economic and political change in 43 societies*. Princeton, NJ: Princeton University Press.

Lukes, S. (1974). *Power, A radical view*. London, GB: Macmillan Press.

March for Life and Family. (2020). Retrieved from https://marsz.org/marsz-dla-zycia-i-rodziny-2019/.

Marcuse, H. (1991). *Człowiek jednowymiarowy [One-dimensional man]*. Warszawa, PL: PWN.

Nixon, R. (2011). *Slow violence and the environmentalism of the poor*. Cambridge, MA/London, GB: Harvard University Press.

Robertson, R. (1992). *Globalization: Social theory and global culture*. London, GB: SAGE Publications.

Spencer, H. (1876). *The principles of Sociology*. London, GB: Appleton-Century-Crofts.

Stiglitz, J. (2002). *Globalization and its discontents*. New York, NY: W. W. Norton & Company.

The Equality Marches. (2019). Retrieved from https://mnw.org.pl/parada-i-marsze-rownosci-2019/.

Wyleżałek, J. (2020). Polityka globalna jako czynnik lokalnych aktywności i zmian społecznych [Global politics as a factor of local activities and social changes]. *Rocznik Lubuski*, 46(2), 23–34.

Zielonka, J. (2018). *Kontrrewolucja. Liberalna Europa w odwrocie [Counterrevolution. Liberal Europe in retreat]*. Warszawa, PL: PWN.

4 The Role of Trust in Business

Elżbieta Kacperska and Katarzyna Łukasiewicz
Warsaw University of Life Sciences

Introduction

The problem of trust has been analyzed within the scope of many research areas. Thus, the trust may be treated as an economic, that is, business problem. This is reflected in the importance of trust in the decision-making process in economic activity. It is essential to be able to rely on the word of a business partner and, as a result, avoid many problems. Loyalty toward a business partner makes it possible to enhance the system's efficiency and thus contributes to the greater production of goods.

The aim of this chapter is to identify the role played by trust in economic activity and to discuss factors determining the development and preservation of trust among partners in the case of both intra-and inter-organizational relationships. Intra-organizational relationships are defined as situations within an organization (relationships between employees and supervisors). In contrast, inter-organizational relationships are purely business relationships. In order to present trust as a key factor in relationships and attempt at a precise definition of this concept in business relationships, a critical, interdisciplinary review of literature is given, and conclusions have been formulated.

The Concept of Trust

Analysis of literature concerning trust shows that it is multifaceted and interdisciplinary (Paliszkiewicz, 2013). It has been the subject of studies in many research disciplines, for example, management, sociology, psychology, and economics (Clawson, 1989; Watson, 1991; Hosmer, 1995). As a result, trust is a concept, which may be interpreted in a variety of ways. The understanding of trust may be divided into at least four categories, according to which trust is (Paliszkiewicz, 2019):

- A feature of character,
- An individual expectation or belief,

DOI: 10.4324/9781003165965-4

- The foundation of human relationships,
- The basis for economic and social exchange.

In terms of personality characteristics, this category may include definitions presented by Luhmann (1979) and Wrightsman (1966), indicating that trust is a personality characteristic, which may be reflected in general expectations toward the intentions of other people. This concept is similarly interpreted by Rotter (1967), who wrote that trust is THIS characteristic of personality, which reflects the general expectation concerning the credibility of others. A different opinion was presented by Gibb (1978), according to which trust is instinctive and as a feeling, it may be classified as resembling love. Another category comprises definitions presented, for example, by such authors as Sako (1992), Mayer et al. (1995), and Das and Bing-Sbeng (1998). Sako (1992) treats trust as a mindset, expecting a partner to behave in a predictable and mutually acceptable manner. According to Mayer et al. (1995), trust is the willingness of the trusting party to be dependent on the actions of another person, based on the expectation that the trusted party will behave predictably from the point of view of the trusting party irrespective of the potential monitoring or control over the trusted party. According to Das and Bing-Sbeng (1998), trust is a positive expectation toward motives for action in situations burdened with risk.

The literature on the subject also provides references to the third category: the individual character of trust treated as a characteristic or belief, thus its relational character is stressed, the willingness to confer one's trust in another person or a thing. Definitions within this category include, for example, that by Coleman (1990), stating that trust is a relationship of mutual calculations between the entity conferring trust and the entity conferred with this trust.

The last of the aforementioned categories focuses on the character of mutual relationships between individuals, in which partners calculate the level of trust. Among the definitions in that group, we may indicate, for example, that, according to which, trust is a mechanism based on the assumption that other members of a given community behave honestly and cooperatively, which stems from the jointly held norms (Fukuyama, 1997); or the one in which trust is a bet taken based on uncertain, future actions of other people (Sztompka, 2007).

Based on the aforementioned definitions, we may indicate the common elements of trust being both internal and external. Trust accompanies all human actions, and it is a component of all life experiences of a human being.

Intra-organizational Trust

A primary issue in the operations of any organization is related to the specific character of employee–supervisor trust. According to Kiyosaki and Lechter (2006), entrepreneurs lacking leadership abilities, thus failing to incite trust, may face problems in running their business.

Trust requires open and effective communication within an organization. Trust is built thanks to the continuous, direct interactions, the open doors policy, staff meetings, and internal communication media (Burton, 2006).

Within an organization, the manager has to exhibit the characteristics of a good leader so that the relationships between him/her and subordinates are beneficial. These relationships may prove to be equally advantageous for the organization and the employees. When employees trust that the supervisor would not abuse their position to introduce measures against their interest or breach their rights, they are more willing to cooperate, fulfill the manager's directions, and become creatively involved in the functioning of the enterprise. They are also capable of gaining greater satisfaction from the performed work (Robbins, 1998).

A leader should be able to cooperate with others. They will cooperate with the leader if they trust him or her. The process of gaining trust is a long-term process comprising various elements such as (Mayer et al., 1995):

- Competences,
- Honesty,
- Kindness,
- Openness,
- Fairness,
- Expressing one's feelings,
- Truthfulness,
- Consistency,
- Confidentiality,
- Self-confidence.

In a situation, when people do not trust their leader or manager, no team success may be attained. Trust is the key to motivating others, giving them the motivation to work hard and achieve common goals. Thus, it is necessary to avoid actions or errors that breach trust. They may include (Shockley-Zalabak et al., 2010):

- Errors in strategy,
- Firing employees,
- Lack of communication and concealing information,
- Low remunerations.

Managers who have greater trust in their subordinates will care for them. According to Paliszkiewicz (2013), when supervisors care for their subordinates, they appreciate their work, help them develop, and progress in their careers. As a result, employees feel distinguished and appreciated, which obliges them to work more efficiently.

Extraorganisational Trust

At present, all actions are undertaken in enterprises, and thus decisions made need to focus on the satisfaction of the customer/consumer. It is the customer that provides the organization with multifaceted benefits, including financial profits. A customer-oriented enterprise in its activities will strive to consider their opinions and adapt and implement their suggestions on their basis. Such actions will provide the enterprise with a competitive advantage. The success of the enterprise expressed in the development potential and ability to win a stable, competitive position on the market is dependent on the capability to enter and maintain permanent relationships with consumers (Mróz, 2009; Rudawska, 2009). It is trust that is the main factor determining the establishment of stable relationships. Satisfied customers will undoubtedly come back, will care for good relationships, and will be able to persuade others, which in turn will be beneficial to the enterprise, thus winning new customers. Consumers, when buying a given product, do not want to incur an excessive risk. That is why they repeatedly select to purchase the goods they have been satisfied with before. They use recommendations of people they know or choose a well-known brand or the one they have verified themselves (Lewicka-Strzałecka 2003).

As it results from market data, enterprises start to perceive the need to be reliable partners for customers. They are aware of the necessity to win trust and loyalty, to engage in responsible business policy. In a country where the level of social capital and trust is still low, it is very difficult to work on this value. Trust toward a firm needs to be built for a long time; however, because of the financial aspects, it is of great value since consumers are not able to test every product in terms of their quality, reliability, safety, and manufacturing conditions. A responsible company strives to be transparent, inform customers on these aspects, and gradually build its reputation. The success of an enterprise depends on the positive opinion of customers. Poor practices and taking advantage of the consumers' lack of knowledge obviously happen, but in the times when such information has been extensively disseminated, the damage to the company's reputation is costly, while the corporate image takes a long time or practically forever to recover (Stawicka, 2015). The literature on the subject confirms that, at present, it is the marketing relationships that are becoming one of the most effective forms of generating the desired impact and attaining competitive advantage. This may result in the development of long-term relationships for the company.

For this reason, fostering partner relations is a crucial element in business activity. The stronger the relationships, the greater the partners' satisfaction and the pressure to maintain and develop such contacts. Trust is essential for the development of relationships (Czakon, 2007). This is perceived as fundamental for any organization's success since it may serve many roles and refer to multiple functions, thus providing various benefits (Sankowska, 2011). Trust contributes to increased loyalty (Vlachos et al., 2009), while a consequence of trust is a long-term relationship (Huang & Wilkinson, 2013).

Trust in Business Relationships

Trust is considered essential for cooperation between entities and organizations. In view of various phenomena such as globalization, intensified innovations, and recurrent crises, the interest in the nature and role of trust in social and economic life has been increasing (Hardin, 2009;Van Zellad-van der Holst & Henseler, 2018). Trust may be perceived as a strategic relational resource for an organization. According to Drucker (1995), the greatest changes in the manner of running a business concern the intensity of relationships based on partnership rather than ownership.

Trust – as was stressed earlier – may be understood in a variety of ways. Economists in their studies treat trust in the institutional (Zucker, 1986) or calculative sense (Willianson, 1993). An economic interpretation of trust is based on rational and calculative analysis. When investigating the problem over a longer time, perspective behavior in cooperation is more profitable than opportunism, as evidenced in nonzero-sum games such as the prisoner's dilemma (Axelrod, 1984). Trust may also be considered within the concept of the rational choice theory. Here, trust is a relationship of mutual calculations between the one who trusts and the one who is trusted (Coleman, 1988). In terms of the economic aspect, trust may be found, for example, in the theory of transactional costs, which points to the unique character of human nature, which is self-oriented. Thus, it is difficult to specify who can be trusted and who cannot (Światowiec-Szczepańska, 2012). It may be stated that for some economists, trust is a good or commodity with a tangible economic value, which increases efficiency; however, it is not a commodity that may be subject to the turnover on the free market (Zucker, 1986).

In their definition of trust, Doney and Cannon (1997) also included the economic element pointing to the aspect of credibility, consisting of the fact that the other party will behave as promised and show kindness and strive to attain a common goal. Thus, it may be stated that in the opinion of the authors, trust in business relationships is associated with reliance on another person, being confident of their kindness, and good intentions.

Studies conducted on the issue of trust in business clearly show the importance of this problem. It may be considered that trust is dynamic and is characterized by high contextuality (Zieliński, 2019). In the opinion of that author, by investigating both sides of the relationship, it was possible to show that evaluation of mutual credibility may be perceived and understood by both buyers and suppliers. At the same time, Zieliński (2019) observed that perception of trust might result from the character of the relationship itself, which assumes interdependence of cooperating parties. Thus, relationships in business are characterized by mutual trust. In view of its dynamic character, trust may be considered dependent on the time and stage in the relationship's life cycle, indicating the transformational character of trust. The transformational model of trust was proposed by Dietz and Den Hartog (2006), who assumed the occurrence of diverse forms of trust, alternating with the development of the relationship (deterrence-based, calculus-based, knowledge-based, relational-based, and identification-based trust). The latter form of trust ensures complete trust related to strong emotional ties and shared goals and interests.

Studies have also confirmed the interpersonal and organizational dimensions of trust (Ashnai et al., 2016). Both dimensions are important for business relationships, but they will be related to a different distribution of factors characterizing trust.

Building of Trust

The importance of trust in business relationships is tremendous. The multitude of definitions, approaches, and models confirms the growing interest of both researchers and practitioners. Trust affects all actions within any organization: it may promote more risky behavior, optimal utilization of owned resources, or human interrelationships. According to Paliszkiewicz (2019), trust is not intrinsic, just the opposite – it requires effort and action. Building trust within an organization plays an important role not only in the functioning of the organization but also in business relationships. Because of the complexity of the trust-building process and its potential loss and recreation, many models have been developed for this process.

The building of trust has a considerable effect on human interrelationships in an enterprise and relationships between business partners (Czakon & Czernek, 2016).

In the literature concerning management, we may distinguish two dominant approaches to trust (Paliszkiewicz, 2019): relational-based trust and trust based on leadership characteristics and relationships. Trust based on characteristics refers to the perception of the manager's personality traits by subordinates. According to Gabarro (1978), these include the following traits: honesty, motivation, consistency, openness, discretion, functional competencies, specific competencies, interpersonal competencies, good judgment, and business sense.

In trust based on formed relationships, the idea is to create conditions conducive to trust development. It is crucial to establish definite goals and a vision in which trust-related behaviors are appreciated. It is essential to foster communication based on sincerity and truthfulness.

Increasing the number of meetings and interactions may contribute to and enhance the potential to build trust.

Trust is a gradual process, requiring time and appropriate interactions between partners. What is crucial is that the trust may be built fast, but it may be lost at least as rapidly. Trust grows with the development of a given relationship (Porras, 2004). In order to recreate trust, it needs to be a naturally progressing process rather than a result of a transaction. Trust cannot be imposed. Covey and Merrill (2009) showed that it is more difficult to rebuild and recover from the loss of trust caused by a lack of positive personality traits (integrity, good intentions) than from the loss of trust resulting from a deficiency in competencies (skills and outcomes).

Among the many models of trust-building, the SEEKER model proposed by Galdorf and Drapeau (2002) needs to be focused on, as it comprises the following elements of trust-building:

- Show that you understand the needs of a person and/or team.
- Establish principles to be followed in your actions.
- Establish resources, which you will be using in your work.
- Key on the principles you have developed.
- Engage in consistent, honest, and feedback-oriented communication.
- Reinforce consistent behaviors.

It may be stated that this model may also be used in business relationships. It comprises critical elements.

Nowadays, in a time of considerable lability and uncertainty, it is necessary to indicate the need to create an organizational culture based on trust (Krot & Lewicka, 2016). In the organization within which the stress will be placed on establishing adequate norms and values, it will be easier not only to create intra-organizational trust, but also to achieve trust in business relationships. This may be confirmed by an example quoting remarks of a manager participating in studies on business relationships (Zieliński, 2019):

> I cannot imagine work without trust or positive relationships with customers and suppliers. I know that with everyone, these relationships are different and are developed on various levels, but I always try to look beyond the financial outcome and to see the person on the other side. I believe that without trust, the relationships formed

> are callous and short-term. At long-term work, a lack of trust poses a threat to any project already at its onset: how can you delegate a task to individuals whom you do not trust?

According to studies presented by Zieliński (2019), depending on the performed tasks, the approach to the manner we perceive trust will vary. For example, sales specialists will emphasize trust leading to success in business (higher sales, limited competition, steady, smooth, and predictable cooperation, and many streamlined processes), reducing risk and uncertainty, facilitating problem-solving, and alleviating conflicts. In turn, marketing managers perceive trust as a tool that will help build and develop relationships between customers and the enterprise, guarantee to reach long-term goals (loyalty, recommendations, business stability, and business development), and reduce the probability of switching to the competition.

The consequences of trust in business relationships may be positive and negative. Among the many approaches stressing the former, we may mention the one presented by Akrout and Akrout (2011), in which relational (e.g., satisfaction, commitment) and economic consequences (e.g., efficiency, effectiveness) are distinguished. In turn, in the category showing negative consequences, we may mention the approach indicated by Skinner et al. (2014), who perceived trust as a process, with the "dark side" being situations when it is unwanted or disadvantageous and at the same time unavoidable for either or both sides of the relationship.

Conclusion

The core of this paper concerned the presentation of the role of trust in business. Theories and conclusions from studies have been briefly discussed, indicating the importance of this phenomenon. Trust needs to be analyzed both in the intra-organizational context and in extra-organizational contacts. Limitations that may be mentioned here include, first of all, the highly multifaceted and complex treatment of trust, which hinders its comprehensive analysis since it would require the adoption and investigation of this concept solely from a single perspective.

The following conclusions may be drawn based on the presented text:

- Trust requires a unique, individual approach, which takes time, precision, and extensive knowledge.
- Despite its definite role in many models, concepts, or approaches, trust needs to be analyzed in-depth using the case study method.
- Because of its place in many disciplines of science, trust should be analyzed in large interdisciplinary teams.

- Trust in business requires numerous studies and conclusions, which will help indicate the importance of its individual aspects and ensure appropriate relationships.
- Trust in business requires adequate preparation of managers and appropriate organizational culture.

In the future, it would be valuable to do the research on the following topics:

- Trust as a factor requiring a specific approach on the part of a business organization: the need to introduce changes versus. steady and consistent operating conditions;
- Trust in online relations (customer relations, relations with suppliers);
- Trust in intra-organizational relations (supervisor–subordinate relations);
- The potential use of intra-organizational trust to modify relations with the business environment of the organization;
- Addressing the need to incur costs related to securing transactions, which could be avoided in the case of mutual trust;
- Analyses of causes for lack of trust in business relations – and thus addressing the need to incur costs related to securing transactions, which could be avoided in the case of mutual trust.

Apart from the above-mentioned elements in research on trust in business relations, it would also be advisable to conduct studies providing answers to the following research questions:

- How to build trust in business relations (case studies)?
- How to restore trust in business relations (is it even possible)?
- What factors make us trust the other party in business contacts?
- How to ensure absolute transaction security because of opportunistic behaviors?

References

Akrout, W., & Akrout, H. (2011). Trust in B-to-B: Toward a dynamic and integrative approach. *Recherche et Applications en Marketing*, *26*(1), 1–21.

Ashnai, B., Henneberg, S. C., Naude, P., & Francescucci, A. (2016). Interpersonal and inter-organizational trust in business relationships: An attitude-behavior-outcome model. *Industrial Marketing Management*, *52*, 127–139.

Axelrod, R. (1984). *The evolution of cooperation*. New York, NY: Basic Books.

Burton, S. K. (2006). Without trust. You have nobody. Effective employee communications for today and tomorrow. *Public Relations Strategist*, *12*(2), 17–29.

Clawson, J. (1989). You can't manage them if they don't trust you. *Executive Excellence*, *6*(4), 10–11.
Coleman, J. (1988). Social capital in the creation of human capital. *American Journal of Sociology*, *94*, 95–121.
Coleman, J. (1990). *Foundations of social theory*. Cambridge, UK: Harvard University Press.
Covey, St., & Merrill, R. R. (2009). *The speed of trust: The one thing that changes everything*. Poznań, PL: Publishing House Rebis.
Czakon, W. (2007). *Dynamics of interorganisational ties within an enterprise*. Katowice, PL: Publishing House: Academy for Economics in Katowice.
Czakon, W., & Czernek, K. (2016). The role of trust-building mechanisms in entering into network competition: The case of tourism networks in Poland. *Industrial Marketing Management*, *57*, 64–74.
Das, T. K., & Bing-Sbeng, T. (1998). Between trust and control: Developing confidence in partner cooperation in alliances. *Academy of Management Review*, *23*(3), 491–512.
Dietz, G., & Den Hartog, D. N. (2006). Measuring trust inside organisations. *Personnel Review*, *35*(5), 557–588.
Doney, P. M., & Cannon, J. P. (1997). Trust in buyer-seller relationship. *Journal of Marketing*, *61*, (2), 35–51.
Drucker, P. (1995). *Management in turbulent times. New challenges – new horizons*. Kraków, PL: Academy for Economics in Cracow.
Fukuyama, F. (1997). *Trust. The social virtues and the creation of prosperity*. Warszawa-Wrocław, PL: Scientific Publishing House PWN.
Gabarro, J. J. (1978). The development of trust, influence and expectations. In A. G. Athos, & J. J. Gabarro (Eds.), *Interpersonal behaviour, communication and understanding in relationships* (pp. 290–303). Englewood Cliffs, NJ: Prentice Hall.
Galdorf, R., & Drapeau, A. S. (2002). *The trusted leader. Bringing out the best in your people and your company*. New York, NY: Free Press.
Gibb, J. R. (1978), *Trust. A new view of personal and organizational development*. Los Angeles: International College, Guild of Tutors Press.
Hardin, R. (2009). *Trust*. Warsaw PL: Publishing House Sic.
Huang, Y., & Wilkinson, I. F. (2013). The dynamics and evolution of trust in business relationship. *Industrial Marketing Management*, *42*(3), 455–465.
Hosmer, L. T. (1995). Trust: The connecting link between organizational theory and philosophical ethics. *Academy of Management Review*, *20*(2), 379–403.
Kiyosaki, R. T., & Lechter, S. L. (2006). *The business school for those who want to help others*. Osielsko PL: Instytut Praktycznej Edukacji.
Krot, K., & Lewicka, D. (2016). *Trust in an innovative organisation*. Warsaw, PL: Publishing House C.H. Beck.
Lewicka-Strzałecka, A. (2003). Trust in the consumer-to-business relationships. *Praxeology*, *143*, 195–207.
Luhmann, N. (1979). *Trust and power*. Chichester, EN: John Wiley and Sons.
Mayer, R. C., Davis, J. H., & Schoorman, D. F. (1995). An integrative model of organizational trust. *Academy of Management Review*, *20*(3), 709–734.
Mróz, B. (2009). Trust in business-consumer relationships. Conditions and dilemmas. In L. Garbarski, & J. Tkaczyk (Eds.), *Controversies concerning marketing in Poland. Uncertainty, trust and buyer behaviour* (p. 486). Warsaw PL: WAiP.

Paliszkiewicz, J. (2013). *Trust in management*. Warsaw, PL: Scientific Publishing House PWN.
Paliszkiewicz, J. (2019). *Leadership, trust and knowledge management in innovative enterprises*. Warsaw, PL: Publishing House CeDeWu.
Porras, S. T. (2004). Trust as networking knowledge: Precedents from Australia. *Asia Pacific Journal of Management*, *21*, 345–363.
Robbins, S. P. (1998). *Behaviour in an organisation*. Warsaw, PL: Publishing House PWE.
Rotter, J. B. (1967). A new scale for the measurement of interpersonal trust. *Journal of Personality*, *35*(4), 651–665.
Rudawska, E. (2009). Bank-consumer relationships under financial crisis conditions. In L. Garbarski, & J. Tkaczyk (Eds.), *Controversies concerning marketing in Poland. Uncertainty, trust and buyer behaviour* (pp. 412–413). Warsaw, PL: WAiP.
Sako, M. (1992). *Prices, quality and trust, inter-firm relations in Britain & Japan*. Cambridge, GB: Cambridge University Press.
Sankowska, A. (2011). *The effect of trust on enterprise management. An intraorganisational perspective*. Warsaw, PL: Publishing House Difin.
Shockley-Zalabak, P. S., Morreale, S. P., & Hackman, M. Z. (2010). *Building the high-trust organization*. San Francisco CA: Jossey-Bass.
Skinner, D., Dietz, G., & Weibel, A. (2014). The dark side of trust: When trust becomes a "poisoned chalice". *Organization*, *21*(2), 206–224.
Stawicka, E. (2015). Socially responsible business practices of enterprises in their relationships with consumers. *Journal of Agribusiness and Rural Development*, *3*(37), 539–540.
Sztompka, P. (2007). *Trust. The foundation of the society*. Kraków, PL: Publishing House Znak.
Świątowiec-Szczepańska 2012 Świątowiec-Szczepańska, J. (2012). *The risk of strategic partnership between enterprises; a model approach*. Poznań, PL: Publishing House of an Economic University in Poznan.
Van Zellad-van der Holst, E. M., & Henseler, J. (2018). Thinking outside the box: A neuroscientific perspective on trust in B2B relationships. *IMP Journal*, *12*(1), 75–110.
Vlachos, P. A., Tsamakos, A., Vrechopoulos, A. P., & Avramidis, P. K. (2009). Corporate social responsibility: Attributions, loyalty and the mediating role of trust. *Journal of the Academy of Marketing Science*, *37*(2), 170–180.
Watson, C. (1991). Doing what's right and doing well in business. *Business Forum*, *16*(2), 28–30.
Willianson, O. E. (1993). Calculativeness, trust, and economic organization. *The Journal of Law and Economics*, *36*(1), 2, 453–486.
Wrightsman, L. S. (1966). Personality and attitudinal correlates of trusting and trustworthy behaviors in a two-person game. *Journal of Personality and Social Psychology*, *4*(3), 328–332.
Zieliński, M. (2019). *Trust in business-to-business relationships. Dynamic perspective*. Poznań, PL: Publishing House of an Economic University in Poznań.
Zucker, L. G. (1986). Production of trust: Institutional sources of economic structure, 1840-1920. *Research in Organizational Behavior*, *8*, 53–111.

5 Establishing Trust in Artificial Intelligence in Education

Maria Elena Corbeil and Joseph Rene Corbeil
The University of Texas Rio Grande Valley

Introduction

Although oftentimes, education organizations are slow in integrating new technologies for teaching and learning, rapid technological advancements and recent unforeseen world events have thrust educators globally into an unprecedented level of technology adoption that could not have been foreseen. While educational institutions at all levels were at different stages of technology adoption prior to the COVID-19 pandemic, in Spring 2020, the vast majority of educators around the world were not prepared to rapidly transition from face-to-face to remote or online instruction. A metaphor frequently used to describe this situation is that educators were tasked with building the airplane mid-flight.

This educational experiment of 2020, coupled with the need from industries across all work sectors for an increasingly technologically and data literate workforce, has created an opportunity for educational institutions to reinvent themselves to better prepare their graduates. One promising tool that can radically impact how education is managed and delivered is Artificial Intelligence (AI). According to Vincent-Lancrin and van der Vlies (2020), "while most innovation in the past decade related to an increased use of computers and the internet in the classroom, the next wave will be based on AI, or on combinations of AI and other technologies" (p. 6). Yet, as we consider the enormous potential of AI in education, we must also recognize a myriad of emerging issues and potential negative consequences, especially to vulnerable student populations who may be unintentionally and inaccurately characterized or labeled through faulty or biased AI-powered algorithms. Unintended or harmful consequences of AI can compound the issues of trust many people have with smart technologies that are able to do things previously attributed only to humans. Issues of data privacy and misuse further complicate the AI–human relationship, making decisions regarding its use complex for educators. In order to help guide informed decisions regarding the selection and implementation of AI, this chapter discusses the benefits and challenges of AI in education, current and emerging

DOI: 10.4324/9781003165965-5

applications of AI at all educational levels, and best practice resources for increasing stakeholder trust in, and responsible use of AI for managing the educational enterprise and preparing learners for the careers of today and tomorrow.

Challenges of Artificial Intelligence in Education: To Trust or Not to Trust?

Regarding the use of AI in education (AIEd), Vincent-Lancrin and van der Vlies, (2020) observed, "the use of digital technologies increases both the production and value of data, creating new opportunities to improve education and education policies, but also new challenges" (p. 6). According to a 2019 report by researchers at Pegasystems, despite the demonstrated advantages of AI, "many consumers aren't sold on the benefits" (p. 2), adding, "perhaps the reason lies less in AI's ability to *think*, and more in its inability to *feel*" (p. 2). A computer making decisions without it being able to discern the value or impact of the decision leads to distrust of AI by many. Trust concerns include fears that AI will take over human jobs, apprehensions related to bias, and lack of transparency regarding how decisions are made and by whom (if made by a person at all). In education, where decisions impact students' lives, the concerns are augmented. The Internet is strewn with stories of decisions that impacted students' lives using big data results that created bias or were made without human scrutiny; students capitalizing on the weaknesses of AI to cheat; and computer systems doing the teaching, among others.

In AIEd, the potential for bias is a major trust concern. It is complex because, on the one hand, AI mitigates bias by removing or reducing human subjectivity in the decision-making process. On the other hand, AI may have unintentional biases baked into the decision-making algorithms created by humans (Silberg & Manyika, 2019). For example, Young (2020) describes an AI feature previously integrated into a popular learning management system that identified students who submitted work late, "suggesting on a dashboard shown to professors that such students were less likely to do well in the class" (para. 3). As a result, "some scholars worry that AI in learning management systems ... could lead to misidentifications ... by doing things like falsely tagging certain students as low-performing, which could lead their professors to treat them differently or otherwise disadvantage them" (Young, 2020, para. 2). An instructor interviewed by Young expressed that there was room in such systems for errors, citing an example of a student who submitted an assignment on time, but in a different format, triggering the system to flag it as a late, or as a nonsubmission. Her concerns were that instructors of large courses who are not able to get to know their students, may get erroneous impressions of them, and students may not even be aware of the information being generated automatically by the learning management system.

Another challenge is that advanced AI systems may be more complex and therefore more expensive to implement and maintain, resulting in less-sophisticated tools being used. According to Corbeil et al. (2017), "this can promote decisions made based on superficial information, instead of more in-depth detailed data that may be more challenging to mine" (p. 5). Leopold (2017) raises another issue of trust regarding who controls student data. He notes, "in an era when information is the coin of the realm, who's to say the system won't be abused" (para. 35)? Other challenges with AI arise from the lack of, or outdated, policies and procedures regarding data collection, analysis, storage, and use. Evgeniou et al. (2020) describe an example where an AI system was used to "determine final grades based on current and historical data" (Evgeniou et al., 2020, Summary, para. 1) after high school students were not able to complete high school exams due to the COVID-19 pandemic in early 2020. "When the results came in, many scores did not correlate with grades that had been predicted" (Evgeniou et al., 2020, Summary, para. 1), and although many students appealed the results, the appeal system had not been updated, resulting in many students not being admitted to their first-choice universities. According to Evgeniou et al., this points out the importance of developing and publishing clear policies regarding when and how decisions are made, as well as how they can be appealed.

Another AIEd trust issue raised is the opportunity it can afford students to cheat. Examples of cheating are frequently attributable to the way some learning systems grade assignments, forcing students to find novel ways to beat the computer to earn passing grades. Chin (2020) describes the experiences of middle and high school students who were failing a subject due to low grades generated for assignments submitted to a popular learning platform. In the examples cited by Chin, the parents or the students figured out that well-written essays did not earn passing grades. Instead, they discovered that inserting a string of keywords related to the topic throughout the essay earned them a perfect (or nearly perfect) grade on the assignment, even when the essay became nonsensical. While this can easily be remedied by the instructor reviewing the graded assignments, in many cases, especially in large enrollment courses, this may not be feasible.

Chatbots, AI-powered text or text-to-speech conversational bots designed to answer users' questions in real-time, are also raising issues of trust in education. Often used to provide instant responses to prospective students' questions while visiting college and university websites, chatbots are now appearing in online courses. Accordingly, "... as AI technology becomes more sophisticated, it might not always be clear if the 'person' you're interacting with is an actual human or machine"

(Pegasystems, 2019, p. 6). While the end-users may think they are talking to a real person, eventually, it may become disconcertingly apparent that they are just querying a database (TechTarget, n.d.). While AI has enormous potential in education, Popenici and Kerr (2017) also warn of the "real limits of AI algorithmic solutions in complex endeavors of learning" (Results and discussion, para. 1). For example, current automated systems cannot manage the subtleties of communication, such as humor, irony, or sarcasm. Similarly, in a recent study, Leopold (2017) reported that AIEd showed less impact in urban and rural areas, noting, "different students require different strategies" (para. 32). Consequently, while some AI algorithms work well with suburban students, they do not work as well with urban and rural students.

While there are certainly many challenges to be addressed regarding the safe and ethical use of AIEd, there are also many benefits that can be reaped through the thoughtful integration of AI into the educational enterprise. Its judicious use necessitates that educators who are decision-makers, users, and/or consumers of AI be aware of AI's limitations in order to use it responsibly. In fact, examples of practical and useful AI applications abound and are presented in the following section.

Benefits and Responsible Use of AIEd

The application of AIEd is not new and is expected to grow in the coming years. According to Behavioral Signals (n.d.), use of AI in education in the United States of America is expected to reach 50% by 2021. This growth is attributable to the explosion of smart products in the education market and a 24-year research trajectory (Zawacki-Richter et al., 2019). Yet, as seen in the previous section, there are risks that need to be planned for and managed. To help educational leaders and practitioners make informed decisions, increase stakeholder trust, and implement AIEd responsibly, this section describes some of the benefits and current applications of AI in primary, secondary, and postsecondary education.

AI for Managing the Educational Enterprise

AIEd today includes products and services that help administrators and educators manage the educational enterprise, that is, to carry out the daily and long-term operations required to plan, implement, and maintain the business side of education. According to Schmelzer (2019), administrators are using AI tools "to help with ... budgeting, student applications and enrollment, course management, educator HR related issues, purchasing and procurement activities, expense management, and facilities management" (Assisting educators with organizational tasks, para. 2).

At all levels, AI-powered systems can help to lower operating costs, help administrators track and project income and expenses, and improve the overall responsiveness of the organization (Schmelzer, 2019). Johnson (2019) adds, "AI improves IT processes and unleashes new efficiencies", para. 8). For example, AI can be implemented to manage campus safety, allowing administrators to monitor student traffic in hallways and identify where students are and where they go. It can also be used at the campus, district, state, or even national level to make predictions of future needs for planning (e.g., facilities, food, course demand, etc.), thereby saving time and money and helping to facilitate an array of educational services tailored to the needs of learners, when and where they need them (Johnson, 2019; Vincent-Lancrin & van der Vlies, 2020). In higher education administration, AI is currently being used to "improve the fairness and quality of the admissions process" as it "provide[s] a more systematic way of handling admissions" (Schmelzer, 2019, Assisting educators with organizational tasks, para. 2).

AI-powered educational data mining is also showing progress in helping to reduce dropouts. Vincent-Lancrin and van der Vlies (2020) observe, "even though identifying risks does not imply solving them, AI solutions help school principals to use existing data in new ways and design interventions to predict and prevent dropout more efficiently" (p. 10). By collecting and analyzing longitudinal data, AI is also helping to improve early warning systems that alert educators of students who are at risk of dropping out (Vincent-Lancrin & van der Vlies, 2020).

AIEd is also helping educators get through the administrative part of teaching, such as "planning lessons, assessing students, grading homework, giving feedback and administrative paperwork" (Barshay, 2020, para. 4), freeing up their time to work directly with learners. On average, "teachers spend 3-5 hours per day grading papers and tests, preparing lesson plans and completing administrative work outside of the classroom…" (Behavioral Signals, n.d., para. 5). In addition to helping to support the work educators do behind the scenes to prepare for or administrate learning, AI is allowing educators to provide a more robust learning experience for learners.

AIEd for Learning and Teaching Support

Examples of AIEd to support teaching and learning are varied and growing. Typical applications involve helping educators create or obtain smart digital content, personalize instruction, and assess learning. Examples of smart content include digital textbooks, audio, video, and micro lessons that can be easily updated and customized for, and by, the learners (Plitnichenko, 2020). According to Plitnichenko (2020), AI-powered smart content presents "new ways of perceiving information, such as visualization, simulation, [and] web-based study environments" (Produce smart content, para. 2). For example, with *Cram101,* presently in use in high school and college courses in the United States, textbooks become guidebooks with in-depth explanations, links to additional sources, and built-in self-assessments (Gupta, 2020). Similarly, *JustTheFacts101* "highlights and formulates summaries by chapter, which are later stored digitally and can be accessed on [commercial sites like] Amazon" (Gupta, 2020, Content technologies, Inc., para. 1).

Taking AIEd to the next level, *Netex Learning* has created a learning platform where educators in all levels of education and the workplace, can create their own smart content. According to Faggella (2019), it "provides a personalized learning cloud platform designed for the modern workplace, in which employers can design customizable learning systems with apps; gamification and simulations; virtual courses; self-assessments; video conferencing; and other tools" (Smart content, para. 3).

Bots and chatbots are another way AI is being used to support teaching and learning at colleges and universities in the United States. According to Foresman (2020), "chatbots powered by AI have helped universities better communicate with students and ensure they are supported on their path to graduation" (para. 1). For example, chatbots provide students support by "texting them reminders of quizzes or assignments, or of events on campus, or suggesting students reach out to academic counselors if they're struggling in class" (Foresman, 2020, para. 5). A famous example of a chatbot used in instruction is Jill Watson, an AI bot developed by a computer science professor who found himself teaching 400 students in an online class. Knowing that neither he nor any human teaching assistant could ever respond to all students' questions in a timely manner, he put Jill into action (Leopold, 2017). According to Leopold (2017), Jill was a "utilitarian message board, set up like Microsoft Outlook; questions and topics are in the left-hand column, each of which opens to a threaded conversation on the right" (Leopold, 2017, para. 7). Although Jill's true identity was not revealed until the end of the semester, she was positively received by students. Regarding Jill's identity as an AI bot, one student noted, "I haven't been able to tell ... I think if you can't tell, it's pretty effective, and I think it's a good thing, because people can get help more rapidly" (Leopold, 2017, para. 7).

AIEd for Personalized Learning

One of the most advantageous features of AIEd is its capability to personalize the learning experience. For example, products such as *ThinkerMath* help students learn math through educational games that reward and motivate learners to boost engagement (Gupta, 2020). Similarly, *Teach to One*, used in lower secondary mathematics, "... relies on data from continuous formative assessment to identify individual learning gaps in maps describing progression in skills" (Vincent-Lancrin & van der Vlies, 2020, p. 8). Vincent-Lancrin and van der Vlies (2020) cite examples in other countries, including China and India, where AI tutoring is also being implemented in and out of the class for topics ranging from mathematics and science, to college entrance exam test preparation, allowing students to learn at their own pace with a system that adapts to their ability level and performance.

It is the power of personalization that has boosted the use of AI by teachers and learners with differing abilities. For example, currently available AI technologies can read text and pictures in books, recognize faces, and even connect students to a person who can act as an interpreter for the visually impaired (Wu, 2019; Vincent-Lancrin & van der Vlies, 2020). Similarly, at a university in Beijing, a speech recognition system has been in use since 2016 that projects what the teacher says as text on a large screen at the front of the class (Vincent-Lancrin & van der Vlies, 2020). Vincent-Lancrin and van der Vlies (2020) note that this is a game-changer for learners with varying abilities as it allows them to access content in multiple formats.

AI is also assisting learners with varying hearing abilities. For example, AI-enabled hearing aids connected to users' cell phones are able to differentiate sounds from the learners' environment as "background noise" or "important noise" (Wu, 2019, para. 2). Wu (2019) observes that this is a very important development as it allows learners to actively participate in the learning activities and interact with the instructor and fellow students.

Similarly, AI tools are helping learners with autism spectrum disorder interact with others and interpret nonverbal and social cues using a digital coach that operates through smart glasses. Vincent-Lancrin and van der Vlies (2020) add, "students with autism can explore and improve social skills through interacting and collaborating with virtual characters and digital objects in a classroom" (p. 9). In addition to helping students develop their social skills, AI technologies allow "children with ASD to focus on the skills taught rather than the need to interpret social cues" (Wu, 2019, AI tools for people with ASD, para. 3). These advancements are helping learners with varying abilities to participate more fully and equitably in learning environments, and this is just the beginning. AIEd is advancing at a rapid pace, to the point where some systems have developed the ability to read human emotions based on the sound of learners' voices. When it detects students, who are frustrated or struggling, the system notifies the teachers, affording them the opportunity to respond to the students just-in-time (Behavioral Signals, n.d., para. 11). Gupta (2020) notes that by personalizing the learning experience, AI tools are actively engaging learners, enabling them to learn at their own pace.

AIEd for Assessing Learning

At the classroom level, educators have been using AI to automate grading and administer assessments. AI-powered grading systems can grade large numbers of papers very quickly, even in multiple languages; learn and update grading so it does not become outdated; integrate easily with other tools such as virtual interfaces and grade calculators; and reduce subjectivity (Kumar, 2020). If students consistently miss a question "by a more significant than average percentage of the class," the system can identify gaps in student performance as well as gaps in the curriculum where additional reinforcement may be needed (Behavioral Signals, n.d.). An added benefit of AI-powered assessments is their ability to help educators provide ongoing and formative feedback based on data that are collected and analyzed from student performance over time (Vincent-Lancrin & van der Vlies, 2020). Additionally, AI-powered game-based assessments and simulations using augmented and virtual reality, currently in use in science, engineering, mathematics, and medical education, can provide fun and engaging ways to assess complex skills (Vincent-Lancrin & van der Vlies, 2020, p. 10). AI can also aid in test preparation in the form of virtual tutors (Gupta, 2020).

Conclusions and Future Directions

AI is not a new technology and has evolved significantly since the mid-1950s. Hence, there has been ample time to explore its benefits and limitations across a wide variety of fields. As noted by Pegasystems (2019), through AI, organizations can be "more understanding and empathetic toward customers, but it's up to these organizations to take control of AI, guide it, and address their customers' concerns" (p. 4). Establishing a foundation of best practices for the responsible implementation of AI in education can go a long way to increase its effectiveness, manage risks, and increase stakeholders' trust.

A good starting point would be to critically analyze the myriad of complex issues related to the thoughtful and responsible implementation of AI in education across the entire enterprise. Khan (2005) proposed a comprehensive framework that stakeholders can use to assess their readiness and ability to implement and manage new technology initiatives across all levels of an organization. Through the careful analysis of factors across eight institutional dimensions: (1) pedagogical, (2) institutional, (3) ethical, (4) technological, (5) interface design, (6) resource support, (7) management, and (8) evaluation, the framework provides a structure to enable stakeholders to "think through every phase of a new initiative to ensure that desired learning outcomes are achieved" (Khan et al., 2016, A framework for analyzing educational issues, para. 2). To this day, "Khan's framework remains a valuable tool for evaluating an organization's educational technology readiness and opportunities for growth" (Khan et al., 2016, A framework for analyzing educational issues, para. 2). There are clear benefits to using Khan's framework when adopting or evaluating the effectiveness of AI in education. First, the framework helps stakeholders identify, and prepare for, any challenges that may arise during the application of AI. Second, trust is enhanced when stakeholders at all levels within the enterprise are able to participate in and contribute to the development of the implementation plan and its assessment. Third, by involving stakeholders from the community, transparency is accentuated, which can go a long way toward building trust and buy-in from students, parents, and the community at large.

In addition to systematically analyzing the benefits and risks, identifying and applying best practices are essential for the successful implementation of AIEd. There are many free, online resources available to help stakeholders with the responsible implementation of AIEd. For example, in May 2019, *The Organisation for Economic Co-Operation and Development* (OECD) adopted and published *AI Principles* that "promote use of AI that is innovative and trustworthy and that respects human rights and democratic values" (n.d., AI Principles overview). These principles "… set standards for AI that are practical and flexible enough to stand the test of time" (OECD, n.d., para. 1). Trustworthy AI addresses "(1) inclusive growth, sustainable development and well-being; (2) human-centered values and fairness; (3) transparency and explainability; (4) robustness, security, and safety; and (5) accountability" (OECD, n.d., Values-based principles, para. 1). Along these lines, Paliszkiewicz (2010, as cited in Paliszkiewicz et al., 2015, p. 20) identified four essential tenets of trust that can apply to the thoughtful application of AIEd:

a. Not act in a way that is harmful to the trusting firm.
b. Act in such a way that it is beneficial to the trusting firm.
c. Act reliably.
d. Behave or respond in a predictable and mutually acceptable manner.

An additional resource for AI best practices is found through *Partnership on AI to Benefit People and Society (PAI)*. With over 100 partners composed of researchers, business people, and academics, their goals are "to develop and share best practices, advance public understanding, provide an open platform for discussion and to identify aspirational effort in AI for socially beneficial purposes" (Partnership on AI to Benefit People and Society, n.d., our goals, paras. 1–4). Companies like Google and Microsoft also provide extensive resources for the responsible implementation of AI. For example, Google's (n.d.) *Responsible AI Practices*, recommend stakeholders "use a human-centered design approach; identify multiple metrics to assess training and monitoring; [and] when possible, directly examine raw data" (Recommended practices, para. 1). They add, it is also important to "understand the limitations of your dataset and model; test, test, test; and continue to monitor and update the system after deployment" (Recommended practices, para. 1).

Similarly, Microsoft (n.d.) published *Guidelines for Responsible AI* for the following six key areas of AI: (1) human–AI interactions; (2) conversational AI; (3) inclusive design; (4) AI fairness checklist; (5) datasheets for datasets template; and (6) AI security engineering guidance (Guidelines for responsible AI, paras. 1–6).

There are also resources available to help educators not only use AI for teaching but also to actually engage learners in the AI development process. For example, the *International Society for Technology in Education* (ISTE) and General Motors (GM) partnered to develop and share a multitude of easy-to-use, online guides and resources by grade level, titled the *Hands-On AI Projects for the Classroom*, available in multiple languages. In these activities, students develop AI products including chatbots, interactive presentations, and video games (ISTE, n.d.).

In summary, if used responsibly, AIEd can magnify education stakeholders' ability to carry out the daily business of teaching and learning at all levels. By adopting a comprehensive framework for identifying and analyzing the benefits and risks and by building a solid foundation for AIEd based on best practices, the education enterprise can leverage the best attributes of AI to improve the quality of education and make learning meaningful and relevant to students. Furthermore, as applications of AI are rapidly being infused into all aspects of people's personal and professional lives, educational institutions will need to prepare today's students to learn and work in environments "where AI is a reality" (Marr, n.d., para. 1).

References

Barshay, J. (2020). Reframing ed tech to save teachers time and reduce workloads. The Hechinger Report. Retrieved from https://hechingerreport.org/ai-in-education-reframing-ed-tech-to-save-teachers-time-and-reduce-workloads.

Behavioral Signals. (n.d.). The impact of AI on education. Retrieved from https://behavioralsignals.com/the-impact-of-ai-on-education.

Chin, M. (2020). These students figured out their tests were graded by AI — and the easy way to cheat. Retrieved from The Verge https://www.theverge.com/2020/9/2/21419012/edgenuity-online-class-ai-grading-keyword-mashing-students-school-cheating-algorithm-glitch.

Corbeil, M. E., Corbeil, J. R., & Khan, B. H. (2017). A framework for identifying and analyzing major issues in implementing big data and data analytics in e-learning: Introduction to a special issue on big data and data analytics. *Educational Technology*, 57(1), pp. 3–9. Retrieved from https://www.jstor.org/stable/44430534.

Corbeil, M. E., Corbeil, J. R., & Khan, B. H. (2019). A framework for implementing responsible data mining and analytics in education. In B. H. Khan, J. R. Corbeil, & M. E. Corbeil (Eds.), *Responsible analytics and data mining in education: Global perspectives on quality, support, and decision making* (1st ed., pp. 3–15). Routledge.

Evgeniou, T., Hardoon, D. R., & Qvchinnikov, A. (2020). What happens when AI is used to set grades? *Harvard Business Review*. Retrieved from https://hbr.org/2020/08/what-happens-when-ai-is-used-to-set-grades.
Faggella, D. (2019). Examples of artificial intelligence in education. EMERO. Retrieved from https://emerj.com/ai-sector-overviews/examples-of-artificial-intelligence-in-education.
Foresman, B. (2020). How chatbots are helping university students stay on track. EdScoop. Retrieved from https://edscoop.com/university-chatbots-educause-2020.
Google. (n.d.). Responsible AI practices. Google AI. Retrieved from https://ai.google/responsibilities/responsible-ai-practices.
Gupta, J. (2020). 7 real-life examples of AI in education – Latest digital transformation trends. Wire 19. Retrieved from https://wire19.com/real-life-examples-of-ai-in-education.
ISTE. (n.d.). Artificial intelligence in education. Retrieved from https://www.iste.org/learn/AI-in-education.
Johnson, A. (2019). 5 ways AI is changing the education industry. eLearning Industry. Retrieved from https://elearningindustry.com/ai-is-changing-the-education-industry-5-ways.
Khan, B. H. (2005). A framework for web-based learning. In B. H. Khan (Ed.), *Web-based training*. Englewood Cliffs, NJ: Educational Technology Publications.
Khan, B. H., Corbeil, J. R., & Corbeil, M. E. (2016). Responsible analytics and data mining in education. Retrieved from https://big-data-in-education.blogspot.com.
Kumar, A. (2020). AI's new role in education: Automated grading. eLearning Industry. Retrieved from https://elearningindustry.com/artificial-intelligence-new-role-in-education-automated-paper-grading.
Leopold, T. (2017). A professor built an AI teaching assistant for his courses — and it could shape the future of education. *Business Insider*. Retrieved from https://www.businessinsider.com/a-professor-built-an-ai-teaching-assistant-for-his-courses-and-it-could-shape-the-future-of-education-2017-3.
Marr, B. (n.d.). How is AI used In education: Real world examples of today and a peek into the future. *Forbes*. Retrieved from https://bernardmarr.com/default.asp?contentID=1541.
Microsoft. (n.d.). Guidelines for responsible AI. Retrieved from https://www.microsoft.com/en-us/ai/responsible-ai-resources?activetab=pivot1%3aprimaryr4.
OECD. (n.d.). OECD AI principles overview. Retrieved from https://www.oecd.ai/ai-principles.
Paliszkiewicz, J. (2010). Organizational trust – A critical review of the empirical research. In *Proceedings of 2010 International Conference on Technology Innovation and Industrial Management*, 16–18 June 2010, Pattaya, Thailand.
Paliszkiewicz, J., Gołuchowski, J., & Koohang, A. (2015). Leadership, trust, and knowledge management in relation to organizational performance: Developing an instrument. *Online Journal of Applied Knowledge Management*, *3*(2), 19–35. Retrieved from http://www.iiakm.org/ojakm/articles/2015/volume3_2/OJAKM_Volume3_2pp19-35.pdf.
Partnership on AI to Benefit People and Society. (n.d.). Retrieved from https://www.partnershiponai.org/about/#!.

Pegasystems. (2019). AI and empathy: Combining artificial intelligence with human ethics for better engagement. Retrieved from https://www.pega.com/system/files/resources/2019-11/pega-ai-empathy-study.pdf.
Plitnichenko, L. (2020). 5 main roles of artificial intelligence in education. eLearning Industry. Retrieved from https://elearningindustry.com/5-main-roles-artificial-intelligence-in-education.
Popenici, S. A. D., & Kerr, S. (2017). Exploring the impact of artificial intelligence on teaching and learning in higher education. *Research and Practice in Technology Enhanced Learning*, *12*(1). doi: 10.1186/s41039-017-0062-8. Retrieved from https://www.ncbi.nlm.nih.gov/pmc/articles/PMC6294271.
Schmelzer, R. (2019). AI applications in education. Forbes Cognitive World. Retrieved from https://www.forbes.com/sites/cognitiveworld/2019/07/12/ai-applications-in-education/?sh=54182d4162a3.
Silberg, J., & Manyika, J. (2019). Tackling bias in artificial intelligence (and in humans). McKinsey Global Institute. Retrieved from https://www.mckinsey.com/featured-insights/artificial-intelligence/tackling-bias-in-artificial-intelligence-and-in-humans#.
TechTarget. (n.d.). What is an IM bot? Retrieved from https://searchdomino.techtarget.com/definition/IM-bot.
Vincent-Lancrin, S., & van der Vlies, R. (2020). Trustworthy artificial intelligence (AI) in education: Promises and challenges. OECD Education Working Papers, No. 218, OECD Publishing, Paris. Retrieved from https://www.oecd-ilibrary.org/docserver/a6c90fa9-en.pdf?expires=1614717629&id=id&accname=guest&checksum=9EA8D808D97B5CC98B9637AFBE4D9057.
Wu, J. (2019). Artificial intelligence is providing special education alternatives: AI tools for visually impaired, hearing impaired, and people with ASD. ArtificialCiti. Retrieved from https://medium.com/artificialciti/artificial-intelligence-is-providing-special-education-alternatives-389b551d16d0.
Young, J. (2020). Researchers raise concerns about algorithmic bias in online course tools. EdSurge. Retrieved from https://www.edsurge.com/news/2020-06-26-researchers-raise-concerns-about-algorithmic-bias-in-online-course-tools.
Zawacki-Richter, O., Marín, V. I., Bond, M., & Gouverneur, F. (2019). Systematic review of research on artificial intelligence applications in higher education: Where are the educators? *International Journal of Educational Technology in Higher Education*, *16*(39). Retrieved from 10.1186/s41239-01 9-0171-0.

6 Virtual Organizations and Trust

Wojciech Pizło and Andrzej Parzonko
Warsaw University of Life Sciences

Introduction

Due to the widespread implementation of information technology, enterprises that were previously organized hierarchically are undergoing intensive changes. The hierarchical structure of organizations blocked and distorted the flow of information (Jarvempaa & Tanriverdi, 2003). The widespread access to IT tools resulted in the flattening of the hierarchical structures in many organizations. The nonhierarchical structures enable the construction of networks sharing internal and external resources and facilitate collaboration in virtual space. Not only is the structure of the organization modified, but also the regional and supra-regional business networks are undergoing changes. The effect of an organization's engagement in a business network is often a dynamic change in the relationships between partners oscillating between competition and cooperation (Håkansson & Snehota, 2006). The development of an organization may be facilitated by "internationalization" (Camagni, 1993), consisting of creating strong relationships between the organization and other entities already operating at the international level. Business networks use modern IT tools and databases, and above all, the creativity of people who are capable of creating new organizational solutions characterized by high degree of flexibility and effectiveness (Snellman, 2014). In the era of the global ICT network, organizations are interconnected by educated, open-minded, and creative people. New challenges and opportunities result mainly from technological changes and contribute to increased work effectiveness. New technologies support establishing cooperation between dispersed experts, stakeholders, organizational units, and enterprises. One of the new ways of organizing work is building effective virtual organizations and virtual teams.

The extant literature indicates that the main factors supporting the idea of creating open virtual organizations are the lack of administrative restrictions on access to innovative production and communication technologies (Gassmann, 2006). The open virtual organization model

DOI: 10.4324/9781003165965-6

starts to proliferate when the processes of economic globalization intensify, the mobility of international capital increases, production costs decrease, and more effective information and communication technologies emerge. The research indicates that the types of businesses most willing to collaborate include: high-tech enterprises (Gassmann, 2006), enterprises offering various types of services (e.g., the medical services sector and healthcare, due to the necessity to apply specialist procedures), and the entertainment sector (computer games) (Chamoso et al., 2018). The development of virtual organizations results from the availability of specialized IT tools supporting knowledge management (Le-Nguyen & Dyerson, 2018), including document management systems (Sun et al., 2020), the Web 2.0 system (Orenga-Roglá & Chalmeta, 2019), systems supporting innovation (Schmidt & von der Oelsnitz, 2020), as well as systems supporting teamwork and decision making.

The aim of this chapter is to identify the research gap concerning the issues relating to virtual organizations and virtual teams operating within their structures, as well as the issue of trust moderating the effectiveness of teamwork. While conducting the literature review, the methodological recommendations of Creswell (2009) were followed and the following keywords were selected: virtual organizations, virtual teams, effectiveness, and trust. The reviewed literature included publications from the databases of *Elsevier* and *SpringerLinks* journals as well as publications of authors available on Researchgate. This study uses a reporting approach that assumes that the research purpose is the recognition and description of individual facts, as well as an explanatory approach, involving the investigation of scientific facts. This approach enables an understanding of social and managerial regularities taking the humanistic perspective as a reference point. The study formulated the following research questions:

1. What is the specificity of virtual organizations and what are the directions of research on their functioning?
2. What characteristics of virtual teams determine their effectiveness?

Some of the cited studies are qualitative studies (Eisenhardt, 1989), relating to small populations, where the Eisenhardt approach (Hung et al., 2021) and Goia's methodology (Gioia et al., 2012) are used, encouraging the use of various research methods and a variety of techniques, and emphasizing that a case study can serve as both a test method and a theory-building method.

Virtual Organizations in Business Operations

The issue of virtual organizations was introduced into the scientific field in the 1990s (Davidow & Malone, 1992), and since then it has been addressed by many authors (e.g., Byrne et al., 1993; Snow et al., 1999). The main research areas included, among others, forms of cooperation, leadership, and directions of evolution of organizational structures under the changing market characteristics. One of the first studied areas was the issue of virtual teams (Lipnack & Stamps, 1997), presenting the impact of many factors on people working in a virtual environment. In the business context, the virtual organization model is based on co-operation mediated by trust and positive personal and social experience (Chamoso et al, 2018). Virtual organizations create a network of connections and use shared resources (Rodriguez et al., 2011), which ensure the possibility of their surviving on the market and achieving the intended goals.

Joint operations of virtual organizations involve minimizing risk and sharing financial, material, and knowledge resources. Virtual organizations are defined as a proactive response to the global competitive situation (Hirsch & Tilebein, 2015). The creation of virtual organizations is often initiated by small and medium-sized enterprises looking for development opportunities through pooling resources within a virtual collaboration. Virtual organizations may emerge from traditional enterprises that attempt to pool dispersed resources while minimizing financial risk. They enable the development of products supported by hybrid services (Hirsch & Tilebein, 2015). However, their ability to achieve goals does not only depend on the complementarity of the shared resources, but also on the willingness to collaborate personified by the level of trust. Virtual organizations are a network of independent organizations that pool their skills and organizational resources to achieve goals and make use of IT technologies to coordinate joint activities but, at the same time, avoid integration (Pizło, 2009). A virtual organization is defined as a temporary network of independent enterprises (Bielecki, 2001) whose purpose is to accomplish a defined task by using the key competencies of individual entities co-creating the organization (Malara, 2006). Virtual organizations rely on digital technologies for communication but still need to build relationships based on trust and co-operation. The core of a virtual organization is a community that creates flexible and secure IT solutions that enable the control of the entire constructed system while maintaining the autonomy of individual entities. The virtual organization system consists of (Hirsch & Tilebein, 2015): (1) IT system including the algorithm for managing the resources of all partners. (2) Knowledge base containing tangible and intangible resources, including, in particular, knowledge about the market and the rules regulating its use by partners. (3) The algorithm of settlements between active partners contributing to creating added value.

The main goal of creating virtual networks is to increase the adaptability and flexibility of the organizations that design them. The key emphasis is on the empowerment of employees, as they are expected to make creative decisions (Malhorta, 1997). The creation of a virtual organization is driven by the vision of benefits that can be obtained by individual entities (i.e., the expected market niches and the expected business advantages). The functioning of a virtual organization can also be perceived as a network of entities co-creating the added value delivered to the market. One of the methods of increasing effectiveness is sharing resources, which involves standardization and digitalization of the resources made available to the partners and their consistent and open network-based management (Rehm et al., 2010). The advantages of digitization and sharing resources include the reduction of total costs, and in particular, the time spent on organizing distributed service processes (Hirsch & Tilebein, 2015).

The Essence of Virtual Teams

Virtual teams are perceived as structural elements of a virtual organization, determining its specificity. The participants of these teams are often culturally and socially diverse employees with different professional experiences. Virtual teams are defined in the literature as "groups of geographically, organizationally and/or time dispersed workers brought together by information and telecommunication technologies to accomplish one or more organizational tasks" (Powell et al., 2004, p. 7). Other authors (Wong & Burton, 2000) perceive a virtual team as: (1) a group coming from culturally diverse backgrounds; (2) brought together by a common goal to be achieved in a defined perspective; (3) geographically dispersed; (4) connected by weak bonds; and (5) performing creative work. At the same time, the same researchers (Wong & Burton, 2000) indicate that there are no "pure" virtual teams that meet all these criteria, because there are teams that meet the requirement of geographical dispersion but, for example, do not meet the requirement of cultural diversity. The features shared by virtual teams include reliance on IT tools for communication and performance of partial tasks, the flexibility of team composition, and going beyond the current (traditional) organizational boundaries. Virtual teams are also portrayed as a group of people who interact through interdependent tasks, driven by a common goal that operates across space, time, and organizational boundaries, with communication enhanced by technology (Lipnack & Stamps, 1997; Hwang & Singh, 2015). A separate category is an open and inclusive virtual team, which, apart from meeting the aforementioned criteria, focuses on building relationships fostering respect for diverse cultures, nationalities, gender identities, values, religions, personalities, and physical appearances (Hung et al., 2021). The aim of the emerging open virtual teams is to develop the possibly most effective work system and to achieve a precisely defined goal, with the perspective of the team being dissolved after the task is accomplished. The success factors of virtual teams indicated in the literature (Hanebuth, 2015) include leadership, clear processes, procedures and norms, transparent organizational structure and efficient communication supported by modern technological solutions, as well as trust and a training system improving employees' competencies. Virtual teams can be described with reference to three categories (Hanebuth, 2015; Hung et al., 2021):

1. Virtual team context – the speed of designing a team to accomplish a task, time of its operation, and dissolution after completing the task. The incidental nature of the existence of a virtual team means that this team has no organizational memory, and therefore it is only the sum of personal experiences. The process of the formation and dissolution of virtual teams is continuous, permanent, and repetitive (Lipnack & Stamps, 1997) and the tasks of the virtual team are partial, creative, and delivered on tight schedules;
2. Virtual team composition – the competencies of team members resulting from their unique organizational experiences and cultural differences. A virtual team accumulates resources possessed by individual workers, including, in particular, knowledge, skills, soft competencies, and cultural resources, which contribute to generating added value offered on the market;
3. Virtual team structure – the structure that should be based on effective institutional patterns. Collaborative structures have to dominate: (a) the lack of interpersonal proximity, and (b) the awareness of the team temporariness.

Some empirical studies point to the ineffectiveness of virtual teams (Wakefield et al., 2008; Bouncken et al., 2020) Despite the fact that they had employed advanced IT technologies, they were ineffective due to the lack of coordination of the teamwork and conflicts. Consequently, assigning competent employees to the team, setting a goal, and providing them with ITC tools do not always guarantee success. An important, but underestimated, role in virtual teams is the ability to gather and share knowledge about the resources of all partners, current research, and the directions of market development. Leveraging knowledge resources requires the management of relevant data needed to achieve economic goals (Kankanhalli et al., 2005). Knowledge sharing is based on the process of encoding, delivering, decoding, and using knowledge (Raghuram et al., 2019). On the organizational level, it involves connecting teams and organizations that transfer knowledge, skills, and experiences so that they can be transformed into economic resources and translate into a greater competitive advantage for the organization as a whole. Sharing knowledge is also moderated by the individual characteristics of team members. It depends on age and gender and also on open organization culture (in-group collectivism, power distance, uncertainty avoidance, and performance orientation) and the openness of the information system (Raghuram et al., 2019). The main individual factor behind knowledge sharing is internal motivation. Virtual teams are believed to be more productive when team members are more able to share knowledge and exchange ideas (Alsharo et al., 2017). Interestingly, the factors improving the effectiveness of a virtual team also include the experience of team members as players of online cooperative games. Online games, and specifically massively multiplayer online role-playing games, reveal similar leadership roles and collaborative skills that are needed in teamwork (Williams et al., 2006; IBM, 2007). The openness of the team and its diversity increases its effectiveness, creates the opportunity to gain access to knowledge resources, experience, and skills of its members. In the research on effectiveness, it was found that such features as trust and creativity are particularly important, similarly to team climate, team cohesion, team confidence, and team knowledge, skills, and abilities (Wei et al., 2018). The openness of a virtual team is influenced by factors such as the age of team members, their functions, and the diversity of attitudes and values. Empirical research on virtual team performance has shown that technological factors have a significant impact on the coordination of teamwork and, consequently, contribute to its increased effectiveness (Wong & Burton, 2000). At the same time, it was found that the degree of digitization does not have a direct impact on the team's creativity, but rather relates to a different level of trust (Wei et al., 2018). To make a virtual team succeed, it is recommended to ease communication, develop trust, and implement transparent procedures to facilitate the coordination of activities. In addition, it is recommended to identify the expectations of individual members of the virtual team regarding the informal organizational rules connecting the team (team culture). Researchers (Wong & Burton, 2000) indicate that tolerance for errors is particularly important for increasing the effectiveness of virtual teams. In those organizations where mistakes cannot be made (tolerance is low), it is recommended to build traditional teams.

The literature also indicates the important role of the leader and leadership in maintaining virtual team cohesion, influencing trust build-up, and team engagement. Leadership roles, (innovator, broker, producer, director, coordinator, monitor, facilitator, and mentor), taken from the leadership theory were verified in terms of their impact on the effectiveness of virtual global teams. Interestingly, the research showed that the members of virtual teams did not identify these roles (Han et al., 2020). However, as reported in the literature (Mysirlaki & Paraskeva, 2019), the role and behavior of the leader is an important factor enhancing the work performance of virtual teams, in particular in the international environment (Barnwell et al., 2014). The significance of the team leader role increases with geographical and global dispersion of the virtual team (Jimenez et al., 2017). The leader binds the team together, motivates its individual members, resolves conflicts, and strives to increase the effectiveness of the team, which requires high emotional intelligence. That is why cooperation with the HR department is recommended to enhance collaborative skills in virtual context (Han et al., 2020). Researchers encourage team leaders to create an inclusive atmosphere in which everyone sees success or failure as the result of a team effort (Hung et al., 2021). The recognition of the contribution of all team members increases team morale and consequently improves team performance. Maintaining a high level of virtual team performance requires the leader to foster the integration of team members and assign tasks that facilitate cooperation (Mysirlaki & Paraskeva, 2019). Additionally, the leader should focus on establishing principles that strengthen the team's performance by building rules facilitating teamwork (Mysirlaki & Paraskeva, 2019).

Better performing virtual teams operate in a social environment that promotes knowledge sharing, collaboration, and social interactions aimed at developing social trust (Mysirlaki & Paraskeva, 2019, pp. 36–55). Virtual team members should be supported with trainings, including social competence training, to increase the level of team trust (Mysirlaki & Paraskeva, 2019, pp. 36–55; Han et al., 2020) (Figure 6.1). The virtual team performance results directly from having the appropriate software and technology supporting the team. Information and communication technology and the professional skills of employees play

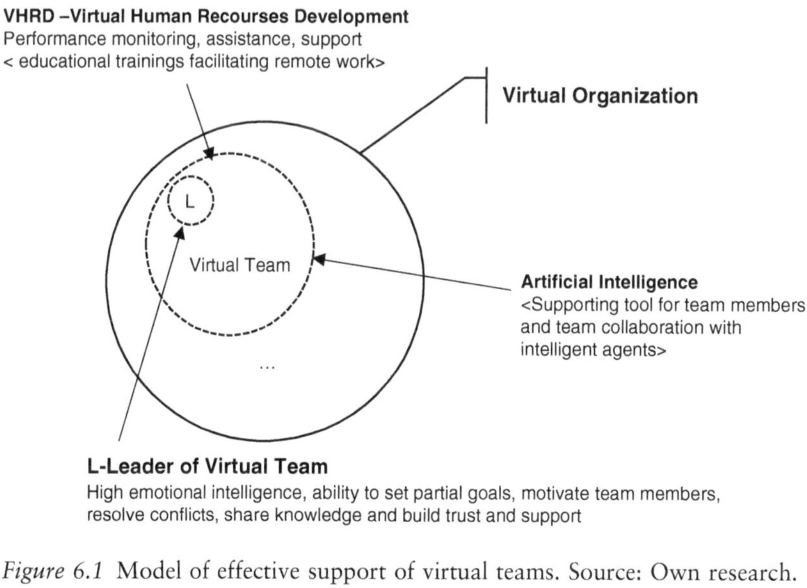

Figure 6.1 Model of effective support of virtual teams. Source: Own research.

a decisive role in increasing team effectiveness. Apart from technologies, the factor impacting the performance of virtual teams is the support of experienced employees or specialized trainers (Germain & McGuire, 2014, pp. 356–370), supporting team design, and self-teaching of team members (Mysirlaki & Paraskeva, 2019, pp. 36–55). The knowledge contribution and absorption increase the innovative capabilities of virtual teams (Hung et al, 2021, pp. 1–12). Improved problem-solving and innovation are related to the active participation of members in accumulating and acquiring knowledge. The lack of direct face-to-face communication means that individual team members may limit their contribution to achieving the team's goal, which reduces the effectiveness of the whole team. The method of increasing the productivity of virtual teams, in this case, is to design group tasks aimed at facilitating interaction between group members (Mysirlaki Paraskeva, 2019, pp. 36–55). Another important factor increasing teamwork effectiveness include common rules and norms regulating the relationships within the group and problem-solving procedures.

The Role of Virtual Agent

The goal of the virtual organization is to create a structure that enables the distribution of resources using algorithms for data identification and data processing, in which virtual agents act as heterogeneous units. The literature proposes insights into the role of virtual agents in open organizations and their adaptive features (Rodriguez et al., 2011, pp. 13005–13023). Virtual agents (VA) are a broad functional group of computer software that manages proprietary information (sniffer agent), facilitate communication via interface agent, or provide assistance through intelligent virtual assistant (Figure 6.2). Some research on virtual organizations focused on the role of virtual agents or multi-agent systems, which are part of the virtual environment (Mirbabaie et al., 2021). Virtual agents can be defined as virtual entities that are human equivalents and fulfill a supporting role toward humans. The intelligent virtual agent can answer questions and even independently (at a higher level of technology advancement) present alternative solutions. Virtual agents are personalized advisers and can be treated as a technical dimension of the interface. There is an interaction between the agent (supported by artificial intelligence with access to the appropriate knowledge base), and the user, during which the agent is learning. When examining the relationships between virtual team members, it was observed that team members supported by virtual agents were more effective. Some of the respondents defined their individual virtual agent as part of their extended self (Mirbabaie et al., 2021). These people were more likely to identify with the virtual team members than other colleagues. It should be pointed out that virtual agents supported by

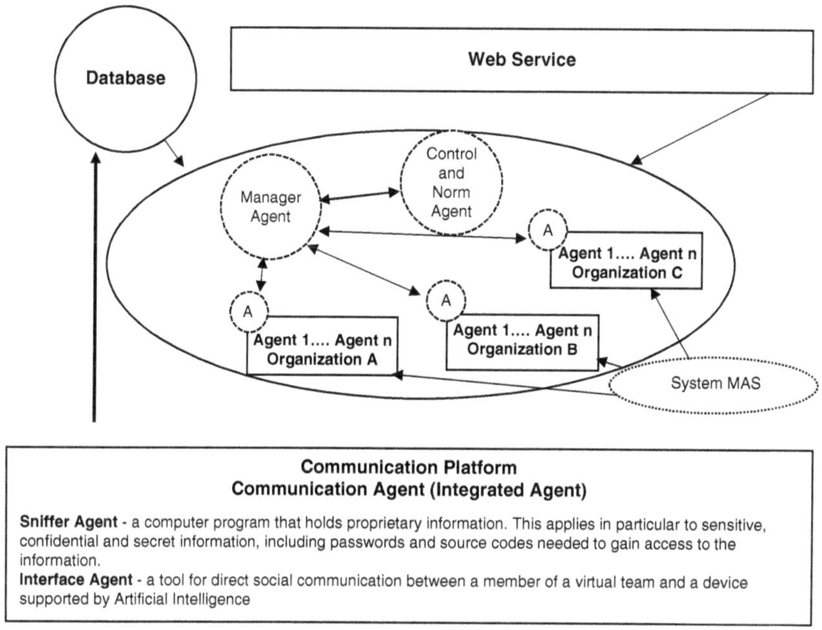

Figure 6.2 Model of supporting organization with virtual agents. Source: Own research.

artificial intelligence are able to self-organize, form groups, coalitions, or suborganizations. These systems are assessed with regard to their ability to solve new types of problems and increase the effectiveness of existing solutions. The single-agent institution has been expanded to include an infrastructure that enables interaction and communication (Figure 6.2).

The multi-agent systems (MAS) are open, noncentralized systems, containing autonomous, heterogeneous, and distributed agents (Huhns & Stephens, 1999). These agents have their own "personality", that is, they may be self-interested or cooperative. This system enables the co-operation of agents who coordinate the exchange of services and information; they can negotiate and reach a compromise and are able to implement other complex social activities. An intelligent virtual agent is a software (model) that uses knowledge resources, can use 3D graphics, and is able to identify changes and undertake defined actions to adapt to the environment. The use of intelligent virtual agents enables the simulation of many areas of business activity from medical services to a virtual production hall based on a library of models of used machines and devices (knowledge base). It is possible to combine various specialized agent models to build complex production structures (Lechevalier et al., 2019). Agents can act autonomously or supplement employee's activity. They can express their behavior just like a living creature, and can also demonstrate awareness of the changes that take place around them. However, the research showed that the introduction of virtual agents to a virtual team requires increased socialization of team members (Mirbabaie et al., 2021) (Figure 6.1).

The Essence of Trust

The issue of trust can be considered at the individual (micro), organizational (mezzo), and social (macro) level of conceptualization. The literature points to the differences in perception and definition of the concept of trust in various scientific disciplines. The differences between social psychology and economic sciences are significant (Paliszkiewicz, 2011). The diversity may result from the ontological differences in defining reality by individual disciplines. Thus, when identifying trust, one can indicate the interdependence between individual and collective (social and organizational) trust. In the case of emerging organizations, collective trust is not a simple sum of individual trusts. Building organizational trust requires positive behavior, being consistent with socially accepted norms, and confirming the purity of intentions and the tendency to act as declared. Trust can change over time and is one of the basic social characteristics of a human being. It is often contrasted with distrust. An important feature of trust or distrust is the level of its grounding in society (Sztompka, 2002). People who have trust in another person or an institution become more spontaneous and innovative. Consequently, trust generates the features that employers are looking for. By putting trust in someone, we offer them a certain "credit" of trustworthiness and, consequently, we liberate ourselves from the need to verify the intentions of the other party, thus incurring lower external costs. Trust is defined as the "willingness of a party to be vulnerable to the actions of another party based on the expectation that the other will perform a particular action important to the trustor, irrespective of the ability to monitor or control that party" (Mayer et al., 1995, pp. 709–734). In this approach, the definition of trust refers to positive expectations and willingness to take risks in social relationships. In the classic Mayer et al.'s (1995) model, trustworthiness is the trustor's perception of the trustee's qualities such as *ability, benevolence*, and *integrity*. *Abilities*, in this model, are understood as "a group of skills, competencies, and characteristics that enable a party to have influence within some specific domain". In turn, *benevolence* is understood as "the extent to which a trustee is believed to want to do good for the trustor". So benevolence represents a special attachment to the person for whom we act. *Integrity*, on the other hand, is "the trustor's perception that the trustee adheres to a set of principles that the trustor finds acceptable". However, if the trustee does not comply with the principles, which we consider a minimum requirement, they will not be seen as an honest person and, in consequence, we will lose trust in them.

Trust in Virtual Teams

Trust in a virtual team is related to its cohesion and external and internal motivations of its individual members (Snellman, 2014). The essence of trust in small groups boils down to interpersonal skills that facilitate communication between group members. Members of virtual teams are usually highly motivated and their motivation results from a clearly defined goal and a tight schedule to complete the assigned task. These factors make it easy to achieve a community effect, provided, however, that team members trust each other. Trust, openness, knowledge management, and mutual understanding are the foundation of effective decision-making. Lack of trust results from many objective and subjective reasons and may result in the need for additional communication effort aimed at strengthening trust and improving knowledge sharing. Factors, which are derivatives of trust and increase the effectiveness of virtual teamwork, include a favorable climate of openness and straightforwardness that mobilizes the team to greater cooperation, knowledge sharing, and knowledge acquisition.

Discussion

Due to the technological revolution, remote work is nowadays performed by administration employees, pupils and students, architects, designers, scientists, and other creative professions. Organizations previously organized hierarchically change their structure and pool resources with other entities looking for development opportunities in competitive markets (Hirsch & Tilebein, 2015). Building open virtual organizations improves the performance of enterprises mainly in the sectors of high technology, medical services, and entertainment. It should be noted that the emergence of virtual organizations will progress along with the development of information technologies and will assume an increasingly holistic dimension. When identifying the specificity of a virtual organization, it is necessary to point out the increased emergence of new organizational forms and the creation of virtual teams within their structures to implement highly specialized goals. Virtual organizations emerge because their activities are more effective and burdened with lower risk, as the complementary resources of the main stakeholders are combined (knowledge, skills, tangible and intangible resources) (Hirsch & Tilebein, 2015). Joint social and business networks make better use of shared resources and avoid integration at the same time. The idea of this new entity – a virtual organization – is based on relationships, trust, and cooperation. The concept of virtual organization involves joint actions of the members, based on a common goal, shared resources (tangible and intangible), an algorithm for managing the resources, as well as the algorithm of settlements.

Virtual teams are functional elements of a virtual organization. Digitized virtual teams use advanced ITC tools and specialized knowledge bases managed by intelligent virtual agents (Lipnack & Stamps, 1997; Hwang & Singh, 2015). The virtual agents are intelligent as they are powered by the "engine" of artificial intelligence. As the relationships between members of the human team emerge, simultaneously relationships between virtual agents are created. In our opinion, isolating the subcategory of "open and inclusive virtual teams" (Hung et al., 2021) is only an unnecessary multiplication of entities. Openness, the ability to share explicit and hidden knowledge, a large margin of tolerance for unforeseen errors, and care for the entire team working to accomplish the task characterize each effective virtual team. The leader has an undeniable role in fostering positive emotions and resolving possible conflicts. Their role is to maintain team cohesion and strengthen the trust and engagement of all team members. Soft, social, and persuasive skills are the ones that facilitate the achievement of the expected performance (Han et al., 2020; Hung et al., 2021). Virtual teams that perform better are teams that operate in a social environment that promotes knowledge sharing, cooperation, and are characterized by a high level of individual and social trust (Mysirlaki & Paraskeva, 2019).

An important factor that proactively affects the speed and effectiveness of delivering the project by a virtual team is team cohesion, assigning tasks requiring cooperation (Mysirlaki & Paraskeva, 2019), and clearly defined rules. Moreover, trust is the resource that must be developed primarily by the leader but has an impact on the effectiveness of the entire team. Trust in a virtual team derives from the consistency of the adopted operating principles and the motivation of virtual team members to achieve the set goal. Trust should also be analyzed with regard to the relationships between the team of employees and the team of intelligent virtual agents supporting their work.

Research studies on work performance within virtual organizations focused on the effectiveness of virtual teams. They draw from many scientific areas including management, economics, and other social sciences. Intra-group processes, leadership behavior, effective communication, and other factors determining the effectiveness of accomplishing tasks are currently being investigated by researchers. However, it should be noted that teams operating within virtual organizations carry out different tasks and take different forms, from human teams to teams of robots (Salas et al., 2008; Stowell & Cooray, 2017). Another problem is the fact that we are also unable to determine the dynamics of virtual research teams, although we already know that team leaders play a crucial role in their management and they should be (apart from high competencies) open, flexible, and above all empathetic and willing to share knowledge, which can increase the level of trust in the team. The creative attitude of employees also requires further research, because their ability to trust others and gain their trust swiftly determines the effectiveness of achieving the goal by a virtual team. Research on virtual team performance is usually carried out on limited research samples and usually covers Anglo-Saxon countries. There is no research on co-operation in global teams of employees coming from distant cultures, and the specificity of societies in Eastern Europe, Asia, and Africa is ignored. In research on trust and trust in virtual organizations, in particular, new methods and tools are being sought to measure team dynamics (Delice et al., 2019).

Conclusions

Technological changes that we observe today, mainly resulting from the so-called "digital revolution", modify the way people communicate with one another and flatten the hierarchy of organizational structures. Enterprises are looking for effective ways to intensify the exchange of information between business partners, which could accelerate the process of creating solutions that are valuable for the market. Modern digital technologies enable the effective aggregation of resources of many organizations, which leads to an increased efficiency of cooperating entities. New technologies stimulate cooperation between geographically distant experts and enterprises with valuable resources. Virtual organizations and virtual teams operating within their structures are a response to the increased competition and the development of modern methods of communication.

When answering the question about the specificity of virtual organizations and the directions of further research on their functioning, it should be noted that modern digital technologies create a unique opportunity for small and medium-sized enterprises looking for their market niche. The earlier research studies on virtual organizations mainly focused on forms of cooperation, leadership, and the directions of development of organizational structures under specific market conditions. Nowadays, the research in this field investigates effective ways of using shared resources, the role of trust, and the importance of personal experiences of individual team members. The literature emphasizes that virtual organizations create increasingly complex networks of connections between entities, share resources using them more and more effectively, and, above all, minimize the risk involved in any business activity. Virtual organization should be defined as a group of organizations that temporarily cooperate with each other, use IT tools for communication, and combine their resources (including knowledge, experience, and capital) in order to achieve common goals. The core of the virtual organization is the IT system, that is, the management algorithm, the knowledge base, and the settlement processing algorithm.

When looking for an answer regarding the characteristics of virtual teams that impact their effectiveness, it should be stated that in the research on virtual teams, a lot of attention is paid to the effectiveness of culturally and socially diverse teams of employees with different professional experience. The answer to the question of whether it is better if the teams are homogeneous or heterogeneous in terms of the cultural structure of the members – is still inconclusive and requires more detailed research. When formulating recommendations resulting from numerous studies, it should be noted that virtual teams are presented as groups of people guided by a common goal and operating in a specific space, time, and within organizational boundaries. The ineffectiveness of virtual teams is mainly due to the lack of teamwork coordination and conflicts. Therefore, it seems crucial to assign competent employees to the team and set precise goals that can be achieved, as well as to provide employees with adequate authorizations to access and share IT resources. The conducted in-depth review of the literature shows that the determinants of virtual team success include the ability of the team as a whole to collect and share knowledge about the resources of all partners. This process is supported by the intrinsic motivation of team members and the speed with which they gain confidence in each other. The tendency to share knowledge depends on not only the individual characteristics of the team members, their age, gender, and personality, but also on cultural openness. This skill seems to be enhanced by team members' experience as players in cooperative games. Sharing knowledge and experience has two dimensions: the organizational dimension, which consists of combining different resources of the organizations, and the socio-cultural dimension, where not only the organizational resources, but also individual experiences, skills, and personalities of all team members are shared. The factors determining effective team performance include leadership, clear procedures and standards, a transparent organizational structure, and effective communication supported by modern technological solutions, as well as trust. Many publications on management in virtual teams indicate the important role of the leader and management in maintaining the cohesion of the virtual team and level of trust in the team. It turns out that the classic leadership roles from the Quinn Model are not identified in the Internet communication environment. Therefore, it would be advisable to conduct research on the position of the leader and leadership in virtual teams, because the team leader must properly motivate team members, resolve conflicts, and ultimately ensure the team's success.

When looking for an answer to the question about further directions of research on virtual organizations and teams and the role of leadership and trust, one should point to the increasing use of various IT tools, such as algorithms and artificial intelligence supporting decision-making. An important research area should involve work on the architecture of virtual teams with an optimal structure designed for various purposes. There is a need to design a specialized architecture of both organizations and virtual teams for medical services, banking services, or virtual police teams. The still unresolved issue is the role of virtual agents (algorithms) supporting the work of individual team members or parts of a virtual organization. Another open question is the issue of synchronizing algorithms, defining their goals, defining their priorities, etc., and, above all, transparency of the actions taken to build trust. It is important to formulate rules regulating cooperation between algorithms – a kind of algorithm checking the readiness for cooperation and the "purity" of intentions. This is because there is an interaction between the agent (supported by artificial intelligence with access to the appropriate knowledge base) and the user, during which the virtual agent is learning. Moreover, the research shows that some members of virtual teams put excessive trust in virtual agents (computer programs) and identify with them – treating them to a large extent as part of the extended self. Moreover, these people identify with virtual members of the team more often than with other colleagues. Research into the factors increasing the efficiency of virtual teamwork should be continued, as the research to date, although promising, still raises various doubts.

References

Alsharo, M., Gregg, D., & Ramirez, R. (2017). Virtual team effectiveness: The role of knowledge sharing and trust. *Information & Management*, *54*, 479–490.

Ayoko, Oluremi B., Konrad, Alison M., & Boyle, Maree V. (2012). Managing conflict and emotions for performance in virtual teams [Online work]. *European Management Journal*, *30*(2), 156–174.

Barnwell, D., Nedrick, S., Rudolph, E., Sesay, M., & Wellen, W. (2014). Leadership of international and virtual project teams. *International Journal of Global Business*, *7*(2), 1–8.

Bielecki, W. T. (2001). *Informatyzacja zarządzania [Computerization of management]*. Warsaw, Poland; PL: Polskie Wydawnictwo Ekonomiczne.

Bouncken, R. B., Kraus, S., Martínez-Pérez, & J. F. (2020). Entrepreneurship of an institutional field: The emergence of coworking spaces for digital business models. *International Entrepreneurship and Management Journal*, *16*, 1465–1481.

Byrne, J., Brand, R., & Port, O. (1993). The virtual corporation. *Business Week*, 43–52. Retrieved from https://www.bloomberg.com/news/articles/1993-02-07/the-virtual-corporation.

Camagni, R. P. (1993). From city hierarchy to city network: Reflections about an emerging paradigm. In T. R. Lakshmanan, & P. Nijkamp (Eds.), *Structure and change in the space economy. Festschrift in honor of Martin J* (Vol. 78). Beckmann, Berlin, Germany: Springer Verlag.

Chamoso, P., Rodriguez, S., de la Prieta, & F., Bajo, J. (2018). Classification of retinal vessels using a collaborative agent-based architecture. *AI Communications*, *31*, 427–444.

Creswell, J. W. (2009). *Projektowanie badań naukowych. Metody jakościowe, ilościowe i mieszane [Designing scientific research. Qualitative, quantitative and mixed methods]* (pp. 49–55). Krakow, Poland: Wydawnictwo Uniwersytetu Jagiellońskiego.

Davidow, W. H., & Malone, M. S. (1992). *The virtual corporation: Structuring and revitalising the corporation for the 21st century*. New York, USA: HarperCollins Publishers.

Delice, F., Rousseau, M., & Feitosa, J. (2019). Advancing teams research: What, when, and how to measure team dynamics over time. *Frontiers in Psychology*, *10*, 1324.

Eisenhardt, K. M. (1989). Building theories from case study research. *Academy of Management Review*, *14*(4), 532–550.

Gassmann, O. (2006). Opening up the innovation process: Towards an agenda. *R &D Management*, *36*(3), 223–228.

Germain, M. L., & McGuire, D. (2014). The role of swift trust in virtual teams and implications for human resource development. *Advances in Developing Human Resources*, *16*(3), 356–370.

Gioia, D. A., Corley, K. G., & Hamilton, A. L. (2012). Seeking qualitative rigor in inductive research, seeking qualitative rigor in inductive research: Notes on the Gioia methodology. *Organizational Research Methods*, *16*(1), 15–31.

Håkansson, H., & Snehota, I. (2006). "No Business is an Island" 17 years later. *Scandinavian Journal of Management*, *22*(3), 271–274.

Han, S. J., Beyerlein, M. K. M., & DeRosa, D. (2020). Leadership role effectiveness as a mediator of team performance in new product development virtual teams. *Journal of Leadership Studies*, *13*(4), 20–36.

Hanebuth, A. (2015). Success factors of virtual research teams – Does distance still matter? Innovation Networks [Special issue]. *Management Review*, *26*(2), 161–179.

Hirsch, M., & Tilebein, M. (2015). Gestaltung und Steuerung von Industrial Service Networks in der Bekleidungsindustrie, Schmalenbachs. *Zeitschrift für betriebswirtschaftliche Forschung*, *69*(15), 95–118.

Huhns, M., & Stephens, L. (1999). Multiagent systems and societies of agents. In Weiss, G. (Ed.), Multi-agent systems: A modern approach to distributed artificial intelligence. (pp. 1–42) Cambridge, US: The MIT Press.

Hung, S., Cheng, M., Hou, Ch., & Chen, N. (May 2021). Inclusion in global virtual teams: Exploring non-spatial proximity and knowledge sharing on innovation. *Journal of Business Research*, *128*, *599–610*.

Hwang, E. H. P. V., & Singh, L Argote. (2015). Knowledge sharing in online communities: Learning to cross geographic and hierarchical boundaries. *Organization Science*, *26*(6), 1593–1611.

IBM. (2007). Virtual worlds, real leaders: Online games put the future of business leadership on display. Global Innovation. Retrieved from https://www.ibm.com/ibm/files/L668029W94664H98/ibm_gio_gaming_report.pdf.

Jarvempaa, S. L., & Tanriverdi, H. (2003). Leading virtual knowledge networks. *Organizational Dynamics*, *31*, 403–412.

Jimenez, A., Boehe, D. M., Taras, V., & Caprar, D. V. (2017). Working across boundaries: Current and future perspectives on global virtual teams. *Journal of International Management*, *23*(4), 341–349.

Kankanhalli, A., Tan, B., & Wei, K. (2005). Contributing knowledge to electronic knowledge repositories: An empirical investigation. *MIS Quarterly*, *29*(1), 113–143.

Lechevalier, D., Shin, S., Rachuri, S., Foufou, S., Lee, Y. T., & Bouras, A. (2019). Simulating a virtual machining model in an agent-based model for advanced analytics. *Journal of Intelligent Manufacturing*, *30*, 1937–1955.

Le-Nguyen, K., & Dyerson, R., & Harindranath, G. (2018). Exploring knowledge management software implementation from a knowing-in-practice perspective. *Information Systems Frontiers*, *20*(5), 1117–1133.

Lipnack, J., & Stamps, J. (1997). Virtual teams: Reaching across space. Time and organisations with technology. New York, USA: John Wiley & Sons, Inc.

Malara, Z. (2006). *Przedsiębiorstwo w globalnej gospodarce. Wyzwania współczesności. [A company in a global economy. The challenges of today]*. Warsaw, PL: Polskie Wydawnictwo Naukowe.

Malhorta, Y. (1997). Virtual corporations. *Human Issues & Information Technology* [Interview]. Retrieved from http://www.brint.com/interview/astdint.htm.

Mayer, R. C., Davis, J. H., & Schoorman, F. D. (1995). An integrative model of organizational trust. *Academy of Management Review*, 3(20), 709–734.

Mirbabaie, M., Stieglitz, S., Brünker, F., Hofeditz, L., Ross, B., & Frick, N. R. J. (2021). Understanding collaboration with virtual assistants – The role of social identity and the extended self. *Business & Information Systems Engineering*, **63**, 21–37.

Mysirlaki, S., & Paraskeva, F. (2019). Virtual team effectiveness: Insights from the virtual world teams of massively multiplayer online games. *Journal of Leadership Studies*, *13*(1), 36–55.

Orenga-Roglá, S., & Chalmeta, R. (2019). Methodology for the implementation of knowledge management systems 2.0. *Business & Information Systems Engineering*, *61*, 195–213.

Paliszkiewicz, J. (2011). Inter-organizational trust: Conceptualization and measurement. *International Journal of Performance Measurement*, *1*, 15–28.

Pizło, W. (2009). *Przedsiębiorstwa w społeczeństwie informacyjnym w świetle teorii ekonomii instytucjonalnej [Enterprises in the information society in the light of the theory of institutional economics]*. Warsaw, PL: Wydawnictwo SGGW.

Powell, A., Piccoli, G., & Ives, B. (2004). Virtual teams: A review of current literature and directions for future research. *The DATA BASE for Advances in Information Systems - Winter 2004*, *35*(1), 6–36.

Raghuram, S., Hill, N. S., Gibbs, J. L., & Maruping, L. M. (2019). Virtual work: Bridging research clusters. *Academy of Management Annals*, *13*(1), 1–34.

Rehm, S., Lau, A., & Hirsch, M. (2010). eCollaboration zur Entwicklung textiler Produkt- und Dienstleistungsinnovationen. *HMD Praxis der Wirtschaftsinformatik*, *47*, 46–56.

Rodriguez, S., de Paz, Y., Bajo, J., & Corchado, J. M. (2011). Social-based planning model for multiagent systems. *Expert Systems with Applications*, *38*(10), 13005–13023.

Salas, E., Cooke, N. J., & Rosen, M. A. (2008). On teams, teamwork, and team performance: Discoveries and developments. *Human Factors*, *50*, 540–547.

Schmidt, S., & von der Oelsnitz, D. (2020). Innovative business development: Identifying and supporting future radical innovators. Leadership, *Education, Personality: An Interdisciplinary Journal*, 2, 9–21.

Snellman, C. L. (2014). Virtual teams, opportunities and challenges for e-leaders. *Procedia – Social and Behavioral Sciences*, *110*, 1251–1261.

Snow, Ch., Lipnack, C., & Stamps, J. (1999). The virtual organization: Promises and payoffs, large and small. Trends in organizational behavior [supplemental material]. *Journal of Organizational Behavior*, 6, Chichester, 15–30.

Stowell, F., & Cooray, S. (2017). Virtual action research for virtual organisation? *Systemic Practice and Action Research*, *30*(2), 117–143.

Sun, J., Lei, K., Cao, L., Zhong, B., Wei, Y., Li, J., & Yang, Z. (2020). Text visualization for construction document information management. *Automation in Construction*, *111*, 1–12.

Sztompka, P. (2002). *Socjologia. Analiza społeczeństwa. [Sociology. Society analysis]*. Krakow, PL: Znak.

Wakefield, R. L., Leidner, D. E., & Garrison, G. (2008). A model of conflict, leadership, and performance in virtual teams. *Information Systems Research*, *19*(4), 434–445.

Wei, L. H., Thurasamy, R., & Popa, S. (2018). Managing virtual teams for open innovation in Global Business Services industry. *Management Decision*, *56*(6), 1285–1305.

Williams, D., Ducheneaut, N., Xiong, L., Zhang, Y., Yee, N., & Nickell, E. (2006). From tree house to barracks: The social life of guilds in world of warcraft. Games and culture. *A Journal of Interactive Media*, *1*(4), 338–361.

Wong, S. S., & Burton, R. M. (2000). Virtual teams: What are their characteristics, and impact on team performance? *Computational & Mathematical Organization Theory*, 6, 339–360.

7 CSR Communication Strategies in Trust-building and Customer Engagement

Jerzy Gołuchowski[1], *Anna Losa-Jonczyk*[1], *Joanna Paliszkiewicz*[2], *and Jeretta Horn Nord*[3]

[1]*University of Economics in Katowice*
[2]*Warsaw University of Life Sciences*
[3]*Oklahoma State University*

Introduction

The digitalization of communication between organizations and stakeholders challenges trust research to reconsider the determinants and strategies for building trust in organizations and creating customer engagement in their relationship with the organization. Numerous trust crises show that trust relationships have become more fragile in the digital world. However, studies show that the Internet offers opportunities to increase trust (Gołuchowski et al., 2018).

Well-managed organizations are aware of the significance of stakeholder trust for the decision-making process related to the purchase of products or services. According to Józefowicz (2012), customers agree to higher prices of brands they trust because if they were to take the risk of searching for other offers and comparing them, they would have to bear the cost of time and the possible risk of wrong decisions. A customer who wants to be satisfied with his purchases is more likely to choose based on the trust he has in particular brands. This is why managers strive to communicate in such a way as to inspire this trust. Nevertheless, there are still many images and economic crises (and often both in connection with each other) of brands and companies, which cause a loss of consumer trust. Organizations are troubled by questions about whether and how the organization should treat communication in the process of building stakeholder trust in the organization as a strategic area. Through the organization's communication, stakeholders are sufficiently involved in the relationship with the organization so that building trust is an ongoing process, resulting in an excellent reputation for the organization and long-term relationships with the environment.

It should be accepted with certainty that trust is variable over time, it can increase, decrease, or disappear, and that relationality is inherent in

DOI: 10.4324/9781003165965-7

the process of creating trust. The literature describes activities that support trust-building or weaken or even destroy it (Paliszkiewicz, 2018). One of them is the organization's communication with the environment. Communication that builds trust is characterized by authenticity, honesty, constancy, and two-way communication. According to S. R. Convey, when the trust account is high, communication is easy, instant, and effective (Convey, 2013). It is also possible to reverse the order of inference and assume that when communication is easy, instant, and effective, the level of trust increases.

The aim of the chapter is to present the role of CSR communication strategies in trust-building and consumer engagement.

In this chapter, the trust and risk of distrust are described. Next, the models of communicating social responsibility as a tool for building trust and engagement are presented and the CSR communication strategies are characterized. Next, the case of Princeton University is presented. The chapter ends with conclusions including limitations and future directions.

Trust and Risk of Distrust

Trust is a concept that is understood differently, even within a single discipline, for example, management sciences. However, it is the subject of research in many disciplines. Apart from the management sciences, it is also the subject of interest in sociology, psychology, and economics (Paliszkiewicz, 2013). Therefore, in the literature, one can find many definitions and typologies of trust and dozens of components of this construct defined by researchers (from several to several dozen components) as components of trust. The most-often-mentioned components of trust in the literature are honesty, benevolence (acceptance), competence, and reliability (Jabłonowska, 2012). Researchers of the subject indicate essential components of trust: compatibility of norms and values, openness, reliability, or compassion (Sankowska, 2011). However, after many years of research on trust, it is still difficult for researchers to determine which component of this concept is the overriding one.

The attitude of trust in an organization begins with an initial trust, a confidence that depends in part on the beliefs, commitments, and attitudes of the environment. In a certain sense, this attitude is a response to risk. Nowadays, when a consumer can "lock" a brand with a single click, organizations must make every effort to ensure that their social media communications convince stakeholders to trust the organization. According to Connolly (2020), the transparency of communication is the best way to gain the trust of stakeholders. Consumers want to know how an organization produces its product, how it relates to its employees and contractors, its attitude to global issues (e.g., ecology or poverty), and its values. They want assurance that it operates ethically and responsibly.

Stakeholders expect organizations to be more human, more engaged, and more trustworthy than ever before (Connolly, 2020). Websites, blogs, and social media accounts are appropriate places where an organization can communicate its activities and values, thus building stakeholder trust. Nowadays, internet users want to be involved by the organization in its activities to react to the published content. They are willing to interact with the organization for the right reasons. A lack of trust or a low level of trust is an opportunity cost for the organization. Therefore, regularly informing consumers, employees, and the environment about the organization's responsible approach to the natural environment and skillfully conducted dialogue with stakeholders, is a challenge for today's enterprises. Therefore, communicating corporate social responsibility (CSR) should be a strategic area in the process of building trust in organizations.

Stakeholders' trust in an organization cannot be fully guaranteed. It is changeable; therefore, managing an organization should assume that building trust through social media is a continuous and multistage process. In the literature, there are models describing levels of maturity and stages of building trust (Dietz & Hartog, 2006; Connolly, 2020). For example, Connolly distinguishes two main stages of creating trust in organizations: (1) initial trust and (2) continual trust. According to him, the organization's task is to prepare a communication strategy in social media in such a way that stakeholders move from one stage of trust creation to the other, increasing their engagement. Initial trust is based on first impressions after getting in contact with a company profile (e.g., a funpage). It is built, for instance, on factors such as the number of followers, ease of site navigation, and site security. These are the factors that shape the acquisition of initial trust. Later, through regular, positive contacts with the organization in social media, stakeholders can move to the second stage of building trust – continual trust. This level of trust is built on the knowledge that stakeholders already have about the organization or brand, their experience with the organization, and the commitment created at the initial trust stage. The process of creating and increasing trust is based on ongoing relationships, dialogue with stakeholders, and evaluation by stakeholders of the organization's activities. In the next stage of building continual trust, stakeholders identify with the organization's values and show empathy toward it.

The process of building trust requires investment by the organization. It is necessary, among other things, to create a communication strategy aimed at building trust in the organization, to operationalize communication with customers in social media, or to provide stakeholders with the knowledge they need (Gołuchowski et al., 2018). However, the costs of lack of trust or loss of trust exceed the costs of building trust.

In the process of designing an organization's communication with stakeholders, not only the content and form of the message are essential, but also the context in which the messages are sent and received. Therefore, when choosing an organization's communication strategy, it should be remembered that social media relations are built not only between the organization and the stakeholder but also between other web users. The comments under the organization's posts, discussions, sharing, and linking mean that other people discuss the topic raised by the organization, and the organization's communication with its stakeholders and its feedback affect the increase or decrease in the level of trust among stakeholders.

A specific way of communicating by the organization to inspire trust among stakeholders (potential recipients of the content of the broadcast messages) is the organization's social responsibility communication. The concept of social responsibility communication is defined in the literature as a process that aims to transparently provide information on integrating business activities with the organization's pro-social and pro-environmental actions and interaction with stakeholders (Morsing & Schultz, 2006).

Models of Communicating Social Responsibility as a Tool for Building Trust

Organizations set various CSR communication objectives (Capriotti & Moreno, 2007; Crane & Glozer, 2016). The main objectives most often mentioned in the literature are to create a positive image and develop a reputation among stakeholders (Ihlen et al., 2011) and to build trust in the organization (Morsing & Schultz, 2006; Cho et al., 2017). Research confirms that communicating social responsibility influences changes in the environment's attitudes toward the organization, enhancing reputation, and increasing trust in the organization's activities (Du et al., 2010), supporting the organization in crises (Stephens et al., 2005).

Of the many different CSR communication models appearing in the literature, two will be cited that most closely match the needs of building trust in a social network: the model by Du et al. (2010) and the model by Korschun and Du (2013).

The model by Du et al. (2010) encompasses three dimensions of communicating CSR, and through this, building trust in the organization of social network actors:

1. Communicating CSR,
2. Organization and stakeholder characteristics,
3. Impact of communication.

Analyzing the first distinguished dimension of building trust through CSR communication, researchers emphasize the role of message content and the type of channel used for communication. In their content, many

CSR messages convey information about the organization's involvement in specific pro-social or pro-ecological activities. In this context, the researchers distinguished elements that the organization should emphasize in messages to the environment. They included such topics as the motives for undertaking CSR activities and the impact that these activities have on the environment. Here, it is worth noting that messages about the organization's real impact on the solution of a social or environmental problem are one of the most interesting for the recipients and stimulate to engage the audience in communication with the organization (Simmons & Becker-Olsen, 2006).

In addition to the content of the messages in building trust, communication channels' choice is equally important. An important feature of the communication channel in the perspective of trust-building is whether the organization prefers to communicate through channels dependent on it, such as websites, nonfinancial reports, press releases, or independent channels such as media coverage and whisper marketing. Studies by Simmons and Becker-Olsen (2006) have shown that greater trust among the recipients is evoked by CSR messages conveyed through channels independent of the organization. That is why social media, which were not included in the Du et al. (2010) model, play such an important role in building trust through CSR communication.

The second dimension of trust-building in the model includes the characteristics of stakeholders and organizations. Their specific features may be treated as moderators of effective communication affecting the growth of trust. These include, among others, the type of industry, reputation of the organization, and type of stakeholder group – their pro-social attitude or lack thereof.

The third dimension of the model includes external and internal effects of the communication process. Research has shown the impact of CSR communication on stakeholders' identification with the organization, loyalty, productivity, an increase in investment capital, and an increase in trust toward the organization.

Although the CSR communication model described earlier is multifaceted, it does not exhaust all the important factors that can affect the building of stakeholder trust, and in this context, the effectiveness of CSR communication. This model does not consider social media as a specific communication channel, which currently seems to be a significant shortcoming of social media trust dimensioning. Research shows (Simmons & Becker-Olsen, 2006) that what channels and tools an organization use to communicate the content it communicates affects the level of stakeholder trust. Trust in what an organization communicates through advertising and marketing materials is significantly lower (41%) than the level of trust in content communicated through direct-to-consumer communications, such as responses to social media comments (EDELMAN, 2018). Although trust in social media has been falling below 50% for several years (in 2019, it was 43% – EDELMAN, 2019), it is still higher than trust in advertising.

Communication through social media is partially dependent only on the organization. The organization can manage this communication. The content, form, and timing of a post are the decisions of the organization. On the other hand, the audience decides how a message with the organization's content and form will be received, and consequently, what new topics will appear in the comments. Social media messaging allows an organization to convey relevant content in posts while at the same time allowing recipients to express their opinions on the topic at a time not far from publication. Stakeholder reactions to an organization's posts show their engagement with the organization and are also the basis for building its reputation in the marketplace. Thus, managing an organization's communication extends to managing dialogue between the organization and social media users.

The impact of advanced Web technologies and social media on trust-building CSR communications is considered in Korschun and Du's (2013) model. This model is based on the recognition of the need for a virtual dialogue about CSR with stakeholders. It enables stakeholders to participate in shaping, implementing, and supporting an organization's socially responsible activities. The tools used in this type of communication are advanced Web technologies and social media. Korschun and Du assume in the model that three dimensions characterize CSR communication: (1) co-creation of CSR, (2) communication platforms, and (3) stakeholder participation in communication. Co-creation CSR is understood as stakeholder input to the selection of CSR project partners, for example, NGOs working on a given social or environmental problem and promoting initiatives in the environment. Communication platforms should enable two-way synchronous communication with the possibility of immediate reaction and feedback and the expression of own opinions, expectations, etc. Stakeholder participation in communication is defined by different stakeholder groups' ability to communicate with each other and participation in communication available to the organization's external environment. The combination of these three dimensions of CSR communication, according to the authors, leads to the creation of shared value for the organization and the stakeholders. These values include a sense of community and identification with the community, strengthening trust in the organization.

The cited models complement each other, and both point to CSR communication's impact on increasing stakeholder trust. One of the shortcomings of the characterized models is the failure to include the communication strategy as an element of the model. Organizations often realize their cooperation with the environment based on the assumption that stakeholder relations strategies and communication strategies are operationally treated as synonyms. However, it should be noted that

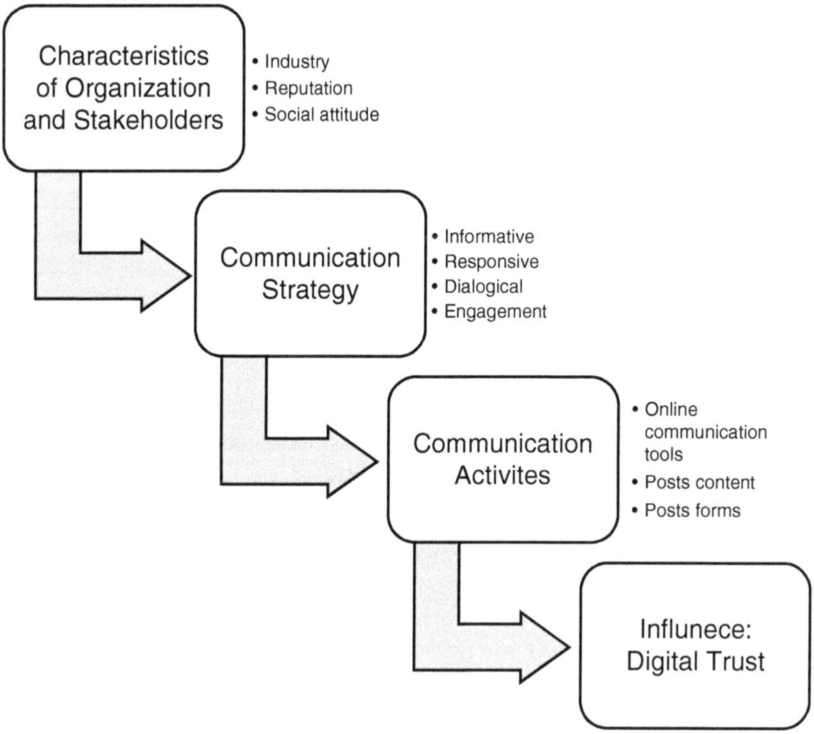

Figure 7.1 Model of CSR communication aimed at building digital trust. Source: Authors' own elaboration based on Du et al. (2010) and the model by Korschun and Du (2013).

building stakeholder relations is a long-term strategic task based on a specific philosophy, whereas communication strategies are a tool for achieving this task (Mitręga, 2008; Fryzeł, 2011). In the opinion of researchers (Stanaland et al., 2011), the choice of an appropriate communication strategy is crucial in the case of such a sensitive topic as CSR in order to gain positive attitudes of stakeholders toward the organization and to eliminate their lack of trust in the rationale behind decisions on CSR activities. The authors have not encountered in the literature a presentation of such a model that would take into account this dimension of the organization's activity.

Considering the dimensions proposed in both presented models, the authors proposed a model of CSR communication aimed at building digital trust. The model includes dimensions and elements of the communication process that affect the organization's increase of stakeholders' trust. The individual elements of the model are presented in Figure 7.1.

The first dimension of the model includes the organization's characteristics and stakeholders concerning the industry. The organization represents the organization's reputation and the attitude of stakeholders to pro-environmental and pro-social activities. The next element of the model is the identification of the type of CSR communication strategy adopted. The choice of a particular type of strategy is related to the adopted main objective of communicating about its responsibility. Types of CSR communication strategies, taking into account their objectives, are discussed in the next section (7.4). Let us note that the choice of strategy determines subsequent activities related to the communication process included in the model, such as: identifying the tool for communication in social media and developing the content and form of messages.

CSR Communication Strategies as Strategies for Building Trust and Engagement of Stakeholders

Research on CSR communication has identified several typologies of communication strategies implemented by organizations. The typologies introduced most often in the literature are cited by Wagner et al. (2009), Drumwright (1996), Kim et al. (2014), Morsing and Schultz (2006), Colleoni (2013). Kim et al. (2014) distinguished three types of communication strategies used by companies based on research: (1) corporate ability strategy, (2) corporate social responsibility strategy, and (3) hybrid strategy. The purpose of corporate ability strategy is to build the organization's image as a specialist in the market by emphasizing the quality of products or services in the communications. Corporate social responsibility strategy is used to communicate the organization's pro-environmental and pro-social activities and build its image as a committed and responsible organization. The third hybrid strategy combines the assumptions of the previous two types of communication strategies. The proposed division of strategies makes it possible to determine, based on the content of posts related to CSR and their frequency, whether the organization is positioning itself on CSR or rather on the quality of the product or service. The analysis based on this typology will not answer whether the communication strategy strengthens trust in the organization. Assuming that the organization builds trust through transparency of communication and engaging stakeholders in dialogue, it can be assumed that the typology proposed by Morsing and Schultz (2006) will be the most adequate to determine whether the communication strategy strengthens the building of trust in the organization.

The typology presented by Morsing and Schultz (2006) includes three dimensions that characterize each type of strategy:

1. The main task of communicating,
2. The role of stakeholders in the communication process as defined by the organization,
3. The decision-making process concerning CSR activities and communication about them in the organization's structure.

The three types of CSR communication strategies are (1) information strategy, (2) responsive strategy, and (3) engagement strategy. Each of the presented strategies sets different overarching tasks. Because the information strategy (1) is characterized by a one-sided approach of the organization to CSR communication, the main task carried out is to inform the environment about the organization's CSR activities, "broadcasting" the organization's CSR messages. These are messages with positive overtones, building a positive image and reputation of the organization. In the responsive strategy (2), on the other hand, the organization assumes that the main task of CSR communication is to collect information among stakeholders that may be needed to understand the nature of the emerging problem (often in the first phase of problem-solving), its scale, background, as well as new current trends in communities. The third type of CSR communication strategy, the engagement strategy (3), enables the organization's environment to be involved in decision-making related to its social responsibility area. The involvement strategy assumes that the main task of communicating social responsibility is to establish lasting relations and cooperation with stakeholders that result from joint analysis of emerging problems and searching for ways to build consensus.

Etter (2014) analyzed organizations' social media communication strategies and similarly distinguished three types of strategies adopted and described them as (1) a broadcasting strategy – information is communicated to an anonymous recipient without a personalized approach, (2) a reactive strategy – when the organization merely responds to questions or comments that arise from stakeholders, and (3) an engaging strategy – which enables a proactive approach to communication by the organization, the organization encourages dialogue and the exchange of ideas.

A strategic approach to social media communication in order to engage customers and gain their trust was also the basis of the communication model proposed by Connolly (2020). He distinguished seven levels of customers (one of stakeholders group) digital trust. The first three levels of the model present how to build initial trust in social media by identifying stakeholders' needs and values. The next stage strengthens brand awareness through financial motivations and maintains interaction between the organization and message recipients. At the next levels, providing the knowledge needed by stakeholders, responding to comments leads to creating long-term relationships of the environment with the organization, increasing loyalty, which results in gaining the continual trust of stakeholders.

Recognizing the gap in the aforementioned typologies of CSR communication strategies (Morsing & Schultz, 2006 typologies; Etter, 2014), the authors proposed to complement them with a fourth type of strategy, which is the dialogue strategy (4). They considered it to be intermediate between the responsive strategy and the engagement strategy. The adoption of the fourth type of strategy – dialogic strategy – results from the need to clarify the role of stakeholders in the CSR communication process and the main task of communication. In a dialogue strategy, it is primarily important to obtain feedback on the organization's proposals and learn about stakeholders' opinions and feelings regarding the organization's CSR activities. The opinions obtained may influence the change of decisions and direction of activities by the organization.

However, it is only the last type of strategy – the engagement strategy that leads to the highest level of stakeholder identification with the organization, building loyalty and trust (Etter, 2014; Lopez et al., 2017). Moving to the operational level, the organization should determine how to leverage social media's power to implement an engagement strategy. Trust is essential to the quality and secure interactions in online social networks (Zhank & Yu, 2012).

The Attempt to Identify the Strategy for Building Trust and Engagement Through CSR Communication in Social Media – the Case of Princeton University

Based on the proposed model, the authors attempted to analyze CSR communication in social media in the context of building trust and stakeholder involvement of one of the most highly ranked universities in the USA and the world – Princeton University (sixth place in the Academic Ranking of World Universities 2020). In the literature, the concept of sustainable development, the topic of communicating and activities related to social and environmental responsibility, is addressed by researchers concerning the companies (Testarmata et al., 2018; Saxton et al., 2019). However, it should be noted that universities are not the only organizations implementing the concept of sustainable development. Additionally, universities play an essential role in promoting sustainable development responsibility among the main stakeholders, as students, candidates, graduates, and employees are crucial due to the opinion-forming role of the world of science among society.

When selecting the subject for the study, three factors were identified that determine the choice: (1) popularity/prestige of the University (assumed: top ten in the international ranking), (2) implementation by the University of activities related to social and environmental responsibility (activities related to Sustainable Development Goals by UN), and (3) communication about these activities in social media. The same criteria were met by Harvard University and Princeton University, among others. However, for the following analysis, it was important that (4) the examined University did not communicate about sustainable development on separate social media accounts explicitly dedicated to this topic, as other universities do, but that the full range of topics to be communicated was contained in one main university account. This is why Princeton University was chosen.

Universities use a variety of communication tools, usually several. The social media communication tool that was chosen for analysis was Instagram. Instagram was chosen for analysis because it is now a rapidly gaining medium in popularity with the public. Instagram is becoming immensely popular among young Internet users (Digital 2020 Report), the group with which universities communicate (students, candidates, and graduates).

The research on social media communication showed that universities' social media communication topic has not been of broad interest to researchers so far. In the authors' opinion, social media should be the primary tool for communicating sustainable development and dialogue with its main stakeholders.

A case study was adopted as the research method. The key research questions posed are:

1. How can one communicate pro-social and pro-environmental (sustainable development) activities in the social media of the studied university based on the model of CSR communication in building digital trust?
2. What type of social media communication strategy does the university implement?
3. How does the university build trust and commitment by communicating pro-social and pro-environmental activities?

To answer the research questions, a text corpus consisting of 211 posts on the official university's Instagram accounts was collected for analysis. The text corpus was created based on the entries posted in the accounts in one year – from January 2020 to December 2020. Then the content of the collected entries was analyzed according to the coding procedure adopted by the authors. From the text corpus, entries concerning sustainable development were separated. The number of sustainable development posts was 76, accounting for 36% of the total number of posts. When analyzing the entries' content, coding tags were indicated, which define the particular areas of sustainability. The posts have been grouped according to sustainable development areas (based on Sustainable Development Goals by UN). The results of the analysis showed that the posts were mainly about three topics: physical and mental health (SDG 3), ecology (SDG 7, 13, 15), and gender and race equality (SDG 5, 10).

The research process's theoretical basis was the typology of social media communication adopted by Kim et al. (2014) and the model of CSR communication aimed at building digital trust proposed by the authors.

The type of social media communication strategy was determined based on the collected quantitative data (total number of entries and the number of entries concerning sustainable development). The number of posts concerning sustainable development posted on the Instagram profile did not exceed 50%; therefore, the communication strategy cannot be described as a CSR strategy. The implemented strategy is a hybrid strategy combining information about the University's services with posts about the University's responsibility toward the environment and society. Since posts from the year 2020 were analyzed, a period of the global pandemic that also significantly affected the USA, it is worth noting that there was a relative increase in posts about the University's responsibility between mid-February and December compared to posts from the first weeks of 2020.

Based on the model of CSR communication in building digital trust, an attempt was made to characterize the strategy implemented by the University to communicate about sustainable development activities in social media. The identification of the strategy was carried out according to the proposed model. The elements of the model requiring identification in the first instance were the organization's characteristics and stakeholders concerning the criteria: reputation, industry, and stakeholders' attitude toward pro-environmental and pro-social activities. The next step was to identify the main objectives of communication, the content and forms of messages to be communicated, and the chosen communication tool. This research process allowed us to identify the communication strategy adopted by the University and its effect on the trust of the group's primary stakeholder groups using the social network Instagram.

The first step of the pilot study carried out was to analyze the organization and its stakeholders: the university is part of higher education, which is endowed with a high level of trust from the public (Trust Global Barometer Report 2018), and consequently, there are expectations of responsibility associated with the university's activities both in the research and educational fields. The researched university has a very good reputation, which is evidenced by, among other things, the high place it occupies annually in the Academic Ranking of World Universities and a large number of positive comments in social media posted by current students and alumni. The stakeholders targeted by social media messages are mainly students, applicants, and graduates of the university. University employees also post comments on posts, but sporadically. Among the recipients of the University's messages, the attitude to the activities related to sustainable development is positive, as evidenced by the high number of likes and positive comments under the posts related to this topic. There are also occasional comments under the posts with doubts or accusations toward the University and its responsibility concerning society or the environment. However, it should be noted that these are comments that demonstrate an understanding among the recipients of the relevance of the University's topics in social media. This characterization of the University and the open and positive attitude of the main stakeholder groups toward the topics communicated in sustainable development in social media increases the possibility of building trust (digital trust) in the university-environment relationship.

The next steps were aimed at identifying the second and third elements of the model, that is, the main objectives of communication, the content and forms of messages posted, and the communication tools adopted, and identifying the communication strategy adopted by the organization. The authors could not access the document of the CSR communication strategy adopted by the University, so the identification of the strategy was based on the study of the content and frequency of the University's comments posted under stakeholder reactions and comments. Considering that the University carries out CSR communication in social media (here, the examined Instagram profile), a tool that enables the recipient to immediately respond to the content posted by the sender, both positive and negative, and to conduct a dialogue with other stakeholders without imposing the topic by the account owner, the implemented communication strategy of the University can be characterized as open and dialogue-oriented. This is also evidenced by the University's frequent responses to stakeholder comments.

The identified strategy can be described as a dialogue strategy with elements of an engagement strategy. The University carries out the dialogue through "likes" under stakeholder comments and responses to questions from the recipients of the messages (e.g., questions about the recruitment process or research reports mentioned in the posts). The posts' content is informative, promotes sustainable development activities undertaken by the University, and less often encourages co-creation of these activities. Stakeholder comments that express doubt or question the credibility of the promoted activities are not discussed by the University and remain unanswered. In some cases, such comments arouse others' interest, and the topic is developed, despite the University's lack of response. However, importantly, negative comments are not deleted by the University's account administrator.

The dialogue strategy's primary purpose is to get stakeholders' feedback on the University's activities described in the posts to find out their opinions and feelings. The information obtained can influence the organization's action plan's adjustment, as the stakeholders' opinion is vital to the organization. Signs of an engagement strategy can be found in posts prepared by the stakeholders: students, alumni, or employees. Not only do they have the opportunity to react and comment on the University's posts, but they are also involved in the creation of content and promotion of sustainable development activities.

Conclusions

As numerous studies show, trust is an intangible value of an organization, which influences both the behavior of employees and the organization's relations with its external environment by improving processes, the quality of services and products, open communication and the company's reputation, and customer loyalty (Józefowicz, 2012). By building trust, the organization reduces transaction costs, increases its value level, and achieves a competitive advantage in the market. The organization must consider that trust is not permanent and may be changeable in time. Many factors influence its increase or decrease, including the quality of communication between the organization and its environment.

In order to meet these challenges, organizations need new communication strategies that, on the one hand, optimize the use of new opportunities and, on the other, provide opportunities to avoid potential pitfalls leading to failures in the organization's communication with its customers online. CSR communication is one of the platforms for building stakeholder trust in organizations. Based on our research of a selected American university, an example of a strategy that organizations can successfully implement when engaging in dialogue with stakeholders on social media to positively influence their trust and engagement is presented. The analysis of other organizations' strategies is a valuable inspiration for entities that want to build digital trust among their stakeholders.

This chapter presents a research model for identifying CSR communication strategies as a tool for building trust under the digitalization of the organization's communication with its stakeholders, especially customers. It outlines the challenges in building trust in organizations that organizations are currently facing due to digital and social platforms' development using CSR communication. Social media platforms facilitate and enable greater transparency of organizations' activities, consumer empowerment, and online activism. Alongside these undoubted benefits, there are negative phenomena, for example, opportunities to abuse online participants' trust and to create fraud on a mass scale. The outlined model was verified based on research to identify the CSR communication strategy applied by one of the prominent American universities – Princeton University.

The strategy followed by Princeton University on Instagram can be described as an intermediate strategy between a dialogic and an engagement strategy. The main objective of the dialogic strategy used is to obtain feedback from stakeholders regarding the University's sustainable development activities described in the posts, and the information obtained can influence the adjustment of the organization's action plan. The purpose of the engagement strategy, on the other hand, is to enable the organization's environment to be involved in decision-making related to its area of social responsibility. The engagement strategy assumes that the main task of communicating responsibility-related activities is to create lasting relationships and cooperation with stakeholders. The realization of the engagement strategy can be described as the university's posts, which are prepared by the stakeholders, where they are involved in creating content and promoting activities related to sustainable development. Such a strategic approach to communicating the organization's responsibility, based on dialogue, transparency, and stakeholder involvement, as previous studies have shown, may contribute to increasing stakeholder trust.

The research presented in this chapter is necessarily limited by the purpose and scope of possible considerations in the chapter. The research on the University's CSR communication strategy was limited to a selected university and only one year of stakeholder communication, moreover specific due to the prevailing global pandemic. It is reasonable to conduct both a broader study of the university's strategic activities in social media and a comparative study – a comparison of the selected university's strategy with other American universities. However, even such a limited study as the one conducted shows that the university is using CSR communication as a strategy to build trust and engagement, and by doing so is achieving the goals set for it.

Based on identified shortcomings of the current literature, future directions in communicating CSR as a strategic area in the process of building trust should include additional research in both universities and corporations considering social media as a communication channel. In addition, due to the global significance of CSR, a comparative study should be conducted among organizations in countries worldwide regarding processes and challenges faced with respect to the role of CSR communication strategies in trust-building and customer engagement.

References

Capriotti, P., & Moreno, A. (2007). Corporate citizenship and public relations: The importance and interactivity of social responsibility issues on corporate websites. *Public Relations Review*, *33*(1), 84–91.

Cho, M., Furey, L. D., & Mohr, T. (2017). Communicating corporate social responsibility on social media: Strategies, stakeholders, and public engagement on corporate Facebook. *Business and Professional Communication Quarterly*, 80, 52–69.

Colleoni, E. (2013). CSR communication strategies for organizational legitimacy in social media. *Corporate Communication: An International Journal*, *18*(2), 228–248.

Connolly, B. (2020). *Digital trust. Social media strategies to increase trust and engage customers*. London: Bloomsbury Business.
Convey, S. R. (2013). *The 7 habits of highly effective people*. New York: Simon & Schuster.
Crane, A., & Glozer, S. (2016). Researching corporate social responsibility communication: Themes, opportunities and challenges. *Journal of Management Studies*, *53*(7), 1223–1252.
Dietz, G., & Hartog, D. (2006). Measuring trust inside organizations. *Personnel Review*, *35*(5), 557–588.
Digital 2020 Report. (2020, October 21). Retrieved from https://wearesocial.com/digital-2020.
Drumwright, M. E. (1996). Company advertising with a social dimension: The role of noneconomic criteria. *Journal of Marketing*, *60*(4), 71–87.
Du, S., Bhattacharya, C. B., & Sen, S. (2010). Maximizing business returns to corporate social responsibility (CSR): The role of CSR communication. *International Journal of Management Reviews*, *49*(1), 82–100.
EDELMAN. (2018). Edelman trust barometer special report. Retrieved from https://www.edelman.com/research/trust-barometer-brands-social-media.
EDELMAN. (2019). Edelman trust global barometer report 2019. (2020, October 21). Retrieved from https://www.edelman.com/sites/g/files/aatuss191/files/2019-02/2019_Edelman_Trust_Barometer_Global_Report.pdf.
Etter, M. (2014). Broadcasting, reacting, engaging – Three strategies for CSR communication in Twitter. *Journal of Communication Manag*ement, *18*(5), 662–674.
Fryzeł, B. (2011). Strategie relacji z interesariuszami: Praktyczny aspekt CSR na przykładzie polskich przedsiębiorstw [Stakeholders relations strategies: The practical aspect of CSR on the example of Polish enterprises]. *Zeszyty Naukowe Ostrołęckiego Towarzystwa Naukowego*, 25, 297–311.
Gołuchowski, J., Filipczyk, B., & Paliszkiewicz, J. (2018). Social media and trust. In J. Liebowitz, J. Paliszkiewicz, & J. Gołuchowski (Eds.), *Intuition, trust, and analytics* (pp. 173–196). New York: CRC Press Taylor & Francis Group.
Gołuchowski, J., Konieczna, D., & Losa-Jonczyk, A. (2018). Building trust in corporate social responsibility reports. In J. Liebowitz, J. Paliszkiewicz, & J. Gołuchowski (Eds.), *Intuition, trust, and analytics* (pp. 121–142). New York: CRC Press Taylor & Francis Group.
Ihlen, O., Bartlett, J., & May, S. (2011). Corporate social responsibility and communication. In O. Ihlen, J. Bartlett, & S. May (Eds.), *The handbook of communication and corporate social responsibility*. Chichester, West Sussex, England: Wiley-Blackwell.
Jabłonowska, L. (2012). Style komunikacyjne w budowie zaufania w organizacji [Communication styles in building trust in an organization]. *Studia i prace Kolegium Zarządzania i Finansów Szkoła Główna Handlowa w Warszawie*, *116*, 70–80.
Józefowicz, B. (2012). Rozważania na temat zaufania we współczesnym przedsiębiorstwie w kontekście badań nad pozytywnym potencjałem organizacji [Reflections on trust in the contemporary enterprise in the context of research on the positive potencial of organizations]. *Studia i prace Kolegium Zarządzania i Finansów Szkoła Główna Handlowa w Warszawie*, *116*, 96–104.

Kim, S., Kim, S. Y., & Sung, K. (2014). Fortune 100 companies' Facebook strategies: Corporate Ability versus social responsibility. *Journal of Communication Management*, *18*(4), 343–362.

Korschun, D., & Du, S. (2013). How virtual corporate social responsibility dialogs generate value: A framework and prepositions. *Journal of Business Research*, *66*, 1494–1504.

Lopez, M., Sicila, M., & Moyeda-Carabaza, A. A. (2017). Creating identification with brand communities on Twitter: The balance between need for affiliation and need for uniqueness. *Internet Research*, 27(1), 21–51.

Mitręga, M. (2008). *Marketing relacji. Teoria i praktyka* [Relationship Marketing. Theory and Practice]. Warszawa: CeDeWu.

Morsing, M., & Schultz, M. (2006). Corporate social responsibility communication: Stakeholder information, response and involvement strategies. *Business Ethics: A European Review*, 15(4), 323–338.

Paliszkiewicz, J. (2013). *Zaufanie w zarządzaniu* [Trust in management]. Warszawa: PWN.

Paliszkiewicz, J. (2018). The foundations of trust. In J. Liebowitz, J. Paliszkiewicz, & J. Gołuchowski (Eds.), *Intuition, trust, and analytics* (pp. 69–81). New York: CRC Press Taylor & Francis Group.

Princeton University Instagram. (2021, January 2). Retrieved from https://www.instagram.com/princeton/.

Sankowska, A. (2011). *Wpływ zaufania na zarządzanie przedsiębiorstwem. Perspektywa wewnątrz-organizacyjna [The impact of trust on corporate governance. An intra-organizational perspective]*. Warszawa: Difin.

Saxton, G. D., Gomez, L., Ngoh, Z., Lin, Y., & Dietrich, S. (2019). Do CSR messages resonate? Examining public reactions to firms' CSR efforts on social media. *Journal of Business Ethics*, 155, 359–377.

Simmons, C. J., & Becker-Olsen, K. L. (2006). Achieving marketing objectives through social sponsorships. *Journal of Marketing*, 70, 154–169.

Stanaland, A. J. S., Lwin, M. O., & Murphy, P. E. (2011). Consumer perceptions of the antecedents and consequences of corporate social responsibility. *Journal of Business Ethics*, 102(1), 47–55.

Stephens, K. K., Malone, P. C., & Bailey, C. (2005). Communicating with stakeholders during a crisis: Evaluating message strategies. *Journal of Business Communication*, 42, 390–419.

Sustainable Development Goals by ONZ. (2020, November 16). Retrieved from https://www.un.org/sustainabledevelopment/sustainable-development-goals/.

Testarmata, S., Fortuna, F., & Ciaburri, M. (2018). The communication of corporate social responsibility practices through social media channels. *Corporate Board: Role, Duties & Composition*, *14*(1), 34–49.

Trust Global Barometer Report. (2018). https://www.edelman.com/sites/g/files/aatuss191/files/2018-10/2018_Edelman_Trust_Barometer_Global_Report_FEB.pdf.

Wagner, T., Lutz, R., & Weitz, B. A. (2009). Corporate hypocrisy: Overcoming the threat of inconsistent corporate social responsibility perceptions. *Journal of Marketing*, 73(6), 77–91.

Zhank, Y., & Yu, T. (2012). Mining trust relationship from online social networks. *Journal of Computer Science and Technology*, 27, 492–505.

8 Trust and the Digital Economy: A Framework for Analysis

Anna Jasiulewicz, Piotr Pietrzak, and Barbara Wyrzykowska
Warsaw University of Life Sciences

Introduction

The digital economy is a new social-economic paradigm, which not only makes the Internet an infrastructure and a communication channel but also a way of creating value. This new type of economy implies not only technological but also and especially structural and process-related opportunities and threats (Zimmermann, 2000). We are shifting from business-to-consumer (B2B) models to bilateral or peer-to-peer (P2P) models (Sarhadi et al., 2012), where we can both buy and sell and link to other users through different platforms.

That is why taking part in the digital economy is an ongoing act of trust, which is necessarily bound up with the image we have on the "other" as an abstract, general entity. We are faced with what has been called "interpersonal trust" (Hassan et al., 2012), which stems from our previous experiences and our willingness to enter into a relationship or transaction in digital settings. Many authors (e.g., Mattila & Seppälä, 2016) attempted to define and discussed the exact notion of digital trust or cyber trust (Thomas & Amon, 2007). Also, plenty of researchers have continually tried to construct models for trust in the era of the digital economy (e.g., Hoffman et al., 1999; Pavlou, 2003; Grabner-Kräuter & Kaluscha, 2008; Kim et al., 2008). However, the majority of these models are case-specific and loosely integrated (AL-Dwairi & Kamala, 2009).

The prevalence of conceptual and illustrative case studies clearly shows the lack of maturity of this phenomenon of digital trust. Reis et al. (2018) emphasize that future research should focus more on setting the theoretical basis for this issue. Thus, this chapter presents the meaning of the digital economy and delivers a framework for analyzing digital trust. To this end, the next section provides a brief description of the methodological approach and is followed by the literature review. The chapter ends with some concluding remarks.

DOI: 10.4324/9781003165965-8

Research Method

The primary research method was a critical evaluation of literature on the topic (Webster & Watson, 2002). This methodology included searching for source materials, their selection, analysis, and synthesis. The critical evaluation included articles from such databases as Scopus and Web of Science. The search for articles was conducted notwithstanding the time impediments but constrained to journal papers and conference proceedings. Over 1,000 different studies were collected for an initial review and subsequently subjected to a selection process (based on selected keywords, abstracts, and titles). Finally, over 70 articles were chosen for in-depth analysis. A synthesis of the collected research material made it possible to identify the definitions, components, participants of the digital economy, and propose a digital trust model.

Digital Economy – A Literature Review

The digital economy is a recently emerging phenomenon of expanding significance (Bukht & Heeks, 2018). That is why there are plenty of definitions of the digital economy in the literature reflecting different scopes of relevance (Brynolfsson & Kahin, 2000; McAfee & Brynjolfsson, 2017). Since first coined in the mid-1990s, the definition of the digital economy has evolved, reflecting the quickly changing nature of technology and its use by enterprises and consumers (Barefoot et al., 2018).

In the late 1990s, analyses were primarily concerned with the adoption of the Internet and early thinking about its economic impacts (Tapscott, 1996; Brynolfsson & Kahin, 2000). As the use of Internet expanded, definitions from the mid-2000s evolved to include analyses of different policies and digital technologies, on the one hand, and the growth of informationand communication technologies (ICTs) and digitally oriented firms as key actors, on the other (OECD, 2012). With improved Internet connectivity in developing countries, and therefore the growth within the numerous digital firms, product, and services, studies of the digital economy have begun to incorporate additional substantial analyses of the situation in developing countries (Babkin 2017; Morrar et al., 2017; Ross et al., 2017; Amelin & Schetinina, 2018; Asadullina, 2018; Ritter & Lettl, 2018).

Analyzing the digital economy definitions, one can identify a number of different perspectives reflected:

- Resource perspective: most obviously this rests on a technology perspective with many definitions identifying the technologies on which the digital economy is founded; however,
- A few encompass a content perspective that typically relates to the handling of data or information (e.g., Brynolfsson & Kahin, 2000),

and a human resource perspective that goes further to incorporate human knowledge or skills or creativity that are enabled by ICTs (e.g., Tapscott, 1996);

- Process perspective: plenty of definitions cover the use of technologies to support particular business processes such as commerce/transactions (e.g., Kling & Lamb, 2000; Mesenbourg, 2001);
- Structural perspective: maybe rather generic in talking about economic transformation (e.g., Brynolfsson & Kahin, 2000) or more specific in identifying the new network-based structures that emerge as part of the digital economy (e.g., Van Gorp & Batura, 2015);
- Business model perspective: lying between the process and structural perspectives, are the few definitions that bring in the idea of the new business models such as e-commerce (e.g., Mesenbourg, 2001) or digital platforms (e.g., Van Gorp & Batura, 2015).

Finally, it should be mentioned that according to the Center for Development Informatics (Nagy, 2020), the core of the digital economy is the "digital sector" (ICT) responsible for providing digital infrastructure, that is, ICT networks (the core digital infrastructure for connectivity); data infrastructure (data centers, submarine cables, and cloud infrastructure); digital platforms; and finally digital devices and applications.

As noted earlier, the digital economy is closely associated with progress in several frontier technologies, including some key software-oriented technologies, such as blockchain, data analytics, and artificial intelligence (AI). These technologies have been the subject of many studies (e.g., Wahid et al., 2019; Wallis, 2019; Caldarelli, 2020; Capece & Lorenzi, 2020; Colomo-Palacios et al., 2020; Jindal et al., 2021; Jung et al., 2021; Saba et al., 2021).

In recent years, increasing attention has been paid to user-facing devices (such as computers and smartphones), 3D printers and wearables, as well as specialized machine-oriented hardware, such as Internet of Things (IoT), automation, robotics, and cloud computing (e.g., Liu & Dhakal, 2020; Masmoudi et al., 2020; Saorin et al., 2020; Kaur, 2021; Zhang et al., 2021).

In order to fully characterize the digital economy, attention must also be paid to its participants. Sanjuán et al. (2018) identified five fundamental groups of participants that interact in the digital economy: traditional companies in the digital conversion process; users; facilitators; hardware and software companies, which provide abilities to the digital economy for its development; purely digital companies, which are at the forefront of innovation and development processes (e.g., Amazon, Apple, Facebook, Google); traditional companies in the digital conversion process; and support entities (investors, higher education institutions, governments, and regulators).

The digital economy has given its participants more opportunities than ever to interact and trade with strangers. The virtual environment facilitates situations in which information asymmetry with respect to "the other" increases. Transparency and the amount of available information are the key components for lubricating the digital system and fostering participation, collaboration, and consumption. This boom in transparency encourages detailed, public, or easily accessible information from any users. That is why, in recent years, the role of trust in the online environment – cyberspace – has received significantce (Pavlou, 2003; Wang & Emurian, 2005; Flavián et al., 2006; Grabner-Kräuter & Kaluscha, 2008; Kim et al., 2008).

It is worth noting that in subject literature (e.g., Trim & Upton, 2016; Górka, 2018; Valja, 2018; Trelikowski, 2019), one can find numerous definitions of cyberspace, and many experts do not agree on whether it is appropriate to use the term as a synonym for the Internet. There are also several alternative approaches to how cyberspace should be regulated in legislation. The most important are (Banasiński & Rojszczak, 2020):

- Introduction of regulations at the level of national law, with complimentary use of international standards;
- Recognition of cyberspace as international space and thus using international law exclusively;
- Attempting to take account of national regulations in the form of a new international agreement to build a supranational cybersecurity framework.

The definition of future concepts concerning the protection and security of cyberspace may not ignore technological aspects, especially because, in this case, not only the technology is subject to regulation, but can also provide tools that will increase the effectiveness of implemented solutions due to automation (Kowalczyk, 2019).

First of all, two main issues need to be taken into consideration – the first concerning the technical feasibility of establishing an entity responsible for regulating the operation of the Internet; the second concerning the extent to which the operation of such an entity can be effective, given today's network architectures (Leineweber et al., 2018).

The first issue boils down to seeking answers to the question of whether the Internet can be regulated. The second of the identified issues results from the observation that in the global network, the choice of the route along which the data is transmitted most often depends on economic considerations (Lu, 2017). This means that data between any two points is usually transmitted along the fastest route, which is not always tantamount with the shortest route. This circumstance makes it significantly more difficult to build effective models for the protection of cyberspace, as it makes it impossible to think of cyberspace as physical space – as an area with precisely defined borders, where focused security checks can be carried out.

The current cybersecurity model – based on multiple regulations, which often lack cohesion, as well as characterized by a lack of a global outlook on the problem – requires not only improvement but also significant restructuring. This in turn should be combined with a change in the approach to internet regulation and the use of our experience in building machine learning systems (e.g., Murphy, 2018; Rojszczak, 2019). Modern law and properly selected technology can be a permanent solution to the majority of today's most common threats (Mazanec & Thayer, 2016). Therefore, the authors of this chapter have attempted to create their own model of trust in the digital economy. At the same time, they hope that it will make a valuable contribution to management theory and practice.

A Model of Trust in the Digital Economy

Figure 8.1 shows a conceptual model of trust in the digital economy. As seen in the framework, we have five basic types of participants that interact in the digital economy. Each of them has different expectations and faces different challenges:

- Traditional organizations are the first parties involved in making decisions concerning digital transformation, as they are interested in the reputation of digital operations that can drive business. This

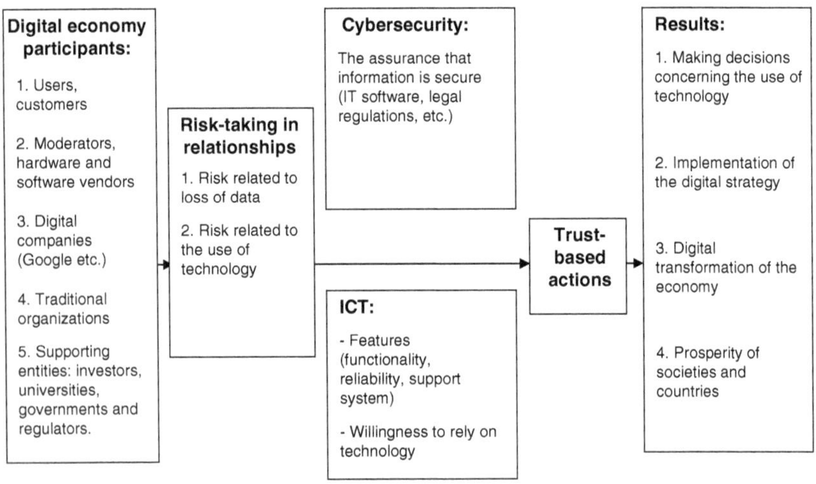

Figure 8.1 A conceptual model of trust in the digital economy. Source: Own compilation.

reputation is often affected by the ICT security assessment of an organization, often tantamount to its reliability;

- Users are the second party involved in digital operations. In many cases, they are individual consumers interested in the privacy of their digital activities;
- Facilitators are companies that support and influence digital operations as vendors, service providers, and other entities – as such they have an impact on the reputation and risk level of the organization and customers. These days they increasingly often are external companies – for example, service providers who offer their resources to external business partners to support the organizations and their customers;
- Purely digital companies, for whom security must be seen as a greater social responsibility. A concept that aims to counteract the risks of progressive digitization and at the same time exploit its potential. Digital social responsibility aims at bringing about the so-called common value of the digital economy for society and companies;
- Supporting entities: investors, universities, governments, and regulators — may exercise regulatory oversight (authorities), make coordinated efforts to influence the opinions of customers (activists), or publish information (media) highlighting decisions that build digital confidence. Of particular importance are authorities providing oversight, which influences the digital operations of organizations by means of various regulations.

Based on our model digital trust activities contribute to the following outcomes:

- Making decisions on the use of ICT technologies that limit, replace, or eliminate human participation. The tendency to make decisions about the use of technology can be analyzed in the context of three features proposed by Lankton et al. (2014): the functionality of the technology, its reliability, and assistance provided to users in achieving their goals and tasks;
- Implementation of the digital strategy. Minimizing the risks associated with cybersecurity is essential for the implementation of digital strategies, and any neglect or oversight at this level may result in a loss of confidence in the organization, as well as threaten its existence due to possible lawsuits, compensation payments, and loss of customers (Richards, 2016). Managing reputation is a key element for individual digital operations and organizations as a whole. Reputation is often ambiguous and challenging – as is confidence itself – due to the fact that it can be influenced in many ways. Organizations, thus, need to understand that cybersecurity risk management is key to survival in the digital world (Kowalczyk, 2018);

- Digital transformation of the economy. Trust in ICT technologies and their use by organizations contribute to the transformation of the economy in a given country;
- The wealth of societies and countries. Using modern information technologies is associated with serious, often-unacceptable risks. However, a complete lack of human trust in technology would prevent its use in everyday life, and thus its development and the development of entire societies (Carr, 2016). Low levels of digital trust mean that the economy is dominated by relationships with low levels of risk and value, built ad hoc, and inherently tactical, which hardly create new economic ties. Thus, much of the world's "economic backwardness" is due to digital distrust.

In our model, we noted that two types of risk can occur in the relationships between participants in the digital economy: risk related to loss of data and risk related to the use of technology. Therefore, in order to create trust in cyberspace, it is necessary to guarantee data protection (cybersecurity) and to ensure appropriate technology.

It should be mentioned that there is no solution in the world that would guarantee full cybersecurity, one can only strive to achieve a certain acceptable level of risk (e.g., Banasiński & Rojszczak, 2020). Cybersecurity thus remains a joint challenge; which means that technical and legal verification based on a common set of standards can provide a basis for building trust. This should come as a result of a joint effort because no single provider, government, or telecommunications operator has the ability to achieve this on their own (Lindstom & Rounds, 2020).

Trust in technology can refer to a general level, which reflects the level of public confidence, to the level of a particular technology, or a particular solution. Trust in technology takes into account the risks, which are defined as the belief in potential, unpredictable, and, most often, negative impacts associated with the use of a given technology and the risks stemming from its use. The risks associated with the marketing and use of new technologies thus require a certain level of confidence, which determines human interaction with technology as a whole (Ejdys, 2018).

Finally, we note that trust built online facilitates interaction in the real world. By combining the elements of the digital and real-world, a new generation of trust is being built. The way we are connected with other people is changing along with the relationships we build, which transforms the models of economic activity around the world (Koohang et al., 2017).

Conclusions

Although the issue of trust in the digital economy has recently become an interesting area of academic discourse, there is a lack of comprehensive research devoted to this issue. This study, therefore, makes a significant contribution to the development of research on online trust. The study resulted in the concept of a trust model in the digital economy.

The current model of cyberspace protection has many limitations, overcoming which requires not so much improving upon existing technical and legal solutions, but proposing new ones to replace them. The presented suggestion to develop a new international agreement to constitute the basis for the implementation of modern cybersecurity systems, taking advantage of machine learning and artificial intelligence, should be treated as a voice in the discussion on the possible direction of change; however, regardless of the selected option, it seems that the current, fragmented and heterogeneous model of cybersecurity does not only limit the effectiveness of actions undertaken in this area but also serve as the best incentive for new criminal groups to be active in cyberspace.

The literature analysis carried out so far indicates the need to continue work on digital trust in management. For future research, the authors suggest verifying the model created by them by conducting empirical qualitative and quantitative researches in different countries and among various groups of entities.

References

AL-Dwairi, R. M., & Kamala, M. A. (2009). An integrated trust model for business-to-consumer (b2c) e-commerce: Integrating trust with the technology acceptance model. *2009 International Conference on CyberWorlds*. (pp. 351–356). New York, NY: IEEE.

Amelin, S. V., & Schetinina, I. V. (2018). Organization of production in the digital economy context. *Production Organizer*, *26*(4), 7–18.

Asadullina, A. V. (2018). Digital economy in Russia: Current status and development problems. *Russian Foreign Economic Bulletin*, *6*, 98–112.

Babkin, A. V., Burkaltseva, D. D., Kosten, D. G., & Vorobyov, Y. N. (2017). Formation of digital economy in Russia: Essence, features, technical normalization, development problems. *Scientific and Technical State Papers of SPbSPU. Economics*, *10*(3), 9–25.

Banasiński, C., & Rojszczak M. (2020). *Cyberbezpieczeństwo [Cybersecurity]*. Warsaw, PL: Wolters Kluwer.

Barefoot, K., Curtis, D., Jolliff, W., Nicholson, J. R., & Omohundro, R. (2018). Defining and measuring the digital economy. *Working paper. Bureau of Economic Analysis*. Retrieved from https://www.bea.gov/system/files/papers/WP2018-4.pdf.

Brynolfsson, E., & Kahin, B. (Ed.) (2000). *Understanding the digital economy: Data, tools, and research*. Cambridge: MIT Press.

Bukht, R., & Heeks, R. (2018). Defining, conceptualising and measuring the digital economy. *International Organisations Research Journal*, *13*(2), 143–172.

Caldarelli, G. (2020). Understanding the blockchain oracle problem: A call for action. *Information (Switzerland)*, *11*(11), 1–19.

Capece, G., & Lorenzi, F. (2020). Blockchain and healthcare: Opportunities and prospects for the HER. *Sustainability (Switzerland)*, *12*(22), 1–17.

Carr, M. (2016). *US power and the internet in international relations. The irony of the information age*. New York, NY: Palgrave Macmillan.

Colomo-Palacios, R., Sánchez-Gordón, M., & Arias-Aranda, D. (2020). A critical review on blockchain assessment initiatives: A technology evolution viewpoint. *Journal of Software: Evolution and Process*, *32*(11), 1–11.

Ejdys, J. (2018). *Zaufanie do technologii w e-administracji* (*Trust in technology in e-government*). Białystok, PL: Oficyna wydawnicza Politechniki Białostockiej.

Flavián, C., Guinalíu, M., & Gurrea, R. (2006). The role played by perceived usability, satisfaction and consumer trust on website loyalty. *Information & Management*, *43*(1), 1–14.

Ghosh, I. (2020). The global trust crisis. *Foreign Policy*. Retrieved from https://foreignpolicy.com/n.

Górka, M. (2018). *Cberbezpieczeństwo jako wyzwanie dla współczesnego państwa i społeczeństwa* (*Cybersecurity as a challenge for the modern state and society*). In Dębowski, T. (Ed.), *Cyberbezpieczeństwo wyzwaniem XXI wieku (Cybersecurity as a challenge of the 21st century)* (pp. 31–45). Łódź-Wrocław: Archage Grap, Wydawnictwo Naukowe.

Grabner-Kräuter, S., & Kaluscha, A. E. (2008). *Consumer trust in electronic commerce: Conceptualization and classification of trust building measures*. In T. Kautonen, & H. Karjaluoto (Eds.), *Trust and new technologies. Marketing and management on the internet and mobile media* (pp. 3–22). Cheltenham-Northampton: Edward Elgar Publishing.

Hassan, M., Toylan, N. V., Semerciöz, F., & Aksel, I. (2012). Interpersonal trust and its role in organizations. *International Business Research*, *5*(8), 33–39.

Hoffman, D. L., Novak, T. P., & Peralta, M. (1999). Building consumer trust in online environments: The case of information privacy. *Communications of the ACM*, *42*(4), 80–85.

Jindal, S., Sharma, A., Joshi, A., & Gupta, M. (2021). Artificial intelligence fuelling the health care. *Lecture Notes in Networks and Systems*, *140*, 501–507.

Jung, J., Maeda, M., Chang, A., Bhandari, M., Ashapure, A., & Landivar-Bowles, J. (2021). The potential of remote sensing and artificial intelligence as tools to improve the resilience of agriculture production systems. *Current Opinion in Biotechnology*, *70*, 15–22.

Kaur, G. (2021). Framework for resource management in cloud computing. *Smart Innovation, Systems and Technologies*, *196*, 25–32.

Kim, D. J., Ferin, D. L., & Rao, H. R. (2008). A trust-based consumer decision-making model in electronic commerce: The role of trust, perceived risk, and their antecedents. *Decision Support Systems*, *44*(2), 544–564.

Kling, R., & Lamb, R. (2000). *IT and organizational change in digital economies*. In E. Brynjolfsson, & B. Kahin (Eds.), *Understanding the digital economy: Data, tools, and research* (pp. 295–324). Cambridge: MIT Press.

Koohang, A., Paliszkiewicz, J., & Goluchowski, J. (2017). The impact of leadership on trust, knowledge management, and organizational performance. *Industrial Management & Data Systems*, *4*(10), 521–532.

Kowalczyk, L. (2018). Zarządzanie organizacją w drodze do cyfrowej transformacji: Zarys problemów [Organization management on the road to digital transformation: Outline of problems]. *Prace Naukowe WSZiP*, *45*(1), 9–15.

Kowalczyk, L. (2019). Znaczenie technologii mobilnych w cyfrowej transformacji [The importance of mobile technologies in digital transformation]. *Prace Naukowe WSZiP*, *48*(2), 9–34.
Lankton, N. K., McKnight D. H., & Thatcher J. B. (2014). Incorporating trust-in-technology into Expectation Disconfirmation Theory. *Journal of Strategic Information Systems*, *23*(2), 128–145.
Leineweber, S., Wienbruch, T., & Lins, D. K. (2018). Concept for an evolutionary maturity based Industrial 4.0 migration model. *Procedia CIRP*, *72*, 404–409.
Lindstom, P., & Rounds, M. (2020). *Digital trust: The key driver for digital transformation*. Retrieved from: https://www.idc.com.
Liu, Y., & Dhakal, S. (2020). Internet of Things technology in mineral remote sensing monitoring. *International Journal of Circuit Theory and Applications*, *48*(12), 2065–2077.
Lu, Y. (2017). Industry 4.0: A survey on technologies, applications and open research issues. *Journal of Industrial Information Integration*, *6*, 1–10.
Masmoudi, F., Maamar, Z., Sellami, M., Awad, A. I., & Burégio, V. (2020). A guiding framework for vetting the Internet of Things. *Journal of Information Security and Applications*, *55*, 102644.
Mattila, J., & Seppälä, T. (2016). Digital trust, platforms, and policy. *ETLA Brief*, *42*, 1–2.
Mazanec, B. M., & Thayer, B. (2016). Deterring cyber warfare. Bolstering strategic stability in cyberspace. Basingstoke, United Kingdom: Palgrave Macmillan.
McAfee, A., & Brynjolfsson, E. (2017). *Machine, platform, crowd: Harnessing our digital future*. New York: W.W. Norton & Company.
Mesenbourg, T. L. (2001). *Measuring the digital economy*. Suitland: U.S. Bureau of the Census. Retrieved from https://www.census.gov/content/dam/Census/library/working-papers/2001/econ/umdigital.pdf.
Morrar, R., Arman, H., & Mousa, S. (2017). The fourth industrial revolution (Industry 4.0): A social innovation perspective. *Technology Innovation Management Review*, *7*(11), 12–20.
Murphy, K. A. (2018). Recent FTC regulation of the Internet of Things. *The Business Lawyer*, *73*(1), 34–36.
Nagy, H. (2020). Assessing the digital economy: Aims, frameworks, pilots, results, and lessons. *Journal of Innovation and Entrepreneurship*, *9*(16), 1–16.
OECD. (2012). *OECD internet economy outlook 2012*. Paris: OECD Publishing.
Pavlou, P. A. (2003). Consumer acceptance of electronic commerce: Integrating trust and risk with the technology acceptance model. *International Journal of Electronic Commerce*, *7*(3), 69–103.
Reis, J., Amorim, M., Melão, N., & Matos, P. (2018). Digital transformation: A literature review and guidelines for future research. In Á. Rocha, H. Adeli, L.P. Reis, & S. Costanzo (Eds.), *Trends and advances in information systems and technologies. WorldCIST'18 2018. Advances in intelligent systems and computing* (pp. 411–421). Cham: Springer.
Richards, J. (2016). *Cyber-war. The anatomy of the global security threat*. United Kingdom: Palgrave Macmillan.

Ritter, T., & Lettl, C. (2018). The wider implications of business-model research. *Long Range Plan*, *51*(1), 1–8.
Rojszczak, M. (2019). Cyberprzestrzeń jako nowa płaszczyzna budowania relacji społecznych (Cyberspace as a new platform for building social relations). In M. Rojszczak (Ed.), *Ochrona prywatności w cyberprzestrzeni z uwzględnieniem zagrożeń wynikających z nowych technik przetwarzania informacji (Protection of privacy in cyberspace, taking into account the threats resulting from new information processing techniques)* (pp. 49–59). Warsaw: Wolters Kluwer.
Ross, J. W., Sebastian, I. M., & Beath, C. M. (2017). How to develop a great digital strategy. *MIT Sloan Management Review*, *58*(2), 7–9.
Saba, D., Sahli, Y., & Hadidi, A. (2021). The role of artificial intelligence in company's decision making. *Studies in Computational Intelligence*, *911*, 287–314.
Sanjuán, C. E., Cárdenas García, M., & Cañizares Arévalo, J. de J. (2018). Architecture of a digital economy policy: A tool to achieve efficiency in the development of the local economy. *Journal of Physics: Conference Series*, *1126*, 1–7. Retrieved from https://iopscience.iop.org/article/10.1088/1742-6596/1126/1/012064/pdf.
Saorin, J. L., Diaz-Alemán, M. D., & Pérez-Conesa, C. M. E. I. (2020). Introduction of digital technologies and 3D printers in the art casting industry. *Dyna (Spain)*, *95*(4), 1–4.
Sarhadi, A., Yousefi, A., & Broumandnia, A. (2012). New method for grid computing resource discovery with dynamic structure of peer-to-peer model based on learning automata. *World Applied Sciences Journal*, *19*(1), 153–158.
Tapscott, D. (1996). *The digital economy: Promise and peril in the age of networked intelligence*. New York: McGraw-Hill.
Thomas, R. C., & Amon, P. D. (2007). *Incentive-based cyber trust - Acall to action*. Retrieved from http://meritology.com/resources/Incentive-based%20Cyber%20Trust%20Initiative% 20v3.5.pdf.
Trelikowski, T. (2019). Bezpieczeństwo cyberprzestrzeni wyzwaniem naszych czasów. System cyberpezbieczeństwa w Polsce (w świetle obowiązującego prawa) [Cyberspace security as a challenge of our times. Cyber security system in Poland (under applicable law]. *Zeszyty Naukowe SGSP*, *71*(3), 81–87.
Trim, P., & Upton, D. (2016). *Cyber security culture. Counteracting cyber threats through organizational learning and training*. New York: Taylor & Francis.
Valja, M. (2018). *Improving IT architecture modeling through automation: Cyber security analysis of smart grids (Doctoral Thesis)*. Stockholm: KTH.
Van Gorp, N., & Batura, O. (2015). *Challenges for competition policy in a digitalised economy*. Brussels: European Parliament. Retrieved from https://www.europarl.europa.eu/RegData/etudes/STUD/2015/542235/IPOL_STU(2015)542235_EN.pdf.
Wahid, F., Ismail, L. H., Ghazali, R., & Aamir, M. (2019). An efficient artificial intelligence hybrid approach for energy management in intelligent buildings. *KSII Transactions on Internet and Information Systems*, *13*(12), 5904–5927.
Wallis, C. (2019). How artificial intelligence will change medicine. *Nature*, *576*(7787), 48.

Wang, Y. D., & Emurian, H. H. (2005). An overview of online trust: Concepts, elements, and implications. *Computers in Human Behavior*, *21*(1), 105–125.

Webster, J., & Watson, R. T. (2002). Analyzing the past to prepare for the future: Writing a literature review. *MIS Quarterly*, *26*(2), 13–23.

Zhang, S., Duan, X., Li, C., & Liang, M. (2021). Pre-classified reservoir computing for the fault diagnosis of 3D printers. *Mechanical Systems and Signal Processing*, *146*, 106961.

Zimmermann, H. D. (2000). Understanding the digital economy: Challenges for new business models. *AMCIS 2000 Proceedings. Paper 402*, 729–732. Retrieved from https://papers.ssrn.com/sol3/papers.cfm?abstract_id=2566095.

9 Trust in Machine-learning Systems

Grzegorz Dziczkowski,
Szymon Głowania, and Bogna Zacny
University of Economics in Katowice

Introduction

The meaning of the terms trust and distrust has changed significantly in the course of research on them, and it also varies depending on the scientific discipline in which they are used. In works published in the 1950s and 1960s, trust was described as the individual's trust in the intentions and motives of another person and was based on the sincerity of a person's statement (Mellinger, 1956). We expect our interests to be protected and safe in the hands of those we trust. Hoping for a frank exchange of information, we are willing to entrust personal information, thus exposing ourselves to the risk of damaging our trust (Read, 1962).

In the 1990s, the meaning of the word trust evolved from a concept based on motives and intentions to a definition based on behavior. Trust is defined as the willingness to be vulnerable to another person's action (Mayer et al., 1995). Researchers defined distrust by analogy with the previous definition as the expectation that third parties would not act in our best interest and may even act harmfully (Barber, 1983). In the late 1990s, researchers suggested that trust is not the opposite of distrust (Lewicki et al., 1998). There are separate factors contributing to the increase and decrease of trust or distrust. Thus, if it is acceptable that love and hatred exist simultaneously, by analogy, trust and distrust can also co-exist. Studies have shown that trust should not be seen as "something good" and distrust as "something bad", because these are different dimensions.

In later years, the term trust had to evolve again. One of the factors of change was the increasing use of Internet tools, social media, recommendation systems, artificial intelligence, and machine learning algorithms. Machines and computers dominated even daily activities to such an extent that it was necessary to interact not only with other system and network users but also with automatons, programs, intelligent agents, and extensive IT systems. Our interactions with machines have become everyday life. In many cases, users' trust is unconscious, and most users of technologies that employ some elements

DOI: 10.4324/9781003165965-9

of artificial intelligence do not think at all about the algorithms that determine its operation. Without information about the role played by artificial intelligence algorithms, we are exposed to the risk of losing our privacy and, what is worse, our subjectivity. The lack of a critical approach and the a priori adoption of trust in artificial intelligence have many reasons. They include three factors: psychological, environmental, and technological (Siau & Wang, 2018; Toreini et al., 2020). The basis for trust is the personality traits of each individual, their ability to trust (resulting from past experience), and their ability to deal with risk. Environmental factors may relate to the nature of the tasks performed by artificial intelligence, the cultural aspects of an individual's origin, and the surrounding setting. The last factor refers to the technology itself and can be considered from three perspectives: the performance of applied tools/methods, the course of a specific task, and its purpose.

Recognizing the dangers of bestowing uncritical trust on AI, legislators in many countries have introduced appropriate laws and regulations requiring state and private institutions to inform their clients on what basis decisions are made in their cases (GDPR, 2016; Journal of Laws, 2019, item 730, Articles 43, 46, 138). Users of technology based on artificial intelligence algorithms have a "right to explanation" (Goodman & Flaxman, 2017; Wikipedia, 2020) of decisions that have a significant impact on an individual, especially when they are health-related, legal, or financial decisions.

Analyses of pandemics and epidemics are an example of how important trust and distrust in machine learning systems are. In order to be able to reduce the spread rate of the H1N1 virus discovered in 2009, it was necessary to get information on the location of new cases of the disease. Information about new outbreaks did not bring the expected results, and the pandemic maps were still out of date. The solution proposed by Google, which consisted of checking the phrases entered by the users in the Internet search engine, proved to be helpful. At that time, the number of questions asked was approximately three billion per day. The algorithm compared more than 50 million of the most popular phrases that were typed into the search engine window by US citizens with data received from the CDC on the spread of influenza from 2003 to 2008. The purpose of the data comparison was to identify the areas where the first outbreaks occurred. The system processed about 450 million different mathematical models, and the results were compared with actual data on the development of influenza in 2007 and 2008. The outcome of the work was the identification of a combination of 45 queries that showed a high level of correlation between program prediction and actual data. This made it possible to determine new disease locations. Each new sick person was identified on an ongoing basis by phrases entered into the search engine. As a result, it was possible to react quickly, isolate patients, and start treatment (Mayer-Schonberger & Cukier,

2017). Currently, systems are still being developed to analyze the scale of development and the emergence of new outbreaks of the pandemic caused by the COVID-19 virus. The level of trust in artificial intelligence decisions should be measurable and analyzable, especially in such sensitive situations and applications.

We need to consider many factors and concepts related to trust in technology. Trust in artificial intelligence and machine learning systems depends – among other things – on the transparency of the models used. Models that are not transparent should, by definition, be explainable and interpretable in order to increase their transparency and consequently increase the users' confidence in the results obtained. This chapter presents the problems of *Interpretable Machine Learning* (IML) and *eXplainable Artificial Intelligence* (XAI). First of all, machine learning algorithms will be discussed in order to present the way in which a machine creates knowledge and makes decisions.

The aim of this chapter is to characterize the concept of trust in the context of artificial intelligence systems and to present methods to increase the level of trust in the results of machine learning algorithms. These methods are described by Interpretable Machine Learning (IML) and eXplainable Artificial Intelligence (XAI). The chapter is divided into the following sections: the first section explains the notion of "trust" and presents the evolution of the term over the years. The second section introduces machine learning and focuses on the nature of the results obtained by using it. The third section presents IML and XAI approaches that explain how ML generates results. The final section summarizes the findings.

Machine Learning – How a Machine Creates Knowledge

Machine Learning Systems (MLS) are based on the application of *Artificial Intelligence* (AI), which provides systems with the ability to automatically learn and improve based on experience without the need for direct programming. Machine learning focuses on the creation of computer programs that have access to data and use them, learning independently. They learn from their erroneous actions, their operation is dynamic, and MLS adapt their actions over time. In a sense, they are able to draw conclusions and modify their previous rules.

There are two approaches to artificial intelligence. The first one is strong AI, according to which a properly programmed machine, as the equivalent of the human brain, would have intelligence at a similar level to that of humans. According to this approach, it is possible to create self-learning systems which – thanks to the knowledge gained – can solve problems or answer questions. According to the second approach, that of weak artificial intelligence, the computer is able to formulate and check hypotheses to some extent. The ways in which the human brain processes information and calculates are not fully understood. At present, we are not able to fully explain the perception and processing of various stimuli before they cause a reaction in mind. As a result, it is possible to create models and implement them only in response to specific objectives (Duch, 1997).

There are three basic types of machine learning that enable both strong and weak intelligence concepts: with supervision, without supervision, and association rules. In order to illustrate how a machine thinks, let us focus on machine learning with supervision. It consists of learning a model by using the previously determined data of the teachers. This allows us to predict and generate new information in the future. The term "supervised" defines a set of samples with the output known in advance. The result of learning is acquired knowledge.

To illustrate the creation of knowledge by machine learning, let us use an academic example from the field of banking. Let us say we want to be able to predict whether a bank should give a loan to a particular person or not. This person for the bank is identified by a set of features. These features describe a particular person and include, for example: age, earnings, education, type of employment, marital status, number of children, place of residence, etc. In order to teach the model of machine learning with supervision, we need a teaching set. In the analyzed example, the teaching set is made up of people, previous customers of the bank, who received or did not receive a loan in the near past. So, we have a large set of people with completed features and feedback on whether the person received a loan or not. On the basis of data from the teaching database, the machine learning model creates knowledge. The way it does, this depends on the algorithm. Knowledge will be created in different ways by the algorithm of decision trees and by the algorithm of neural networks. At the moment when the knowledge is extracted, we no longer need the teaching base, and we are able to assign a loan decision to a completely new person based on their characteristics.

Machine learning models built by the use of such algorithms can be divided into two types (Biecek & Burzykowski, 2021):

- *White-box* models (*glass-box*, *transparent-box*) are models whose structure allows for interpretation of its elements. A transparent structure (visualizable) and a small number of estimated parameters allow for a precise understanding of the relationship of all the features used in the model.
- *Black-box* models are models whose structure is impossible to interpret. This difficulty most often results from the complexity of these models – the number of estimated parameters and the complexity of mathematical transformations is so great that a human is not able to see (and visualize) all the relations modeled by the algorithm.

In order to be able to analyze the confidence in algorithms, they should be explainable, and in some way, we aim to understand (even for *black-box* models) how machine learning algorithms have created knowledge. For example, knowledge in the decision tree algorithm is represented by a graph that is understandable to humans. The clarity of a created graph is not a problem. However, the transparency of knowledge discovered by a neural network algorithm is completely different. It is a completed weight matrix between neurons. Weights will be determined during the teaching stage – this process is called retro gradient propagation in neural networks. It is impossible to interpret the result in any way, the weights point to the appropriate output for a given input. We must therefore introduce an explanation of the operation of a neural network to introduce measures of trust and distrust.

It is worth noting that machine learning answers the question of what we should receive or do but does not provide an analysis of its decision. Thus, it does not explain the reasons for the decision and does not answer the question "why". Historically, humanity has tried to answer the emerging questions by analyzing the world around us. The development of mathematics and physics allowed for an analytical distribution of the problem and obtaining results by calculating the relationships we are interested in. When building a bridge, engineers calculate the necessary stresses of the construction materials by selecting the appropriate technologies and materials so that the final product meets a particular specification. In machine learning, we obtain answers. We do not receive an analytical explanation, but we rely on statistical calculations. The ideal application of machine learning is, therefore complex analyses for which we are not able to calculate the result due to the lack of appropriate mathematical transformations.

Let us use an example to explain what kind of knowledge we get from an MLS. We will treat our planet as a closed automatic system. We want to predict the price of tuna in Ohio next month – April. We know that currently, in March, the fires in Australia are causing smoke in the territorial waters. A consequence of this phenomenon is the migration of shark populations to the north. In the Sea of Japan, the economy is focused on tuna fishing that ultimately leads to less tuna fishing, and the natural supply-demand relation will cause prices to rise. This example can be extended with further features and continuously developed. It is impossible to take all factors into account in analytical terms. The possibilities of today's mathematics make it impossible to analyze such a large number of features. However, thanks to machine learning, we are able to get the correct price results for tuna in Ohio.

Ultimately, using statistical machine learning algorithms, we will not get the answer to the question "why". We will not know the decision-making process or the factors that influenced the feedback we received. We will get the result of "how much", but we will not know the answer to the question of why the given result is correct. Statistically obtained answers are fully correct – but can we trust them? For this reason, the interpretability and explainability of these models are important to gain user confidence in ML algorithms and their results.

Interpretability and Explainability of Machine Learning Models

The basis of human trust in artificial intelligence is the ability to understand all models generated by means of machine learning algorithms applied. As mentioned earlier, some models become more understandable than others due to their structure. The inability to interpret some models of machine learning (lack of their transparency) does not mean that their operation cannot be explained.

White-box models are inherently interpretable and thus explainable. The relationship between the data and parameters of a *black-box* model can be explained (presented) thanks to an established testing strategy. The distinction between interpretation and explainability of the models is important from the point of view of preparing a strategy to explain a decision made about the users to them. *Black-box* models cannot be interpreted, but they should be explained. In order to meet these expectations (and in cases specified by law, even orders), a number of techniques have been developed to explain the behavior of a model. Such techniques include model simulation/testing strategies (*Local Interpretable Model-agnostic Explanations*, *Shapley Additive Explanations*) and methods for visualizing the results of such simulations (*Individual Conditional Expectation Plots*, *Partial Dependence Plots*, *Accumulated Local Effects Plots*, *Merging Path Plots*) (Molnar, 2020; Biecek & Burzykowski, 2021).

Interpretability consists of describing the model mechanics, that is, the relationship between data and parameters of a given algorithm. Interpretation possibilities integral to a specific algorithm allow analysts to predict changes in the model following algorithm parameters or input data modification. It is enough for an expert to look at a decision tree graph to understand what is happening in it, to determine the causes and effects of such and not other behavior in the model without the need to know the field of the analyzed model. The model's interpretability guarantees an understanding of how the model will formulate forecasts, which in turn will allow understanding of why the model makes mistakes. Interpretable models are therefore characterized by understandability and thus by communicativeness. Understandability is a feature of a model which tells us that a human is able to understand how the model works without the need to analyze the way in which data is processed, whereas communicativeness is the ability to represent the knowledge of the model in a manner that a human can understand

(Craven, 1996; Gleicher, 2016; Montavon et al., 2018; Fernandez et al., 2019).

Another feature that allows increasing trust in the MLS is the explainability of a model. A number of techniques allowing us to determine which of the built models have better explainability, regardless of whether they are interpretable or not, is called *eXplainable Artificial Intelligence* (XAI). One of the main definitions of XAI describes them as AI systems whose operation is more comprehensible to humans by providing the user with appropriate explanations (Gunning et al., 2019). This concept mainly assumes the creation of AI systems, where the creation of a suitable environment for the end user is as important as performance so that in addition to obtaining information about the result of the algorithm, they will also be able to find out about the way of reasoning applied, or the grounds for the decision made (Bellotti & Edwards, 2001). Thus, it can be noted that the ability to interpret the results of an interpretable model can be successfully used in building an XAI system as an extension of its capabilities.

The key element of the XAI explainability is the human and his place in creating and using AI. It is his trust and understanding of AI algorithms that are essential for their real use in a company. In Barredo Arrieta et al. (2020), we can find a division of AI users according to their roles in the process of creating and using AI:

- Field experts and AI users (e.g., doctors, insurance agents) using the results of AI's operation – their confidence in the model and gaining knowledge based on the results of its operation is crucial,
- Agencies and regulators evaluate models and prepare legal regulations,
- Managers and decision-makers take decisions about the allocation of funds to AI and the profitability of these solutions,
- AI researchers and developers – AI solution developers who check and improve product performance, research new development opportunities,
- People affected by the consequences of decisions based on the use of AI.

XAI is an opportunity to explain to a person (both a machine learning expert and a layman) how the model works in a specific field problem. It means a literal explanation of what is happening (Gall, 2018). This means that explanation covers a broader range of tasks than interpretation. For example, using the linear regression algorithm, model interpretation will involve formulating a description for each slope of the model specifying the relation between the features and the target and the intercept. Representation of the knowledge of regression models is most often expressed by means of a clear equation, for example, $y' = .25*x_1 + 15$ (where

y is a target, e.g., food expenses and x_1 is a feature, e.g., income), that is, the slope of feature x_1 equal to 0.25 indicates how much food expenses will change when income increases by 1 unit and the intercept (here equal to 15) indicate how much food expenses will be when income equals 0. Because not all machine learning algorithms allow for a clear representation of knowledge, it will be impossible to interpret their results. In such cases, it is necessary to apply methods of explaining the model, which are not based on knowledge representation but some estimated (simulated) behavior of the model. These methods can also be successfully used to explain interpretable models. Using the example presented earlier to simulate the behavior of the linear regression model for different scenarios, the following observation can be made: "If the client's income is PLN 2,500, his food expenses will be PLN 640" or "If the client earns PLN 1,000 more, his food expenses will increase by PLN 250". By converting the mathematical presentation of the model into a statement in natural language, the information is comprehensible to a broader audience and will allow to increase the understanding of the solutions obtained by means of machine learning algorithms and thus increase confidence in AI.

Lack of trust, the ability to review future results, and uncertain stability of results due to the way *black-box* algorithms work can be key factors blocking the use of AI in a company. As can be observed, for example, based on the number of publications on XAI, a growing group of scientists dealing with the subject of AI indicates that the approach based on performance increase is insufficient, and they emphasize the importance of understanding ML.

What is important is that the methods developed for explaining the behavior of a noninterpretable model can be successfully applied to interpretable models. Thus, it is possible to present the results of different models in a consistent way and – what is even more important – to compare the quality and effectiveness of the generated models.

Regardless of whether interpretable or noninterpretable models are used in the process of building artificial intelligence systems, a very important issue is to assess the quality of the estimated models. It can be noted that as the accuracy of a model increases, its interpretability decreases significantly. Decision trees, due to their design, are one of the easiest to interpret and most intuitive ML algorithms, unfortunately, the accuracy of their prediction compared to other ML methods are relatively low. *Deep Learning* solution, on the other hand, achieves some of the best results in terms of performance, but its operation is based on the *black-box* approach, which makes it the least interpretable and comprehensible. This has a significant negative impact on confidence in the use of this approach, and in certain disciplines, due to significant responsibility and legal requirements, its use is impossible.

The picture (ref. Figure 9.1) shows a diagram for estimating trust in MLS using interpretability and explainability. The goal is to maximize

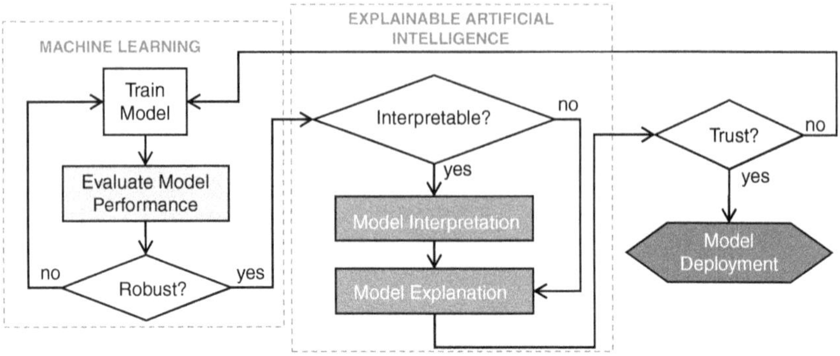

Figure 9.1 The model explanation process. Source: Own research.

the value of trust in the received model. In the picture, you can see a model trained with a teaching base. Then the model evaluation stage is carried out in order to estimate the efficiency of the model obtained. The presented stages are machine learning techniques, and they follow iteratively in order to select the best model in terms of its predictive abilities. Sometimes it happens that several models show similar results in their prediction accuracy evaluation. In such cases, several best models can be admitted to the next stage, where they will be compared in terms of the trust. Then, another phase begins, and it depends on the type of algorithm used to build the model – if the algorithm allows to build an interpretable model, the interpretation of estimated parameters, discovered patterns, and trends takes place.

The models obtained by using machine learning algorithms store very extensive knowledge. It is possible to extract a lot of very diverse information from them, used to explain different aspects of a given model. As the main task of the models is to predict the behavior of the analyzed objects, questions arise that concern both individuals, phenomena, and the whole set of objects. This division has a key impact on the process of explanation, which may depend on the willingness to understand how the model works locally (case-focused) or globally (many cases treated as a whole). Moreover, from both the local and global perspectives, it is possible to understand the impact of individual features used in model building and prediction. Depending on the method used, it is possible to detect which of the features most strongly determined the final result of the prediction or how the result would change if only some of the features changed (*what-if* analysis). A consequence of explaining the model behavior may be the detection of the causes of incorrect model predictions, removal of irrelevant features from the input base, or of cases that stand out and make the model produce false results (Biecek & Burzykowski, 2021).

For *black-box* models, it will be desirable to use methods of model explanation. There are two basic categories of the explanation process (Barredo Arrieta et al., 2020). The first category (*Model-Agnostic Method*) includes groups of methods that can be applied regardless of the algorithm used, the way the data is processed by the model, or the subsequent presentation of information. The next category contains groups of methods that can be used only on selected algorithms (*Model-Specific Method*), for example, *Multi-Layer Neural Networks*, *Convolutional Neural Networks*, *Recurrent Neural Networks*, *Support Vector Machine* or *Ensembles*, and *Multiple Classifier*. These methods are *Model-Agnostic* solutions adapted to the specific structure of internal data processing by the ML algorithms mentioned above.

The first group – the *Model-Agnostic Method* – allows us to build another model based on the results of the original model but with the use of algorithms enabling interpretation. Such a model is a simplification of the original model, which only provides an approximate image of the results. The most popular of these methods is *Local Interpretable Model-Agnostic Explanations* (LIME) (Ribeiro et al., 2016). LIME does not explain the whole (global) model but selects one case (it can be a forecasted case) and builds local explanatory models around it. The construction of the explanatory model consists of determining the linear regression function on the basis of randomly selected cases situated near (locally to) the forecasted case. The parameters of this function allow us to identify the importance of the features on the basis of which *black-box* model decisions are made.

When analyzing *Model-Specific Methods* constructed to enable behavior analysis of specific algorithms, it is worth noting that they are a specific implementation of *Model-Agnostic Methods*. This adjustment makes it possible to take into account the specific, multilayer structure and internal transformations performed.

The most common techniques for explaining and understanding the operation of multi-layer neural networks (MLN) are: methods to simplify the model, feature accuracy estimators, text descriptions, explanations based on local analyses, and visual models (Barredo Arrieta et al., 2020). One of the algorithms allowing for simplification in multilayer neural networks is Deep RED (*Rule Extraction from Deep Neural Networks*). It involves extracting rules (neuron level) by adding more decision trees and rules (Barredo Arrieta et al., 2020).

In explaining *Convolutional Neural Networks* (CNN), whose main applications are image analysis, object classification, and detection, there are two dominant approaches. The first one is based on understanding the decision-making process by mapping the output data to the input data and understanding which elements of the input data determined the result. On analyzing the CNN operation using heatmaps or Grand-CAM (*Gradient-weighted Class Activation Mapping*), the user will obtain visual information about the reason for the conclusion. A filter will be applied to the image so that the part of the image which contributed the most to the decision will be marked with an appropriate warm distinct color, whereas the other fragments will remain in cold blue-green colors (Barredo Arrieta et al., 2020). The second approach relies on its analysis of the interpretation of individual network layers and their meaning (Barredo Arrieta et al., 2020). Appropriate layers are assigned to recognize increasingly complex patterns. In the case of face recognition, the first layer could be responsible for distinguishing shapes, the next one for selected elements of the face (e.g., eye, ear), whereas the task of the last one would be to classify the whole face.

In the case of *Recurrent Neural Networks* (RNN), used primarily in sequential data analysis, natural language processing, and time series analysis, there are two main approaches to explaining their operation. The first one consists of understanding the knowledge gained by the model. For this purpose, methods to explain the significance of traits are used. The other approach is to rebuild the structure of the RNN, which makes it possible to monitor the decisions made through local explanations. (Barredo Arrieta et al., 2020)

Going through the process of building a model of machine learning, one should consider its usefulness both from the perspective of its effectiveness and the possibilities of its interpretability and explainability. Using appropriate XAI methods and techniques, it is possible to compare the above-mentioned parameters for a selected algorithm and choose the best solution.

Conclusion

The continuous growth of AI's popularity, and machine learning, in particular, is reflected in the increasing use of these solutions. International Data Corporation (IDC) forecasts that global spending in this area will continue to grow and could reach 52.2 billion U.S. dollars in 2021. Such great potential and still growing popularity translate into a desire to use AI more and more.

This chapter presented the role of the level of trust in machine learning systems. The use of Big Data algorithms revolutionizes our cognition, and we have access to new knowledge. However, before we can fully use the new technology, we need to be able to trust it. The level of our trust in the acquired knowledge determines its use in commercial and scientific projects. As shown in this chapter, trust in MLS depends on their interpretability and explainability.

The *eXplainable Artificial Intelligence* approach allows us to create AI systems where the performance of a machine algorithm or the precision of the model in decision making are not the only areas of concern, but it is also important to create the right environment for the end-user. As indicated in the chapter, the complexity of the models resulting from the application of various machine learning algorithms is so great that it is necessary to develop new methods of explaining their results and presenting the way in which a model takes decisions.

Both the creators and users of these technologies keep challenging the algorithms, and thanks to XAI, they are no longer only effective but also more understandable and interpretable for humans so that we can trust them and gain new knowledge from them. We should remember, however, that despite a significantly growing interest in XAI, there is still a number of challenges and difficulties that researchers must face, such as the choice between focusing on the human or on the machine, emphasizing accuracy or interpretability, or explaining AI's abilities or decisions (Gunning et al. 2019). It is worth noting, however, that more and more organizations, that is, AI4EU, XAI-Project, DARPA – Explainable Artificial Intelligence (XAI) Project, SoBigData, Humane AI, Google Brain, or Explainable Machine Learning Models engage in the development of XAI, and the solutions themselves are increasingly appreciated.

References

Act of February 21, 2019, amending certain acts in connection with ensuring the application of Regulation 2016/679 of the European Parliament and of the Council of April 27, 2016, on the protection of individuals with regard to the processing of personal data and on the free movement of such data and repealing Directive 95/46/EC (General Data Protection Regulation). Journal of Laws 2019, item 730.

Barber, B. (1983). *The logic and limits of trust.* New Brunswick, NJ: Rutgers University Press.

Barredo Arrieta, A., Díaz-Rodríguez, N., Del Ser, J., Bennetot, A., Tabik, S., Barbado, A., Garcia, S., Gil-Lopez, S., Molina, D., Benjamins, R., Chatila, R., & Herrera, F. (2020). Explainable artificial intelligence (XAI): Concepts, taxonomies, opportunities and challenges toward responsible ai. *Information Fusion*, *58*, 82–115.

Bellotti, V., & Edwards, K. (2001). Intelligibility and accountability: Human considerations in context-aware systems. *Human Computer Interaction*, *16* (2-4), 193–212.

Biecek, P., & Burzykowski, T. (2021). *Explanatory model analysis: Explore, explain and examine predictive models.* New York, Chapman and Hall/CRC.

Craven, M. W. (1996). *Extracting comprehensible models from trained neural networks* (tech. rep.). University of Wisconsin-Madison Department of Computer Sciences. Retrieved from https://minds.wisconsin.edu/bitstream/handle/1793/60078/TR1326.pdf?sequence=1.

Duch, W. (1997). *Fascynujacy swiat komputerow* [*The fascinating world of computers*]. Poznań: Wydawnictwo NAKOM.

Fernandez, A., Herrera, F., Cordon, O., Jose del Jesus, M., & Marcelloni, F. (2019). Evolutionary fuzzy systems for explainable artificial intelligence: Why, when, what for, and where to? *IEEE Computational Intelligence Magazine*, *14*(1), 69–81.

Gall, R. (2018). Machine learning explainability vs interpretability: Two concepts that could help restore trust in AI. Kdnuggets. Retrieved from https://www.Kdnuggets.com/2018/12/machine-learning-explainability-interpretability-ai.html.

Gleicher, M. (2016). A framework for considering comprehensibility in modeling [PMID: 27441712]. *Big Data*, *4*(2), 75–88.

Goodman, B., & Flaxman, S. (2017). European union regulations on algorithmic decision-making and a right to explanation. *AI Magazine*, *38*(3), 50–57.

Gunning, D., Stefik, M., Choi, J., Miller, T., Stumpf, S., & Yang, G. Z. (2019). XAI-explainable artificial intelligence. *Science Robotics*, *4*(37), eaay7120. 10.1126/scirobotics.aay7120

Lewicki, R. J., McAllister, D. J., & Bies, R. J. (1998). Trust and distrust: New relationships and realities. *Academy of Management Review*, *23*(3), 438–458.

Mayer, R. C., Davis, J. H., & Schoorman, F. D. (1995). An integrative model of organizational trust. *Academy of Management Review*, *20*(3), 709–734.

Mayer-Schonberger, V., & Cukier, K. (2017). *Big data: The essential guide to work, life and learning in the age of insight*. London, GB: John Murray.

Mellinger, G. D. (1956). Interpersonal trust as a factor in communication. *The Journal of Abnormal and Social Psychology*, *52*(3), 304.

Molnar, C. (2020). *Interpretable machine learning*. Lulu.com.

Montavon, G., Samek, W., & Müller, K. R. (2018). Methods for interpreting and understanding deep neural networks. *Digital Signal Processing*, *73*, 1–15.

Read, W. H. (1962). Upward communication in industrial hierarchies. *Human Relations*, *15*(1), 3–15.

Regulation (EU) 2016/679 of the European Parliament and of the Council of April 27, 2016, on the protection of natural persons with regard to the processing of personal data and on the free movement of such data, and repealing directive 95/46/EC (General Data Protection Regulation). (2016-05-04). *Official Journal of the European Union, L 119/1*.

Ribeiro, M. T., Singh, S., & Guestrin, C. (2016). "Why should I trust you?": Explaining the predictions of any classier. *Proceedings of the 22nd ACM SIGKDD International Conference on Knowledge Discovery and Data Mining*, 1135–1144. 10.1145/2939672.2939778

Siau, K., & Wang, W. (2018). Building trust in artificial intelligence, machine learning, and robotics. *Cutter Business Technology Journal*, *31*(2), 47–53.

Toreini, E., Aitken, M., Coopamootoo, K., Elliott, K., Zelaya, C. G., & van Moorsel, A. (2020). The relationship between trust in ai and trustworthy machine learning technologies. *Proceedings of the 2020 Conference on Fairness, Accountability, and Transparency*, 272–283.

Wikipedia. (2020). Right to explanation Wikipedia, the free encyclopedia [Last modified December 12, 2020]. Retrieved from https://en.wikipedia.org/wiki/Right_to_explanation.

Part II

Trust in the Digital Economy: Issues and Challenges

10 Trust and Modern Internet Technology Solutions in the Banking Sector

Ewa Stawicka
Warsaw University of Life Sciences

Introduction

The Internet of Things (IoT) started as a vision of all digital objects being connected and acting in smart ways. This vision has been evolving over the years since 2000. The IoT is the main constituent of Industrial Revolution 4.0 (Want et al., 2015). The development of branchless banking services via multiple communication channels has made it possible to create a new kind of added value for customers in the banking and financial service sector. The growing use of mobile phones, especially other wireless devices such as wearable and sensors, has made the IoT a tool to improve customer experience, a logical development in electronic banking. Potential applications of the IoT in these sectors include insurance through telematics, life and health insurance, investment management, and worker's compensation in the commercial arena. IoT will definitely enhance the customer experience and enhance overall network infrastructure in banks. However, IoT implementation becomes effective if and only if the big data analytics and cloud accessibility are integrated with the IoT structures. Although today, in the banking and financial service sector, online and mobile banking systems deliver a high-quality service to consumers, and the quality of services could be made a bet by using IoT technologies. To the best of our knowledge, there is no framework using IoT and analytics for banks and financial organizations today (Urban & Wójcik, 2019). On the other hand, banks play very important functions in economic and social life, as well as commercial and service functions. They are responsible for providing shareholders with material benefits, and, on the other hand, they have obligations toward the community in which they operate, bank employees as well as future generations and stakeholders (Zhao et al., 2019).

In banking, the technologies used to make noncash payments are more convenient and provide greater security to market participants, but many people still use cash. Coins and banknotes are part of the cultural heritage, carry a message, and are sometimes a work of art. Cash was and is

DOI: 10.4324/9781003165965-10

one of the basic forms of payment, especially in retail trade. Despite the intensive promotion of noncash payments, over 80% of transactions in the Polish economy are concluded in a traditional way (Badania Mastercard, 2020). The tendency to accumulate money at home is a derivative of the limited access to points where you can withdraw or deposit cash. Especially in rural or suburban areas, there is a shortage of ATMs. On the other hand, the evolution of society caused by the introduction of thInternetet to almost all spheres of human life forces banks to automate and digitize all banking processes and products to meet the requirements of modern customers (Druszcz, 2017). The problem is customer trust in Big Data, mobile payments, biometrics, and the IoT. Trust management in the era of modern technologies involves a number of uncertainties and verification of solutions whether they are consistent with the assumption. As a consequence, modern solutions create trust but can also lead to its loss in relation to the company, brand, or product. Technology users bear a certain risk of trusting that the activities performed using technology will produce the desired results. As long as a given solution brings the expected results, it strengthens trust. Possible undesirable effects undermine confidence. The aim of the article is to recognize the use of modern technologies and user confidence in IoT solutions in the Polish banking sector. Specifically, this study focuses on three research questions:

1. What is the situation regarding modern IoT solutions in banking in Poland?
2. Which IoT solutions in banking do users most often use?
3. How is users' trust in modern IoT solutions in banking shaped?

The chapter is divided into six parts. The main problems and findings are outlined first. The second part presents synthetic contemporary views on modern internet technology solutions in the banking sector and users' trust in modern solutions, based on a critical review of the literature. The third part presents the methodological process with research steps and questions. The next chapter presents the results of research on the behavior, attitudes, and trust of banking service users in modern IoT solutions in banking. The fifth part is a discussion of the results of other studies. The chapter ends with a summary and research implications.

Theoretical Background

Polish banking in the free market edition has a shorter history than in most developed economies. Compared to countries from the former Eastern bloc, such as Slovakia, Romania, or Hungary, the banking situation is in favor of Poland. The banking sector is mostly controlled by domestic capital (the share of Polish capital is around 56%) (Janik,

2018). The latest data from the European Commission (2020) show that despite the impressive growth in the last decade, Polish banking still plays a marginal role on a global scale.

Despite the development of electronic payment instruments, cash is still dominant, even in economically advanced economies. Virtual payments are very popular in the Scandinavian countries, South Korea, and the Netherlands. In countries such as Austria, Germany, Japan, and even Switzerland, cash rules (Bohdziewicz, 2017). Cash is the most important emergency means of payment, the cheapest method of paying small retail payments. It is treated as a payment instrument as well as a store of value. It turns out that in an era of uncertainty, COVID-19 is likely to change that. The form of cash payments may not match the realities of the electronic economy more and more, on the other hand, types of terrorism or hacker attacks are becoming a threat. (Żołyński, 2017). The government program "Cashless, Paperless Poland" (Cashless, 2020) provided for, among other things, the taking of excess cash from the market and transferring it to bank accounts. It was related to the emergence and popularization of ATMs with the function of depositing cash. However, especially in rural and suburban areas, there is a shortage of ATMs, and it is characteristic to keep savings in private places. Society's possession of mobile devices, that is, smartphones, portable computers, laptops, and tablets, is changing the situation. Almost every adult inhabitant of the Earth has a smartphone, and the development of thInternetet makes communication instantaneous. Poles are more and more willing to use financial services on smartphones. Over 63% of respondents declare that they "banking" in a mobile way (average 52%), and already more than half of the Polish consumers (52%) use various forms of mobile payments offered by banks, whereas in the countries of Central and Eastern Europe this indicator remains up to 40% (Marciniak, 2019). Mastercard's research (2020) shows that Polish consumers are enthusiasts of digital services, appreciating above all the speed, convenience, and the ability to use services anywhere, anytime. More than half of Polish consumers pay by mobile and online shopping is the most popular digital service among Poles.

Today's banking is based on advanced electronic systems. Banks use new technologies, want to be friendlier, reach more customers, and expand the package of services. The activities are aimed at reducing costs, maximizing profits, and becoming more competitive in the market. In the segment of payment services, the Internet of Thinks is increasingly dominating, a trend that popularizes new purchasing and transaction mechanisms, thanks to which paying becomes easier and faster than ever before. Often, online purchases and payments are made by the machine, according to criteria defined by us regarding the subject of the transaction, its amount, etc. (Szafrański, 2017). The IoT is the inseparability of man and devices and a very high level of communication between them, which ultimately is to leads to an almost complete connection of each type of device in the network. The rapid development of the IoT concept is favored by customers' openness to new solutions and their basic knowledge to use the technology. Technical background, such as the widespread possession of a smartphone or internet network at home and in workplaces, favors the development of new technologies. The argument for IoT solutions is convenience. Bank customers have positively received online banking, mobile applications, and contactless payments, which are gaining more and more popularity (Zajączkowski, 2016).

The banking sector is changing its technological face extremely quickly. IT in banking is developing very dynamically in order to keep up with the growing needs, especially in terms of the security of transactions and stored data (Ibrahim, 2016). The hardware layer and data distribution, and thus their security, are no longer the biggest challenge. Bank data resources, including information about customers or transactions, are becoming more important. The analysis of giant data sets is an issue known as Big Data (Dawei et al., 2018). The vast amount of information, its governance, and its global integration are used in all decision-making processes, and they are, therefore, an element of strategic importance in the development process and in the survival of every company, thanks to the potential for transforming all information sources into knowledge and quantifying reality in all its elements (objects, places, phenomena, people, and human behavior). Having a large volume and a wide variety of information (i.e., Big Data) shared within an organization is crucial for the interactive and multidirectional process of risk assessment and management (Grazia et al., 2019). Due to the dynamic development of the Big Data industry, financial institutions can now use many advanced analytical tools tailored to the specifics of their operations. One of the basic Big Data solutions used by financial institutions is systems for collecting and analyzing user data. After determining the profiles of individual clients, a client base is created. As a result, the bank can conduct a complex segmentation of customers and create individual offers tailored to the needs and behavior of each of them. Extensive knowledge of the client allows additionally to propose answers to his real needs in a natural way (mobile channels, social media, etc.) (Kathuria, 2016). This solution reduces costs related to advertising and increases the efficiency of customer acquisition, and this translates into sales efficiency and an increase in the financial results of the institution.

Another issue is biometrics. A technique of measuring living things for the purpose of automatic recognition of persons. Biometric methods are divided into two subgroups:

- Examining physical characteristics; we include here the biometrics of fingerprints (fingerprints), the iris of the eye, the retina of the eye, the pattern of blood vessels in the finger and hand, the shape (geometry) of the face or hand;

- Examining the characteristics of behavior (behavioral); these methods include biometrics of the way of voice intonation, biometrics of a handwritten signature (examining, among others, the dynamics of a signature), as well as biometrics examining brain waves or ways of moving (Kowańska, 2018).

Biometrics, as an alternative to passwords and PINs, has many advantages, but also – from the point of view of the customer and the bank – disadvantages. The advantage is convenience, security, and certainty of authentication. Some customers are reluctant to accept this method of identity verification, fearing identity theft. The limitation is the implementation costs in the bank and in some customer systems. Currently, the most popular methods are: fingerprint scanning, the blood vessel system of the hands and fingers, the iris of the eye, voice, and facial image recognition (Kearney, 2014). The simplicity of using most of the solutions limited to expanding the capabilities of their devices instead of using them completely new increased the level of confidence in new solutions among many users. Many of them did not undergo any approval process due to the fact that individual new "smart" add-ons were introduced gradually and over a longer period of time, thus not creating any problem for the user in the adaptation process. In the case of the IoT, the potential of technology has definitely been used correctly. Efficient use of IoT helps to save natural resources, electricity, and reduce pollution produced into the environment, thus directly or indirectly saving money in the public and private sectors. The industries that are the biggest beneficiaries of IoT are (Ministerstwo Cyfryzacji, 2019):

- Finance and insurance,
- Smart cities and buildings,
- Healthcare,
- Agriculture,
- Transport and logistics.

Each device connected to ICT networks is exposed to hackers' attacks. Many financial organizations consider biometric solutions to be one of the most promising acquisitions of modern technology, whereas cybercriminals see them as a new opportunity to steal confidential information (Polaczek, 2017). Financial sector development, ensured by trust in the banking system, is an essential prerequisite for sustainable economic and social growth. Trust management plays an important role in IoT for reliable data fusion and mining, qualified services with context-awareness, and enhanced user privacy and information security. It helps people overcome perceptions of uncertainty and risk and engages in user acceptance and consumption of IoT services and applications. However, current literature still lacks a comprehensive study on trust management in IoT.

Research Methodology

The snowball type assessment and sampling technique were used to collect the data. The survey was conducted at the turn of May and September 2020. On the Internet, using Google Forms, the author prepared an electronic version of the survey. The study's target population was adult (18+) employees, using the services of the banking sector, and the sampling location was in Poland. There were no other inclusion or exclusion criteria for sampling. Each of the respondents completed the questionnaire independently. Efforts were made to collect as much data and answers as possible from the widest age groups and their level of education. After data collection, 124 fully completed questionnaires were obtained for data analysis. Women were 72.6% of the 124 respondents; over 36% of them were under 35 years old; however, the largest group were people aged 36–55. Most of the respondents have a university degree, are employed, and live in a city of over 500,000 inhabitants. The review and analysis of the literature allowed for drawing conclusions and formulating recommendations, and also indicated the limitations of the research.

Results

Research on a group of market users has shown that modern solutions related to banking and the IoT are gaining popularity. More and more services can be provided digitally. Some services have become so established that it is difficult to imagine how you can function without them. Some of them have already gained an established position, among the most popular among Poles are sending e-mails (76%), searching for information on thInternetet (76%), and using social media (75%). Other digital services include field navigation applications (66%), electronic calendar use (65%), loyalty programs (63%), online weather checking (54%), streaming music and video content "on-demand" (50%), or booking accommodation (38%) and purchasing travel tickets (34%). In some areas, digitization is still in the initial phase of development, as it is in the case of reading books – the use of an e-book reader is declared by only 14% of respondents. On the other hand, Poles are enthusiasts of online shopping and the most advanced users of electronic payments in Central and Eastern Europe (Marciniak, 2019). On the other hand, the analysis of data among the 124 surveyed users showed that the respondents used various forms of banking services and technical innovations. 93% of the respondents most often used online banking solutions, whereas 88.7% of respondents indicated mobile payments (Figure 10.1).

The respondents indicated that they very often use payment cards, Skykash applications, phone payments, blik, and even 16.1% indicated

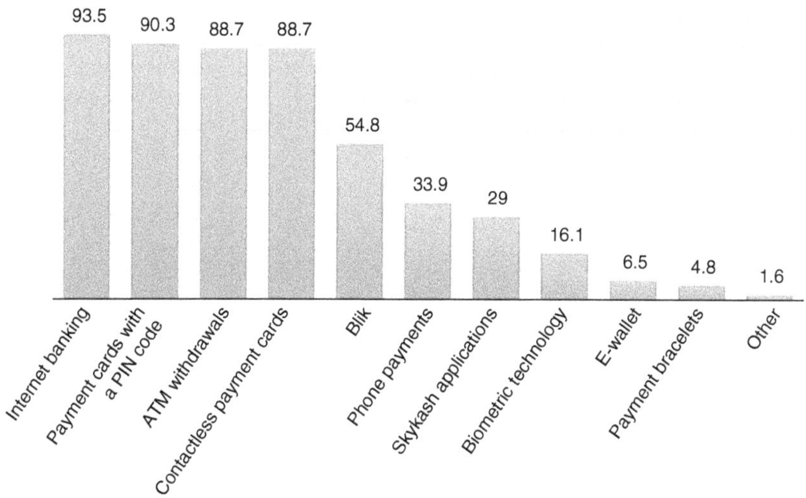

Figure 10.1 IoT solutions are most often chosen by the respondents [%], N = 124.

Source: Author's own calculation.

biometric technology. Modern solutions such as phone payments and blik were usually indicated by younger users, up to 35 years old. They confirmed that they are so-called early adopters. The respondents were asked about their trust in modern solutions. The trust that man and technology can create between themselves is important because it takes care of many human tasks. The proper functioning of technology is very often responsible for facilitating everyday activities. On the other hand, it raises many concerns. More than 17% of respondents admitted that they absorb new products early, they were not afraid of changes. The aforementioned group of early adopters also confirmed that they do not remember having had a bad experience with the banking sector in terms of data security or the use of IoT. Figure 10.2 shows how the respondents assessed the level of trust in modern IoT solutions in banking. Over 48% of the respondents trusted banking services. Only 5% of respondents showed fears and a lack of confidence in new banking.

The respondents expressed a high level of trust in Internet banking and new banking solutions. It was interesting what, in the opinion of the respondents, influenced the creation of trust in banking services. Trust becomes an effective link between the producer and the consumer, as well as internal communication, which in turn brings profit. Trust is growing in importance as a resource that is hard to come by and at the same time of high value in life and management. Among the respondents, brand recognition was of great importance in creating confidence in

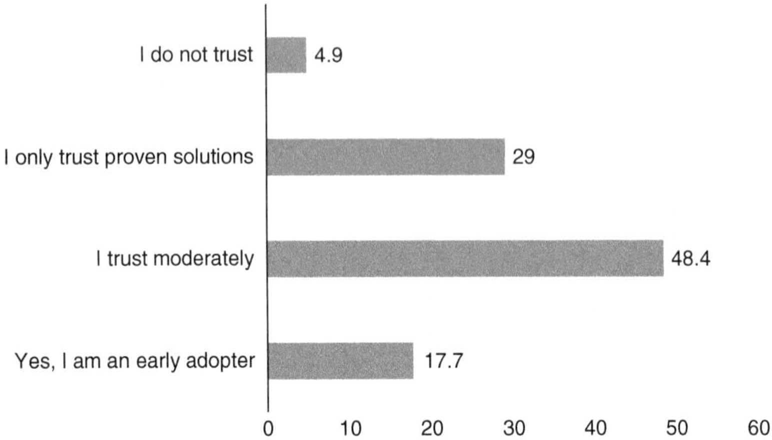

Figure 10.2 Trust in IoT in Banking [%], N = 124.

Source: Author's own calculation.

banking, as indicated by 30% of respondents, as well as socially responsible practices of banks. Social responsibility in banking influences good relations and creates a competitive advantage in the market. The transparency of banks and information on responsibility was used for an informed and responsible decision-making process. An important aspect of CSR as creating trust in banks was indicated by 23% of the respondents (Figure 10.3).

Each of these factors played a role in building trust. Confidence in the individual choice of specific banks by the respondents was influenced, among others, by the history of the bank, country of origin, recommendations of other trusted persons, and advertising. As previously mentioned, the

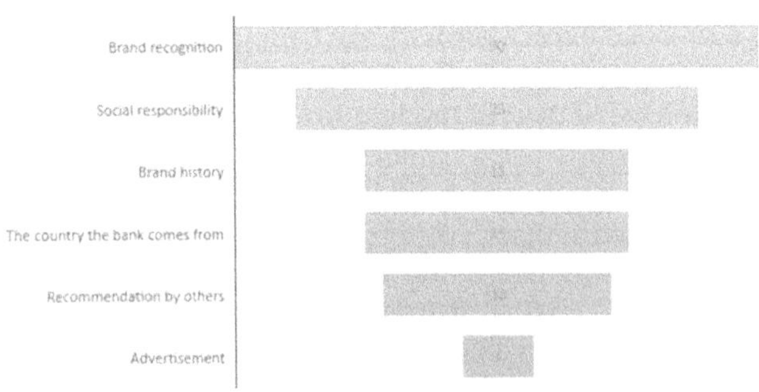

Figure 10.3 Factors that contribute to the creation of trust in banking [%], N = 124.

Source: Author's own calculation.

respondents emphasized the greatest trust in brand recognition and socially responsible practices of banks. New banking offers and specialized IT technologies contribute to the development of banking services. New technologies allow us to adjust the banking offer to the individual needs of customers. As form-banking, the trust could help in reducing customers' fears and concerns regarding the privacy of their personal data and security of banking transactions carried out through mobile devices. A factor that has been proposed to be an important antecedent of loyalty is trust.

Discussion

The results of this study showed not only that the quality of banking services is a factor significantly related to customer satisfaction, but also trust in electronic banking services. Creating trust is the strongest dimension that affects customer satisfaction. This is supported by previous studies (Dawei et al., 2018; Urban & Wójcik, 2019), which suggested that trust has a significant impact on service quality and customer satisfaction. The results also showed that improvements and modern solutions improve the quality of banking services. Electronic banking services have a significant impact on customer satisfaction in the Polish banking sector. Poles are early adopters of IoT news in banking. These results are supported by previous research (Kowańska, 2018; Ministerstwo Cyfryzacji, 2019), which empirically shows that there is a direct relationship between the dimensions of internet banking services, service quality, and customer satisfaction with banks' services.

An important dimension of the quality of services is the efficiency and ease of use of this service. According to Polaczek (2017), the use of bank electronic services gives customers such an opportunity to be profitable in carrying out transactions, not only by saving money, but also by saving time (RAPORT, 2020).

The results of the analyzes in this study are consistent with studies carried out in other markets (Wirtz & Bateson, 1995; Hammoud et al., 2018), which suggested that higher levels of efficiency increase customer satisfaction. IoT, biometrics, electronic banking, and reliability for banking services are important elements of service quality. Protection in banking against hacker attacks is also emphasized (Grazia et al., 2019).

Effective communication and education in the field of digital services can be important for customers who have problems with e-banking services, and this seems to significantly affect customer trust and satisfaction.

Conclusion

Realizing the need to change the bank's strategy and the current business model is the first and most important challenge facing bank presidents.

The scope of changes related to digital transformation shows that digitization is a difficult and complex undertaking. Seizing transformational opportunities and opportunities will require banks to invest, carefully plan, and bank-wide coordinated decision-making. The IoT is the next phase of the digital revolution that will change the lives of consumers. While the Internet doesn't typically go beyond the electronic world, connected objects are the extension of the Internet to things and places. IoT is revolutionizing the financial sector with its services. Today, the financial industry is becoming more visible than ever (Dineshreddy & Gangadharan, 2016). Next time, it will revolutionize retail banking, core banking, and other banking software. IoT will continue to transform other industries. However, managing the balance between trust in a service provider and individuals' need for privacy becomes a major challenge when considering automatic multi-person exchanges. The greater experience of banks in providing services using IoT, Big Data, and biometric methods also mean modern security. The study showed that:

- Users' trust in modern IoT solutions is growing;
- The interest in modern solutions is growing due to the convenience;
- The considerations indicate the need for education about modern technologies and getting used to the concept of the IoT. The need to shape digital competencies among the population should also be emphasized;
- Research indicates the need to transfer knowledge about the opportunities and threats related to the use of IoT in banking practice.

The research has numerous theoretical and practical implications; from the theoretical implication, this research fills the gap in the literature by examining the drivers for and resistance to the adoption of the IoT in one conceptual model. Furthermore, it investigates the reasons that affect the drivers for adoption of and resistance to the IoT with the user behavior of the banking sector. Regarding the managerial implications, focusing on innovation through a resistance approach would help organizations avoid or reduce innovation failure. The research emphasizes that managers in the banking sector should increase consumers' awareness of using the banking sector and eliminates the factors that lead to consumer resistance. The use of the banking sector would lead to reducing the workload of branches and would save consumers' time and effort. The presented proposal encourages further research to determine the impact of building trust in banking services on Internet services by users, for example, of different ages or levels of education. It is worth considering the factors influencing trust in the IoT usage.

References

Badania Mastercard. (2020). *Polacy doceniają bankowośc cyfrową* [*Poles appreciate digital banking*]. Retreived from http://briefs/badanie-mastercard-polacy-fanami-cyfrowych-uslug-z-elektronicznych-platnosci-korzystaja-najczesciej-w-europie-srodkowo-wschodniej/.

Bohdziewicz, J. (2017). Świat kocha gotówkę [The world loves cash]. *Bank*, *9*(291), 20–21.

Cashless. (2020). Cashless, paperless Poland. Retrieved from https://www.cashless.pl/9256-cashless-pay-2020-cashless-live.

Dawei, L., Anzi, H., & Gen, L. (2018). *Big data technology: Application and cases, Handbook of Blockchain, Digital Finance, and Inclusion* (1st edition, Vol. 2, pp. 65–82). Amsterdam, Netherlands: Elsevier Inc.

Dineshreddy, V., & Gangadharan, G. R. (2016). Towards an Internet of Things framework for financial services sector. *Published in 2016 3rd International Conference on Recent Advances in Information Technology (RAIT)*.

Druszcz, P. (2017). Digitalizacja produktów bankowych jako cel strategiczny uczestników polskiego sektora bankowego [Digitization of banking products as a strategic goal of the participants Polish banking sector]. *Ruch Prawniczy, Ekonomiczny i Socjologiczny*, *79*(1), 237–250.

Grazia, D., Galeone, G, Zappimbulso, E., & Dell'Atti, V. (2019). Risk management 4.0: The role of big data analytics in the bank sector. *International Journal of Economics and Financial Issues*, *9*(6), 40–47.

Hammoud J., Bizri R. M., & Baba I. El. (2018). The impact of e-banking service quality on customer satisfaction: Evidence from the Lebanese banking sector. *Business and Management*, *8*(3), 1–12.

Ibrahim, M. H. (2016). Business cycle and bank lending procyclicality in a dual banking system. *Economic Modelling*, *55*, 127–134.

Janik, R. (2018). Sektor bankowy w Polsce i za granicą. Porównanie aktywów i struktury własnościowej [The banking sector in Poland and abroad. Compare assets and structure] *Polski Sektor Bankowy*. Retrieved from https://www.najlepszekonto.pl/sektor-bankowy-w-polsce-i-za-granica.

Kathuria, A. (2016). Impact of big data analytics on banking sector. *International Journal of Science, Engineering and Technology Research*, *5*(11), 3138–3141.

Kearney, A. T. (2014), *Going digital: The banking transformation road map*. Retrieved from https://www.atkearney.com/documents/10192/5264096.

Komisja Europejska. (2020). Usługi bankowe i finansowe [Banking and financial services]. Retrieved from https://ec.europa.eu/info/policies/banking-and-financial-services_pl.

Kowańska, B. (2018). Application of biometric technologies in the banking sector. Economy, business economy/management, human resources in economy. ICT *Information and Communications Technologies*, *10*(1), 225–234.

Marciniak, A. (2019). Badania mastercard [research mastercard]. Retrieved from https://newsroom.mastercard.com/eu/pl/news-polacy-fanami-cyfrowych-uslug-z-elektronicznych-platnosci-korzystaja-najczesciej-w-europie-srodkowo-wschodniej/.

Ministerstwo Cyfryzacji. (2019). IoT w polskiej gospodarce [IoT in the Polish economy]. Retrieved from https://www.gov.pl/web/cyfryzacja/grupa-robocza-ds-internetu-rzeczy-internet-of-things-iot.

Polaczek, K. (2017). Bankomaty Zombie [Zombie ATMs]. *Bank*, 9(291), 48–49.

Raport. (2020). RAPORT o sytuacji ekonomicznej banków [REPORT on the economic condition of banks] *Związek Banków Polskich*, 10/2020. Retrieved from https://www.zbp.pl/aktualnosci/wydarzenia/Raport-o-sytuacji-ekonomicznej-bankow-BANKI-2020.

Szafrański, B. (2017). Banki w świecie nowych technologii [Banks in the world of new technologies]. *Bank*, *1*, 80–82.

Urban, M. A., & Wójcik, D. (2019). Dirty banking: Probing the gap in sustainable finance. *Sustainability*, *11*, 1745.

Want, R., Schilit, B., & Jenson, S. (2015). Enabling the Internet of Things. *Computer 1*, 28–35.

Zajączkowski, J. (2016). Cyfrowa rewolucja trwa [The digital revolution continues]. *Bank*, *11*, 86–89.

Wirtz, J., & Bateson, J. E. (1995). An experimental investigation of halo effects in satisfaction measures of service attributes. *International Journal of Service Industry Management*, 6(3), 84–102.

Zhao, Q., Tsai, P., & Wang, J. (2019). Improving financial service innovation strategies for Enhancing china's banking industry competitive advantage during the fintech revolution: A Hybrid MCDM model. *Sustainability*, *11*, 1419.

Żołyński, M. (2017). Klienci preferują swobodny wybór form płatności [Customers prefer a free choice of payment methods]. *Bank*, 9(291), 26–27.

11 Trust as a Factor Influencing the Willingness to Pay Taxes

Piroska Dobos[1] *and*
Katalin Takács-György[2]
[1]*Óbuda University Doctoral School on Safety and Security Sciences*
[2]*Óbuda University, Faculty of Business and Management*

Introduction

Our aim – beyond the microeconomic examination of tax fraud – is to approach the willingness to pay taxes from a behavioral point of view, to examine the reasons that lead individuals to make decisions on tax avoidance and the means by which the size of the hidden economy can be reduced. Based on an analysis of the relevant international special literature and a questionnaire survey, we sought to answer the question of the impact of trust in government, the stability of the tax system, and the respectful treatment of taxpayers as partners by tax authorities on tax evasion and fraud. Based on the analysis, we came to the conclusion that the higher level of citizens' trust in the government, tax authorities and other legal institutions, the friendly and respectful treatment of taxpayers, their treatment as partners, and the direct political participation and involvement of citizens in political decisions and democracy also have a significant positive effect on tax morals. Empirical studies on the topic of deterrence and mood also found that taxpayers' tax morals increase when officials treat them with respect, whereas deterrence leads to tax evasion.

Human Nature in the Context of Tax Behavior

Taxation is a very complex and complicated set of tools, which is why tax fraud, tax evasion, and tax denial are often accompanied by very complex, intricate phenomena. Taxation has been a concept that has existed since the inception of states. Different and varied forms of tax evasion have emerged in different historical eras. In a rapidly changing economic environment, tax abuses are difficult to typify because human ingenuity knows no barriers.

The concept of "tax morals" is not new, but it has received surprisingly little attention in the special literature on tax compliance. Some preliminary tax morality research was conducted in the 1960s at the "Cologne Tax Psychology Department" by Schmölders (1960) and

DOI: 10.4324/9781003165965-11

Strümpel (1969) who attempted to build a bridge between the economy and social psychology, emphasizing that economic phenomena should not be analyzed from a traditional neoclassical perspective only. Tax morals have been seen as an important and integrated attitude closely linked to non-compliance with tax payment (Alm & Torgler, 2005). The general concept of tax morals can be divided into several components that – although to varying degrees – both theoretically and empirically, affect the informal economy in the same direction as trust in and satisfaction with public institutions, perception of government corruption, observance of the law, observance of the norms, and besides conformity, tax awareness is a part of it (Torgler, 2003).

Trust – Can It Be Untied from Attitudes of Taxpaying Behind the Internet?

As it is increasingly the case in the field of personal human relations – everything is rearranged to the field of social media – in practice, communication and liaison between taxpayers and the authority take place on the Internet. This means that it is increasingly happening in the form of all electronic administration, online, through the customer portal, company portal, e-government portal, e-paper. The year 2016 was a key turning point for the Hungarian Tax Authority, when the change of attitude began, which makes the tax authority not "merely" an office that collects tax revenues, but also a service-oriented institution acting in a supportive way toward taxpayers. The aim of the transformation is to create a tax and customs office that, in cooperation with customers, effectively meets social and governmental expectations, encouraging taxpayers to pay taxes adequately by transforming the culture of administration and making services accessible. Thus, more emphasis has been placed on customer-friendly administration. By this, a process has started in Hungary as well – the friendly and respectful treatment of taxpayers by the authorities – which method, for instance, has long been recognized in Switzerland as an important resource for increasing compliance with tax rules. This tendency also shows well that the quality of the relationship between taxpayers and the state and state institutions has a significant impact on the willingness to pay taxes, that is, one of the main determinants of tax morals is trust in government and legal institutions. Almost at the same time, serious tightening was introduced, such as the online cash register system in 2014, the road freight control system in 2015, and the online invoicing program system in July 1, 2018, as a result of which the invoices are issued in real-time and the tax authority receives the data on the account turnover of enterprises at the same time. On July 1, 2020, the next level of the online invoice data service was introduced, according to which all domestic taxpayers must provide data on the issued invoice to the tax authority. The measure is expected to further whiten the economy, clean up the market, increase VAT revenues, and introduce more targeted controls. Systems similar to online invoicing have already been introduced in other countries, but only in very few places for the time being, so Hungary is definitely at the forefront with this form of digitization. Based on these, what could be a more effective means of whitening the economy on the part of the authorities – supportive partnership or rigorous, coercive efforts? In the middle of a pandemic, in 2020, while businesses aim for survival, the issue of trust in government institutions is even more significant.

Connections Between Trust in the Government, the Legal and Judicial System and Willingness to Pay Taxes

Most often, one of the leading causes of the black economy is attributed to high tax burdens; however, several studies have shown that tax cuts are not necessarily accompanied by an increase in tax revenues. Tax compliance depends on a number of factors. Alm et al. (1995) conducted experiments on compliance with tax rules in Spain and the United States. The two countries are very different both in culture and in history. Subjects were found to consistently show higher compliance in the United States than participants in the same experiments in Spain, and these differences were attributed to compliance with higher social standards in the United States.

Strümpel (1969) conducted an international comparative survey in Europe comparing both the tax systems of different European countries and the levels of tax morals among taxpayers in each country. Tax morals were relatively low in Germany while relatively high in England. In his view, the main difference also stemmed from the fact that the German government used coercive tax control techniques, whereas the English system treated taxpayers with more respect and less control. Empirical surveys carried out by Scholtz (1998) also show that trust in government is a determinant of the development of tax morals, which rather influences the payment of taxes than the fear of getting caught.

According to Frey and Feld (2002), taxpayers' tax morals increase when tax officials treat them with respect. In contrast, when tax officials rely solely on deterrence of taxpayers, they tend to respond by actively trying to avoid paying taxes. In addition, it has been shown that an authoritarian approach more strongly displaces tax morals, as well as when citizens have fewer rights of political participation. In contrast, a respectful approach and high political participation rights of citizens greatly increase tax morals. According to Frey and Torgler (2006), the direct political participation of taxpayers is also of great importance for the willingness to pay taxes, as it leads to lower tax fraud and higher internal motivation in paying taxes. The quality of political institutions has a strong observable impact on tax morals, and political stability, non-violence, government efficiency, quality of regulation, the rule of law, and the control of corruption also have a strong impact on tax morals. Weakening trust in public institutions and the perceived high level of government corruption go hand in hand with the more likely acceptance of forms of payment in the face of tax fraud. Dissatisfaction with state institutions is particularly strong in Hungary compared to other European countries, and this can be a very detrimental factor in tax morals (Fazekas et al., 2010).

Cummings et al. (2004) suggest that coercive effort can increase compliance with tax rules, but extreme punitive items can even have the opposite effect – resulting in lower tax payments and a loss of overall trust in public institutions. Botswana and South Africa, although geographical neighbors, they are very different in terms of their social history. In South Africa, tax fraud is treated as a serious crime, whereas in Botswana the attitude of the tax authorities is much more helpful. British colonial rules have achieved visible success in Botswana as it has been the fastest growing economy in the world for the past 35 years.

Alm et al. (2005) examined the tax payment attitudes, tax morals, or internal motivation of citizens to pay taxes in the Russian economy during the beginning of the transition (1991), during the transition (1995), and somewhat later (1999). The results suggest that a higher level of trust in the state has a positive effect on tax morals. Tax fraud is widespread in countries in transition. Citizens' tax-paying attitudes depend on a number of factors. One of the main determinants of tax morals is trust in government and legal institutions. In the 1990s, the Russian tax enforcement strategy was based on strong coercive methods, mainly to increase the mandate of the growing law enforcement agencies. The results of the research show that in parallel, tax morals have fallen sharply in Russia. "The weight of trust as an emotional attitude in the functioning of a modern market economy is so significant that many areas and phenomena of the economy cannot be analyzed without a clear picture of the role of trust, but fraud is inextricably linked to the topic, which is such a phenomenon which – if emerges – undermines trust" (Hámori, 1998).

Kirchler et al. (2007) argue that the strength of the tax authority and the appropriate level of trust in the tax authority require an understanding of forced and voluntary tax payments. In a hostile environment, taxpayers and tax authorities work against each other, whereas in a synergistic climate they work together. In a hostile environment, there is likely to be a great social distance, little respect toward the authorities, so voluntary tax payments are negligible and citizens take advantage of tax evasion. In contrast, with a "service and customer" authority approach, the authorities aim to support taxpayers. In Switzerland, for example, the friendly and respectful treatment of taxpayers by the authorities has long been recognized as an important resource for increasing compliance with tax rules. The power of the tax authority and the trust in the tax authority together affect the level of tax compliance. If trust in the authorities is low and the power of the authorities is weak, it is likely that citizens will seek to maximize their individual results by evading taxes.

Schneider and Buehn (2012) analyzed the shadow economy in 39 OECD countries using the MIMIC method in the period from 1999 to 2010 (including Hungary). The impact of the higher shadow economy on official GDP data will result in an expected negative value as well as reduce government revenues. Tax policy and government regulatory factors also affect the black economy, which, if they grow, the black economy will also grow with them. Schneider (2000) cites high tax burdens as only one of the reasons for the hidden economy, but there may be more reasons, such as the impact of regulations, the complexity and transparency of the tax system, and the behavior of taxpayers toward the state. "In states where the tax payment process is easier, they can expect more revenue, more trust is given to the taxpayer. Besides high tax rates and high administrative burdens, trust also declines" (Herich, 2011). In analyzing the relationship between tax payment and trust in the state, it is also important to take into account that tax morals develop not only at the level of the individual but also at the level of society. In the case of a government that is perceived to be corrupt, tax fraud is taken for granted by society as a whole, and they do not think about harming other citizens. The social acceptance of tax fraud has a repercussion on the level of the individual and tax morals continue to deteriorate. In a high trust environment, the opposite process takes place, where the social rejection of tax fraud can improve the tax morals of individuals independently of other factors (Győrffy, 2007).

Methodology – Hungarian Survey

The shadow economy can be measured through micro-level surveys, questionnaires, interviews, observation, or indirect methods such as the approach to currency demand or hidden variables, using macroeconomic indicators. From the listed methods, we chose the method of the questionnaire survey to measure the factors and attitudes motivating the entry into the black economy, with the aim of supporting the correlations revealed on the basis of the international literature presented earlier. Sampling was performed using a non-probabilistic theoretical/expert procedure. The questionnaire was specifically interviewed among the managers of small and medium-sized enterprises of different sizes and activities in Hungary who are competent in tax decisions. The questionnaire was available online in the fall of 2018 over a 2-month period, during which 345 responses were received. The dimensions of a large number of data sets were reduced by principal component analysis to the extent that the variance present was retained as much as possible. Based on the Bartlett test and the Kaiser-Meyer-Olkin (KMO) criterion, we examined whether the data were suitable for principal component analysis and continued to work with these principal components.

Names of principal components:

F1.1. Moral dilemma

F1.2. The relationship of business partners and competitors with the black economy

F1.3. Tax fraud in the Hungarian economy

F1.4. The impact of the correct information and the effect of improvement of tax culture

F1.5. Personal consumption as corporate expense

F1.6. Purchase of fictitious cost invoice

F1.7. Means to increase the willingness to pay taxes

F1.8. The effect of the black economy on the competitive position of other companies

F2.1. The relationship between citizens and government

F2.2. The relationship between taxpayers and the tax authority

F2.3. Impact of the tax system

To support international research findings, we used Pearson's correlation study to find out whether there is a significant correlation between the different variables.

Some Results of a Survey Among Leaders of Enterprises (Hungarian Case)

Based on the level of significance of the "Moral dilemma" (F1.1) (sig = $0.000 < 0.05$), the null hypothesis can be rejected. The alternative (H_1) hypothesis is fulfilled; and there is a significant correlation between the variables. Based on the correlation coefficient ($r = -0.236^{**}$), there is a weak negative relationship between the "Moral dilemma" (F1.1) and the "Relationship between citizens and government" (F2.1), which means that if the value of one indicator increases, it also entails a decrease of the other indicator. Regarding the order in which the questions can be answered, it can be stated that the better the relationship between the citizens and the government, the more certain it is that the activities related to the hidden economy are perceived by the respondents as tax fraud. The less good the relationship between citizens and government, the more certain it is that activities related to the hidden economy will not be perceived by respondents as tax fraud.

According to the significance level of the "Tax fraud in the Hungarian economy" (F1.3) (sig = 0.000 < 0.05), the null hypothesis can also be rejected, so the alternative (H_1) hypothesis is fulfilled, that is, there is a significant correlation between the variables. Based on the correlation coefficient (r = 0.267**), there is a positive weak relationship between "Tax fraud in the Hungarian economy" (F1.3) and "Relationship between citizens and government" (F2.1), if the value of one of the indicators increases, it also implies an increase in the other indicator. In terms of the order in which the questions can be answered, the worse the relationship between citizens and government, the more certain it is that activities related to the hidden economy are present in an economy. The better the relationship between citizens and government, the more certain it is that activities related to the hidden economy are less present in the economy.

The null hypothesis can also be rejected according to the significance level (sig = 0.001 < 0.05) of "Personal consumption as corporate expense" (F1.5). The alternative (H_1) hypothesis is satisfied, so there is a significant correlation between the variables. The correlation coefficient (r = 0.178**) means that there is a weak positive relationship between "Personal consumption as corporate expense" (F1.5) and "Relationship between citizens and government" (F2.1) (Table 11.1.). The higher the level of confidence of citizens in government, the less common this form of tax evasion is in the economy.

Table 11.1 F1. The Relationship Between Tax Fraud and F2.1 the Relationship Between the Citizens and the Government

	Pearson Correlation	*Sig.*	*Hypothesis*
F1.1	-.236**	.000	H_1
F1.2	0.022	.689	H_0
F1.3	.267**	.000	H_1
F1.4	-0.091	.093	H_0
F1.5	.178**	.001	H_1
F1.6	0.084	.119	H_0
F1.7	-0.069	.205	H_0
F1.8	0.064	.235	H_0

Source: Own research.

Notes

**Correlation is significant at 0.01 level (2-tailed).

*Correlation is significant at 0.05 level (2-tailed).

The significance level of "The relationship between business partners and competitors with the black economy" (F1.2) (sig = 0.044 < 0.05), based on this, we can reject the null hypothesis. The alternative (H_1) hypothesis is fulfilled; there is a significant correlation between the variables. According to the correlation coefficient (r = 0.109*), there is a weak positive relationship between "Relationship between business partners and competitors with the black economy" (F1.2) and "Relationship between taxpayers and the tax authority" (F2.2).

According to the significance level of "Tax fraud in the Hungarian economy" (F1.3) (sig = 0.032 < 0.05), we can also reject the null hypothesis. According to the alternative (H_1) hypothesis is fulfilled, so there is a significant correlation between the variables. The correlation coefficient (r = 0.116*), there is a weak positive relationship between "Tax fraud in the Hungarian economy" (F1.3) and "The relationship between taxpayers and the tax authority" (F2.2).

The null hypothesis can also be rejected according to the significance level of "personal consumption as a firm cost" (F1.5) (sig = 0.031 < 0.05). Thus, the alternative (H_1) hypothesis is satisfied, there is a significant correlation between the variables. According to the correlation coefficient (r = 0.116*) means that there is a weak positive relationship between "Personal consumption as corporate expense" (F1.5) and "The relationship between taxpayers and the tax authority" (F2.2) (Table 11.2.). Based on the above, we can say that treating taxpayers as partners, respectfully, and a good relationship between taxpayers and the tax authorities have a positive effect on the willingness to pay taxes.

Based on an analysis of the correlations between the "impact of the tax system" (F2.3) and tax morals (F1), that is, tax legislation is extremely complex and difficult to navigate and that most forms used in taxation are difficult to understand, the significance level of "The impact of the

Table 11.2 F1. Tax Fraud and F2.2 the Relationship Between Taxpayers and the Tax Authority

	Pearson Correlation	*Sig.*	*Hypothesis*
F1.1	–.017	.758	H_0
F1.2	.109*	.044	H_1
F1.3	.116*	.032	H_1
F1.4	–.081	.132	H_0
F1.5	.116*	.031	H_1
F1.6	.065	.232	H_0
F1.7	.059	.273	H_0
F1.8	.040	.465	H_0

Source: Own research.

Notes

**Correlation is significant at 0.01 level (2-tailed).

*Correlation is significant at 0.05 level (2-tailed).

Table 11.3 F1. Relationship Between the Tax Fraud and F2.3 the Impact of the Tax System

	Pearson Correlation	*Sig.*	*Hypothesis*
F1.1	–.034	.530	H_0
F1.2	.066	.220	H_0
F1.3	–.016	.773	H_0
F1.4	–.022	.681	H_0
F1.5	.027	.612	H_0
F1.6	.061	.257	H_0
F1.7	–.285**	.000	H_1
F1.8	–.128*	.017	H_1

Source: Own research.

Notes
**Correlation is significant at 0.01 level (2-tailed).
*Correlation is significant at 0.05 level (2-tailed).

black economy on the competitive position of other companies" (F1.8) (sig = 0.017 < 0.05), the null hypothesis can be rejected. The alternative (H_1) hypothesis is fulfilled; there is a significant correlation between the variables. Based on the correlation coefficient (r = –0.128*), there is a negative weak relationship between "The impact of the black economy on the competitive position of other companies" (F1.8) and "The impact of the tax system" (F2.3), that is, the complexity and difficulty in understanding the tax system affect negatively the willingness to pay taxes (Table 11.3).

Discussion and Conclusion

Despite the fact that the most obvious means of tax policy to enforce and regulate tax payments is the policy of deterrence – that is, the prospect of higher penalties and fines, as well as coercion, it can even have the opposite effect on taxpayers. Coercion and extremely high taxes and penalties can result in lower taxes, and in general, a loss of trust in public institutions. It is definitely worth noting that American tax morals outperform all countries because tax morality proves to be more effective in terms of better treatment of taxpayers and unforced intervention by government agencies. In addition, the high value of tax morals measured in the United States and Switzerland may mean that tax morals can be increased through strengthening direct democratic elements. A comparative study of the English and German tax systems showed that tax morals were lower in Germany than in England. The difference may also stem from the specificities of the two tax systems, while in Germany coercive tax control techniques were typical, in England, the respectful treatment of taxpayers. Empirical studies on the topic of deterrence and mood also find that taxpayers' tax morals increase when officials treat them with respect, whereas deterrence leads to tax evasion. The quality of political institutions, the stability of the tax system, and non-violence have a strong impact on tax morals, and direct political participation also leads to higher internal motivation to pay taxes. In the state, a higher level of trust has a positive effect on tax moral, whereas tax enforcement based on highly coercive methods reduces the willingness to pay taxes. If trust and respect for the authorities are low, tax moral will decrease. In contrast, we can cite the example of Switzerland, where friendly and respectful treatment by the authorities is an important resource for increasing compliance with tax legislation. Thus, it can be concluded that tax policy and state regulatory factors have a significant impact on the shadow economy.

Although the sample could not be considered representative of the entire population, the aim was specifically to select a specific, specialized group that can provide valuable information for our theory. Based on the size and other characteristics of the selected companies, we were also able to examine the tax attitudes of natural persons and individuals. Although 87.8% of the respondents are managers, owners, sole proprietors, or managers and owners at the same time, 12.2% are competent managers in financial and economic decisions. Thus, the principle of voluntary compliance prevails in their decision-making, which, however, may be overridden by their personal values, attitudes, willingness to take risks, and other moral issues. Thus, the individual taxpayer's decision has an impact on both the success and effectiveness of the business and the psychological and living conditions of the natural person.

Due to the change of attitude in the Hungarian tax office since 2016 and the reform of the leading austerity measures in digitalization, further examination of the factors influencing tax moral is even more timely and necessary. We hope that by examining the impact of the measures and reforms introduced on tax morale, we can clarify the results already obtained and answer the question of what can be the most effective means of whitening the economy on the part of the authorities – a supportive cooperation or rigorous and coercive efforts, extending our research to the effects of the current pandemic on the economy.

References

Alm, J., & Torgler, B. (2005). Culture differences and tax morale in the United States and in Europe. *Journal of Economics Psychology*, 2, 224–246.

Alm, J., Martinez-Vazquez, J., & Torgler, B. (2005). Russian attitudes toward paying taxes – Before, during, and after transition. *International Journal of Social Economics*, *12*, 832–857.

Alm, J., Sanchez, I., & de Juan, A. (1995). Economic and noneconomic factors in tax compliance. *Kyklos*, *48*(1), 3–18.

Cummings, R. G., Martinez-Vazquez, J., Mckee, M., & Torgler, B. (2004). Effects of culture on tax compliance: A cross check of experimental and survey evidence. *CREMA. Working Paper, 13*. 10.2139/ssrn.661921.

Fazekas, M., Medgyesi, M., & Tóth, I. J. (2010). Az informális munkavégzést meghatározó tényezők Magyarországon, *MTA KTI*, Budapest.

Frey, B. S., & Feld, L. P. (2002). Deterrence and moral in taxation: An empirical analysis. *CESifo Working Paper, 760*.

Frey, B. S., & Torgler, B. (2006). Tax moral and conditional cooperation. *Journal of Comparative Economics, 1*, 136–159.

Győrffy, D. (2007). Társadalmi bizalom és költségvetési hiány, *Közgazdasági Szemle, 54*, 274–290.

Hámori, B. (1998). Érzelemgazdaságtan, *Kossuth Kiadó*, Budapest, HU: Kossuth Kiadó.

Herich, Gy. (Ed.). (2011). Nemzetközi adózás, Adózás az Európai Unióban, *Penta Unió*, Pécs.

Kirchler, E., Hoelzl, E., & Wahl, I. (2007). Enforced versus voluntary tax compliance: The "slippery slope" framework. *Journal of Economic Psychology, 2*, 210–225.

Schmölders, G. (1960). *Das Irrationale in der öffentlichen Finanzwssenschaft*. Hamburg: Rowolt.

Schneider, F. (2000). The increase of the size of the shadow economy of 18 OECD countries: Some preliminary explanations. Retrieved from http://www.econstor.eu/bitstream/10419/73324/1/wp0008.pdf.

Schneider, F., & Buehn, A. (2012). Shadow economies in highly developed OECD countries: What are the driving forces? Retrieved from http://www.econstor.eu/bitstream/10419/67170/1/727543865.pdf.

Scholtz, J. T. (1998). Trust, taxes and compliance, trust and governance. In V. Braithwaite, & M. Levi (Eds.) (pp. 135–166). New York, NY: Russell Sage Foundation.

Strümpel, B. (1969). The contribution of survey research to public finance. In Alan T. Peacock (Ed.), *Quantitative analysis in public finance* (pp. 14–32). New York, NY: Praeger Publishers.

Torgler, B. (2003). Tax morale: Theory and empirical analysis of tax compliance. Doctoral Dissertation, Universität Basel.

12 The Crucial Role of Trust in Adapting Logistics to the New Conditions

Konrad Michalski
Warsaw University of Life Sciences – SGGW

Introduction

Functioning in the conditions of scattered consumption and digital links between the participants requires trust between them. It becomes even more important when unforeseen events occur that influence the existing reality, destroy it, and cause the emergence of a new state of affairs. Such phenomenon is defined as the Black Swan (Taleb, 2020b) or the Gray Rhino (Wucker, 2017), the example of which can be, for instance, the pandemic. Increasingly more information indicates that the world could have been more prepared for the COVID-19 pandemic that we have witnessed since 2020 when it was officially announced (see Horton, 2020), which would indicate the case of Gray Rhino.

Comprehensively understood trust should be treated as a significant determinant of a transformation of digital logistics, being an element of a wide spectrum of changes defined by the concept of Industry 4.0 (Schwab, 2018). But these changes are slowed down by more frequent crises, such as the one related to the COVID-19, resulting in freezing all areas of life and economy sectors. This crisis, like in a lens, showed the critical role of stability and quality not only of virtual relations in the conditions of severing the physical connections, but also human ties and trust. For this reason, the COVID-19 pandemic can be treated as a training ground for changes in global logistics.

At the same time, managers should be convinced that the change ought to be a natural stage of the organization's development – antifragile, reinforcing it for the future (Taleb, 2020a). The knowledge of trust determinants, being the condition for change as such, and also of the factors that support and weaken it, creates an opportunity to develop permanent foundations of the organization, anchored in the emerging socio-economic reality that is another stage of human development, not yet completely defined (Kelly, 2017). For logistic organizations, the goal should be to avoid the phenomenon of blockage: limiting oneself to the current systemic framework, preventing opening oneself to new challenges (Mączyńska & Okoń-Horodyńska, 2020).

DOI: 10.4324/9781003165965-12

The main goal of the chapter is to introduce the term of trust in the context of changes in contemporary logistics taking into account current obstacles such as the COVID-19 crisis. Identification of the research gaps in the scope of management is also intended.

The chapter presents the impact of the Industry 4.0 concept on strategic changes in logistics. Then, the concept of trust as a key success factor in making changes to adapt logistics to new operating conditions was defined. The next parts present the assumptions and results of the study among the major logistics operators in Poland, whose strategic changes were disrupted by the crisis related to the coronavirus pandemic. The chapter includes conclusions with implications for theory and practice.

The Industry 4.0 Concept as a Direction of Strategic Changes in Logistics

In the preface to the Polish edition of his book *The Fourth Industrial Revolution*, Schwab characterizes the ongoing revolution as follows: "(...) it is based on the intelligent, connected technology not only within the organization but also in everyday life. Its essence is transferring most decisions from people to the competence of machines and blurring the boundaries between what is biological and what is digital", further mentioning technologies that will become leading ones, like the Internet of Things, artificial intelligence, blockchain, autonomous vehicles, 3D printing, and robots (2018, p. 14). In short, the concept of Industry 4.0 consists of an integration of the human world with machines and algorithms operating on large data sets (Big Data) and incorporating them into the economy, including the industry, thanks to which it would become not only more efficient, effective, and economical, but also secure and environmentally friendly. Digital transformation of manufacturing or – more broadly – business is the cloud of the whole concept.

The "new logistics" is included in the set of areas that are under the influence of the Industry 4.0 concept (Mączyńska Okoń-Horodyńska, 2020, p. 17). In particular, for the logistics, the following possibilities for improvement arise:

- Utilization of resources and processes optimization;
- Use of assets;
- Work efficiency;
- Quality (Ślusarczyk, 2019).

The aforementioned areas of potential improvement correspond to the essence of logistics management; therefore, they are its basic criteria of evaluation, identified more with the economics of operation. However, the view is postulated of implementing the elements of the Industry 4.0

concept also in terms of management and social requirements, where the following should be subject to alteration: strategic thinking, innovation culture, building development scenarios, involving staff in decision making, cooperation between management and employees, the flexibility of penalty policy, creation of new professions and places of work, openness to new trends, motivating in the process of technological transformations (Mączyńska & Okoń-Horodyńska, 2020). Looking at the implications for the management, one can distinguish three levels (from the highest) of locating the changes within the framework of logistics transformation:

- Logistic support system (see Chaberek, 2002) – representing the entire potential of the organization to offer possibilities to carry out the logistics activities (decisions and activities of strategic nature);
- Logistics management – deciding about the system configuration and the course of logistics processes constituting the basis of logistics (the sphere of management tactics);
- Organizational and technological solutions – on which the execution of logistics processes (operational management) is based.

Trust as a Key Factor of Strategic Changes in Logistics

Trust is defined by the representatives of many disciplines: philosophers, psychologists, sociologists, economists, management (Paliszkiewicz, 2013, p. 13), and IT experts (Daudi et al., 2016, p. 19). Legal (Wiewiórski, 2019, pp. 619–674) and ethical (ACM, 2019, pp. 665–674) aspects of IT, building trust for partners, institutions, and the state are also subject to scientists' interest. Trust is interdisciplinary.

One can find many definitions of trust relating to management (Paliszkiewicz, 2019, pp. 37–44), placed in many of its detailed theories (Paliszkiewicz, 2013, pp. 23–48). For the needs of this chapter, the author defines trust as a faith of an entity trusting that it will experience in its surroundings such behaviors and results of activities that will have a beneficial influence on the functioning of that entity in its environment.

Change in an organization usually falls into three areas: structure and scheme of the organization, technique, operations, and people (Griffin, 2018, p. 404). Each of these areas can relate to logistics, and when the change is of transformative nature, it will touch each one of them, as it brings the necessity of redefining the established patterns of operation and resulting from their habits and convenience, so also reduction of routine. At the same time, transformation causes a natural increase in the concerns of the participants in the changes, being the elements of the networks of connections and internal relations, developed over a long period of time.

The aforementioned outline of the essence of digital transformation on logistics should lead to the perception of trust as an exceptionally important factor of the success of change processes. Trust in logistics is not, however, widely undertaken in the scientific literature. The results of the review carried out in September 2021 of scientific articles from the years 2010–2020 present on three databases: Ebsco, Elsevier, and ProQuest indicate that in the largest of the three (Elsevier), after selecting the keywords "trust" and "logistics" 53 were obtained, and after adding "change" – only nine positions appeared. This proves that there is little interest in the trust issues concerning logistics, which can be the result of treating it like any other sphere of organization. Meanwhile, logistics is the field of fundamental, but also controversial changes that require taking into account such aspects as the influence of artificial intelligence and algorithms on the demand for human work, defining a new role of an employee in the digital world, or even negative results of dehumanization. Few scientific papers undertake specific, although important, and interesting threads of trust in the supply chains being the field of the most complex logistic activities. Ha et al. (2011) distinguish two types of trust influencing the effective operation of the supply chain: affective trust and trust in competency. Daudi et al. (2016) emphasize the critical role of uncertainty in cooperation and building trust between partners. On the other hand, Yuan et al. (2018) consider trust, next to involvement and orientation to knowledge, as important components of effective logistic service.

The literature lacks a comprehensive approach to the role of trust – in its various sections and perspectives – examined from the perspective of creating conditions in the organization for the development of logistics, influenced by so many strong in their course trends in the surrounding, additionally disturbed by more frequent crises. When we assume, following Dyduch (2019), that building the climate of trust is the condition of innovative, and thus new, unknown, and unchecked values, that trust becomes a strategic issue for any organization that wants to develop. The logistics environment creates newer and potentially better possibilities for development, which is the aftermath of the technological revolution. But when direct human relations (in its essence built over a long time) are replaced sometimes with single electronic transactions, the trust between its partners is essential – the example is the concept of sharing logistics (see Michalski, 2020c).

From the point of view of logistics organization, several entities, objects, and directions of reference of trust can be distinguished, together forming a culture of trust in the organization advantageous for wide-ranging changes toward the digital transformation (Figure 12.1):

- Individual's trust for oneself – manifesting in the certainty resulting from being an important and strong element of the organization, through the fulfillment of its expectations and realization of the delegated tasks;

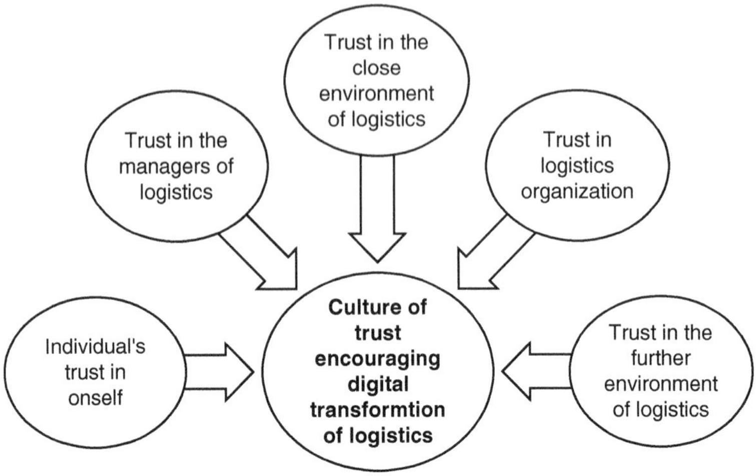

Figure 12.1 Culture of trust in the logistics organization.

Source: Own work.

- Trust in managers – perceived as an expectation of shaping by the decision-makers of the closest surroundings (microenvironment) of the organization;
- Trust in the close surroundings (co-workers, clients, etc.) – understood as the expectation of the possibility of cooperation with the organization based on professionalism and partner relations allowing in the longer perspective to develop permanent and resistant to various crises links;
- Trust in the organization – relating to the anticipation by all elements of the organization of the advantageous for them directions of changes, influencing the conditions and results of work and the possibilities of further growth;
- Trust in the further environment (international organizations, government, public institutions, etc.) – in practice, coming down to the expectations that no barriers with a negative impact on the functioning of the organization as a whole are created.

Trust management in any organization is a continuous process. The goal of that process should be developed by that organization of such level of trust that will be a significant component of its organizational culture, supporting its continuous development, through alterations. What is specific for the logistics organization, in addition to the aspects outlined in the second part of the chapter, is a growing share in the surroundings of logistics of factors with a hardly predictable time of occurrence, force, and direction. That in itself is a serious hindrance for the necessary construction by the logistics organization of the comprehensive "plan of digital transformation", that acts as an azimuth for all organizations in the industry. The author believes that the crisis relating to the COVID-19 pandemic can be treated as a test for the changes related to the digital transformation of logistics, taking place "live".

Research Method

In the research conducted in 2020 in the logistic companies in Poland, a qualitative method was used, as by Dźwigoł (2018): a structured interview using a questionnaire survey.

The goal of the study was to learn about the experiences from the first period after the introduction (March 2020) of the freezing of the economy in Poland. In April 2020, a questionnaire was sent to 12 deliberately selected, in terms of varied activities profile, logistics companies operating in Poland. In terms of the scale of activity these were global firms, European and Polish, often being leaders in their sectors. The questionnaire was aimed at high-level logistics managers, including the CEO.

Responses were obtained from six companies (50% of those approached): two of the global scale of activity and four of European reach. They were companies with different core-business: courier services, international transport, distribution logistics, the so-called home-delivery, as well as with full TFL (transport, forwarding, logistics) service range. Answers to the following questions were obtained:

- Which measures were introduced in the initial period of pandemic (March–April 2020), to secure the operational continuity?; what were the factors in succeeding in switching to new lines of operation?
- Which activities does the firm treat as an innovative success?; what will remain permanently of the changes?
- What advantages (chances) does the company identify after three months (March–May 2020) of operating in the changes of socio-economic reality?

Results of the Research

Experiences from the First Period after Freezing the Economy in Poland

Maintaining business continuity, including logistics operations, was key for all companies. For this purpose, the undertaken actions by virtually all companies were:

- Appointment of a crisis team with strong support in the company's structure;
- Development of the continuity plan, under the general guidelines of the state and sanitary authorities, as well as the controversy of recommendations for internal regulations;
- Carrying out a staff training with the particular emphasis on the employers having contact with the client;
- Large-scale introduction of remote work (even up to 95% of office personnel in Poland within several days of the announcement of lockdown) and the dissemination on an even wider scale of electronic forms of work (chats, teleconferences, instant messaging, etc.);
- Reorganization, including more flexibility in terms of working hours, of internal logistics processes: warehousing, contemplational, transport;
- Introducing quickly available measures minimizing the risk of infection in the relations with the client, including electronic communication channels in the highest possible amount, contactless implementation, and touch-free forms of delivery confirmation.

Most of the surveyed companies emphasized that the following could not be overestimated in that period:

- Having at least advanced plans of the wide introduction of electronic solutions in internal and external relations;
- Understanding among the recipients of services of the necessity of adjusting to the limitations in the functioning of the logistics supplier and real possibilities of fulfilling by him the obligations related to, for example, completeness and timeliness of delivery;
- Understanding the necessity for changes among the employees, their high discipline in the implementation of tasks, and a joint search for possibilities of maintaining a high quality of work;
- Having clearly defined workflows, including roles of individual participants and procedures of conduct in the case of deviations;
- Having at their disposal (in the understanding of integration with the client) the IT solutions, allowing quick implementation of alternative scenarios of action;

All organizations emphasized the role of having at least general crisis plans and earlier use of solutions, which in the initial period of pandemic became common tools of work. This determined how much time and with what result from the first stage of lockdown would end. The activities in that time had a similar character for all researched companies, but the time of the beginning of preparations for the probable freeze of activity was earlier in the case of global companies (even in the mid-

February 2020), or in such that has an organizational structure in China. On the other hand, the question of whether the company has an appropriate potential to successfully implement innovative solutions in a time of crisis, depended on the representative sector of activity, creating specific possibilities for development.

Determinants of Implementation of Innovation in the Time of Freezing the Economy in Poland

Based on the classic Schumpeter definition, the innovations are distinguished: product, organizational, process and marketing. What is the essence of innovation is novelty; in logistics *"innovatio"* can mean "different", "more efficient", "quicker", "more attractive", or "safer", which in the initial period of the considered crisis was most important.

As the pandemic crisis progressed, the conscious organizations wondered how this time should be used for development. For it can be assumed that after the crisis a new state of the industry will emerge, where there will be losers and winners. The winners will be the entities that could not only maintain business but also offer new solutions to the client. Whilst only the strongest entities use the time of pandemic for the conversion of the organization into new, not fully known state and order (Michalski, 2020a).

The researched logistics companies, assessing after three months of crisis whether they identify some chances of development for their organizations, spoke positively in this respect, at the same time identifying a series of conditions for success in this scope:

- It was necessary to constantly penetrate the market in the search for niches and new needs of clients arising as the consequence of crisis (for instance, the cargo-partner company already in March 2020 launched dedicated teams of specialists and services of air transport for the automotive, pharmaceutical, and personal protection services, so the areas strongly affected by the severed supply chains – in this case, the presence in Asia was used, primarily in China);
- One must have at their disposal the proven IT solutions ensuring effective counteraction to threats related to the implementation of the global supply chains, which is critical, for example, to manufacturing firms based on the deliveries from many sources (for instance, one of the company, thanks to the prior investment in the technology of supply chain transparency, based on the artificial intelligence and algorithms of machine learning, was able to provide its partners an insight in the real-time into the implemented transportation networks – this helped dealing with much more frequent unexpected events bringing threats of the inefficiency of deliveries);

- It is necessary to have an organizational potential flexible enough and quickly adaptable to the altered expectations of the clients, to benefit from the new market trends (for the courier service company the challenge was not only handling the surge in the number of packages purchased online in the conditions of necessity to minimalize the direct contact with the client but also undertaking such activities so that the change of shopping and consumption model could be accommodated for permanently);
- The quality of cooperation to date is important, as well as relations with the clients based on trust (for instance, the TFL company continued the participation in the tender procedures and allowed the potential clients the virtual tours of logistics facilities, where it was possible to "touch" any storage place in the warehouse – thanks to the dedicated sales platform and the VR (Virtual Reality);
- Strong relations with the employees must be supported by the organization not sporadically, but constantly, through creating a proactive, professional, and conscious significance of the organizational culture that in the crisis is an asset (the strategy of cultivating the culture of continuous improvement is an example of systematic action, and a certificate such as "great place to work" or an award for "the best employer", are evidence of strong internal ties).

At the same time, many of the above-mentioned solutions shall remain in the companies permanently, because:

- The pandemic made it possible to believe that many projects can be implemented remotely with the identical result, generating lower costs – in the view of one company;
- Implementations do not have to take a long time, but on condition that the solutions are already pre-developed – as stated by another company;
- Temporary decline in business, as well as the altered organization of work, can be used for professional development, which met with the high interest of the employees – emphasized one of the company, which launched the "home office academy" project, with the help of which a series of training was carried out on the subjects of work security in the time of the pandemic, as well as business-related ones;
- Flexible working hours, primarily home-office, met with a positive assessment of employees – according to all surveyed companies.

Preparing an Organization for the Subsequent Crises

Mature organizations should assume that the time of COVID-19 ought to be the beginning of preparations for the next crisis. Even though the current one has not yet ceased, it is necessary to think of the next turbulence.

This would indicate the rationality and predictability in thinking of contemporary life in the global village. A significant difficulty, however, is the fact that no one knows the nature of the next crisis and how exactly it would manifest itself. Nonetheless, based on the COVID-19 pandemic, once again one can imagine severed supply chains, even larger scale of electronic communication, subsequent business processes realized virtually, or limitations in the direct human contacts (Michalski, 2020b, p. 68).

Virtually all surveyed managers stated that the success of logistics company providing services in turbulent, crisis-disturbed, and so unpredictable in terms of future shape operating conditions depends on the following factors:

- Further digitalization of processes in the entire organization, based on the integration of systems and detailed solutions, possible to combine with the solutions of partners in the supply chain and the end customers – it is the *sine qua non* condition for participation in the emerging form of logistics corresponding with the concept of the Industry 4.0, based on the connection networks between people, machines, robots and other objects, such as, for example, drones, or even every-day use appliances;
- Implementation of AI solutions and other, advanced technologies from the scope of the Internet of Things that can replace a human, which can also be safer from the point of view of threats (e.g., the transmission of virus) in the interhuman relations;
- Strong internal and external relations based on trust and mutual understanding of limitations in the operation in the conditions of a crisis, which is not a state easy to build in the short time perspective;
- Staff's support for the necessity of changes, because assuming that as long as the logistic processes based on the physical flows of material objects have no virtual alternative, the participation of a human in their implementation will remain dominant – meanwhile, all changes going toward further mechanizing and electronification, digitalization and virtualization of the processes will be inducing the sense of threat in people.

Conclusions

Strategic changes in logistics have to be based on solid foundations. A specific binder, in this case, is trust, considered on at least a few levels presented in the chapter. The issue of trust in logistics, as shown in the literature review, has not yet been raised frequently in research. It seems that the reason for this is that the general assumptions of trust in an organization are similar for all areas of its activity, for example, logistics. However, already at the level of considering a given industry, for example, TFL, the specific impact of the industry's environment and the conditions in which it develops cannot be ignored.

Undoubtedly, logistics is the area of science and practical knowledge that is under the strong influence of socio-economic megatrends in the environment. The very confrontation of assumption of the concept of Industry 4.0 with the requirements toward logistics that, to maintain the role of an efficient tool of an enterprise's competitiveness, must be the subject of comprehensive transformation based on the dominant share of information digitalization, virtualization of business processes, dispersing competition and decision in blurry organizational structures. But the plans for the development of logistics in the above-mentioned direction are disturbed by unpredictable events that on the one hand are destructive, but on the other – releasing energy and creativity in the quick search for new solutions. As shown by the research conducted among logistics companies in Poland, the COVID-19 pandemic only sped up mostly inevitable activities, but their success depended on widely understood cooperation between key participants of changes. Key partakers of transformations were employees and external partners (clients), and the critical factors – understanding, openness, and determination, conclusively influencing trust. Technologies and broadly comprehended progress create for the industry of logistics service providers enormous possibilities of accelerating actions, reducing errors, making cost savings, etc. In contrast, work and cooperation in the technologically advanced system require an appreciation of the importance of trust, starting with the individual's faith in own capabilities, through trust directed by the individual to its environment, close one and further afield.

The study aimed to show the role of trust as a necessary glue that unites elements of change in logistics for which the concept of Industry 4.0 has to be the main direction. The key problem is that strategic changes in the area of logistics are being hindered by current crises, as exemplified by COVID-19. For this reason, the next planned step is to identify the detailed factors supporting and weakening the digitization of logistics as a milestone in the compass of the strategic transformation of logistics. Then, the goal will be to investigate the strength of the impact of change actors on the success of digital transformation in logistics.

In the context of further, detailed studies on trust as an indispensable factor of transformation of logistics organizations, two cognitive directions can be indicated, corresponding to two levels of management:

- Strategic: presenting, based on the experiences related to the COVID-19 crisis, the point of view of the individuals (employees) on the directions of changes taking place on logistics; is it optimistic in the case of managers and logistics owners?
- Tactical – concerning the increasingly popular concept of sharing logistics, assuming trust as a condition of any cooperation between partners: what are the barriers for building stable links and the possibility of their growth in the emerging socio-economic reality departing from the culture of possession toward access?

References

ACM. (2019). ACM code of ethics and professional conduct. In S. Wrycza & J. Maślankowski (Eds.), *Informatyka ekonomiczna. Teoria i zastosowania* [Economic IT. Theory and applications]. Warsaw, PL: PWN.

Chaberek, M. (2002). *Makro- i mikroekonomiczne aspekty wsparcia logistycznego* [Macro and microeconomic aspects of logistic support]. Gdańsk, PL: Gdańsk University Press.

Daudi, M., Hauge, J. B., & Thoben, K.-D. (2016). Behavioral factors influencing partner trust in logistics collaboration: A review. *Logistics Research*, 9(1), 1–11.

Dyduch, W. (2019). Organizational design supporting innovativeness. *Przegląd Organizacji*, 6, 16–22.

Dźwigoł, H. (2018). *Współczesne procesy badawcze w naukach o zarządzaniu. Uwarunkowania metodyczne i metedologiczne* [Contemporary research processes in management sciences. Methodological and metedological conditions]. Warsaw, PL: PWN.

Griffin, R. W. (2018). *Podstawy zarządzania organizacjami* [Management]. Warsaw, PL: PWN.

Ha, B-Ch., Park, Y.-K., & Cho, S. (2011). Suppliers' affective trust and trust in competency in buyers. *International Journal of Operations & Production Management*, *31*(1), 56–77.

Horton, R. (2020). The COVID-19 catastrophe. What's gone wrong and how to stop it happening again. Cambridge-Medfod, GB: Polity Press.

Kelly, K. (2017). *Nieuniknione. Jak inteligentne technologie zmienią naszą przyszłość* [The Inevitable. Understanding the 12 technological forces that will shape our future]. Warsaw, PL: Poltext.

Mączyńska, E., & Okoń-Horodyńska, E. (2020). Przedsiębiorstwo i jego otoczenie w obliczu czwartej rewolucji przemysłowej [The Company and its environment in the face of the fourth industrial revolution – Challenges, opportunities and threats]. *Przegląd Organizacji*, *1*, 9–21.

Michalski, K. (2020a). Innowacje w branży logistycznej w dobie COVID-19 [Innovations in the logistics industry in the COVID-19 era]. *Logistics*, *3*, 62–65.

Michalski, K. (2020b). Innowacje w branży logistycznej w dobie COVID-19 – część 2. Jak przygotować organizację do kryzysu? [Innovations in the logistics industry in the COVID-19 era – part 2. How to prepare an organization for a crisis?]. *Logistics*, *4*, 68–71.

Michalski, K. (2020c). Logistics in the era of sharing. In J. Paliszkiewicz (Ed.), *Management and information technology: New management*. Warsaw: Warsaw University of Life Sciences Press.

Paliszkiewicz, J. (2013). *Zaufanie w zarządzaniu* [Trust in management]. Warsaw, PL: PWN.

Paliszkiewicz, J. (2019). *Przywództwo, zaufanie i zarządzanie wiedzą w innowacyjnych przedsiębiorstwach* [Leadership, trust and knowledge management in innovative enterprises]. Warsaw, PL: CeDeWu.

Schwab, K. (2018). *Czwarta rewolucja przemysłowa* [The fourth industrial revolution]. Warsaw, PL: Studio Emka.

Ślusarczyk 2019 Ślusarczyk, B. (2019). Potencjalne rezultaty wprowadzania koncepcji Przemysłu 4.0 w przedsiębiorstwach [Selected results of introducing the Industry 4.0 concept in enterprises]. *Przegląd Organizacji*, *1*, 4–10.

Taleb, N. N. (2020a). *Antykruchość. Jak żyć w świecie, którego nie rozumiemy* [Antyfragile: things that gain from disorder]. Poznań, PL: Zysk i S-ka.

Taleb, N. N. (2020b). *Czarny łabędź. Jak nieprzewidywalne zdarzenia rządzą naszym życiem* [The Black Swan: The impact of the highly improbable]. Poznań, PL: Zysk i S-ka.

Wucker, M. (2017). *The gray rhino*. New York, NY: St. Martin's Press.

Wiewiórski, W. R. (2019). Prawne aspekty informatyki [Legal aspects of computer science]. In S. Wrycza, J. Maślankowski (Eds.), *Informatyka ekonomiczna. Teoria i zastosowania* [Economic IT. Theory and applications]. Warsaw, PL: PWN.

Yuan, Y., Feng, B., Lay, F., & Collins, B. J. (2018). The role of trust, commitment, and learning orientation on logistic service effectiveness. *Journal of Business Research*, *93*, 37–50.

13 Mutual Trust in the City Strategy Implementation

Vesa-Jukka Vornanen[1] *and Josu Takala*[2]
[1]*City of Kotka*
[2]*University of Vaasa*

Introduction

Based on the Local Government Act, municipalities must produce financial statements annually. In accordance with the law, municipalities assess the impact of exceptional circumstances and the success of crisis management. The purpose of this chapter is to present the use of a spreadsheet-based situational log in a way that develops mutual trust in order to simultaneously implement the security strategy of society and the city strategy.

The phenomenon under study is the action researcher's observation of knowledge management before and during the year 2020s COVID-19 crisis. The city's target organization reacts proactively to the threats. Performance has improved by joint exercises. The region's authorities with the city had conducted several readiness exercises in the previous year, analyzed these events, and even produced an international research article on the metrics of the preparedness process (Vornanen & Takala, 2020). The collaboration had improved joint performance, and urgency was controlled. Neither time was the weakness of competitiveness factors nor costs or flexibility. A quality was. Unknown threat increased uncertainty about customer-oriented use of resources to achieve strategic goals. The increased need for knowledge management directed the search of solution models for how measurement data should use in practice in a way that increases mutual trust.

Let us look at a slightly broader picture of the situational factors. Digitalization in the public environment has grown over the past decades, and simultaneously the criticality of digitalized services to service suppliers and customers has grown too. Digitalization taking place through community servitization, more and more at the channels of social media. Municipalities are the platforms and at the same time competitors of business investments and jobs that they create in the digital era. To control this balance in all circumstances, security management requires practical, trustful steps and collaboration to implement strategies of the cities. Planning and training build confidence in the

DOI: 10.4324/9781003165965-13

successful implementation of the multi-strategies with the constantly evolving ability to secure value chains in every level of organization on the public platform. Performing joint operations shares a common goal as a mutually supportive and complementary process. Situational factors, their context, and content form the basis for process control. The preparedness process is sustained situational awareness of the common resource-based view (Wernerfelt, 1984; Barney, 1991).

The digital public environment includes three levels: physical, logical, and user-level. Levels form a manageable context. The physical level includes touchable things such as buildings, furniture, roads, bridges, trucks, surfaces, facemasks, network cables, and so on. The logical level controls the interaction with the physical level, including, for example, laws, codes, work safety policies, applications, software, and protocols. The user-level means high-performing people. The level consists of user-related details that connect individuals and organizations to interact through networks.

Where is the problem? High-performing people's confidence in crisis management will decreases if resource follow-up measures from the physical level do not support their continuity management responsibilities. At its meeting on Friday, March 11, the city's Emergency Management Team (later in the text EMT) notes, "*we have to shut down some public services in order to protect our residents*". The network of large Finnish cities has made similar observations. At this point, cities were not entitled to do so. In the evening of the same day, the Prime Minister of Finland spoke in a television interview about the activities of the public sector. She highlights the challenge of the activities of the EMT's city and the current situation as an example. On Monday, March 13, the Government, together with the President of Finland, state that there are exceptional circumstances in Finland. To manage the exceptional situation, Finnish society uses the Emergency Powers Act. The law gives the government temporary powers to bypass the fundamental rights of the individual to protect the entire community. Referring to joint experiences of history, Finnish society has a strong mutual trust in the force of this law.

Why look at the software choice from a logical and high-performing people's mutual trust-building perspective? First, because the number of resources is limited, unnecessary additional work increases costs and execution time and finally reduces opportunities for the development of competitiveness. Therefore, knowledge management procedures should add value to the situation and continuity management. If the crisis continues or expanding, the amount of un-analyzed data will increase, and the benefits created by the common forum during the crisis will be lost. The platform and collaboration methods on it should support and secure the functionality of the value chains.

Secondly, spreadsheet software is widely in use, just like word processing and presentation graphics software. The advanced utilization of widely used standard-like tools is cost-effective and meaningful. Using spreadsheet software as a situational log supports joint managerial actions. The spreadsheet measures the content written about the events. The measured and analyzed situational factors and operational priorities lead to common situational awareness, conclusions; decision-making; effective implementation of decisions; monitoring, and learning from influences (Vornanen, 2017).

The commonly agreed writing procedure is a base for value giving and use of the columns of the spreadsheet. With the help of review columns, the data written in the cells of a row can be filtered, grouped, and classified, thus producing statistical information from qualitative data. Pivot tables help analyze the data collected in spreadsheet software, study trends or frequencies, and present a situational picture of the direction of development. The EMT's advanced use of spreadsheet software develops collaboration and increases the organization's competitiveness.

There is also personal interest in research because exceptional circumstances are very rare possibilities, especially in action research. The corresponding author, as a director of the technical services division, is a member of the EMT. Action research is a research strategy that includes action development and influencing perceived problematic factors (Lewin, 1946). As stated in the phenomenon presentation above, the problem identified as a quality problem in the technical dimension of quality (Grönroos, 1984). The choice of an appropriate tool affects continuity management, first into analysis reliability and interpretation of the results, then to situational awareness and decision-making ability. At worst, the risk remains that mistakes will recur. Uncertainties weaken psychological resilience during a crisis. Therefore, the choice is important.

Methodology

Actions with the Log Data

The Act on the Openness of Government Activities, Section 24.1, 8. § underlines that documents concerning preparations for accidents and emergency conditions are secret. Therefore, the study focused on the public part of data of crisis management and describing the analysis of log data. The research subject of content analysis is a spreadsheet-based situational log. The content analysis included quantitative and qualitative research. Quantitative analysis helps to find out the cause-and-effect relationships of phenomena, the connections between them, or the frequency and occurrence of phenomena with the help of numbers and statistics. A qualitative analysis aims to understand the quality, properties, and meanings of an object holistically. Both methods explain the same research subjects in different ways. The Log's data will be grouped and categorized to highlight so-called PESTLE perspectives (Newton & Bristoll, 2013). In the study, a PESTLE is a framework tool used to identify, analyze, and organize factors of the city strategy. The framework builds a strategic crisis management model of COVID-19 threat from the legal, social, technological, environmental, political, and economic perspectives to develop continuity planning.

Actions with the Target Organization

In practice, the researcher's goal is to affect the procedures in the target organization by participating and influencing by example and leadership. The members of the EMT lead their processes. These city's core processes maintain the public environment as an operational platform for the residents. The platform consists of different kinds of public services, such as buildings, streets, HVAC-, electric- and ICT-networks, ports, parks, sports facilities, and so on. Management measures occur by the manner manager writes the date, personal initials, and situation-based activity information as well as any additional information about the command in the log. By common column content model, managers can copy data on their mobile phones or tablets to a common spreadsheet page of the information system. The city regulations define duties for EMT-managers. Their units implement the city strategy approved by the city council. Manager's preparedness planning and preventive actions are the way implement of the security strategy of society, both strategies at the same time. The outputs and impacts of the city's preparedness process can be described as a matrix. As a horizontal input, the city's EMT monitors relevant situation factors, and as an output, the core functions and systems (processes) are realized into operational reliability, which reduces uncertainty. As a vertical input, EMT gathers and controls the platform's resources, quantity, and quality of the service network based on situational awareness, to achieve as a vertical output necessary effects to common strategic goals through the core processes. A mayor, who introduces issues of strategic decision-making to decision-makers, leads EMT. At the same time, he/she is a Chairman of the region's security and preparedness organization, which works with EMT in risk management activities.

Actions with the Community

The assessment of the implementation of the city strategy in exceptional circumstances is justified because the Strategic Management Society of Finland awarded an honorary diploma for the City of Kotka's strategy and its implementation in 2018. On a Finnish scale, the strategy of the City of Kotka and its implementation are noteworthy and exceptional. The City of Kotka residents came up with ideas and highlighted what they considered important for the city. In exceptional circumstances, tasks in the processes will be adapted to the situation, for example, by closing or concentrating some services together. Referring to the lessons learned from history, In Finland, everyone's lives matter. Securing the vital functions of society based on the concept of comprehensive security. The Finnish concept for comprehensive security means that the citizens, organizations, the business community, and the authorities in collaboration secure society's vital functions, or in other words, the value chains on the platform. The key success factor is everyone is a security actor. Thus, the joint performance of hybrid organizations arises from the successful implementation of multi-strategies to manage various threats (Vornanen, 2017).

Results

Results from the Log Data

The EMT's first COVID-19 related statistical signal is on January 22, one week before the first disease case occurs in Finland. The organization has had time to review contingency plans, resources and take the necessary operative actions before the declaration of exceptional circumstances. The exceptional situation lasted three months, from March 13 to June 16, 2020. The data cover the period from January to June, in which EMT produced 579 commands to the log. In the quantitative content analysis, their written log data were grouped into four more manageable categories (Table 13.1). In the qualitative content analysis, the actions written in the log were examined in relation to the city strategy and PESTLE-perspectives. Some of the cross-administrates measures targeted several strategic entities and thus combined core processes and resources. In this case, the total sum of the log entries is larger than the sum of individual entries. Figure 13.1 summarizes the qualitative content analysis.

From the point of view of joint efforts, the measurement results show the balance of operations of critical services in relation to the PESTLE-perspectives, and at one time, the implementation of the city strategy. There are two highlighting perspectives from the content analysis; the common manageability and the desired social impacts. The diagram has value in securing the common value chains. There is a need to consider how to achieve the best possible customer-oriented outcome, how to add value to all residents.

Results from the Target Organization

On the proposal of the action researcher, the method of maintaining the situation diary was changed in the target organization from separate

Table 13.1 Monthly Variation in Operating Frequency

Category	*Core Functions and Systems*	*Commands Per Month*					
		I	*II*	*III*	*IV*	*V*	*VI*
Management	Municipal management and decision-making, Payroll and financial management, Information management, and Communication and information	1	4	109	89	34	7
Well-being	Pre-primary education and early childhood education, Basic education, Primary health care, social security and social care, and Environmental health	-	-	59	86	28	1
Circular economy	Energy supply, Waste disposal, Water and wastewater supply, Logistics and public transportation	-	-	24	16	-	-
Critical services	Infrastructure maintenance (streets, bridges, machinery, etc.), Building maintenance (cleanliness, backup power, renovations, etc.), Food services and catering, and Situational awareness (permits, registers, etc.), CCTV's and HVAC technical supervision	4	4	63	26	14	10

Source: Own research.

pages of the word processing software to the use of spreadsheet software to manage the possible long-lasting continuum of the exceptional circumstances. The mutual trust created through the readiness exercises before disruption was beneficial.

When the crisis escalated, the mayor decided to include the Chairman of the City Board in the EMT. In this way, decision-makers were part of operational activities and the team underwent continuous performance evaluation. The benefit of situational awareness by using spreadsheet software is that the chart and graphs are automatically updated every time data added. As a result, the performance of each member of EMT is equally important for the management of the whole, which strengthens mutual trust, and creates opportunities to recognize and build dynamic capabilities (Vornanen & Takala, 2014).

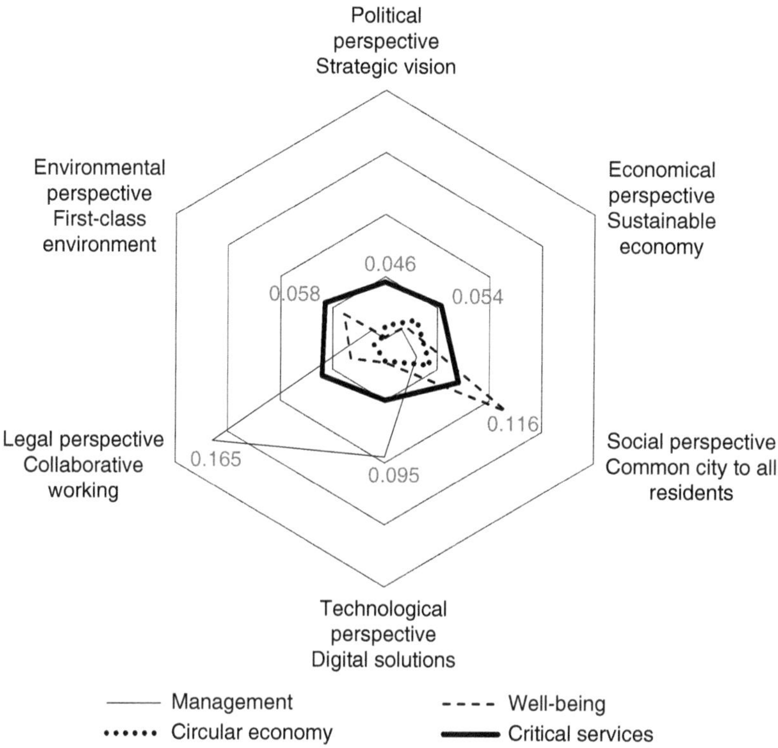

Figure 13.1 PESTLE-strategy – diagram about the city's strategy implementation during COVID-19 crises. Source: Own research.

The author concludes that the above-mentioned PESTLE-Strategy-diagram is a pandemic local threat profile. It refers to EMT observations made after the first wave of crisis and at the beginning of the second wave. A pandemic seems to be by nature a hybrid threat that generates a wide variety of indirect effects. For example, activities that require human control and supervision may require isolating or work phasing solutions to protect the service continuum. Therefore, there is a risk that increasing the steps in the processes will increase variability in the whole service network, threatening to improve execution time and costs.

The impact of the pandemic was on human supply chains and logistics services. The group size and mutual distances influenced residents gathering. Findings on the characteristics and influences of the pandemic evaluated together with the joint performance of the target organization and its service network. The need for a new type of services testing and training space that offers different conditions and changes became clear.

Results from the Community

State-organized measures against COVID-19 threat included mandatory and voluntary quarantine, closure of state borders, and territorial isolation. The content analysis of the EMT log describes the city's action. EMT maintained situational awareness, informed residents, and led operations in the city. These included, among others, the addition of handwashing points, the transition to teleworking, the closure of certain public services, and unauthorized access to technical services division bases prevented.

Municipalities have a lot in common, and in some cases, different core functions. For example, coastal municipalities may have port functions that inland municipalities do not have. During the crisis, some key public services such as schools and sports facilities closed. In the target organization, the closing time of services was utilized flexibly for cleaning, maintenance, and construction work.

The results of the action research presented to the Safety Park project's steering group on October 30. At the meeting were represented several public organizations: City of Kotka, Southeast Finland Police Department, Carelia Brigade, Army Academy, Finnish Border Guard, Kymenlaakso Fire Department, Merikotka Maritime Safety and Transport Research Center, University of Applied Sciences of Southeast Finland, and the Federation of municipalities in Social and Health Services in the region of Kymenlaakso. There were private organizations as well: Port of HaminaKotka Ltd, Image Wear Ltd, Innocode Ltd, and Steveco Ltd. The steering group was pleased with the presentation and especially the city council's decisions.

The above-mentioned extensive co-operation started at the beginning of 2019 to establish the Southeast Finland Safety Park, promoting a change in the safety culture in the city's port and industrial areas ecosystem. This forthcoming safety park, as its project phase, is already unique in Finland. It brings together all security actors in the region to manage comprehensive security. The need for change arises from megatrends such as the inevitability of an energy revolution, the integration of technology into everything, and the adaptation of the community to climate change (Vornanen & Takala, 2020).

During the crisis, EMT monitored the variation in the number of employees. In this way, it was possible to react to changes in the demand for services. By reducing the amount of variation, had the potential to affect the flow efficiency of the preparedness process. A temporary, employee-based resource bank for new crisis-related tasks was established. For example, a new task was to distribute school meals to schoolchildren's families with volunteers.

The quality of service monitoring is based on feedback from residents. Feedback channels included the city's website and social media channels. According to the author's observations, residents were satisfied with the services.

Conclusion

The limitations are as follows. The action research of mutual trust examines only one city's EMT. It is too early to reflect on success in all situations. The COVID-19 crisis continues globally. Referring to CDC (Centers for Disease Control and Prevention, 2021), more rapidly infectious variants of the SARS-CoV-2 virus are emerging. The third wave of the COVID-19 crisis is possible (Murovska et al., 2020). Asynchronized vaccinations have uncertainties (Jeyanatham et al., 2020). The threat itself, uncertainties, and time-criticalness characterize strategic crisis management, and thus, the future we can see. Despite these, the future direction of mutual trust research is to look at the interoperability of a larger entity that the local level.

The new thing that the chapter brings to strengthen mutual trust in theory and practice is as follows. Management and recovery from the crisis require monitoring of situational factors and constant securing of value chains. The selection and use of a standard tool facilitate the simultaneous production and processing of data. The procedure promotes the management of time-critical activities and cumulates the development of the organization's core competencies to add value.

Referring to Hämeri and Gahmberg (2020), in an uncertain world, the importance of science is emphasized. This action research utilizes the management of production economics in public operational impacts and the achievement of the community's well-being goals. EMT has used a spreadsheet-based situational log for crowdsource-based knowledge management purposes (Vornanen et al., 2016). Co-producing and co-processing of data have been simultaneous activities. The implementation method of the security strategy of society and the city strategy leaves no space for fake news. The choice of the tool has been of fundamental importance for EMT's mutual trust and joint efforts in extreme situations.

According to Hall and Saias (1980), the 'structure follows the strategy' operation principle, the technical director concluded that the target organization had to restructure to achieve new kind of goals and respond to rising threats. Therefore, a new manufacturing strategy was planned for the division. It takes place by evaluating the structures and resources, processes and workflows, organizational and information system through success, are they relevant to experience or has the capabilities to fulfill new expectations. The experience of the COVID-19 crisis will utilize as a driver for technology management. The city council approved the technical director's organizational restructuring proposal (70§) and over 900,000 EUR security investment in developing hybrid organization's competitiveness (71 §). The city acquired a large port building for safety park purposes to develop common safety culture (72 §). These decisions verify mutual trust in a resource-based approach.

From the point of view of the successful management of a hybrid organization, it is desirable that the local organization has its own strategic knowledge management team, which also designs and coordinates local data collection, for example, against combined threat situations. In this way, a quantitative content analysis serves the construction of a common resource-based view, maintenance of situational awareness, and even the state's decision-making.

When using word processing or presentation graphics software as situation diaries, the compilation of situation factors and other data material has to transfer to spreadsheet software to produce a situational picture or to do analyses. It is desirable that spreadsheet software be a common tool with pre-agreed column entries before, during, and through the observations, including after the crisis. From the point of view of continuity management, it is advantageous that in the preparedness process, situational factors and operational priorities are continuously analyzed from a sense-and-response perspective (Vornanen et al., 2013).

Although the author paints a picture of an analytically implemented shared leadership tactic in the target organization, the qualitative material from EMT's diary with the author's observations conveys a more realistic picture of the mayor's management in the COVID-19 crisis. In a situation where residents' concerns are needed to listen and encourage towards a common goal, to care and to communicate it is wisdom. The mayor plays a leading part in the team communicating the direction of development convincingly, usefully, and inspiringly to residents. Leadership is relevant and, depending on the situation, even critical to the success of strategies. The target organization had the right leader in the right place at the right time.

The actions of the mayor had an inspiring effect on the EMT and its joint performance. The right tool's choice has been affected to cooperation as a team's key instrument to tell, crowdsource, measure, and analyze strategic actions. Utilizing the tool have help to strengthening mutual trust, which promoted resilience. The implementation of the city strategy was successful by identifying welfare-critical choices and the use of resources to manage the crisis and accelerate recovery from the exceptional circumstances.

References

Barney, J. (1991). Firm resources and sustained competitive advantage. *Journal of Management*, *17*(1), 99–120.

Centers for Disease Control and Prevention. (2021, February 27). *Emerging SARS-CoV-2 variants*. Retrieved from https://www.cdc.gov/coronavirus/2019-ncov/more/science-and-research/scientific-brief-emerging-variants.html.

City council of the city Kotka. (2020, August 17). *Kotka 2025 city strategy*. Retrieved from https://www.kotka.fi/wp-content/uploads/2020/01/Kotka2025_strategia_kvhyv111119.pdf (Original in Finnish).

City council of the city Kotka. (2020, August 17). *Changing the administrative rule, § 70.* Retrieved from http://hallijulkaisu.kotka.fi/ktwebbin/ktproxy2.dll?doctype=3&docid=477711 (Original in Finnish).

City council of the city Kotka. (2020, August 17). *Acquisition budget for I-5 storage building, § 71.* Retrieved from http://hallijulkaisu.kotka.fi/ktwebbin/ktproxy2.dll?doctype=3&docid=477713 (Original in Finnish).

City council of the city Kotka. (2020, August 17). *Acquisition of I-5 storage building, § 72.* Retrieved from http://hallijulkaisu.kotka.fi/ktwebbin/ktproxy2.dll?doctype=3&docid=477715 (Original in Finnish).

EMT of the city of Kotka. (2020). *Joint situation diary January-June 2020.* Not publicly available (Original in Finnish).

Grönroos, C. (1984). A service quality model and its marketing implications. *European Journal of Marketing, 18*(4), 36–66.

Hall, D. J., & Saias, M. A. (1980). Strategy follows structure! *Strategic Management Journal, 1*(2), 149–163.

Hämeri, K., & Gahmberg, C. G. (2020, December 31). *Epävarmassa maailmassa tieteen merkitys korostuu.* Retrieved from https://www.hs.fi/mielipide/art-2000007712844.html (Original in Finnish).

Jeyanatham, M., Afkhami, S., Smaill, F., Miller, M. S., Lichty, B. D., & Xing, Z. (2020). Immunological considerations for COVID-19 vaccine strategies. *Nature Reviews Immunology, 20*, 615–632.

Kozuch, B., Magala, S. J., & Paliszkiewicz, J. (Eds.). (2018). *Managing public trust.* Palgrave Macmillan. Vornanen, V.-J. (Et al.). *Mutual Trust: Joint Performance of an Operations Strategy Implementation – Securing the Value Chain by Preparedness.* 175–190.

Lewin, K. (1946). Action research and minority problems. *Journal of Social Issues*, 2(4), 34–46.

Ministry of Finance. (2012). *Local government act.* Retrieved from https://www.finlex.fi/en/laki/kaannokset/1995/en19950365_20120325.pdf.

Ministry of Justice. (2015). *Act on the openness of government activities.* Retrieved from https://www.finlex.fi/en/laki/kaannokset/1999/en19990621_20150907.pdf.

Murovska, M., Sokolovska, L., Sultanova, A. & Cistjakovs, M. (2020). COVID-19: The third wave of coronavirus outbreak. *Journal of Translational Science, 7*(1), 1–5.

Newton, P., & Bristoll, H. (2013). *Pestle analysis.* Free management e-books. Retrieved from https://pdf4pro.com/view/pestle-analysis-free-management-ebooks-1f52d7.html.

The Strategic Management Society of Finland. (2018). *Strategy work of the year 2018.* Retrieved from https://www.ssjs.fi/toiminta-ja-tapahtumat/vuoden-strategiateko/2018/ (Original in Finnish).

Vornanen, V.-J., & Takala, J. (2020). Metrics in the preparedness process. *Acta Logistica, 7*(3), 145–154.

Vornanen, V.-J. (2017). *Joint performance – Preparedness in the municipal transformation 2009-2015: Securing the value chain by operations strategy implementation.* Doctoral Thesis. Acta Wasaensia, 369. University of Vaasa.

Vornanen, V.-J., Sivula, A., & Takala, J. (2016). Hybrid management in preparedness: Utilizing cooperation and crowdsourcing to create joint performance in the logistic society. *Management, 11*(2), 152–170.

Vornanen, V.-J., & Takala, J. (2014). Towards joint performance: Building dynamic capabilities for public critical asset maintenance. *Management*, 9(3), 239–257.

Vornanen, V-J., Liu, Y., & Takala, J. (2013). Implementing Sustainable Competitive Advantage To The Public Sector's Management System – by sense and respond methodology in facilities services unit's preparedness. *Management and Production Engineering Review*, 4(3), 76–86.

Wernerfelt, B. (1984). A resource-based view of the firm. *Strategic Management Journal*, 5(2), 171–180.

14 The Role of Trust in Modern Food Production Through Blockchain and Related Technologies

Sławomir Jarka, Agnieszka Biernat-Jarka, and Monika Gębska
Warsaw University of Life Sciences

Introduction

Today food chains are extremely complex and sophisticated. Among other things, the following has contributed to this: world trade liberalization, growing competition among agricultural and food processing sector companies, and product and process innovations. Not only the number of operators involved in the processes of food production, distribution, and sales has grown, but also the number of offered food products. This means the occurrence of numerous problems connected with the production and processing of food materials or, finally, the sales of food products, as well.

The following can be listed among the most important problems related to the food products value chain: cheating in the food trade, providing false information on the producer and food production processing; illegal food production, and its marketing and circulation without required documentation. Another issue important for producers is the cost of withdrawal from circulation of food failing to satisfy legally regulated requirements in a certain market.

All these factors specified above decrease the level of consumers' trust, both in B2B and B2C markets, which certainly translates into negative trends of the sales and profitability of businesses creating a market chain of food.

At the same time, we observe the evolution of modern digital technologies, which give practically unlimited potential for improving management quality for individual food chain elements. Implementation of blockchain technology in the food chain may contribute to the elimination or reduction of the problems listed above.

New digital technologies change the functioning and competition conditions for business operators involved in the production of raw materials for food and foodstuffs. Operators belonging to the food chain take more and more advantage of the opportunities given by the digital revolution.

DOI: 10.4324/9781003165965-14

The purpose of this article is to determine the effect of blockchain technology on the level of consumers' trust in the food production process. Apart from that, the authors formulate a hypothesis that blockchain technology increases consumers' trust in individual food chain elements. The article presents the results of literature studies and surveys research indicating that the implementation of blockchain technology has a positive effect on the level of consumers' trust in the food production process.

Consumers' Trust in Food Production Process

Consumers' trust in the food production chain is a very often discussed and analyzed food economy problem (Sapp et al., 2009; Hobbs & Goddard, 2015; Cao et al., 2021). As regards food safety, this trust may indicate a hidden belief that the consumption of food products will have no adverse effects on the consumers' health. Consumers' confidence in food safety is defined as the condition, in which consumers find food safe and harmless both for their own health and for the environment (de Jonge et al., 2007).

Trust determines consumers' attitude to food technologies, food production and processing methods, food origin and source, and reliable transfer of information (Hobbs & Goddard, 2015). It is the result of gathered positive experience, whereas negative incidents related to food quality may induce a visible decrease in consumers' confidence in food safety. Numerous studies carried out so far prove that consumers may have a highly negative reaction to any information on foodstuff contamination or poor quality of food products, especially showing an adverse effect on their health. Here, we can refer to the studies by Setbon et al. (2005) describing consumers' behaviors due to the information about a possible connection between bovine spongiform encephalopathy (BSE), commonly called the "mad cow disease" (MCD), and lethal neurological disease known as a new variant of the Creutzfeldt-Jakob disease. A serious sanitary, sociopolitical and economic crisis arose in France, a country affected by BSE. As a consequence, the fear of getting sick after meat consumption grew rapidly, which triggered off beef market collapse, causing drop in its consumption of even 20–30% (Setbon et al., 2005). Both the dioxin affair in Belgium in 1999 and the BSE disease in Great Britain induced immense problems in foreign trade of many countries (Berg, 2004). In spite of many information campaigns and preventive measures, the loss of trust in food safety became a valid problem (Baron et al., 2000; Setbon et al., 2005). Our trust in food depends on how the food market is functioning and how public authorities control it. (Fischler, 1988) points out that more and more complicated and technologically advanced food production process makes people know less and less about what they eat. Does that mean that the lack of knowledge on the consumed foodstuffs must be compensated for by an abstract trust? The blockchain system may help in building customers' trust, because the process of food production, processing, and distribution is controlled at each production stage, and information gathered in this system can always be verified and checked by the consumer. Let consumers' trust not be like Fischler (1988) stated – oblivious and based primarily on the lack of bad experience, but let it become the effect of the acquisition of knowledge and conviction of high quality of food products confirmed by the blockchain system.

In order to distinguish consumers' approach to food safety, Berg (2004) used two dimensions: trust – distrust and reflexivity – non-reflexivity. Thus, he differentiated:

- *Sensible consumers*, who try to choose healthy food for their everyday diet. They are sure that the food they consume is not harmful either for them and for their families.
- *Skeptical consumers*, who are afraid to select foodstuffs for their everyday diet. Although the consumers are careful, they still think that the food they consume may be detrimental for themselves and for their families.
- *Naïve consumers* that is those who do not care about choosing healthy food for their diet, but are still convinced that the food they consume is not harmful either for them and for their families.
- *Denying consumers*, who, on the one hand, are afraid that the food they consume is detrimental for themselves and for their families, nevertheless they make no attempt to select healthy foodstuffs either for themselves or for their families.

Although trust is an important issue for the public, yet it is first of all analyzed individually. The trust and distrust level experienced by individuals is of key importance for their satisfaction and wellbeing. Therefore, it can be stated that our trust in food quality we consume in everyday meals and use in food production process is essential for the quality of our life itself (Berg, 2004).

The lack of consumers' trust in the offered products is a very serious problem, therefore in current situation food products are more and more often placed on the market with declarations of their healthiness, shelf-life, and authenticity. The lack of confidence in food chain operators can always decrease the number of consumers (de Jonge et al., 2007). Consumers cannot verify many features of food products, and their evaluation is based on the information received from the producers. Healthiness, production according to sustainable development principles, origination from a specific supplier, and/or safety are food features, which cannot be found by consumers on their own, and which should be delivered by a reliable seller or supplier (Verbeke et al., 2013). After all, consumer is unable to verify whether in fact certain product has composition as specified on its packaging, if the product has been actually produced, processed and sold in accordance with specific rules, for example, for storage and transport (Macready et al., 2020). Authenticity of food products is another factor affecting consumers' confidence level. This confidence can be also built by way of confirming reliability of food products by the blockchain system. Trust in food chain elements may help consumers compensate for their lack of knowledge on cultivation and food production processes (De Jonge et al., 2007).

Consumers' trust in individual food chain elements may be an important factor increasing overall consumers' confidence in food safety (Grunert, 2002; Berg et al., 2005). What can build this trust? Presumably, an identification and control system showing the quality of raw materials being used in the production process, and proven product processing technology strictly following verified processes, which will be confirmed by blockchain.

Possibilities of Using the Blockchain Technology in Food Chain

Among other things, the challenges of today encountered by food producers concern food safety, which is the reason why enterprises continuously need new solutions to strengthen their competitive position in the market. Its improvement is possible, for example, through holistic approach to building of confidence between food producers and consumers, based on viable considerations, data available for all parties interested in modern food production. One of the responses to them is the development of industry 4.0 (the fourth industrial revolution), meant as implementations of new technologies, including blockchain, Internet of Things, Big Data, as well as development of artificial intelligence, nanotechnology and improved prototyping (Wolfert et al., 2017). Digitization is an element of processes taking place in the markets in recent years. It is a challenge and at the same time in many cases the solution for producer's attempts to adjust to consumers' needs, and in the future also to offer them goods of highest possible quality (Azzi et al., 2019). Contemporary food delivery chains include producers, suppliers, carriers, wholesalers, retailers, other dealers, and even customers themselves. They consist of many highly diversified interested parties making efforts to achieve their own autonomic targets. Managing them in a conventional way often becomes an ineffective process, in fact even impossible, especially in the face of progressing globalization. Progressing globalization is just the reason why enterprises need new methods and solutions facilitating delivery chain management (Iansiti & Lakhani, 2017). The need to implement innovations and innovativeness in economy triggers off implementation of new, previously unknown solutions, or updating and use of those already existing ones. Moreover, according to management theoreticians and practicians, developing and implementing of innovations is a guarantee of long-term economic growth (Gusc et al., 2021). Here, it is worth referring to the already classic study by J. Schumpeter, who developed the economic theory of innovation in the first half of the 20th century. The author distinguished its 5 types: the production of a new good, the implementation of a new method for the production of a good produced to date, the development of a new market, acquiring a new source of raw materials, effecting enterprise restructuring process (Schumpeter & Backhaus, 2003).

Blockchain is one of the innovative digital technologies of particularly high potential for the food chain in the context of consumers' trust-building (Wang et al., 2019). Blockchain technology was developed in response to the confidence crisis, which seized the world as a result of the financial crisis in 2008. From the very beginning of its creation it has been used only to distribute cryptocurrencies by way of keeping unchanging, scattered books in thousands of scattered nodes, demonstrated by Satoshi Nakamoto in 2008 (Nakamoto, 2008). However, it has been found very quickly that this technology can be also useful for the greater digitization of individual business operators and institutions, sectors, and as a consequence entire economies.

This is a relatively new technology, which may revolutionize the functioning of food delivery chains. Blockchain provides an opportunity to store information on transactions and products in a decentralized and scattered database, which is not susceptible to modifications and manipulations (Werbach, 2018). Blockchain works as a public book, where each transaction is authorized by consensus of the majority of people involved in the system, which ensures transparency of the whole delivery chain. As regards food chain, the following are subject to authorization and verification: individual economic operations and processes carried out in individual elements of the market chain (Jarka, 2019). New digital technologies change the functioning and competition conditions for business operators in various branches involved in the production of raw materials for food and foodstuffs. Operators belonging to the food chain take more and more advantage of the opportunities given by digital revolution (Zambon et al., 2019).

The most important problems related to the value chain of food products include (Michalczyk, 2019):

- Frauds in food trading, providing false information regarding the producer and technological process of food production;
- Illegal production and marketing of foodstuffs without adequate documentation;
- Diseases transmitted via alimentary route;

- The costs of withdrawing from market circulation foodstuffs failing to satisfy legally regulated requirements in a given country.

Implementing the blockchain technology into the food chain may contribute to the elimination or reduction of the problems listed above. These chains are currently extremely complex and sophisticated. Undoubtedly, the blockchain technology is an example of reorganization of processes in an enterprise, and later delivery chain as well. Besides, it can be used in a holistic way, that is from monitoring the quality of raw material deliveries to finished products supplied to the consumers, taking into account commercial element (De Filippi et al., 2020). Thus, it can be classified as organizational and technological innovation.

The basic advantage of using this technology is increased transparency of operation of food delivery chains. Applications based on the blockchain technology allow improving the efficiency of systems for tracking and identifying agricultural and food products in a delivery chain (Leng et al., 2018). As a result, they may help to reduce the number of cases of foodstuffs falsifying and unauthorized use of food quality certificates (Saberi et al., 2019).

Research Method

The studies on the effect of blockchain technology on consumers' trust in individual food chain elements were carried out in the fourth quarter of 2020. The data was gathered using a survey questionnaire. The sample was selected in a targeted manner, and survey participants had knowledge on the blockchain system. The respondents were residents of Central and Eastern Poland (the areas around Warsaw) – from Masovian, Lublin, and Podlaskie Voivodeships.

256 respondents took part in the survey, 65% were women, and 35% were men. The respondents were in the working-age, aged mainly 18–30 (76%). The participants had university degrees (80%) and secondary education –20%.

To evaluate income per household, the majority of people declared income between 5000 and 1000 PLN (more than 32%), and persons declaring income between 3000 and 5000 PLN (more than 31%). People with highest income level, that is over 10,000 PLN constituted more than 17% of survey sample. Among the respondents there were people belonging to households consisting of two persons – this group constituted more than 24%, and to households consisting of three persons – this group constituted more than 23%. Every fifth respondent declared to have a one-person household.

Another interesting finding was to determine the sectors represented by respondents declaring their jobs. And thus, 71% of respondents specified working in enterprises using the newest digital technologies including IoT, Big Data, AI, or at last blockchain.

Research Results

In order to assess the impact of blockchain on the confidence of consumers in the food production a quantitative analysis of survey data has been carried out. The main hypothesis states that:

H1. The overall belief in importance of blockchain in the agricultural production impacts the confidence of consumers in the agricultural production and this impact is positive.

In order to quantify these dependencies, we have developed regression models with variables expressing consumers' trust in blockchain positive impact on the fairness of agricultural production (Y) as the dependent variables and consumers' beliefs in the importance of blockchain in the overall agricultural production (B) as the independent variable.

The Y variables (dependent variables) included the following questions from the survey (all of them are expressed on a scale of 1–5 where 1 denotes full disagreement and 5 full agreement). Variables Y1–Y5 show the beliefs concerning resources and Y6–Y10 concerning the final agricultural product.

Below are the definitions of variables – dependent variables:

Y1	-	Blockchain affects the production of agricultural raw materials in a sustainable way (that is environment-friendly, resource-efficient, and ethically responsible):
Y2	-	Blockchain affects safety of agricultural raw materials.
Y3	-	Blockchain affects fairness of agricultural raw materials production.
Y4	-	Blockchain affects agricultural raw materials storage processes.
Y5	-	Blockchain affects raw materials transport processes.
Y6	-	Blockchain affects safety of food products.
Y7	-	Blockchain affects authenticity of food products origin (compliance with the declared origin).
Y8	-	Blockchain affects the production of foodstuffs in a sustainable way (that is environment-friendly, resource efficient and ethically responsible).
Y9	-	Blockchain affects authenticity of foodstuffs production technology.
Y10	-	Blockchain affects production of healthy food products.

The B variables included the following questions from the survey, expressed on the same scale:

B1	-	Blockchain affects transport conditions for food products.
B2	-	Blockchain affects foodstuffs storage processes.
B3	-	Blockchain affects keeping expiry dates of food products.
B4	-	Blockchain affects authenticity of food products origin.

These variables have been processed using the PCA method (Eigenvalue = 2.39929, cumulative variance extracted = 0.5998) in order to extract one score of the general importance of Blockchain in the agricultural production.

On top of this in the model, we have controlled for the level of overall confidence, extracted from the following variables using the PCA (eigenvalue = 2.41322, cumulative variance extracted = 0.8044).

Independent definitions are presented as follows:

C1	-	Generally, I trust other people
C2	-	I think that people generally are trustworthy
C3	-	I feel that people generally are trustworthy

We have also controlled for the demographic data using the following variables (values coded as in the survey).

The following are the independent variables and demographic data:

D1	-	Sex
D2	-	Age
D3	-	Education
D4	-	Volume of income per household
D5	-	How many family members are there in your household?
D6	-	Place of residence
D7	-	Employment

The research was based on survey results from N = 256 respondents. There were no missing values in the data. Table 14.1 present the main descriptive statistics of the dependent and independent variables (components extracted from PCA).

Table 14.1 Descriptive Statistics of Variables

Variable	*Obs*	*Mean*	*Std. Dev.*	*Min*	*Max*
Y1	256	3.656	0.766	1	5
Y2	256	3.613	0.851	1	5
Y3	256	3.676	0.916	1	5
Y4	256	3.594	0.920	1	5
Y5	256	3.770	0.875	1	5
Y6	255	3.667	0.829	1	5
Y7	256	3.844	0.907	1	5
Y8	256	3.602	0.765	1	5
Y9	256	3.688	0.819	1	5
Y10	256	3.363	0.964	1	5
C	256	0.000	1.553	–4.349	3.279
B	256	0.000	1.549	–5.776	2.704

Source: Own study.

The impact of blockchain on the trust of consumers in the fairness of agricultural production has been quantified using OLS linear regression models for each of the ten dependent variables from the Y block. Models have been estimated using all the available data. We have used robust standard errors to account for possible heteroscedasticity. Standard 0.05 significance level was used to select statistically significant variables. Results of the models are presented in Table 14.2. The coefficients of the variable of interest (B: Importance of blockchain) are presented on Figure 14.1.

In all the 10 models, the belief in the importance of blockchain has a statistically significant impact on the belief of blockchain positive influence on the trust in the fairness of agricultural production. In all the models this variable (B) is highly significant with p-value close to 0. Moreover, in all the models this impact is positive (parameter estimates greater than 0). This confirms that blockchain plays an important role in creating consumers' trust in the agricultural production. The values of parameter estimates are quite similar across the models, ranging from 0.149 for Y1 (greater trust in blockchain positive impact on sustainable production of resources) to 0.311 for Y10 (production of healthy agricultural products). In general the impact is slightly higher for questions Y6–Y10 then for Y1–Y5 which means the impact of blockchain is more visible in case of the final agricultural product than in the case of resources.

On top of the impact of blockchain per se we have observed that the overall confidence of the respondents has some positive impact, but only in case of variables Y2, Y6, and Y10. In case of the demographic variables no clear pattern has been observed, with different demographic characteristics showing statistical significance for different dependent variables. Interestingly, the employment (including employment in the new technology sector) shows no impact on the relations between blockchain and the fairness of food production.

Survey Limitations and Discussion with the Results of Other Surveys

Limitations of this survey include data gathering method that is the survey questionnaire, which affects reliability and trueness of submitted answers. Therefore, the respondents were clearly informed about using this information for scientific purposes only.

Survey sample is the second constraint. The targeted selection of respondents was applied also because these people had to know the blockchain technology. Information from people unfamiliar with this technology would be useless and would lead to false survey results. Considering the applied data selection method, obtained results are not valid for the entire community, but the surveyed sample only.

Table 14.2 Results of Models

Block	*Variable*	*Y1*	*Y2*	*Y3*	*Y4*	*Y5*	*Y6*	*Y7*	*Y8*	*Y9*	*Y10*
Importance of Blockchain	B (Importance of Blockchain)	0.149	0.223	0.239	0.299	0.289	0.245	0.298	0.236	0.230	0.311
		0.032	0.034	0.035	0.034	0.032	0.031	0.032	0.029	0.031	0.036
		0.000	0.000	0.000	0.000	0.000	0.000	0.000	0.000	0.000	0.000
Overall Confidence	C (Overall trust)	0.055	0.030	−0.015	−0.016	0.010	0.084	0.017	0.034	0.037	0.073
		0.032	0.034	0.035	0.035	0.033	0.032	0.033	0.029	0.031	0.037
		0.088	0.381	0.668	0.634	0.766	0.009	0.602	0.244	0.241	0.047
Demographics	Sex										
	Male	−0.049	−0.217	−0.215	0.026	0.176	−0.014	−0.049	0.048	−0.141	0.049
		0.109	0.116	0.119	0.116	0.110	0.108	0.111	0.099	0.106	0.123
		0.656	0.062	0.073	0.827	0.111	0.894	0.663	0.630	0.185	0.694
	Age										
	31–50	−0.133	−0.023	0.015	0.253	0.235	0.051	0.018	−0.233	−0.278	−0.073
		0.122	0.130	0.133	0.130	0.123	0.120	0.125	0.111	0.119	0.138
		0.277	0.858	0.910	0.054	0.058	0.670	0.886	0.036	0.020	0.597
	over 50 years of age	0.321	0.293	0.080	0.481	0.325	0.215	0.592	0.108	0.022	0.395
		0.343	0.366	0.376	0.368	0.347	0.339	0.351	0.312	0.334	0.389
		0.350	0.423	0.831	0.192	0.350	0.527	0.093	0.729	0.948	0.311
	Education										
	university	0.337	−0.259	0.065	−0.124	−0.931	−0.131	−0.366	0.332	−0.448	0.593
		0.926	0.987	1.014	0.992	0.936	0.916	0.948	0.842	0.902	1.050
		0.716	0.793	0.949	0.901	0.321	0.887	0.700	0.694	0.620	0.573
	secondary	0.324	−0.183	0.103	−0.277	−0.853	−0.186	−0.157	0.246	−0.466	0.251
		0.936	0.997	1.024	1.002	0.945	0.925	0.957	0.850	0.912	1.061
		0.730	0.854	0.920	0.782	0.368	0.841	0.870	0.773	0.610	0.813

Income per household										
up to 3000 PLN	−0.180	0.018	−0.315	−0.118	0.054	−0.326	−0.128	0.013	−0.184	0.195
	0.147	0.157	0.161	0.157	0.149	0.146	0.150	0.134	0.143	0.167
	0.222	0.907	0.052	0.454	0.718	0.027	0.397	0.922	0.200	0.243
3001 – 5000 PLN	−0.182	−0.164	−0.589	−0.352	−0.092	−0.235	−0.375	−0.195	−0.133	0.113
	0.124	0.132	0.136	0.133	0.125	0.123	0.127	0.113	0.121	0.141
	0.145	0.216	0.000	0.009	0.466	0.057	0.004	0.086	0.273	0.422
over 10000 PLN	−0.067	−0.008	0.037	−0.528	−0.312	−0.014	0.192	0.151	0.270	−0.218
	0.152	0.162	0.166	0.163	0.154	0.150	0.156	0.138	0.148	0.172
	0.658	0.960	0.823	0.001	0.044	0.928	0.218	0.274	0.069	0.208
How many family members are there in your household?										
2	−0.149	0.085	−0.195	−0.026	−0.003	−0.078	0.012	−0.323	−0.375	−0.175
	0.144	0.153	0.157	0.154	0.145	0.143	0.147	0.131	0.140	0.163
	0.302	0.582	0.216	0.864	0.986	0.584	0.934	0.014	0.008	0.285
3	−0.033	0.048	−0.027	−0.021	0.065	−0.109	−0.074	−0.144	−0.307	0.008
	0.146	0.155	0.159	0.156	0.147	0.144	0.149	0.132	0.142	0.165
	0.819	0.755	0.866	0.892	0.661	0.450	0.621	0.278	0.031	0.962
4	0.050	0.059	0.049	0.054	0.174	0.000	0.060	−0.140	−0.336	−0.023
	0.153	0.163	0.167	0.164	0.154	0.152	0.156	0.139	0.149	0.173
	0.743	0.719	0.768	0.741	0.261	0.998	0.704	0.315	0.025	0.892
5 and more	0.107	0.097	−0.018	−0.006	0.028	−0.205	0.087	−0.171	−0.274	0.052
	0.183	0.195	0.200	0.196	0.185	0.181	0.187	0.166	0.178	0.207
	0.559	0.620	0.927	0.975	0.881	0.259	0.643	0.305	0.125	0.804
Place of residence										
	−0.366	0.202	0.061	0.069	0.181	0.277	0.270	−0.402	−0.349	−0.252

(Continued)

Table 14.2 (Continued)

Block	*Variable*	*Y1*	*Y2*	*Y3*	*Y4*	*Y5*	*Y6*	*Y7*	*Y8*	*Y9*	*Y10*
	- population 30,000 – 100,000										
		0.547	0.583	0.598	0.585	0.552	0.541	0.559	0.497	0.533	0.620
		0.504	0.730	0.919	0.906	0.744	0.609	0.630	0.419	0.513	0.684
	5,000 – 30,000	-0.476	0.130	-0.297	0.034	0.201	0.111	0.194	-0.445	-0.568	-0.463
		0.571	0.608	0.625	0.611	0.577	0.564	0.584	0.519	0.556	0.647
		0.405	0.831	0.636	0.955	0.728	0.844	0.740	0.392	0.309	0.476
	over 100,000	-0.337	0.291	-0.254	-0.069	0.011	0.154	0.404	-0.359	-0.291	-0.480
		0.536	0.571	0.586	0.574	0.541	0.530	0.548	0.487	0.522	0.607
		0.530	0.610	0.665	0.904	0.984	0.771	0.461	0.461	0.578	0.430
	rural	-0.447	0.098	-0.454	-0.237	-0.124	0.258	0.327	-0.232	-0.352	-0.139
		0.545	0.581	0.597	0.583	0.551	0.539	0.557	0.495	0.531	0.618
		0.413	0.866	0.447	0.684	0.822	0.633	0.558	0.639	0.508	0.822
	Employment sector of conventional technologies	-0.039	0.019	-0.022	0.136	0.069	0.003	0.007	-0.050	-0.184	-0.063
		0.105	0.112	0.115	0.112	0.106	0.104	0.107	0.095	0.102	0.119
		0.707	0.865	0.848	0.228	0.518	0.976	0.947	0.604	0.074	0.596
Constant	Constant	3.883	3.690	4.225	3.882	4.516	3.808	3.912	3.886	4.993	3.242
		0.769	0.819	0.842	0.823	0.777	0.760	0.786	0.699	0.749	0.872
		0.000	0.000	0.000	0.000	0.000	0.000	0.000	0.000	0.000	0.000
Statistics	N	256,000	256,000	256,000	256,000	256,000	255,000	256,000	256,000	256,000	256,000
	r2	0.143	0.211	0.281	0.318	0.329	0.284	0.359	0.290	0.287	0.304
	aic	589,822	622,397	636,146	624,807	595,083	581,816	601,497	540,893	576,462	654,192
	bic	660,725	693,301	707,049	695,711	665,987	652,641	672,401	611,797	647,365	725,095

Source: Own study based on completed research.
Legend: For each variable the first row denotes parameter estimate, the second the standard error of the estimate, and the third the p-value.

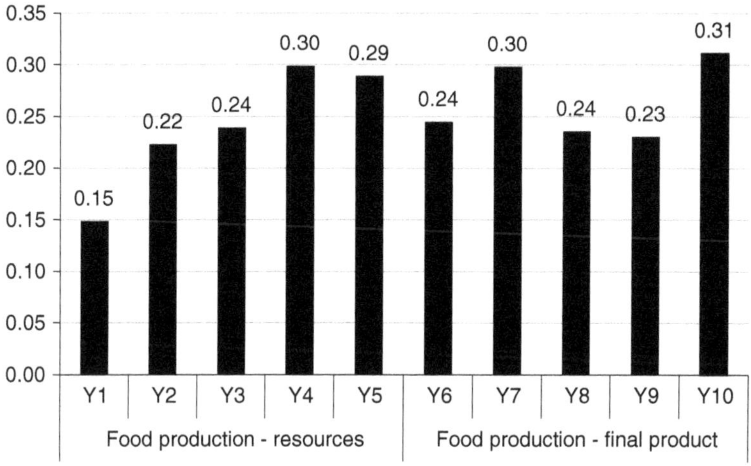

Figure 14.1 Parameter estimates for variable of interest in models. Source: Own study.

Selection of measures in statistical analysis is the third constraint. There are many methods used to measure confidence, but there is no single tool, which could be used in practice. Besides, the completed studies are innovative as regards the impact of blockchain technology on consumers' trust and in the future development of a single measure to determine the level of consumers' confidence in food production process may become another research challenge.

Discussion

Many surveys of consumers' trust applied to selected food chain elements. Yee et al. (2005) focused on farmers, breeders of farm animals, and analyzing causal relationship between factors determining consumers' trust in food safety, and thus meat purchase probability. Completed analyses confirm that the producers should deliver reliable and true information to the consumers, which will surely have positive effect on their purchases. Moreover, the surveys concerning trust in food producers carried out by James (2006) pointed out consumers' expectations regarding foodstuffs reliability. Results of these studies proved unambiguously that the consumers were able to pay higher prices for higher food safety standards. On the other hand, analyzing trust in food retail trade, Kenning (2008) proved that both overall confidence resulting from buyer personality trait and trust in a specific seller positively affect shopping behaviors.

Conclusion

Many surveys carried out so far concerned the level of confidence in food chain elements. Their authors were focusing on determining the level of consumers' trust in food safety, how the level of confidence in individual food sector elements affects overall confidence, and what it results from. However, the surveys carried out to date miss those referring to the impact of blockchain technology on consumers' trust in food chain. Regarding this, the completed surveys are innovative and show the need to implement modern technological solutions that would contribute on the one hand to food safety improvement, and on the other hand, to increasing consumers' trust in information delivered by farmers, processors, and retailers, that is the entire food production process.

Completed surveys indicate that the context, in which present-day consumers function (i.e. rapid development of digital technologies, the appearance of new products and consumption patterns, favorable changes in the economic situation, digitization of socioeconomic life), generates changes in the general consumption model. Consumer of the 4.0 era uses digital tools more and more often and expects that food purchases will be supported by tools improving its quality. Modern digital solutions, for example, blockchain technology were received very well by the consumers, who have considered that they contribute to the building of higher level of confidence in food market chain.

Undoubtedly, one of the reasons why blockchain technology should be used in food delivery chain is building of consumers' trust – B2C and B2B, which will increase as a result of process monitoring, and at the same time will ensure higher quality of foodstuffs. This, in principle, should bring higher profits to business operators involved in its production and distribution.

Limitations of this survey include data gathering method, survey sample, and selection of measures in statistical analysis. There are many methods used to measure confidence, but there is no single tool, which could be used in practice. Besides, the completed studies are innovative as regards the impact of blockchain technology on consumers' trust, and in the future development of a single measure to determine the level of consumers' confidence in food production process may become another research challenge.

References

Azzi, R., Chamoun, R. K., & Sokhn, M. (2019). The power of a blockchain-based supply chain. *Computers & industrial engineering*, *135*, 582–592.

Baron, J., Hershey, J. C., & Kunreuther, H. (2000). Determinants of priority for risk reduction: The role of worry. *Risk Analysis*, *20*, 413–427.

Berg L. (2004). Trust in food in the age of mad cow disease: a comparative study of consumers' evaluation of food safety in Belgium, Britain and Norway. *Appetite*, *42*(1), 21–32.

Berg, L., Kjaernes, U., Ganskau, E., Minina, V., Voltchkova, L., Halkier, B ... Lotte, Holm. (2005). Trust in food safety in Russia, Denmark and Norway. *European Societies*, *7*(1), 103–129.

Cao S., Powell W., Foth M., Natanelov V., Miller T., & Dulleck U. (2021). Strengthening consumer trust in beef supply chain traceability with a blockchain-based human-machine reconcile mechanism. *Computers and Electronics in Agriculture*, *180*, 105886.

De Filippi, P., Mannan, M., & Reijers, W. (2020). Blockchain as a confidence machine: The problem of trust & challenges of governance. *Technology in Society*, *62*, 101284.

De Jonge, J., Van Trijp, H., Jan Renes, R., & Frewer, L. (2007). Understanding consumer confidence in the safety of food: Its two-dimensional structure and determinants. *Risk Analysis*, *27*, 729–740.

Fischler, C. (1988). Food, self and identity. *Social Science Information*, *27*(2), 275–292.

Grunert, K. G. (2002). Current issues in the understanding of consumer food choice. *Trends in Food Science and Technology*, *13*(8), 275–285.

Gusc, J., Jarka, S., & de Zwarte, I. (2021). IoT as a means of strengthening individual farmers' position in collaboration for transformation to sustainable farming. In W. S. K. Sharma, B. Bharat, N. C. Debnath, S. K. Sharma, B. Bharat, & N. C. Debnath (Eds.), *IoT Security Paradigms and Applications: Research and Practices* (pp. 217–236). Boca Raton, FL: CRC Press.

Hobbs, J. E., & Goddard, E. (2015). Consumers and trust. *Food Policy*, *52*, 71–74.

Iansiti, M., & Lakhani, K. (2017). The truth about Blockchai. *Harvard Business Review*, *95*(1), 118–127.

James, H. (2006). Trust in scientists and food manufacturers: implications for the public support of biotechnology. *Journal of Agribusiness*, *24*(2), 119–133.

Jarka, S. (2019). Food safety in the supply chain using blockchain technology. *Acta Scientiarum Polonorum. Seria: Oeconomia*, *18*(4), 41–48.

Kenning, P. (2008). The influence of general trust and specific trust on buying behaviour. *International Journal of Retail & Distribution Management*, *36*(6), 461–476.

Leng, K., Bi, Y., Jing, L., Fu, H. C., & Van Nieuwenhuyse, I. (2018). Research on agricultural supply chain system with double chain architecture based on blockchain technology. *Future Generation Computer Systems*, *86*, 641–649.

Macready A., Hieke S., Klimczuk-Kochańska M., Szumiał Sz., Vranken L., & Grunert K. (2020). Consumer trust in the food value chain and its impact on consumer confidence: A model for assessing consumer trust and evidence from a 5-country study in Europe, *Food Policy*, *92*, 101880.

Michalczyk, J. (2019). Bezpieczeństwo żywnościowe z perspektywy państw Unii Europejskiej (eng. Food security from the perspective of European Union countries). *Ekonomia Międzynarodowa*, *25*, 18–45.

Nakamoto, S. (2008). *Bitcoin: A peer-to-peer electronic cash system*. Retrieved from https://bitcoin.org/en/bitcoin-paper.

Saberi, S., Kouhizadeh, M., Sarkis, J., & Shen, L. (2019). Blockchain technology and its relationships to sustainable supply chain management. *International Journal of Production Research*, *57*(7), 2117–2135.

Sapp, S.G., Arnot, C., Fallon, J., Fleck, T., Soorholtz, D., Sutton-Vermeulen, M., & Wilson, J.J.H. (2009). Consumer trust in the US food system: An examination of the recreancy theorem. *Rural Sociology*, *74*(4), 525–545.

Schumpeter, J., & Backhaus, U. (2003). The theory of economic development. In Backhaus J. (Eds.), *Joseph Alois Schumpeter. The European Heritage in Economics and the Social Sciences*, vol. 1. Boston, MA: Springer.

Setbon, M., Raude, J., Fischler, C., & Flahault, A. (2005). Risk perception of the "mad cow disease" in France: Determinants and consequences. *Risk Analysis*, *25*, 813–826.

Verbeke, W., Rutsaert, P., Bonne, K., & Vermeir, I. (2013). Credence quality coordination and consumers' willingness-to-pay for certified halal labelled meat. *Meat Science*, *95*(4), 790–797.

Wang, Y., Singgih, M., Wang, J., & Rit, M. (2019). Making sense of blockchain technology: How will it transform supply chains? *International Journal of Production Economics*, *211*, 221–236.

Werbach, K. (2018). *The blockchain and the new architecture of trust (information policy)*. Cambridge, MA: The MIT Press.

Wolfert, S., Ge, L., Verdouw, C., & Bogaardt, M. J. (2017). Big data in smart farming—A review. *Agricultural Systems*, *153*, 69–80.

Yee, W. M. S., Yeung, R. M. W., & Morris, J. (2005). Food safety: Building consumer trust in livestock farmers for potential purchase behaviour. *British Food Journal*, *107*(11), 841–854.

Zambon, I., Cecchini, M., Egidi, G., Saporito, M.G., & Colantoni, A. (2019). Revolution 4.0: Industry vs. agriculture in a future development for SMEs. *Processes*, *7*, 36.

15 The Role of Digital Technologies in Building Trust in Agriculture

Henryk Runowski[1]
Warsaw University of Life Sciences

Introduction

Trust is a fundamental social life component (Sztompka, 2002, 2007; Domański, 2009). It is an informal norm that allows for reducing transaction costs, that is, the prices of control and contract processing, without the need to employ legal procedures (Mularska-Kucharek, 2011). Trust increases the sense of security and comfort of life, not only in social life but also in economic life and in agriculture. Agriculture plays a leading role in providing food security for society, which translates into a state where all people have access to safe and valuable food. Its importance raises concerning the growing world population and increasing income of the population, which results in increasing demand for food, both on local and global scales. The global balance of food demand indicates the need to increase agricultural and food production (Wicki, 2010; Szczepaniak, 2017). However, the situation in this matter varies globally. Some continents record food overproduction, whereas others suffer noticeable food shortages (Herausforderungen, 2015). This implies the necessity of transporting food, often over long distances. It includes the need for multiple transshipments of agricultural stock and food products, and consequently, the extension of logistic chains. This does not promote food safety. Food safety is the set of required conditions and actions that have to be taken during all stages of the food production and trading processes to ensure consumer life and health safety.

In pursuit of increasing food production and improving economic effectiveness in agriculture, new, more efficient production methods have been sought that raise consumer doubts and concerns. They correspond to the emergence of new problems and threats, especially of environmental and health nature, but also of ethical nature, that relate to the development of new agricultural production technologies and the ongoing intensification processes (Runowski, 2004; Majewski, 2008). Climate changes, environmental degradation, growing competition for land and water from the side of non-agricultural sectors, long-term increases in prices of energy and other industrial inputs, as well as high cost of

DOI: 10.4324/9781003165965-15

implementing innovation, or occasional climatic disasters and livestock diseases increase risk and uncertainty in agricultural production and food trading. The consequence of those phenomena are problems related to keeping consumer trust in agriculture and food, as well as the trust of agriculture producers in various surrounding stakeholders. Given the existing development conditions, it becomes necessary to look for ways of enhancing consumer trust in farmers and food producers, as well as farmer trust in entrepreneurs and surrounding institutions, or mutual trust within the group of agricultural producers. The level of trust in a product depends considerably on the available information on its production method and origin, the possibility to track the path that a given product traveled from the producer to the consumer, and whether it is branded or not. The collection of such knowledge was relatively easy in traditional, short, and direct supply chains, where the consumer was purchasing food products directly from the producer. As supply chains extended, it became more difficult to get this information. Only the development of digital technologies allows providing the consumer with numerous important information on the product, methods of its production, and about what happened to the product before it was delivered to the final consumer from the producer. The development of digital technologies also allows for better and faster communication of agricultural producers and agribusiness surroundings entities, which facilitates building trust between the transaction participants and gives them mutual benefits.

The purpose of this study is to indicate the possibilities of improving trust levels in agriculture by the implementation and use of digital technologies in agriculture and food chains.

The chapter introduces the concept and importance of trust in agriculture and presents research on overall trust in agriculture and consumer trust in agriculture and food products. It characterizes digital technologies, their types, and directions of application in agriculture, and indicates the limitations and benefits of using digital technologies, including building trust in agricultural and food sectors.

Concept and Importance of Trust in Agriculture and the Food Sector

Trust is understood as a factor that significantly affects an organization's success, especially in the conditions of a rapidly changing environment (Paliszkiewicz, 2012). Some authors (Badaracco, 1991; Bennett, 1996) consider trust as the key factor of a relationship and the expectation that the partners can be relied upon to meet their obligations in a predictable manner and to act honestly when given various opportunities. Such acceptance of others' existence and ruling out any hostile actions on their part is a critical success factor in most relationships in business and between employees (Lewicki & Bunker, 1996).

Trust stimulates learning processes by generating social bonds that become informal communication channels, expanding the scope of perceived responsibility, or expanding the area of potential learning opportunities (Paliszkiewicz, 2014). It is especially needed in conditions of uncertainty and complex environment. Trust affects knowledge management and supports learning, creativity, and innovation (Yilmaz & Atalay, 2009). Employees tend to work more willingly in teams in an atmosphere of trust. It promotes the free flow of information. Trust is extremely important for establishing cooperation both within an organization and among market partners. Trust is the belief that the other party will not act against the organization, act in a way that gives it benefits, be reliable, and behave in a predictable and generally acceptable manner (Paliszkiewicz, 2012).

Trust helps people to overcome the uncertainty gap in relation to other people, organizations, or brands; thus, it is necessary to build lasting trust (Breunig & Ermann, 2017). Digital technologies can be used for this purpose.

Trust is assigned with a measurable economic value (Rudzewicz, 2017). Trust is also the key to motivating people, mobilizing them to work and achieve common goals (Rudzewicz, 2017).

Trust in broadly understood interpersonal and economic relations in agriculture and the entire food sector is becoming more and more important. The increasing awareness of today's consumers in the areas of production methods, food quality and safety, ethics of food producers' behavior requires building mutual trust. It is essential in the conditions of increasing competition and the pursuit of profit, where behavior non-compliant with applicable moral and ethical norms or trading principles cannot be ruled out. The lack of trust raises suspicions, annihilates enthusiasm and a positive attitude (Grudzewski et al., 2007), and reduces the willingness to share experience and knowledge that is so much needed (Paliszkiewicz, 2013). The lack of trust makes people overly cautious and consequently less creative. On the other hand, the existing trust builds a company's reputation, improves the atmosphere in an organization, and gives it a competitive advantage. A higher level of trust promotes innovation and increases the level of customer satisfaction. It is especially significant in relation to food products.

Trust represents the intangible value of a given company. It is one of the major factors that ensure the company's development. It also allows controlling hidden knowledge that cannot be controlled with formal mechanisms. It activates the learning process by establishing social relationships with the use of various communication channels (Paliszkiewicz, 2012). Agriculture and the food sector find it important to maintain consumer trust in the origin, quality, and safety of agriculture and food products.

Trust in Agriculture and Food Products

Research indicates that the level of trust in certain types of food in Poland is moderate (Maciejewski, 2020). Surveyed customers place the greatest trust in organic products (trusted by 46% of respondents) and functional food products (almost 43%) of all food types analyzed. A statistically significant relation was observed between trust in new types of food products and the interest in purchasing them. Thus, the great trust in agriculture can be considered not only in psychological but also in economic terms. Research indicates that consumers not only purchase products they trust more willingly but are also ready to pay more for those products. Research conducted as a part of the project "Changes in food consumption models in Poland" reveals that consumers expect the food sector entities to offer a complete overview of information on products and their supply chains. They want to know about what they eat (Macready et al., 2020). The ability to build relations with consumers is crucial in the process of increasing trust in the food sector. Respondents, in general, demonstrated a positive attitude towards marketing activities in the form of advertising and the participation of socially recognized persons in the promotion of products, considering those activities helpful in choosing products. However, some respondents criticized such practices, finding them unreliable. The respondents also negatively evaluated those forms of relationship building that provided unilateral benefits to producers and advertising companies. Research indicates that emerging temporary crises, as well as revealed reprehensive trading practices, threaten the level of trust (Maciejewski, 2020). Research confirms that the issue of trusting in products to be of high quality and safe for health becomes up-to-date and relevant. The use of digital technologies can facilitate the building of trust, as confirmed by other research.

Research conducted by DNV GL indicates that ensuring food safety is more important (89% of respondents) than environmental protection issues (Raport z badania..., 2020). Health issues are of comparable importance (83% of respondents). Care for the environment (38%) and social aspects indicated by every third respondent (35%) were ranked lower. Furthermore, food safety, marked by 55% of respondents, was found more important than such problems as environmental protection (38% of respondents) or broadly understood social aspects (35%). There was a surprisingly low assessment of such activities as reducing greenhouse gas emissions (10% of respondents), respecting human rights (13% of respondents), and ensuring animal welfare (16% of respondents). This may be explained by the fact that the sample included respondents from all over the world, where there are still areas of hunger and malnutrition. Research also proves that trust in "unbranded" food is lower (69% of respondents) than in "branded" food (85% of respondents).

Two-thirds of consumers in Germany expressed a positive attitude towards German agriculture. Good quality and safety of products are highly appreciated. Only 6,5% of respondents said a negative opinion on domestic agriculture, bringing up such arguments as low production and supply of organic food, low quality, and occasionally emerging food scandals.

Research conducted in the European Union as part of the 2020 Eurobarometer indicates that Poles demonstrate less interest in food safety (33% of respondents) than the EU average (41% of respondents). Moreover, the greatest interest in food safety was declared by respondents over 20 years of age and respondents from the middle and upper-income classes. In the EU they were 45% and 51% of respondents, respectively, whereas in Poland, 37% and 43%. Interestingly, only 19% of respondents from the upper class in Poland pay attention to food safety, whereas the EU average is 41%. Food origin is important for 53% of consumers in the EU and 43% of consumers in Poland. The most important thing for Polish consumers was the product taste – 58% of respondents, compared to 49% of the EU consumers, as well as the product price, 53% of respondents in Poland and 51% of respondents in the EU, respectively (Eurobarometer 2020).

The main sources of information on products and their safety for respondents across the EU are TV and the Internet. Poland does not differ from the EU statistics in this respect. Those sources are indicated by 70% of the EU respondents and 46% of respondents from Poland, respectively. Newspapers and magazines are of less importance in Poland (23% compared to 38% in the EU). The source of knowledge obtained from a specialist (e.g., a doctor or a dietitian) is indicated by 11% and 18% of respondents, respectively, and from trade magazines by 7% and 12%, respectively. Information heard or read on the threat related to food permanently changes the consumption behavior of 33% of the EU respondents and 22% of Polish respondents. Polish consumers also demonstrate a greater tendency for temporary rather than permanent changes in their consumption behavior.

Information on food safety is often very complicated and technical for 31% of Poles and 36% of Europeans. Its complexity decreases trust in the source of information for 29% of Poles and 23% of the EU-28 citizens. The major concern for consumers is food safety (Eurobarometer 2020).

The data in Table 15.1 shows that, in the opinion of 43% of respondents in the EU and 34% in Poland, there are regulations in force ensuring that the available food is safe for health.

Forty-three percent and 52% of respondents, respectively, believe that food contains a lot of harmful substances. According to 29% of the EU respondents and 23%, respondents from Poland, domestic, and the EU institutions protect against food-related threats. Expert scientific advice on food safety is referred to by 28% of respondents in the EU and 15% in Poland. Only 21% of respondents in the EU and 14% in Poland believe that advice is independent of commercial and political interests.

Table 15.1 Results of the Consumer Research on the Perception of Food Product Safety (% of Respondents Confirming a Given Statement)

No.	*Description*	*Consumers in the EU*	*Consumers in Poland*
1.	There are regulations in force ensuring that the food we eat is safe	43	34
2.	Food contains plenty of harmful substances these days	43	52
3.	Institutions in our country, together with the EU, protect us against food-related threats	29	23
4.	The EU is referring to expert scientific advice in order to determine how risky it would be to eat a given product	28	15
5.	Scientific advice on food-related threats are independent of commercial and political interests	21	14
6.	There is a separate institution in the EU that issues scientific advice on food safety	19	16

Source: Own elaboration based on the 2020 Eurobarometer data.

Consumers are primarily interested in extended information on food safety and its effect on health. As indicated by the data in Table 15.2, consumer concerns on food safety mainly arise from the possible presence of harmful substances in food. This applies to the antibiotic,

Table 15.2 Results of the Consumer Research on Factors Decreasing the Safety and Quality of food products in the EU-28 and Poland (% of Respondents Confirming the Importance of a Given Factor)

No.	*Description*	*Consumers in the EU*	*Consumers in Poland*
1.	Antibiotic, hormone, and steroid residues in meat	44	49
2.	Additives such as colors, preservatives, or flavorings added to food and beverages	36	45
3.	Genetically modified ingredients in food and beverages	27	39
4.	Animal diseases	28	37
5.	Environmental contamination in fish, meat, or dairy	37	29
6.	Bacterial infection of food	30	26
7.	Pesticide residues in food	39	24
8.	Allergic reactions to food or beverages	20	18
9.	Toxins of mold fungi in crops used for the production of food or feed	11	16
10.	Crop diseases	9	14

Source: Own elaboration based on the 2020 Eurobarometer data.

hormone, and steroid residues in meat, colors, preservatives, or flavorings added to food and beverages, genetic modifications. Other concerns relate to possible animal diseases, pesticide residues, bacteria and fungi in food, or crop diseases.

The data presented in Table 15.2 indicate that the greatest concerns relate to the antibiotic, hormone, and steroid residues in food products, as confirmed by 44% of respondents in the EU and 49% of respondents in Poland. A similarly high percentage of respondents is concerned about the effects of adding preservatives to food (36% and 45%, respectively), genetic modifications (27% and 39%, respectively), as well as pesticide residues in stock and food products (39% and 24%, respectively) or resulting from animal diseases (28% of respondents in the EU and 37% of respondents in Poland, respectively).

The aforementioned research results indicate that consumers express concerns mainly about food safety. The elimination of these concerns, and thus the increasing trust in agriculture and food products, can rely on the greater use of digital technologies to monitor the production and trade of food products.

Digital Technologies in Agriculture, Their Types, Development, Benefits, and Limitations

Technologies that use digital solutions begin to play a more and more important role in monitoring production processes in agriculture. Digitization effectively supports production and information processes in this sector (Skudlarski, 2012; Areshko et al., 2013). The implementation of digital technologies in agriculture originates at the beginning of the last decade of the 20th century (Reichardt et al., 2009). The concept of precision agriculture emerged at that time. It is a management system consisting of the extensive acquisition, collection, and processing of information, including spatial information (Batte & Arnholt, 2003; Reichardt et al., 2009; Reichardt & Jürgens, 2009). At first, satellite technologies were used to support work processes in agriculture. Then, they were used for the precise dosing of fertilizers adjusted to the local soil nutrient content and nutritional needs of plants. This allowed for the limitation of mineral fertilizers use, without the reduction of crop yields and with the reduction of environmental pollution. Precision agriculture can save production resources, energy consumption, and labor. Smaller doses of pesticides and mineral fertilizers are used to bring not only economic savings but also reduce environmental pollution with industrial chemicals, which is of significant importance in ensuring food safety.

The consecutive phase of using modern technologies in agriculture should be associated with the term smart agriculture (Foray et al., 2009; Aubert et al., 2012). This concept emerged at the very beginning of the

21st century. It uses, that is, a system of sensors and computer software to examine the condition of agricultural events and possibly respond to them in real-time (Harms & Wendl, 2018; Schäffler & Harms, 2018).

The concept of digital farming, sometimes called agriculture 4.0 (Hornung & Hofmann, 2017; Runowski, 2020), was introduced in the second decade of this century. It represents such system solutions that use the Internet, machine-to-machine communication, data storage and processing in the cloud, Big Data analysis, artificial intelligence, and robotics-related both to stationary and mobile devices. It allows the farmer to collect a lot of information, as well as to react faster and more accurately to the events that require intervention. The use of a large number of observations collected over the long term promotes more accurate economic and marketing decisions. Those decisions allow for a specific situation and location of production (Eckert, 2013; Horstmann, 2014). However, the implementation of the above concept requires the provision of adequate infrastructure and architecture of this system (Dressler et al., 2015; Westerkamp, 2015). It consists of, that is, such components as: the Internet of Things (IoT), Cloud systems, Big Data and artificial intelligence, blockchain or RFID (radio-frequency identification).

The Internet of Things corresponds to the complete set of technologies that use the Internet to collect and exchange data in order to analyze it and then use the analysis results for making decisions and controlling machines (Matern & Flörkemeier, 2015). Cloud systems can be listed among other components (Fischer, 2013). Modern agriculture requires the collection of a massive amount of information. It relates not only to the production sphere but also other areas of the farm's operation. It is necessary to create and process a large amount of information in each of those spheres (Eberspraecher & Wohlmuth, 2013). The elimination of the existing information gaps, as well as the information asymmetry, ultimately serves to build consumer trust in farmers and agriculture and farmer trust in other surrounding stakeholders.

Components of digital farming also include Big Data and artificial intelligence. Big Data represents information collections of high volume, great variability, and great variety that require new forms of fast processing in order to support decision-making, discover new phenomena and optimize processes. Another element, business intelligence, is a process of transforming data into information and information into knowledge, which is ensured by analyses and transformations in real-time, providing necessary information and knowledge to the company and surrounding stakeholders, including consumers (Dygaszewicz, 2014). Another component of digital farming is the blockchain system (Linsner et al., 2019). It is a decentralized and distributed database in the open-source model on the Internet without central servers and central data storage. The documentation range includes, that is, records of fertilizer and plant protection product use, records of livestock, data on microclimate in livestock housing, its health conditions, as well as collecting and processing data on accounting records. Solutions based on blockchain technology allow companies to track and share the actual story of the products they offer. The QR code printed on the label grants immediate access to the product characteristics. The consumer can learn, for example, the evidence of the safety, origin, and authenticity of food, which makes its history transparent and promotes consumer trust in the product.

This implies that digital farming can use various components of the system. Each of them is associated with certain possibilities and barriers. Similarly, the entire system of digital farming has its advantages and disadvantages. Digitization can provide agriculture with the development of intelligent farming, allowing to optimize resource use, improve the operation of the food chain, reach new markets, etc. The digital revolution in agriculture brings about expectations related to the need to increase global food production and to growing consumer requirements regarding not only products but also the methods of production. Representative research conducted in 2020 in Germany by Bitkom Research on the group of 1005 people revealed that two-thirds of consumers aged 16 and over expect extended contact with farmers via digital technologies, including the possibility to track the camera feed of livestock housings and fields (Bitkom Resaearch, 2020). As many as 92% of respondents expect that animal breeding and husbandry, in particular, will provide greater transparency using digital technologies. Almost 84% of respondents are interested in the production cycle course and elements, including, for example, information on the origin and composition of livestock feed. Two-thirds of the respondents declare that farmers should use digital technologies to a greater extent than before in order to make it easier for consumers to observe their work, treatments, and livestock keeping. About half of respondents (43%) expect the possibility to visit farm webpages. Every third respondent is interested in tracking production processes in agriculture via social media (Facebook, LinkedIn, Instagram, etc.). However, only 6% of consumers confirmed they used that opportunity in the past. Every third respondent declared an interest in watching the Internet camera feed of livestock housings, production hall,s, and farmlands. However, only 2% of respondents confirmed they used this form of visiting a farm. The communication between producers and consumers is of great importance in building trust. The need to talk to farmers and producers was postulated by 25% of respondents. This research indicates that societies with a higher level of development experience an increase in the interest in agriculture production methods, whereas digital technologies are perceived as a chance to facilitate the tracking of production processes in agriculture.

Research conducted by DNV GL indicates that customers consider digital technologies, such as QR codes that provide the product history, useful in building trust. Consumers are willing, that is, to pay a higher price for products they trust. Solutions based on blockchain technology help track and share the entire knowledge and history of a product, whereas QR code printed on the label grants quick access to product characteristics. Therefore, the customer is able to learn the evidence of product origin and authenticity, its safety, and, consequently, develop greater trust in the product.

However, the above expectations become a reality only if farmers are ready to share their data with other stakeholders. Studies conducted in Australia, Europe, and North America suggest that farmers are not always open to using digital technologies (Fleming et al., 2018; Jakku et al., 2019; Regan, 2019). The reason is they do not trust other farming, processing, or trading enterprises. They fear that their data can be used to build competitive advantages by those enterprises.

Given the absence of clear and adequate ways of dealing with ethical, legal, and social consequences of digital technologies in agriculture for farming enterprises and relationships, the stakeholders (farmers, farmer organizations, and enterprises, that manufacture or provide digital technologies for agriculture as well as individual countries and their associations) started to develop their guidelines, in order to systemize practices of data management in agriculture and provide a foundation for trust. The privacy and security policies in agriculture as well as data codes of conduct have been developed in various regions of the world. Legislators in Australia, New Zealand, North America, and Europe have only recently started to recognize problems related to managing data collected on farms (Wiseman et al., 2018). First of all, the problem concerns the protection of privacy, therefore the farmers want to control data, including information on their farms (Sykuta, 2016). On the other hand, there are some doubts about who is the owner of the data and who is entitled to use it for commercial purposes (Kshetri, 2014; Rasmussen, 2016; Schuster, 2017). Other concerns of the farmers relate to sharing their data with the authorities. All the earlier issues raise questions about the fair distribution of benefits and responsibilities in a given network (Kshetri, 2014; Jakku et al., 2017; Rodriguez et al., 2017; Wolfert et al., 2017). Similar principles were developed in the European Union. The EU code of conduct is based on the belief that the greater transparency of the conditions for data access and use will make the farmers trust the method of managing their data. Trust relationships in digital farming are not unambiguous. In many contexts, digital technologies fundamentally affect changes in the social network surrounding the farm (Wolfert et al., 2017). Trust in digital technology is more likely to be established if it is introduced in association with previous relations and cooperation or if the ones that implement digital technology devote time and effort to build trusted social relationships before introducing their technologies. The main purpose of agriculture data exchange principles and codes of conduct developed in this regard is to build trust between farmers and farming enterprises and other data recipients as well as to build consumer trust in agriculture and the food sector.

Conclusions

Due to the ongoing demographic development and increasing income of the population, there is also a growth in global demand for food. New, more efficient, and science-based technologies have been introduced in order to ensure the production increase in agriculture and the entire food sector. So far, their implementation has employed a wide use of industrial means of production, genetic engineering, and new technology. This direction of development raises consumer concerns related to food safety, quality of agriculture and food products, as well as the condition of the environment or livestock welfare. The path of food products, from the producer to the consumer, was relatively short in traditional agriculture. Nowadays, the supply chains are long. This situation does not favor the building of consumer trust in agriculture and food products, as well as farmers' trust in their surrounding stakeholders. This study indicates the possibilities to increase trust in agriculture and the food sector using digital technologies. Digital technologies offer a wide range of opportunities for perfecting production processes in agriculture, improving their effectiveness, learning the product sources by consumers, tracking the product path, learning product composition, and quality and safety characteristics. The use of digital technologies in agriculture allows for the establishment of more transparent relationships between agriculture producers and agricultural stakeholders. Consequently, the use of digital technologies can promote building trust in agriculture and the food sector. Trust is a fundamental component of social life. It is an informal norm that allows for reducing transaction costs, that is, the costs of control, contract drafting, and processing, dispute settling, without the need to employ legal procedures. Trust facilitates cooperation, strengthens the sense of security and comfort of not only social but also economic life. While accepting the positive aspects of digital technologies development in agriculture, it is worth noticing farmers' concerns about this process. Those concerns are associated with privacy protection and the use of massive data sets they share for purposes incompatible with their economic interest. Some institutional principles for data and its protection, including privacy protection and data protection in agriculture, and data codes of conduct have been developed to prevent those threats. Those activities have also been undertaken in the EU.

This study explains the nature and importance of trust in agriculture and the food sector, based on the literature, presents selected results of the research in this area, and summarizes opportunities and limitations of digital technologies used in the process of building trust. This is of great importance both for theory and practice, as the problem is up-to-date and relatively unexplored. This study may serve as an inspiration for future research in this area and contribute to a wider interest in using digital technologies in agriculture by agriculture producers and agriculture and the food industry stakeholders. Due to the crucial role of the issue, it is important to undertake further research on the possibilities to use digital technologies in building trust in agriculture, which is fundamental for the improvement of agriculture and food producer perception by consumers as well as for the assurance of food safety.

References

Areshko, D. M., Izdebski, W., Sajganov, A. S., Skudlarski, J., & Zając, S. (2013). Application of modern satellite technology in management of work of machinery park and quality of production in agricultural farms. Doklady Miezdunarodnoj nauchno-prakticheskoj konferencji Pererabotka i upravlenije kachestvom selkohozjastvennoj produkcji Białoruski Uniwersytet Techniczno-Rolniczy. Minsk, Białoruś, 21-22 marca 2013, section 4, pp. 303–305.

Aubert, B. A., Schroeder, A., & Grimaudo, J. (2012). IT as enabler of sustainable farming. An empirical analysis of farmers' adoption decision of precision agriculture technology. *Decision Support Systems*, *54*, 510–520.

Badaracco, J. L. (1991). *The knowledge link: How firms compete through strategic alliances*. Boston, MA: Harvard Business School Press.

Batte, M. T., & Arnholt, M. W. (2003). Precision farming adoption and use in Ohio. Case studies of six leading-edge adopters. *Computers and Electronics in Agriculture*, *38*, 125–139.

Bennett, J. L. (1996). Building relationships for technology transfer. *Communications of the ACM*, *39*(9), 35–36.

Bitcom Research. (2020). Vertrauen & IT-Sicherheit 2020. Retrieved form https://www.bitkom-research.de/de.

Breunig, P., & Ermann M. (2017). Digitalisierung als Vertrauensmaschine"? Retrieved form https://www.topagrar.com/panorama/news/digitalisierung-als-vertrauensmaschine-11893163.html.

Domański, H. (2009). *Społeczeństwa europejskie. Stratyfikacja i systemy wartości. [European societies. Stratification and value systems]*. Warsaw, PL: Wydawnictwo Naukowe Scholar.

Dressler, N., Gundermann, S., Keese, S., Aulbur, W., Zhang, J., Amichi, S., Marinoni, A., Nagashima, S., & Cherkin, E. (2015). Business opportunities in precision farming: Will big data feed the world in the future? Roland Berger Strategy Consultants. Retrieved from https://www.rolandberger.com/publications/publication_pdf/roland_berger_business_opportunities_in_precision_farming_20150803.pdf.

Dygaszewicz, J. (2014). Big data w statystyce publicznej [Big data in public statistics]. In G. Szpor (Ed.) *Internet. Publiczne bazy danych i big data* (pp. 49–62). Warsaw, PL: C.H. Beck.

Eberspächer, J., & Wohlmuth, O. (2013). *Big Data wird neues Wissen*. München DE: Münchner Kreis – Übernationale Vereinigung für Kommunikationsforschung e.V, 184.

Eckert, C. (2013). *IT-Sicherheit. Konzepte – Verfahren – Protokolle*. München, GE: Oldenbourg.

EUROBAROMETR (2020). *Eurobarometr*. Retrieved from https://www.efsa.europa.eu/sites/default/files/corporate_publications/files/eurobarometer19/country-factsheets/EB91.3_EFSA_fact_pl_pl.pdf.

Fischer, B. (2013). Umowy świadczenia usług w chmurze obliczeniowej. *Gazeta MSP*, 7(135), 19–20.

Fleming, A., Jakku, E., Lim-Camacho, L., Taylor, B., & Thorburn, P. (2018). Are big datasets intended for large farms or for all farms? Perception of the Australian Grain Industry. *Agronomy for Sustainable Development*, *38*, 24–31.

Foray, D., David P. A., & Hall B. (2009). Smart specialisation – The concept. *Knowledge Economists Policy. Brief*, *9*, 1–5.

Grudzewski, W. M., Hejduk, I. K., Sankowska, A., & Wańtuchowicz, M. (2007). *Zarządzanie zaufaniem w organizacjach wirtualnych. [Trust management in virtual organizations]*. Warszawa. PL: Difin.

Harms, J., & Wendl G. (2018). Möglichkeiten der Digitalisierung nutzen: Tierhaltung Bayerische Landesanstalt für Landwirtschaft, Institut für Landtechnik und Tierhaltung. *Bayerische Landesanstalt für Landwirtschaft*. München DE: Bayerische Landesanstalt für Landwirtschaft (LfL). 57–68.

Herausforderungen. (2015). *Herausforderungen für die Landwirtschaft (2015)*. Leverkusen DE: Herausgeber Bayer AG, Communications and Public Affairs.

Hieke, S. Klimczuk-Kochańska, M., Szumiał, Sz., Vranken, L., & Grunert, K. G. (2020). Consumer trust in the food value chain and its impact on consumer confidence: A model for assessing consumer trust and evidence from a 5-country study in Europe. *Food Policy*, *92*, 1–15.

Hornung, G., & Hofmann, K. (2017). Rechtsfragen bei Industrie 4.0: Rahmenbedingungen, Herausforderungen und Lösungsansätze. In G. Reinhart (Ed.), München DE: Handbuch Industrie 4.0 – Geschäftsmodelle, Prozesse, Technik.

Horstmann, J. (2014). Moderne Kommunikationssysteme in der Landtechnik. In L. Frerichs (Ed.), *Jahrbuch Agrartechnik 2015* (pp. 1–7). Braunschweig GE: Institut für mobile Maschinen und Nutzfahrzeuge.

Jakku, E., Taylor, B., Fleming, A., Mason, C., Fielke, S., Sounness, C., Thorburn, P. et al. (2019). If they don't tell us what they're doing with it, why should we trust them? Trust, transparency and benefit sharing in smart farming. *NJAS Wageningen, Journal of Life Sciences*. Volumes 90-91. 10.1016/j.njas.2018.11.002

Kshetri, N. (2014). The emerging role of big data on key development issues: opportunities, challenges and concerns. *Big Data & Society*, *1*, 1–20.

Lewicki, R. J., & Bunker, B. B. (1996). Developing and maintaining trust in work relationships. In R. M. Kramer, & T. R. Tyler (Eds.), *Trust in organizations: Frontiers of theory and research* (pp. 114–139). New York, NY: Sage Publications.

Linsner, S., Kuntke F., Schmidbauer-Wolf G. M. Reuter Ch. (2019). Blockchain in agriculture 4.0 – An empirical study on farmers expectations towards distributed services based on distributed ledger technology proceedings of mensch. Technische Universität Darmstadt – PEASEC (Wissenschaft und Technik für Frieden und Sicherheit). Retrieved from https://dl.acm.org/doi/pdf/10.1145/3340764.3340799.

Maciejewski, G. (2020). Zaufanie konsumentów do nowych rodzajów żywności [Consumer confidence in new types of food]. In A. Dąbrowska (Ed.), *Bezpieczeństwo konsumentów (na rynku żywności)*, (pp. 143–155). Warsaw, PL: Oficyna Wydawnicza SGH w Warszawie.
Macready, A. L. Retrieved from https://www.sciencedirect.com/science/article/pii/S0306919220300828 -!.
Majewski, E. (2008). *Trwały rozwój i trwałe rolnictwo: Teoria a praktyka gospodarstw rolniczych. [Sustainable development and sustainable agriculture: Theory and practice of farms]*. Warsaw, PL: Wydawnictwo SGGW.
Matern, F., & Flörkemeier, C. (2015). Vom internet der computer zum internet der dinge. *Informatik Spektrum*, 33(2), 107–121.
Mularska-Kucharek, M. (2011). Zaufanie jako fundament życia społecznego na przykładzie badań w województwie łódzkim [Trust as the foundation of social life on the example of research in the Łódź Province]. *Studia Regionalne i Lokalne*, *2*(44), 76–91.
Paliszkiewicz, J. (2012). Zaufanie a zarządzanie wiedzą – przegląd literatury. Retrieved from http://ptzp.org.pl/files/konferencje/kzz/artyk_pdf_2012/p050.pdf.
Paliszkiewicz, J. (2014). Rola zaufania w zarządzaniu przedsiębiorstwami. Retrieved from http://www.ptzp.org.pl/files/konferencje/kzz/artyk_pdf_2014/T1/t1_409.pdf.
Paliszkiewicz, J. O. (2013). *Zaufanie w zarządzaniu. [Trust in management]*. Warszawa, PL: Wydawnictwo Naukowe PWN.
Raport z badania wykonanego na próbie 4500 mieszkańcach świata. (2020). Retrieved from https://www.dnvgl.pl/assurance/viewpoint/viewpoint-surveys/2020Q2/podsumowanie.html.
Rasmussen, N. (2016). From precision farming to market manipulation: The new frontier in the legal community. *Minnesota Journal of Law, Science & Technology*, *17*, 489–516.
Regan, Á. (2019). Ireland's smart farming: Risk perception study with key government actors. *NJAS-Wageningen Journal of Life Sciences*, *90*, 100292.
Reichardt, M. Jürgens, C., Kloble U., Hüter J., & Moser, K. (2009). *Dissemination of precision farming in Germany. Acceptance, adoption, obstacles, knowledge transfer and training activities*. In *Precision Agriculture*. JRC Scientific and Technical Reports. Brussell, BE: European Commission.
Reichardt, M., & Jürgens, C. (2009). Adoption and future perspective of precision farming in Ger-many. Results of several surveys among different agricultural target groups. *Precision Agriculture*, *10*, 73–94.
Rodriguez, D., de Voil, P., Rufino, M. C., Odendo, M., & van Wijk, M. T. (2017). To much or crunch? Large big data modeling. *Agricultural Systems*, *153*, 32–42.
Rudzewicz, A. (2017). Zaufanie w przedsiębiorstwie – znaczenie i pomiar. [Trust in the enterprise – Meaning and measuremen]. *Zarządzanie i Finanse. Journal of Management and Finance*, *15*(2/1), 291–304.
Runowski, H. (2004). Gospodarstwo ekologiczne w zrównoważonym rozwoju rolnictwa i obszarów wiejskich. *Wieś i Rolnictwo*, *3*(124), 25–28.
Runowski, H. (2020). Digitalization in agriculture – Development opportunities and barriers. In J. Paliszkiewicz (Ed.), *Management and information technology: New challenges* (pp. 233–246). Warsaw, PL: Warsaw University of Life Sciences Press.

Schäffler, M., & Harms, J. (2018). Möglichkeiten der Digitalisierung nutzen: Futter und Fütterung/Tierhaltung. In *Tagungsband Nutztierhaltung – Basis der Land-wirtschaft in Bayern, vom 5.7.2018* (pp. 90–93). München DE: Schriftenreihe der Bayerischen Landesanstalt für Landwirtschaf LfL.

Schuster, J. (2017). Big data ethics and the digital age of agriculture. *Resource, 24*(1), 20–21.

Skudlarski, J. (2012). Smart farming, czyli inteligentne rolnictwo. *Agromechanika, 12*, 14–17.

Sykuta, M. (2016). Big data in agriculture: Privacy, property rights and competition in ag Data Services. *International Food and Agribusiness Management Review, 19*, 57–74.

Szczepaniak, I. (red.) (2017). *Konkurencyjność polskich producentów żywności i jej detrminanty [Competitiveness of Polish food producers and its detrminants]*. Instytut Ekonomiki Rolnictwa i Gospodarki Żywnościowej, Warsaw, PL: Państwowy Instytut Badawczy.

Sztompka, P. (2002). *Socjologia. Analiza społeczeństwa. [Sociology. Society analysis]* Kraków, PL: Znak.

Sztompka, P. (2007). *Zaufanie. Fundament społeczeństwa. [Trust. The foundation of society.]*. Kraków: Znak.

The Federation of the American Farm Bureau (2019). *Farm data privacy and security issues, century*. Retrieved from https://www.fb.org/issues/technology/data-privacy/privacy-and-security-principles-for-farm-data.

Westerkamp, C. (2015). Wie verändern digitale Plattformen die Landwirtschaft? In A. Baums, M..Schössler, & B. Scott (Eds.), *Kompendium Industrie 4.0. Wie digitale Plattformen die Wirtschaft verändern – und wie die Politik gestalten kann* (pp. 66–71). Berlin, GE: Stiftung neue Verantwortung e.V.

Wicki, L. (2010). *Efekty upowszechniania postępu biologicznego w produkcji roślinnej. [Effects of disseminating biological progress in plant production]*. Warszawa, PL: Wydawnictwo SGGW.

Wiseman, L., Sanderson, J., & Lachlan Robb, L. (2018). A new approach to ag data ownership. *Farm Policy Journal, 15*(1), 71–77.

Wolfert, S., Ge, L., Verdouw, C., & Bogaardt, M. J. (2017). Big data w inteligentnym rolnictwie – Przegląd. *Agricultural Systems, 153*, 69–80.

Yilmaz, A., & Atalay, C. G. (2009). A theoretical analyze on the concept of trust in organizational life. *European Journal of Social Sciences, 8*(2), 342.

16 Influence of Trust Level on Insurance Decisions of Farmers

Adam Wąs, Ludwik Wicki, and Piotr Sulewski

Warsaw University of Life Sciences

Introduction

Trust is a crucial constituent of all human relationships (Das & Teng, 2004) and an essential determinant of society's economic success and security (Sztompka, 1999; Glaeser et al., 2000). The concept of trust is not entirely clear and can be understood in three different ways: as a perception ("subjective trust"), as various personal and situational factors that lead to subjective trust ("trust antecedents"), and as the actions resulting from a subjective trust ("behavioral trust") (Das & Teng, 2004). Paliszkiewicz (2013) underlines that trust is a belief that the other party will not act against us, will be reliable, and will act predictably and in a manner beneficial for us. In economic relations, trust is the basis of all transactions, and its lack leads to an increase in transaction costs (Dasgupta, 2000; Dyer & Chu, 2003).

Bauer and Freitag (2017) underline that trust means a trustor's existence that trusts a trustee regarding some behavior in some context and at the specified time. This hypothetical situation can be transferred to the relationship between the insured and the insurer. When buying an insurance contract, the policyholder (insured) must trust the insurer that the latter will pay compensation in the case of a loss. Thus, the level of trust in insurance depends mainly on whether the insured can receive the compensation due, and the lower it is, the more claims are rejected (Gennaioli et al., 2020; Ngoma et al., 2018). This issue is critical in agricultural production insurance, a specific and challenging subsector of the insurance market.

The main objective of the research is to examine the determinants of farmers' trust in insurers based on previous business experiences. An attempt is also made to determine farms' characteristics, presenting different trust levels regarding insurance companies. Particular attention is paid to the role of trust in farmers' insurance decisions. The chapter consists of the following sections: literature review, description of the methodology, results of the research, and the discussion, followed by the implications and conclusions.

DOI: 10.4324/9781003165965-16

Literature Review

The specificity of farmers' lack of trust in agricultural insurance results from the nature of agricultural production, which is a risky activity, and farmers are always faced with adverse events that increase income variability both in the short term and long term (Huirne et al., 2000; Hardaker et al., 2004; Meuwissen et al., 2008). The production risk is of particular importance – the analyses carried out using the AGLINK–COSIMO model show that yield volatility is also responsible for more than half of the volatility of agricultural prices (OECD, 2011).

Due to the ongoing climate changes, the importance of production risk in agriculture has been growing recently (OECD, 2020; Olesen et al., 2011). The increasing frequency of adverse events such as droughts, hurricanes, torrential rain, hailstorms, and animal epidemics such as BSE, swine fever, or ASF (Ogurtsov, 2008; van Asseldonk et al., 2003; OECD, 2020) make skillful risk management increasingly challenging.

One of the primary methods of reducing the consequences of risk in agriculture is buying insurance. The general idea of insurance is based on von Neumann's and Morgenstern's theory of expected utility (1953), which says that a risk-averse actor is willing to reduce his expected income exchange for reducing faced risk to an acceptable level. Creation of an adequate insurance market requires to fulfill such conditions like (Hardaker et al., 2004; Rejda & McNamara, 2017):

- Existence of a sufficiently large number of homogeneous clients (insured) with independent but similar risks,
- Losses must be accidental and unintentional – unforeseeable, unexpected, and beyond the control of the insured,
- Losses must be identifiable and measurable – this applies to the cause, time, place, and amount of claim,
- Losses cannot be of a massive (systemic) nature, that is, they cannot concern too many insured persons at the same time,
- The probability of a loss must be calculable,
- The insurance premium must be economically feasible – acceptable (attractive) to buyers, and profitable for the insurance company.

Creating an effective insurance system for agricultural production is difficult due to the systemic character of risk and high information asymmetry, which leads to the phenomenon of adverse selection and moral hazard, which leads to high transaction costs (OECD, 2011; Goodwin & Smith, 2013; Stiglitz & Rosengard, 2015). To reduce the impact of adverse selection and moral hazard, insurers use exclusions of many weather risks in the policies they offer, while farmers consider them to be one of the most important. Restrictions on the insurance scope lead to a reduction of farmers' trust in the insurance offered and in insurers (Girdžiūtė, 2012; Wicka, 2018). As a result, the market mechanism is insufficient to create an effective insurance system, and public funds support the existing agricultural insurance systems (OECD, 2011; Smith & Glauber, 2012). Insurance programs, for example, in the USA, are set so that premiums are actuarially fair for farmers. However, for example, Pearcy and Smith (2015) noted that the catastrophic risk-loading factor increases the premium rate. Thus, premiums established by the Risk Management Agency, on average, overestimate the actuarially fair premiums with which most farmers usually take out insurance (Coble & Barnett, 2013). If the premium subsidy level decreases, even risk-neutral farmers may not use insurance because they consider the premium too high (Ramirez & Shonkwiler, 2017).

Two of the primary forms of agricultural insurance are Multiple Peril Crop Insurance (individual farm plans) and Index Insurance (area plans). Within these forms, one can indicate (Smith & Glauber, 2012): "Yield and Revenue Insurance"; "Weather Insurance"; "Vegetation Insurance"; "Commodity Price Insurance"; and "Livestock Margin Insurance (revenues – costs)". Generally, results show that some farmers have less trust in financial markets and choose in-farm risk management strategies (Meraner & Finger, 2019). Another issue is the low level of popularization of agricultural insurance in some countries. They are not known to farmers, which results in a low level of trust in such solutions (Ehiogu & Joseph, 2019).

Poland's agricultural insurance system has the form of Multiple Peril Yield Insurance, which was introduced in 2005 (Dz.U.Nr150.poz.1249). The critical assumption of the authorities was to make agricultural insurance a universal system. Hence, the assumption was to co-finance insurance premiums up to 50%, while the value of the premium could not exceed 6% of the insured sum (in subsequent years, these levels were increased, and currently, they are up to 65% and 9%, respectively). Selected insurance companies sign an agreement with the Ministry of Agriculture and receive co-financing contributions from the state budget. The Ministry also sets the maximum permissible levels of the insured sum. Despite the expectations, the introduction of subsidized agricultural production insurance did not result in farmers' massive participation in the insurance system. The available data show that the area of insured crops in 2009–2015 ranged from 2.8 million ha to 3.3 million ha, while the total area of arable land in Poland is nearly 14 million ha (Janowicz-Lomott & Łyskawa, 2016). This means that the share of the insured agricultural area did not exceed 23–24%. The same source shows that the number of insurance contracts in the period mentioned earlier was at the level of 140,000–150,000, while the number of commercial farms estimated by Farm Accountancy Data Network (FADN; with standard output value above EUR 4,000) was at the level of over 700,000 farms. The FADN data show that the share of farms paying premiums for crop insurance is on average at the level of about 21% and is strongly depends on the area of the farm – in the smallest farms (<5ha), it is only about 2%, while in the largest farms (>50 ha) around 40%. In this context, it should be emphasized that, according to the assumptions of the Act (Agricultural Insurance Act, 2005), farmers receiving direct payments under the Common Agricultural Policy of the EU are obliged to buy insurance for more than half of the sown area, although sanctions for noncompliance with this provision are somewhat symbolic [2 EUR/ha].

Methodology

Trust is a latent variable characterized by subjective and context-specific nature, and thus "trust measurement" is a challenging task (Bauer & Freitag, 2017). Bauer (2015) underlines that "trust measurement" can be seen as a topic of its own. However, we can generally indicate two approaches to measuring trust, that is, a direct approach based on asking people directly (self-report measures) or indirect measures based on observation of people's behavior (behavioral measures). The classic self-report measures refer to various forms of the question frequently used in sociological questionnaires, which sounds, "Generally speaking, would you say that most people can be trusted, or that you can't be too careful in dealing with people?". In contrast, behavioral measures are based on lab behavioral experiments or hypothetical games (such as the prisoner's dilemma) (Bauer, 2015). Glaeser et al. (2000) revealed that experiments could be integrated with surveys to measure individual-level variation in hard-to-measure characteristics such as trust and trustworthiness.

The study uses data from interviews with a representative sample of 600 farmers, drawn from the Polish commercial farmers' population in 2017, using the Neyman optimal allocation scheme and multiannual financial data form FADN. Based on the interview, the level of farmers' trust in insurance companies is estimated and compared with their purchasing production insurances. During interviews, farmers were asked questions about their experiences and opinions on using crop and animal insurances. Based on the answers, the trust level in the insurance companies has been assessed. Additionally, based on the methodology developed by Kobus (2019) based on the work of Eckel and Grossman (2008) and Dohmen et al. (2011), the farmers' risk aversion was estimated. The stepwise logistic regression was used to examine the determinants of trust in buying insurance(s). The optimal model was estimated using the Akaike information criterion (AIC) (Akaike, 1974). The goodness of model fit was assessed using McFadden's (1973) and McKelvey and Zavoina (1975) corrected R^2 measure.

In the research, it was assumed that trust in insurance companies is reflected by the decision to join the insurance system. This assumption results from the fact that trust is not only a belief or a conviction, but it also involves taking action and risk – by trusting someone without even a guarantee that it will be successful (Sztompka, 2007; Marzec, 2017). In this approach, we can assess the level of trust based on the actual actions/behavior of decision-makers, which eliminates the problem of subjectivity of assessments characteristic of self-report measures and reflects trust situations in real life (Bauer & Freitag, 2017).

Results

The characteristics of the analyzed sample, taking into account the essential variables related to confidence in agricultural insurance, are presented in Table 16.1. The farmers' description is presented in groups specified by economic size, attitude toward risk, farming experience, and farm production type. On average, less than half of the respondents insured their crops in the year preceding the research, suggesting a relatively low trust level in the insurance system. It can also be noticed that a higher percentage of farmers using insurance was observed in the group of the economically largest farms. However, no statistically significant differences were observed in insured farms' rates between farmers with different risk aversion levels.

Similarly, experience in running a farm measured by the number of years did not turn out to be a feature that differed significantly between farmers in using insurance. There were, however, apparent differences in the percentage of the insured between production types. Agricultural insurances were often used in pig farms, which usually produce cereals for feed (which are relatively easy to insure). On the other hand, insurance was used least frequently in cattle farms, which devote most of the sown area to nonmarketable crops, such as grasses, which in practice are not covered by insurance. Insurance was also rarely used in mixed farms, probably due to its diversified production structure and thus lower exposure to income risk. It can be also noticed that farmers who reported a loss in the previous 5 years more often participated in insurance (89%). Similarly, farmers who received public compensation for damage used insurance quite often (64%). We can observe a logical relationship that relatively few farmers used insurance among respondents declaring problems with obtaining compensation (only 21% of respondents) or indicating incomprehensible procedures by insurers (only 16% of respondents in this group used insurance). It was also observed that the variables related to the development of confidence in insurance significantly differ, mainly if the groups were divided by farm economic size and farm production type. The exception is the experience of underestimating claim value and the experience of severe damage. Farmers with strong risk aversion were more vulnerable in this context.

Table 16.1 Characteristics of the Analyzed Farm Population

Specification		Total	Economic Size				Risk Aversion				Experience in Farm Management			Production Type				
			Small	Medium	Big	p-Value*	Netural to Risk	Risk Averse	Strong Risk Averse	p-Value*	Low	High (> 10 Years)	p-Value*	Cattle	Crop	Mixed	Pig	p-Value*
		% of Farms																
Farmers experience	Share of farms	100	51	40	9	–	23	53	24	0	18	82	0	24	42	28	6	100
	Using agri- insurance	48	36	59	71	0	43	50	48	0.3839	52	47	0.3964	37	51	46	82	0
	Damage has occurred within 5 years	89	86	91	96	0.0382	86	92	87	0.0542	86	90	0.2642	90	89	88	97	0.3555
	Received public compensation for damage	64	58	70	68	0.0151	62	65	64	0.8662	66	63	0.5677	76	57	63	71	0.0009
	Received insurance compensation	28	22	32	39	0.004	23	30	27	0.3141	33	27	0.205	17	33	28	34	0.004
	Experienced difficulties or too low insurance compensation	21	15	29	21	0.0007	17	20	27	0.1493	19	22	0.5554	16	24	19	32	0.1072
Farmers opinions	Insurers use incomprehensible procedures	16	21	1	11	0.0006	14	17	14	0.5878	1	16	0.7595	13	19	13	13	0.2571
	Insurers underestimate claims	42	49	39	21	0.0002	44	36	53	0.0029	35	44	0.0733	51	41	39	32	0.0512
	Insurers hamper getting compensation	36	39	35	20	0.0206	41	33	37	0.2372	31	37	0.2655	42	33	33	37	0.2477
	Insurance compensation reduces losses	48	34	59	73	0	43	49	50	0.3629	50	48	0.6422	33	52	49	74	0
	I have experienced severe damage in the past	37	29	43	54	0.0002	28	39	41	0.047	36	37	0.8784	25	44	34	50	0.0006
	I want to fulfill the statutory obligation	36	26	44	52	0	30	38	35	0.3031	39	35	0.3838	26	36	38	53	0.0135
Farmer character-istics	Share of women	13	19	8	4	0.0001	14	13	12	0.8119	17	12	0.1587	11	17	12	0	0.0139
	At least secondary education	59	58	58	64	0.6502	68	58	50	0.01	75	55	0.0002	57	67	44	68	0
	Farmer has successor	25	29	21	16	0.0386	21	24	28	0.3988	17	26	0.0512	20	31	19	21	0.0127
	Age of farmer [years]	46.52	46.92	45.38	49.27	0.056**	44.47	46.84	47.79	0.082**	35.25	49.05	0.000**	44.76	46.06	48.1	49.47	0.025**

Source: Own elaboration. *Chi^2; **Kruskal–Wallis test.

Table 16.2 Results of the Logit Regression Model

	Estimate	*Std. Error*	*p-Value*
Intercept	−0.29772	0.76154	0.69583
I have received insurance compensation within the last 5 years	1.23836	0.41128	0.0026
Insurers use incomprehensible procedures	−1.08306	0.49966	0.03019
Insurers underestimate claims	−0.9581	0.38779	0.01348
Insurers hamper getting compensation	−0.78642	0.40167	0.05025
Insurance compensation reduces losses	2.53535	0.38176	0
I have experienced a severe loss	1.61647	0.39919	0
I want to fulfill the statutory obligation	1.19174	0.40389	0.00317
Farm type – crop production*	−0.27331	0.40805	0.503
Farm type – mixed production	−0.61296	0.44915	0.17235
Farm type – pig production	1.85346	0.70917	0.00896
Farmers age	−0.02692	0.01572	0.08682

Source: Own elaboration.
*Cattle farms are reference; McFadden R^2= 0.6634, McKelvey–Zavoina R^2 = 0.9602.

The logit regression analysis was performed to identify factors increasing/decreasing the probability of a farmer's participation in the insurance system. It was assumed that in the constructed model, participation in insurance reflects the trust in the insurance system (behavioral trust). As parameters explaining participation in the insurance system, variables illustrating farmers' experiences with insurance (subjective trust) and variables describing the type of production were used. The selection of these variables generated the best (and high) explanatory power (Table 16.2). The model results indicate that the variables related to the insurance process and obtaining compensation influence statistically significantly the behavioral dimension of trust, i.e., decisions on participation in the system. It can be observed that the probability of joining the insurance system significantly increases after receiving compensation from the insurance company in the past. Also, "farmer's belief that the insurance contributes to the reduction of losses" and "experience of losses in the past" as well "willingness to fulfill the statutory obligation to insure at least half of the area sowing" increase the probability of participation in the insurance system. The probability of participation in the insurance system is also enhanced by running a pig farm.

On the other hand, the probability of participation in the system is weakened by the farmer's opinion of "incomprehensive insurance procedures", "underestimated the claims", and the belief that insurance companies "make it difficult to receive compensation". These variables illustrate farmers' subjective distrust of insurers. The probability of participation in the system is also reduced by running farms in a mixed and crop type (what results from production characteristics).

Discussion

The conducted analyzes showed that the use of production insurance by farmers, which is a reflection of their "behavioral trust" to insurers, is determined by some variables related mainly to the subjective perception of the relationship with the insurer, which is the result of past experiences (subjective trust). It turned out that farmers who have had positive experiences with obtaining compensation more often join the system than those who have negative experiences (had problems receiving compensation in the past). Thus, obtained results are consistent with the works of other researchers who have shown that if farmers believe that they receive compensation or positive experiences receiving compensation, they were more likely to insure themselves (Gennaioli et al., 2020). Similarly to our results, other authors indicated that negative experiences with an incorrectly defined scope of risk insurance, complicated damage assessment procedures, difficulties in obtaining compensation, and incomplete coverage of damages lead to a decline in farmers' confidence in insurance, and its rebuilding requires active actions by insurers (Prabhakar et al., 2013; Olajide-Adedamola & Akinbile, 2017; Wicka, 2018; Ahmed et al., 2020). We also noticed that the rate of farmers' participation in the insurance system is varied between the farm's economic size – generally, farmers from bigger farms insure their production more often than smaller ones. Similarly, farmers in India who insured crops had higher production inputs, so they trusted that they would earn adequate income regardless of the weather (Cole et al., 2017). It should be mentioned that the level of trust in insurance may also be lowered due to the existence of so-called background risks. Farmers may be more risk-tolerant, which can lead to more cautious behavior and less confidence/trust in the insurance offered on the market (Franke et al., 2006; Harrison et al., 2007; Guiso & Paiella, 2008). Our research, however, did not show a significant relationship between the level of risk aversion and the level of trust in insurance (both in the categories of "subjective trust" and "behavior trust"). Risk aversion turns out to be a factor that significantly differentiated only the percentage of farmers convinced that "Insurers underestimate claims" and "experienced severe damage in the past" as well as farmers with at least secondary education. Generally, the literature indicates that the level of farmers' trust in the insurance also depends on the understanding of the insurance program, level of education, age and gender of the farmer, and his financial literacy (Bratt, 2003; James, 2011;Akter et al. 2016; Masara & Dube, 2017). Some authors suggest that to obtain higher confidence in insurance, insurers should develop the insurance education system, as even in developed countries, a lack of knowledge among farmers can be observed (Ramm & Steinmann, 2014; Syll & Wiengaertner, 2019).

Implications

Considering that our analyses show that the level of farmers' trust in insurance depends on their subjective experiences, insurers and regulators should ensure that the system is as transparent and straightforward as possible. However, it is worth noting that both the "behavioral trust" measured by the farmers' rate of participation in the system, and the "subjective trust", reflected in the perception of selected relationships with insurers, are strongly differentiated between the economic size and farm production type. It concludes that the production insurance system in agriculture should be more flexible and consider the specificity of various categories of farms (currently, identical rules apply to all categories of farms). Insurance companies should remember that farmers are a specific category of clients, which should be considered when preparing an insurance offer. No insurance company can probably offer insurance for all risk factors, but the offer should indicate what the farmer can insure and the terms of the contract (particularly, receiving compensation). Misunderstandings in this area (including unclear rules of compensation payment) lead to a decline in farmers' trust in insurance companies.

Conclusions

The paper provides insight into determinants of farmers' trust in insurers using quantitative analysis based on a survey performed on farmers' representative samples. The research on the role of trust in the sale of agricultural insurance conducted so far in Poland has not had such a factual basis in empirical data. The obtained results confirmed a number of the regularities indicated in the literature. One novelty is the clear indication of a negative impact on the willingness to conclude a contract due to complex legal provisions. This factor is essential for farmers who have experienced problems with the payment of compensation as a result.

A limitation of the conducted research is narrowing the studied population only to Poland, a country with a relatively fragmented agrarian structure. This limitation makes it difficult to generalize the research results, especially in countries with different farm structures.

Indication of the significance of the contract's wording as an essential factor determining success in cooperation between the farmer and the insurer provides the basis for further research to determine the shape of the contract acceptable to farmers.

References

Ahmed, S., Bangassa, K., & Akbar, S. (2020). A study on trust restoration efforts in the UK retail banking industry. *British Accounting Review*, *52*(1), 1–18.

Akaike, H. (1974). A new look at the statistical model identification. *IEEE Transactions on Automatic Control*, *19*(6), 716–723.

Akter, S., Krupnik, T. J., Rossi, F., & Khanam, F. (2016). The influence of gender and product design on farmers' preferences for weather-indexed crop insurance. *Global Environmental Change*, *38*, 217–229.

Bauer, P. C. (2015). *Three essays on the concept of trust and its foundations | Semantic Scholar* [University of Bern]. Retrieved from https://www.semanticscholar.org/paper/Three-essays-on-the-concept-of-trust-and-its-Bauer/4ae73363a36e5d4d15ef3f9b63ef4b4e605eac4c.

Bauer, P. C., & Freitag, M. (2017). Measuring trust. In *The Oxford Handbook of Social and Political Trust* (pp. 15–36). New York. NY: Oxford University Press. 10.1093/oxfordhb/9780190274801.013.1

Bratt, R. G. (2003). Policy review. *Housing Studies*, *18*(4), 607–635.

Coble, K. H., & Barnett, B. J. (2013). Why do we subsidize crop insurance? *American Journal of Agricultural Economics*, *95*(2), 498–504.

Cole, S., Giné, X., & Vickery, J. (2017). How does risk management influence production decisions? Evidence from a field experiment. *The Review of Financial Studies*, *30*(6), 1935–1970.

Das, T. K., & Teng, B. S. (2004). The risk-based view of trust: A conceptual framework. *Journal of Business and Psychology*, *19*(1), 85–116.

Dasgupta, P. (2000). Trust as a commodity. In D. Gambetta (Ed.), *Trust: Making and breaking cooperative relations* (pp. 49–72). Oxford, UK: Basil Blackwell.

Dohmen, T., Falk, A., Huffman, D., Sunde, U., Schupp, J., & Wagner, G. G. (2011). Individual risk attitudes: Measurement, determinants, and behavioral consequences. *Journal of the European Economic Association*, *9*(3), 522–550.

Dyer, J. H., Chu, W. (2003). The role of trustworthiness in reducing transaction costs and improving performance: Empirical evidence from the United States, Japan, and Korea. *Organization Science*, *14*(1), 57–68.

Agricultural Insurance Act. (2005). (Dz.U.Nr150.poz.1249).

Eckel, C. C., & Grossman, P. J. (2008). Forecasting risk attitudes: An experimental study using actual and forecast gamble choices. *Journal of Economic Behavior and Organization*, *68*(1), 1–17.

Ehiogu, C. P., & Joseph, A. (2019). Effect of agricultural insurance on agriculture sector in Nigeria. *Journal of Agriculture and Food Sciences*, *17*(1), 123.

Franke, G., Schlesinger, H., & Stapleton, R. C. (2006). Multiplicative background risk. *Management Science*, *52*(1), 146–153.

Gennaioli, N., La Porta, R. La, Lopez-de-Silanes, F., & Shleifer, A. (2020). Trust and insurance contracts. In *NBER Working Papers 27189*. Cambridge, MA: National Bureau of Economic Research, Inc. doi 10.3386/w27189.

Girdžiūtė, L. (2012). Risks in agriculture and opportunities of their integrated evaluation. *Procedia - Social and Behavioral Sciences*, *62*, 783–790.

Glaeser, E. L., Laibson, D. I., Scheinkman, J. A., & Soutter, C. L. (2000). Measuring trust*. *Quarterly Journal of Economics*, *115*(3), 811–846.

Goodwin, B. K., & Smith, V. H. (2013). What harm is done by subsidizing crop insurance? *American Journal of Agricultural Economics*, *95*(2), 489–497.

Guiso, L., & Paiella, M. (2008). Risk aversion, wealth, and background risk. *Journal of the European Economic Association*, *6*(6), 1109–1150.

Hardaker, J. B., Huirne, R. B. M., Anderson, J. R., & Lien, G. (2004). *Coping with risk in agriculture*. Wallingford, UK: CABI Publishing.
Harrison, G. W., List, J. A., & Towe, C. (2007). Naturally occurring preferences and exogenous laboratory experiments: A case study of risk aversion. *Econometrica*, *75*(2), 433–458.
Huirne, R., Meuwissen, M., Hardaker, J., & Anderson, J. (2000). Risk and risk management in agriculture: An overview and empirical results. *International Journal of Risk Assessment and Management*, *1*, 125–136.
James, P. (2011). Building awareness and institutional capacity for agriculture insurance. *ASCI Journal of Management*, *41*(1), 111–118.
Janowicz-Lomott, M., & Łyskawa, K. (2016). *Funkcjonowanie dotowanych ubezpieczeń upraw w Polsce. [How does subsidized crop insurance work in Poland?]*. Retrieved from www.sejm.gov.pl/archiwum.
Kobus, P. (2019). *Wielowymiarowe modelowanie ryzyka dochodowego w rolnictwie. [Multidimensional modeling of income risk in agriculture]*. Warsaw, PL: Wydawnictwo SGGW.
Marzec, M. (2017). Levels of the analysis of trust in public organisations. In B. Jałocha, R. Lenart-Gansiniec, E. Bogacz-Wojtanowska, & G. Prawelska-Skrzypek (Eds.), *The complex identity of public management: aims, attitudes, approaches*. Kraków, PL Jagiellonian University Institute of Public Affairs.
Masara, C., & Dube, L. (2017). Socio-economic factors influencing uptake of agriculture insurance by smallholder maize farmers in Goromonzi district of Zimbabwe. *Journal of Agricultural Economics and Rural Development*, *3*(1), 160–166.
McFadden, D. (1973). Conditional logit analysis of qualitative choice behavior. *Frontiers in Econometrics*. New York, NY: Academic Press.
McKelvey, R. D., & Zavoina, W. (1975). A statistical model for the analysis of ordinal level dependent variables. *The Journal of Mathematical Sociology*, *4*(1), 103–120.
Meraner, M., & Finger, R. (2019). Risk perceptions, preferences and management strategies: Evidence from a case study using German livestock farmers. *Journal of Risk Research*, *22*(1), 110–135.
Meuwissen, M. P. M., van Asseldonk, M. A. P. M., & Huirne, R. B. M. (2008). Income stabilisation in European agriculture: Design and economic impact of risk management tools. In *Income Stabilisation in European Agriculture: Design and Economic Impact of Risk Management Tools*. Wageningen, NL: Wageningen Academic Publishers. 10.3920/978-90-8686-650-2
Ngoma, H., Mason-Wardell, N. M., Samboko, P. C., & Hangoma, P. (2018). *Switching up climate-smart agriculture adoption: do 'green' subsidies, insurance, risk aversion and impatience matter?* Feed the Future Innovation Lab for Food Security Policy Research Papers 303524, Lansing, MI: Michigan State University, Department of Agricultural, Food, and Resource Economics, Feed the Future Innovation Lab for Food Security (FSP).
OECD. (2011). *Managing risk in agriculture: Policy assessment and design*. OECD Publishing.
OECD. (2020). Strengthening agricultural resilience in the face of multiple risks. In *Strengthening Agricultural Resilience in the Face of Multiple Risks*. OECD.

Ogurtsov, V. (2008). *Catastrophic risks and insurance in farm-level decision making*. Retrieved from https://research.wur.nl/en/publications/catastrophic-risks-and-insurance-in-farm-level-decision-making.

Olajide-Adedamola, F. O., & Akinbile, L. A. (2017). Inhibitors and motivators of adoption of agricultural insurance in Nigeria. *International Journal of Agricultural Management and Development (Ijamad)*, *9*(3), 285–292.

Olesen, J. E., Trnka, M., Kersebaum, K. C., Skjelvåg, A. O., Seguin, B., Peltonen-Sainio, P., Rossi, F., Kozyra, J., & Micale, F. (2011). Impacts and adaptation of European crop production systems to climate change. *European Journal of Agronomy*, *34*(2), 96–112.

Paliszkiewicz, J. (2013). *Zaufanie w zarządzaniu, [Trust in management]*. Warsaw, PL: Wydawnictwo Naukowe PWN.

Pearcy, J., & Smith, V. (2015). The tangled web of agricultural insurance: Evaluating the impacts of government policy. *SSRN Electronic Journal*, *40*(1), 80–111.

Prabhakar, S. V. R. K., Abu-Bakar, A., Claudio, C., & Hung, H. V. (2013). *Promoting Risk Financing in the Asia Pacific Region: Lessons from Agriculture Insurance in Malaysia, Philippines and Vietnam*. Kamiyamaguchi, JP: Institute for Global Environmental Strategies.

Ramirez, O. A., & Shonkwiler, J. S. (2017). A probabilistic model of crop insurance purchase decision. *Journal of Agricultural and Resource Economics*, *42*(1), 10–26.

Ramm, G., & Steinmann, R. (2014, October 24). Agriculture insurance: Freeing farmers from extreme weather risk. *The Guardian*. Retrieved from: https://www.theguardian.com/global-development-professionals-network/2014/oct/29/agricultural-insurance-smallholder-farmers-risk-financial-inclusion.

Rejda, G., & McNamara, M. (2017). *Principles of risk management and insurance*. Harlow, UK: Pearson Education Limited.

Smith, V. H., & Glauber, J. W. (2012). Agricultural insurance in developed countries: Where have we been and where are we going? *Applied Economic Perspectives and Policy*, *34*(3), 363–390.

Stiglitz, E. J., & Rosengard, J. K. (2015). *Economics of the public sector / Joseph E. Stiglitz*. (4th ed.). New York – London: W.W. Norton & Company, Inc.

Syll, M. M. A., & Wiengaertner, L. (December 19, 2019). *Bundling weather index-based crop insurance and credit: A Cautionary Tale Against Misunderstood and Misinformed Take-Up*. (December 19, 2019). Retrieved from: https://papers.ssrn.com/sol3/papers.cfm?abstract_id=3507421.

Sztompka, P. (1999). *Trust: A sociological theory*. Cambridge, UK: Cambridge University Press. Retrieved from https://books.google.pl/books?id=ZrwvSrK5I8AC.

Sztompka, P. (2007). *Zaufanie: fundament społeczeństwa. [Trust: The foundation of society]*. Kraków, PL: Znak.

van Asseldonk, M. A. P. M., Meuwissen, M. P. M., & Huirne, R. B. M. (2003). *A risk financing model for livestock epidemics in the European Union*. Wageningen, NL: IRMA Wageningen University.

von Neumann, J., & Morgenstern, O. (1953). *Theory of game and economic behavior*. Prncenton, NJ: Princeton University Press.

Wicka, A. (2018). Crop insurance with subsidies in poland—Do it works. *Economic Science for Rural Development*, *49*, 178–186.

17 Building Trust and Managing Brand Relationships with Stakeholders

Marek Matejun[1] *and Marcin Ratajczak*[2]
[1] *University of Lodz*
[2] *Warsaw University of Life Sciences*

Introduction

Modern economic organizations operate in complex socio-economic systems interacting with specific groups of interest/pressure, as emphasized in the stakeholder theory. These challenges also apply to micro-, small-, and medium-sized enterprises (SMEs), which operate in dynamic and complex environments with many support instruments offered by specific institutions as a part of regional, national, or international initiatives and assistance programs for small businesses. The exploitation of these instruments requires the development of direct relations between SMEs and stakeholders (support institutions), which should be based on social and formal trust. From the perspective of small businesses, this trust includes both the ability to build the brand of a trustworthy entity and the assessment of the reliability of support institutions and instruments.

Taking this into account, the aim of this chapter is to identify and assess the role of trust in managing relationships with stakeholders on the example of external support exploitation processes for small businesses. The achievement of this objective is based on the results of the international survey research in a random sample of 1,741 SMEs from the European Union. This publication was financed with funds from the research project 2015/17/B/HS4/00988 from the National Science Centre, Poland.

Literature Review and Development of Hypotheses

The stakeholder theory focuses on specific parties (defined as stakeholders), which can affect or are affected by the achievement of the organization's objectives (Freeman, 2010). This theory includes both the identification and evaluation of specific stakeholders of an organization (the normative theory of stakeholder), as well as the interpretation of the conditions and formulation of the principles of managing the relationship with these stakeholders (the descriptive theory of the stakeholder) (Phillips, 2003).

DOI: 10.4324/9781003165965-17

In terms of classification, stakeholders include specific organizations, groups, or individuals, which, from the point of view of the direction of dependence on a given organization, are divided into the following (Atkin & Brooks, 2015, pp. 36–37):

- Internal stakeholders: owners, the board of directors/managers, employees, labor unions (members of the organization in general),
- External stakeholders: customers, suppliers and vendors, and competitors, coopetitors, shareholders/investors, financial institutions, NGOs, media, government and regulatory institutions, and communities.

Phillips (2003) lists normative stakeholders as those to whom an organization has a moral and fairness obligation, and derivative stakeholders, whose actions and claims must be accounted for by managers due to their potential effects upon the organization. More recent studies identify stakeholders according to other axes (Jakhar, 2017; Milani, 2019, pp. 132–136): Primary vs. secondary, positive vs. neutral vs. negative, active vs. passive, or domestic vs. international.

The stakeholder theory is key to the strategic understanding, interpretation, and balance of an organization's commitment to individual groups of interest, including their power, interest, legitimacy, and urgency (Ackermann & Eden, 2011; Lin et al., 2018). To this end, a stakeholder analysis is conducted to identify all the parties, their contribution to the organization, pressure (needs, claims), and their hierarchy (Schilling & Shankar, 2020, p. 127). This theory also explains the transition from a firm-centric to stakeholder-centric approach in economic, environmental, and social value co-creation (Samant & Sangle, 2016) and forms the basis for the development of the CSR concept (Marques et al., 2019). It is important in the management of inter-organizational dialog processes, public relations and marketing communication (Cardwell et al., 2017), and in project management (Derakhshan et al., 2019).

The development of stakeholder relations plays a major role in small business management, both in terms of the company's position and performance (Nejati et al., 2014) and in terms of the implementation of ownership and governance principles (Zhang & Thiam, 2014). A specific group of stakeholders for SME sector companies are the institutions included in support infrastructure. These include (Lisowska & Stanisławski, 2015; Daniluk, 2017; Hausberg & Korreck, 2020):

- Centers of entrepreneurship, including consultation points, training and advisory centers, entrepreneurship incubators, and accelerators,
- Centers of technology and innovation, for example,: technology transfer centers, technology incubators, technology parks, and science, research & development centers,

- Non-bank financial institutions, including loan and guarantee funds, seed capital funds, and business angel networks.

From the stakeholder theory point of view, these institutions are classified as secondary, external, derivative stakeholders, with a positive impact on small businesses. Their impact on the organization can be both passive, by creating general conditions for the development of entrepreneurship in a given area, and active, by offering specific (usually public) formal support instruments for SMEs, such as: Non-returnable, external or equity financing, organizational, administrative and legal instruments, consulting, training and information services, or technological and pro-innovation services (Matejun & Woźniak, 2020). Through active relations, these institutions create economic and social value for SMEs in the form of specific support advantages including resource benefits (e.g., access to limited resources, development of unique resources, improvement of human capital quality) and market benefits (e.g., extension of the company's offer, increase in innovation and flexibility) (Bodas-Freitas & Corrocher, 2019; Alkahtani et al., 2020). These relationships and the role of support in the development processes of SMEs are an important direction of research in the field of entrepreneurship and small business management (Urbano et al., 2019).

Exploitation of this support involves the entry of SME sector companies into relations with support stakeholders, including the identification of benefits and risks of support, the preparation of necessary information and documentation, as well as the control and evaluation of the effectiveness of support. However, companies face many barriers in their exploitation of support (Matejun & Woźniak, 2020; Ropega, 2020), therefore, systematic and persistent exploitation of support, often expressed by many attempts to obtain various support instruments, becomes very important. These assumptions lead to the formulation of the H1 hypothesis: Exploitation of support activities directly, significantly, and positively determine the extent of the support advantages achieved by SME sector companies.

Studies by Mole et al. (2017) also show the importance of entrepreneurial orientation and the characteristics of owner-managers of SMEs in the actions for exploitation of support. They also stress that the scope of support advantages is determined by (1) concerns about access to information and advice, (2) doubts about the costs, benefits, and value of support, and (3) relationship issues. Within these dimensions, the problem of building trust in relations between SMEs and support stakeholders is emerging. It concerns, among other things, lack of trust that there is an appropriate type of support for the company, lack of certainty as to the potential value of the aid, concerns about the advisors' understanding of the specifics of the business, and lack of confidence as to contacting anyone for support. Additionally, entrepreneurs are discouraged by their own previous experiences or those of others. In earlier studies, this problem was pointed out, among others, by Johnson et al. (2007) and Kautonen et al. (2010).

This trust is therefore of an inter-organizational nature (Villena et al., 2016), including a belief in the beneficial, reliable, predictable, and mutually acceptable action of the other party (Paliszkiewicz, 2019), as well as of an interactional nature (Henisz, 2017), based on dialog and joint involvement in decision-making. A review of the literature by Agostini and Nosella (2019) indicates that trust is one of the key social features and success factors of inter-organizational relationships involving SMEs. Due to the specificity and scope of the relationship with support stakeholders, it is important to distinguish two dimensions (capitals) of this trust relevant for SMEs sector companies: (1) The ability to assess support stakeholders' reliability and (2) A trustworthy image/brand of the company for support stakeholders (Grudzewski et al., 2008, p. 20, 37–38). In the first case, it is primarily important to identify positive examples of the use of support in the company's environment, and the ability to objectively assess the support stakeholders offered and the support instruments, as well as one's own positive experiences of co-operation with the support infrastructure. The second dimension consists of an openness to the environment, an ethical approach to the exploitation of support, and orientation to long-term partnership relations with support stakeholders.

Changes in this trust result, among other things, from interpretations of partner behaviors that depend on the performance that has been achieved during earlier stages of cooperation (Vlaar et al., 2007) and relationship frequencies (Brattström et al., 2018). This is also supported by the observations of A. Rad (2017), concerning the positive impact of the period and scope of interaction on the level of trust in inter-organizational relationships. This, therefore, leads to the formulation of the H2 hypothesis: Trust in relationships with support stakeholders mediates the impact of exploitation of support on the support advantages achieved by SME sector companies. Taking this into account, the general assumptions adopted in this paper are presented as a research model in Figure 17.1.

Research Methodology

Sample Procedure and Data Collection

A survey conducted by the author on a random sample of 1,741 SMEs was devoted to the implementation of the objective of the study and verification of the adopted research model. As a research technique, the Computerized Self-Administered Questionnaire was used (Callegaro et al., 2015, pp. 17–25), and the research tool was an original electronic questionnaire made available to respondents in the www.questionpro.com system.

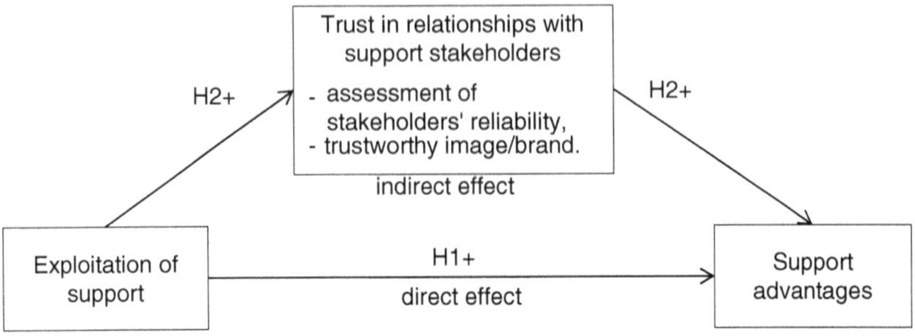

Figure 17.1 Research model. Source: Own work based on theoretical considerations.

The geographical scope of the survey covered 22 selected European Union countries: Austria, Belgium, Bulgaria, Croatia, the Czech Republic, Denmark, Finland, France, Germany, Greece, Hungary, Italy, Lithuania, the Netherlands, Poland, Portugal, Romania, Slovakia, Slovenia, Spain, Sweden, and the United Kingdom. The study considers those countries with the largest number of economic entities in the European Union. According to The World Bank (2015) indicators, the area covered by the study covers more than 4 million km^2 (over 95% of the EU) and is inhabited by nearly 500 million people (98% of the EU population). According to Eurostat (2016) data and European Commission (2016) SME Performance Review data, there are more than 21 million enterprises in the area concerned, more than 98% of which are SMEs. The share of entities according to particular size classes is as follows: micro – 92.52%, small – 6.25%, medium – 1.03%, and large – 0.20%.

The size of the surveyed enterprises was determined on the basis of respondents' declarations based on the criteria of a uniform, formal definition of micro-, small-, and medium-sized enterprises formulated by the European Commission (2015). They take into account the average annual level of employment in full-time equivalents, the level of turnover, and the balance sheet total. In addition, only autonomous enterprises are included in the SMEs category. These are entities completely independent in terms of capital and/or ownership from other entities or having one or more minority partnerships (each less than 25%) with other enterprises. On this basis, 1,183 (68%) micro companies, 399 (23%) small companies, and 159 (9%) medium-sized companies were identified in the sample.

Most of the surveyed companies operate as sole proprietorships (45%) or as limited liability companies (35%). These are enterprises operating primarily in the service sector (60%), less frequently in the production sector (21%) or trade (19%). The majority of the surveyed companies (73%) are active on the market with at least national coverage. The sample included entities with a relatively long period of market activity, amounting to more than 20 years (36%) or companies with a period of 5 to 10 years (21%).

Respondents in the surveys were mainly owners (74%), less frequently senior managers (19%), or employees authorized and empowered by the management to participate in the surveys (7%). On the basis of their answers (opinions) empirical data on the surveyed companies from the SME sector were collected. The questions were answered mainly by men (70%), people between 31 and 40 years old (30%) or over 50 years old (35.5%), with higher education (81%), and in technical (40%) or economic/managerial (26%) majors.

Measures and Variables

The variables (constructs) used in the research model are complex and latent. For this reason, an approach based on synthetic variables was used to analyze the relationships between them. They have been operationalized by means of sets of specific items (indicators) that can be directly identified and assessed in the economic practice of SME companies (Eisend & Kuss, 2019, p. 124). The content of individual items resulted directly from the theoretical characteristics of the variables under consideration. They were all evaluated by respondents on a visual analogue scale, used to measure traits and/or attitudes in social studies (Yeung & Wong, 2019), scaled from 1 (fully not applicable to the company) to 100 (fully applicable to the company).

In this study several methods to test reliability and validity of analyzed variables were implemented. To measure internal consistency reliability, Cronbach's alpha was used, taking a minimum acceptable value of $\alpha Cr > 0.7$ (Taber, 2018). To test convergent validity, confirmatory factor analysis (KMO = 0.958, Bartlett's test of sphericity = 27,052, $p < 0.001$) was used (Üzüm et al., 2018). All factor loadings were found to be above 0.5, and most of them were above 0.7. On this basis, composite reliability (CR) and average variance extracted (AVE) were analyzed, which for each of the analyzed variables were CR > 0.7 and AVE > 0.5 (Ahmad et al., 2016). The results of reliability and validity of adopted variables are presented in Table 17.1. In addition, the synthetic variable "Trust in relationships with support stakeholders" covering the two dimensions considered together was used in further calculations: (1) "Assessment of support stakeholders' reliability" and (2) "Trustworthy image/brand of the company". This variable obtained an acceptable level of internal consistency reliability $\alpha Cr = 0.917$.

Additionally, four control variables were used in the analyses, which were measured on orderly scales based on respondents' answers: (1) The size of the company, (2) The age of the company, (3) The market coverage, and (4) The technological level of the company.

Table 17.1 Scales, Reliability, and Validity of Adopted Variables

Variable	*Items*	*Factor Loading*
Exploitation of supportαCr = 0.731CR = 0.835AVE = 0.507	The owner/manager is an entrepreneurial person, focused on taking advantage of market opportunities	0.75
	The company makes many attempts to obtain various support instruments	0.77
	The company is systematic and persistent in exploitation of support	0.81
	The company has great skills in preparing documentation necessary for the exploitation of support	0.56
	The company controls the effectiveness and profitability of exploitation of support	0.64
Support advantagesαCr = 0.920CR = 0.935AVE = 0.643	Access to resources necessary to achieve development goals	0.76
	Development of unique resources to build a competitive advantage for the company	0.77
	Intensification of the company development in the assumed direction	0.85
	Increase in company innovation	0.85
	Improving the quality of human capital	0.80
	Increase in company flexibility	0.80
	Expanding the scale of operations and market offer of the company	0.82
	Protection against barriers to company development	0.75
Assessment of support stakeholders' reliabilityαCr = 0.865CR = 0.894AVE = 0.517	There are favorable conditions for the support offered in our environment	0.60
	There are good examples of companies that use support in our company environment	0.55
	We can objectively assess the costs, benefits, and risks arising from the use of different support instruments	0.69
	The owner/manager has positive experience of using previous support	0.73
	The company monitors information necessary to use the support	0.80
		0.78

Table 17.1 (Continued)

Variable	*Items*	*Factor Loading*
	The company observes other entities and draws on their experience in using support	
	The company learns through its own experience in using support	0.78
	The company can evaluate and select the most important support stakeholders	0.78
Trustworthy image/brand of the companyαCr = 0.832CR = 0.876AVE = 0.502	Management and employees are committed to acquiring and using support	0.76
	We use support in an ethical and socially responsible way	0.68
	The owner/manager is cooperative and open-minded in dealing with the environment	0.63
	The company develops long-term relationships with support stakeholders	0.76
	The company develops network relations with other entities, facilitating the use of support	0.74
	The company uses various techniques to build links between partners	0.66
	The company is open to changes that encourage the use of support	0.72

Source: Own work based on survey results.

Based on the collected empirical material, a statistical analysis was conducted using IBM SPSS Statistics (Field, 2017). The quantitative statistical methods used were as follows: Mean (m), as a positional measure, and Pearson's (r_{xy}) and Spearman's (r_s) correlation coefficients and their significance tests as measures of interdependence of phenomena and linear regression analysis. To assess the strength of interdependence of phenomena, an approach based on the proposal of J. Cohen (1992) was used, adapted to the specificity of social research, assuming the following levels of dependence as limit values of correlation coefficient: 0.1 – weak; 0.3 – medium; 0.5 – strong; 0.7 – very strong.

Research Results

The results indicate that the surveyed enterprises undertake activities for exploitation of support to a moderate extent (m = 50.4), with the main stimulant being the entrepreneurship of owners/managers and their focus on taking advantage of market opportunities ($m = 69.7$). On the other hand, active activities in the form of multiple attempts and systematic and persistent acquisition of various support instruments were implemented in the companies surveyed to the least extent ($m = 36.1$ and $m = 33.1$, respectively). The involvement in exploitation of support activities increased to a small extent as the size of enterprises increased, r_s (N = 1,741) = 0.19, $p < 0.001$ and with their market coverage, r_s (N = 1,741) = 0.16, $p < 0.001$. The results indicate that this involvement translates strongly into support advantages, r_{xy} (N = 1,741) = 0.53, $p < 0.001$. Among the detailed benefits, the respondents mentioned most the extension of the scale of operations and market offer of the company ($m = 56.4$), increase in innovativeness ($m = 54.4$), and intensification of development in the planned direction ($m = 53.5$).

At the same time, actions for exploitation of support are strongly connected with the increase of trust in relations with institutions supporting SMEs, r_{xy} (N = 1,741) = 0.80, $p < 0.001$. This trust is developed in the surveyed sample to a moderate extent ($m = 47.2$), with slightly more respondents assessing their trustworthy image/brand ($m = 51.7$) than the reliability of business support institutions ($m = 43.3$). Trust in relationships with support stakeholders is also strongly linked to the extent of the benefits of using support, r_{xy} (N = 1,741) = 0.62, $p < 0.001$, which initially confirms the assumptions made in the research model.

In order to assess in detail the trust as an intermediary between the exploitation of support activities and the benefits of using support, a mediation analysis was carried out (Warner, 2013, pp. 645–687) using the approach by R.M. Baron and Kenny (1986) involving three steps:

- Step 1: demonstrating that the predictor statistically significantly determines the level of the dependent variable,
- Step 2: demonstrating that the predictor statistically significantly determines the variability of the mediator,
- Step 3: demonstrating that the mediator is an important predictor of the dependent variable, with additional consideration for the impact of the independent model variable. At the same time, the previously significant impact of the independent model variable on the dependent variable should become insignificant or its significance should be clearly reduced.

In order to carry out this procedure and verify the research model, a regression analysis was conducted, the results of which are presented in Table 17.2.

Model 1 is control and analysis of the impact of control variables on the dependent variable. Despite the fact that the impact of the three variables proved to be statistically significant, this model explains only to

Table 17.2 Verification of the Research Model, Based on the Regression Analysis

Variables:		*Models:*				
Dependent variable:		1 *Support Advantages*	2 *Support Advantages*	3 *Trust in Relationships with Stakeholders*	4 *Support Advantages*	5 *Support Advantages*
Independent variable(s)	Exploitation of support		0.52**	0.79**	0.10*	0.10*
	Trust in relationships with stakeholders				0.53**	
	Assessment of stakeholders' reliability					0.32**
	Trustworthy image/ brand of the company					0.24**
Control variables	Company size	0.11**	0.00	0.00	0.00	0.00
	Company age	–0.08**	–0.04	–0.05*	–0.02	–0.02
	Market range	0.07*	0.01	0.01	0.00	0.01
	Tech. adv.	0.03	0.02	0.04*	0.00	0.00
Model statistics	Observations	1741	1741	1741	1741	1741
	R^2	0.02	0.28	0.64	0.38	0.38
	R^2 corrected	0.02	0.28	0.64	0.38	0.38
	F-stat	10.25**	135.23**	608.80**	180.22**	154.49**

Source: Own work based on survey results.
Multiple linear regression analysis. Standardized coefficients presented.
*significant at 0.01; **significant at 0.001.

a residual extent (R^2 = 2%) the variability in the benefits of using support, and therefore has very little cognitive value. Model 2 analyzed the impact of the predictor "Measures for exploitation of support" on the dependent variable of the "Support advantages" model (step 1). This impact proved to be statistically significant, with no impact of control variables. At the same time, it explains R^2 = 28% of the variability of benefits from the use of support in the SME sector companies under analysis. Also, actions for exploitation of support determine significantly the level of trust in relations between SME companies and support stakeholders (model 3, step 2). This interaction is characterized by a very high degree of matching, amounting to R^2 = 64%.

The key to explaining the mediation effect is model 4 (step 3), which results in a statistically significant impact of trust in relations with institutions supporting small businesses on the level of benefits resulting from the use of support by SME sector companies, with simultaneous controlling assessment of the impact of actions in the scope of support use on the dependent variable. The previously significant impact of the independent model variable on the level of benefits from the use of support is reduced both from the point of view of impact strength (about five times less impact than that of the mediator) and from the point of view of the level of significance (reduction from $p < 0.001$ to $p < 0.01$).

This indicates, therefore, the occurrence of trust as an intermediary factor between the actions for exploitation of support and the benefits resulting from the use of support by SME companies. The further specification of this analysis is model 5, in which the effect is visible in relation to both trust dimensions under consideration: (1) "Assessment of support stakeholders' reliability" and (2) "Trustworthy image/brand of the company for support stakeholders". In order to statistically confirm the identified mediation effect, Sobel's test was performed (Myers, 2019, pp. 237–241), which proved that the impact of actions for exploitation of support on the level of benefits resulting from the use of support is statistically significantly mediated by the level of trust of SME sector companies in relations with support stakeholders, $t = 16.12$, standard error = 0.03, $p < 0.001$.

Discussion

The results indicate a moderate range of activities for exploitation of support in the surveyed companies. This is in line with a number of previous studies that have shown a limited interest of SMEs sector companies in the support offered by support infrastructure, which however contributes to many benefits for small businesses (Lisowska & Stanisławski, 2015; Daniluk, 2017; Galvão et al., 2020). At the same time, the results confirm the direct, significant, and beneficial impact of exploitation of support activities on the support advantages achieved by

SME sector companies, which positively verifies the H1 hypothesis. This proposal is an important voice in the discussion on the effectiveness of public support for SMEs (Radas et al., 2015; Barajas et al., 2016), confirming the microeconomic impact of support on the development benefits of small business.

An important and original contribution of the article to the development of management sciences is to highlight the role of inter-organizational and interactional trust in the management of SMEs' relations with support stakeholders. The results show that this trust acts as a mediator of the impact of exploitation of support activities on the level of benefits resulting from the use of support, which positively verifies the H2 hypothesis. They are at the same time a novel conceptual and empirical contribution to the identification and evaluation of factors determining support performance in small businesses. So far, the research has focused mainly on the impact of personal characteristics of entrepreneurs and SME characteristics on the scope and effects of the use of support (Gicheva & Link, 2015; Rojas & Huergo, 2016). Although theoretical considerations stressed the importance of trust in the effectiveness of SMEs' relations with support stakeholders (Kuhn et al., 2016; Mole et al., 2017), there was a lack of conceptualization and operationalization of this issue and empirical verification of model assumptions in economic practice.

This gap is filled by the research results presented in this chapter. They identify the intermediary role of inter-organizational and interactional trust in the effectiveness of public support for SMEs. This conclusion complements previous analyses showing that trust is an important mediator in the internal processes of SMEs (e.g., Yu et al., 2018) as well as a mediator in the effectiveness of SMEs' relations with other stakeholder groups: Suppliers (Ferro et al., 2016), banks (Saparito et al., 2004), and coopetitors (Hameed & Naveed, 2019).

Based on the conceptual basis of inter-organizational trust management (Brattström & Bachmann, 2018), the results further enhance the instrumental stakeholder theory (Jones et al., 2018), considered from a resource-based view perspective (Verbeke & Tung, 2013). In this context, social exchange theory explains the increase in trust in support stakeholders resulting from the involvement of SMEs in exploitation of support. This involvement is the result of the entrepreneurs' rational calculation of the expected support advantages (rational choice theory). The positive impact of trust on the growth of these advantages is at the same time related to the reduction of transaction costs of cooperation between SMEs and support stakeholders (transaction cost economics). As a result, trust, according to neo-institutional theory, becomes a key factor inducing stability and predictability as well as facilitating coordination in interactions between small businesses and support infrastructure.

From the point of view of SMEs, both dimensions of trust also play an important role in building a sustainable competitive advantage based on exploitation of support. Trustworthy image/brand can be a valuable, rare, inimitable, and non-substitutable resource for SMEs, harmonizing cooperation with many support stakeholders as well as with other stakeholder groups (Barney, 2018). The ability to assess stakeholders' reliability, on the other hand, expresses a specific dynamic capability directed at enhancing the resource potential of SMEs based on opportunities arising from environmental conditions (Teece, 2014). In this context, both dimensions contribute to the identification and assessment of opportunities and threats resulting from the exploitation of support, provide absorptive pension related to above-average support advantages, and positively influence the sustainability and dynamics of relationships with support stakeholders.

These qualities are particularly important in stormy market conditions such as the worldwide COVID-19 pandemic. In this case, many countries have decided to introduce a number of solutions supporting the economy, including SMEs (Brülhart et al., 2020; Goniewicz et al., 2020; Razumovskaia et al., 2020), which intensifies the scope and importance of relations between small businesses and support stakeholders. SMEs with a higher level of trust in relationships with support stakeholders will be able to adapt more quickly to changing conditions and use support more quickly and effectively by preventing or reducing the adverse impact of the COVID-19 pandemic economic shock on the company's development processes.

The results also provide an important voice in the discussion on the role, desired market behavior, and performance evaluation of support policy and institutions for SMEs (Barajas et al., 2016; Juergensen et al., 2020). In this context, these institutions should develop a transparent and reliable communication policy aimed at increasing trust in the eyes of entrepreneurs. From their point of view, the ability to assess the reliability of SMEs using the support is also becoming important. Taken together, these actions should improve the relationship between SMEs and support stakeholders and increase the scope and effectiveness of the use of support translated into microeconomic benefits for SMEs and macroeconomic socio-economic outcomes.

Conclusions

This chapter focuses on identifying and evaluating the role of trust in managing relationships with stakeholders on the example of external support exploitation processes for small businesses. The results obtained indicate that support exploitation contributes significantly to a number of benefits for SMEs. Therefore, it is worth encouraging entrepreneurs and managers of small business to engage in relations with support infrastructure. These relationships further strengthen trust in support stakeholders and instruments, which then translates into above-average resource and market benefits from the use of support. In theoretical terms, the results strengthen the relationship between trust management, stakeholder theory, and a resource-based view by treating the individual dimensions of trust (assessment of stakeholders' reliability and trustworthy image/brand of the company) as specific dynamic resources/capacities to build a sustainable competitive advantage for SMEs based on exploitation of support. These qualities are particularly important in the case of crisis situations requiring fast and radical systemic solutions addressing support for small businesses (e.g., the global COVID-19 pandemic).

However, when implementing the solutions formulated in this chapter, one should take into account the limitations of the research conducted. These are mainly due to the research method used, which is characterized by a high level of subjectivity of the respondents' assessments. On the other hand, the surveys allowed for verification of the research model on a large sample, ensuring an acceptable level of consistency and reliability of responses. Among the limitations, it should also be noted that the constructs considered in this paper are characterized by high cognitive complexity and multidimensionality. As a result, their operationalization was based only on selected items. However, their selection was directly related to the theoretical considerations presented in the literature review and verified in the pilot studies.

The importance of the issues addressed for the management of relations between SMEs and stakeholders also indicates the need to continue research. Interesting research problems include the analysis of the influence of personal factors of entrepreneurs on the development of inter-organizational trust in relations with various stakeholder groups, as well as the identification of other factors mediating or moderating the effectiveness of using external support in small business development processes. From a methodological point of view, it is also recommended that inter-organizational trust as a mediator or control variable be considered in research on the effectiveness of public policy and support instruments towards SMEs.

References

Ackermann, F., & Eden, C. (2011). Strategic management of stakeholders: Theory and practice. *Long Range Planning*, *44*(3), 179–196.

Agostini, L., & Nosella A. (2019). Inter-organizational relationships involving SMEs: A bibliographic investigation into the state of the art. *Long Range Planning*, *52*(1), 1–31.

Ahmad, S., Zulkurnain, N. N. A., & Khairushalimi, F. I. (2016). Assessing the validity and reliability of a measurement model in structural equation modeling (SEM). *British Journal of Mathematics and Computer Science*, *15*(3), 1–8.

Alkahtani, A., Nordin, N., & Khan, R. U. (2020). Does government support enhance the relation between networking structure and sustainable competitive performance among SMEs?. *Journal of Innovation and Entrepreneurship*, 9, 14.

Atkin, B., & Brooks, A. (2015). *Total facility management* (4th ed.). Chichester: John Wiley & Sons.

Barajas, A., Huergo, E., & Moreno, L. (2016). SME performance and public support for International RJVs. *Journal of Small Business Management*, *54*(4), 1206–1228.

Barney, J. B. (2018). Why resource-based theory's model of profit appropriation must incorporate a stakeholder perspective. *Strategic Management Journal*, *39*(13), 3305–3325.

Baron, R. M., & Kenny, D. A. (1986). The moderator-mediator variable distinction in social psychological research: Conceptual, strategic, and statistical considerations. *Journal of Personality and Social Psychology*, *51*(6), 1173–1182.

Bodas-Freitas, I.-M., & Corrocher, N. (2019). The use of external support and the benefits of the adoption of resource efficiency practices: An empirical analysis of european SMEs. *Energy Policy*, *132*, 75–82.

Brattström, A., & Bachmann, B. (2018). Cooperation and coordination: The role of trust in inter-organizational relationships. In R. H. Searle, A.-M. I. Nienaber, & S. B. Sitkin (Eds.), *The Routledge companion to trust* (pp. 129–142). Abingdon: Routledge.

Brattström, A., Faems, D., & Mähring, M. (2018). From trust convergence to trust divergence: Trust development in conflictual interorganizational relationships. *Organization Studies*, *40*(11), 1685–1711.

Brülhart, M., Lalive, R., Lehmann, T., & Siegenthaler, M. (2020). COVID-19 financial support to small businesses in Switzerland: Evaluation and outlook. *Swiss Journal of Economics and Statistics*, *156*, 15.

Callegaro, M. Manfreda, K. L., & Vehovar, V. (2015). *Web survey methodology*. London: Sage Publications.

Cardwell, L. A., Williams, S., & Pyle, A. (2017). Corporate public relations dynamics: Internal vs. external stakeholders and the role of the practitioner. *Public Relations Review*, *43*(1), 152–162.

Cohen, J. (1992). A power primer. *Psychological Bulletin*, *112*(1), 155–159.

Daniluk, A. (2017). Cooperation between business companies and the institutions in the context of innovations implementation. *Procedia Engineering*, *182*, 127–134.

Derakhshan, R., Turner, R., & Mancini, M. (2019). Project governance and stakeholders: A literature review. *International Journal of Project Management*, *37*(1), 98–116.

Eisend, M., & Kuss, A. (2019). *Research methodology in marketing: Theory development, empirical approaches and philosophy of science considerations*. Cham: Springer.

European Commission. (2015). *User guide to the SME definition*. Luxembourg: Publications Office of the European Union.

Eurostat (2016). *Eurostat data*. Retrieved from http://epp.eurostat.ec.europa.eu

Ferro, C., Padin, C., Svensson, G., & Payan, J. (2016). Trust and commitment as mediators between economic and non-economic satisfaction in manufacturer-supplier relationships. *Journal of Business & Industrial Marketing*, *31*(1), 13–23.

Field, A. (2017). *Discovering statistics using IBM SPSS Statistics* (5th ed.). London: SAGE Publications.

Freeman, R. E. (2010). *Strategic management: A stakeholder approach*. Cambridge: Cambridge University Press.

Galvão, A. R., Mascarenhas, C., Marques, C. S. A., Braga, V., & Ferreira, M. (2020). Mentoring entrepreneurship in a rural territory – A qualitative exploration of an entrepreneurship program for rural areas. *Journal of Rural Studies*, *78*, 314–324.

Gicheva, D., & Link, A. N. (2015). The gender gap in federal and private support for entrepreneurship. *Small Business Economics*, *45*, 729–733.

Goniewicz, K., Khorram-Manesh, A., Hertelendy, A. J., Goniewicz, M., Naylor, K., & Burkle, Jr. F. M. (2020). Current response and management decisions of the European Union to the COVID-19 outbreak: A review. *Sustainability*, *12*(9), 3838.

Grudzewski, W. M., Hejduk, I. K., Sankowska, A., & Wantuchowicz, M. (2008). *Trust management in virtual work environments: A human factors perspective*. Boca Raton: CRC Press.

Hameed, W. U., & Naveed, F. (2019). Coopetition-based open-innovation and innovation performance: Role of trust and dependency evidence from Malaysian high-tech SMEs. *Pakistan Journal of Commerce and Social Sciences*, *13*(1), 209–230.

Hausberg, J. P. & Korreck, S. (2020). Business incubators and accelerators: A co-citation analysis-based, systematic literature review. *The Journal of Technology Transfer*, *45*(1), 151–176.

Henisz, W. J. (2017). *Corporate diplomacy: Building reputations and relationships with external stakeholders*. Abingdon: Routledge.

Jakhar, S. K. (2017). Stakeholder engagement and environmental practice adoption: The mediating role of process management practices. *Sustainable Development*, *25*(1), 92–110.

Johnson, S., Webber, D. J., & Thomas, W. (2007). Which SMEs use external business advice? A multivariate subregional study. *Environment and Planning A: Economy and Space*, *39*(8), 1981–1997.

Jones, T. M., Harrison, J. S., & Felps, W. (2018). How applying instrumental stakeholder theory can provide sustainable competitive advantage. *Academy of Management Review*, *43*(3), 371–391.

Juergensen, J., Guimón, J., & Narula, R. (2020). European SMEs amidst the COVID-19 crisis: Assessing impact and policy responses. *Journal of Industrial and Business Economics*, *47*, 499–510.

Kautonen, T., Zolin, R., Kuckertz, A., & Viljamaa A. (2010). Ties that blind? How strong ties affect small business owner-managers' perceived trustworthiness of their advisors. *Entrepreneurship and Regional Development*, *22*(2), 189–209.

Kuhn, K., Galloway, T., & Collins-Williams, M. (2016). Near, far, and online: Small business owners' advice-seeking from peers. *Journal of Small Business and Enterprise Development*, *23*(1), 189–206.

Lin, X., Ho, C. M.-F., & Shen, G. Q. (2018). For the balance of stakeholders' power and responsibility: A collaborative framework for implementing social responsibility issues in construction projects. *Management Decision*, *56*(3), 550–569.

Lisowska, R., & Stanisławski, R. (2015). The cooperation of small and medium-sized enterprises with business institutions in the context of open innovation. *Procedia Economics and Finance*, *23*, 1273–1278.

Marques, P., Bernardo, M., Presas, P., & Simon, A. (2019). Corporate social responsibility in a local subsidiary: Internal and external stakeholders' power. *EuroMed Journal of Business*, *15*(3), 377–393.

Matejun, M., & Woźniak, M. (2020). Strategic determinants of the support absorption process in the SMEs sector companies. *Journal of Economics & Management*, *41*(3), 5–24.

Milani, F. (2019). *Digital business analysis*. Cham: Springer.

Mole, K., North, D., & Baldock, R. (2017). Which SMEs seek external support? Business characteristics, management behaviour and external influences in a contingency approach. *Environment and Planning C: Politics and Space*, *35*(3), 476–499.

Myers, R. (2019). *Data management and statistical analysis techniques*. Waltham Abbey: ED-Tech Press.

Nejati, M., Amran, A., & Ahmad, N. H. (2014). Examining stakeholders' influence on environmental responsibility of micro, small and medium-sized enterprises and its outcomes. *Management Decision*, *52*(10), 2021–2043.

Paliszkiewicz, J. (2019). Information security policy compliance: Leadership and trust. *Journal of Computer Information Systems*, *59*(3), 211–217.

Phillips, R. (2003). Stakeholder legitimacy. *Business Ethics Quarterly*, *13*(1), 25–41.

Phillips, R. (2003). *Stakeholder theory and organizational ethics*. San Francisco: Berrett-Koehler Publishers.

Rad, A. (2017). The importance of trust for inter-organizational relationships: A study of interbank market practices in a crisis. *Qualitative Research in Accounting & Management*. *14*(3), 282–306.

Radas, S., Anić, I.-D., Tafro, A., & Wagner, V. (2015). The effects of public support schemes on small and medium enterprises. *Technovation*, *38*, 15–30.

Razumovskaia E., Yuzvovich, L., Kniazeva, E., Klimenko, M., & Shelyakin, V. (2020). The effectiveness of Russian government policy to support SMEs in the COVID-19 pandemic. *Journal of Open Innovation: Technology, Market, and Complexity*, *6*(4), 160.

Rojas, F., & Huergo, E. (2016). Characteristics of entrepreneurs and public support for NTBFs. *Small Business Economics*, *47*, 363–382.

Ropega, J. (2020). Novice and habitual entrepreneurs and external business support exploitation. *Interdisciplinary Description of Complex Systems*, *18*(2-B), 271–285.

Samant, S. M., & Sangle, S. (2016). A selected literature review on the changing role of stakeholders as value creators. *World Journal of Science, Technology and Sustainable Development*, *13*(2), 100–119.

Saparito, P. A., Chen, C. C., & Sapienza, H. J. (2004). The role of relational trust in bank-small firm relationships. *The Academy of Management Journal*, *47*(3), 400–410.

Schilling, M. A., & Shankar, R. (2020). *Strategic management of technological innovation* (6th ed.). Chennai: McGraw-Hill Education.

Taber, K. S. (2018). The use of Cronbach's Alpha when developing and reporting research instruments in science education. *Research in Science Education*, *48*, 1273–1296.

Teece, D. J. (2014). The foundations of enterprise performance: Dynamic and ordinary capabilities in an (economic) theory of firms. *Academy of Management Perspectives*, *28*(4), 328–352.

The European Commission (2016). *The SME Performance Review data*. Retrieved from https://ec.europa.eu/growth/smes/business-friendly-environment/performance-review-2016_en.

The World Bank (2015). *The World Bank indicators*. Retrieved from http://data.worldbank.org/indicator.

Urbano, D., Aparicio, S., & Audretsch, D. (2019). Twenty-five years of research on institutions, entrepreneurship, and economic growth: What has been learned? *Small Business Economics*, *53*(1), 21–49.

Üzüm 2018 Üzüm, H., Karlı, Ü., & Yıldız, N. O. (2018). Perceived coach attitudes and behaviors scale: Development and validation study. *Journal of Education and Training Studies*, *6*(3), 160–169.

Verbeke, A., & Tung, V. (2013). The future of stakeholder management theory: A temporal perspective. *Journal of Business Ethics*, *112*, 529–543.

Villena, V. H., Choi, T. Y., & Revilla, E. (2016). Revisiting interorganizational trust: Is more always better or could more be worse?. *Journal of Management*, *45*(2), 752–785.

Vlaar, P. W. L., Van den Bosch, F. A. J., & Volberda, H. W. (2007). On the evolution of trust, distrust, and formal coordination and control in interorganizational relationships. *Group & Organization Management*, *32*(4), 407–428.

Warner, R. M. (2013). *Applied statistics: From bivariate through multivariate techniques*. Thousand Oaks: SAGE Publications.

Yeung, A. W. K., & Wong, N. S. M. (2019). The historical roots of visual analog scale in psychology as revealed by reference publication year spectroscopy. *Frontiers in Human Neuroscience*, *13*, 86.

Yu, Y., Li, M., Li, X., Zhao, J. L., & Zhao, D. (2018). Effects of entrepreneurship and IT fashion on SMEs' transformation toward cloud service through mediation of trust. *Information & Management*, *55*(2), 245–257.

Zhang, X., & Thiam, M. (2014). Assessing the role of stakeholders in the implementation of SMEs governance principles in France. *International Journal of Business and Commerce*, *3*(5), 69–81.

18 Building Trust for Start-ups' Development

Michał Borowy and Daria Murawska
Warsaw University of Life Science

Introduction

The contemporary reality, especially the fourth industrial revolution – *Industry 4.0,* forces enterprises to use new activities to achieve market success. The digitization of economic processes made it necessary to compete on the Internet, as well. Entrepreneurs who want to increase sales create an image of their enterprise on the website as a trustworthy partner. For this purpose, they mainly use websites and social media, as well as other tools to confirm their credibility and the fact that they operate transparently.

This chapter is aimed at defining the role and indicating possibilities of using the Internet in building trust for the products and services offered by innovative start-ups in Poland. The chapter presents the results of the analysis carried out on a sample of 100 enterprises selected from a group of Polish Positive Impact Enterprises (PIE). Such a nomination was obtained by enterprises that combine the pursuit for better economic performance and welfare with the natural environment.

The chapter verifies the following research hypotheses:

H1. Modern start-ups strive for a market position by building trust on the website.

H2. Polish successful start-ups build trust on the Internet, based on credibility and transparency.

The chapter consists of five substantive parts: A critical review of the subject-matter literature, research methodology, presentation of research results, discussion on other author's research results, as well as summary and conclusions with information about possible implications for theory and practice.

Critical Review of Subject-matter Literature

Trust is an issue undertaken by different social sciences and interpreted in various dimensions (Paliszkiewicz, 2018). Due to this context, another

DOI: 10.4324/9781003165965-18

aspect of trust is emphasized, concerning not only the relationship between individuals or groups but also those in business relationships. It is assumed that trust is "a bet made about the uncertain future actions of other people" (Sztompka, 2007, pp. 69–70). To be precise, trust, "by the reduction of complexity, discloses possibilities for action which would have remained improbable and unattractive without trust (...)" (Luhmann, 1979, p. 25).

When analyzing trust in economic sciences, the dimension of rational and calculation analyses is primarily indicated. In this context, trust is perceived as a complement to various types of control and coordination mechanisms, which may have a positive impact on reducing transaction costs (Kramer & Cook, 2004). When talking about trust in business relations, it is emphasized that it is related to the expectation of goodwill by a partner and related activities that translate into benefits from cooperation. This is also done by taking into account some possible risks of such an action (Blomqvist, 2002).

Trust in business relations is distinguished by three key factors – partner's competencies, kindness, and honesty (Van Lange et al., 2017). These are basic categories taking into account such areas as partner's experience, knowledge, and obtained confirmations of external authorities, including various types of certificates. Trust in business is associated with transparency, honesty, responsibility, and keeping commitments, as well. It is a basis for building trust between organizations. Moreover, they can be developed in impersonal relationships (except for kindness) (Mayer et al., 1995).

The spread of trust in a given society is influenced by social capital. It is indicated that trust lays the foundations on which it is based, and this has a positive effect on cooperation. In a broader context, it affects the functioning of business and the state of the economy (Rymsza, 2007). It also shows how trust and social capital significantly affect economic development and testify, among other things, to the ability of organizations to pursue related interests (Putnam et al., 1993). As R.B. Harris says: "a good business is built on trust" (Harris, 1993, p. 15).

The results of the international Edelman Trust Barometer (2020) research show that trustworthy enterprises perform better on the market. It is also confirmed that once built trust positively influences their relations with the economic environment, including consumers, employees, regulators, and investors (Edelman Trust Barometer, 2020). Trust is therefore a key element in building a position on the market and while making relationships with customers. In the changing social and economic environment, which is increasingly moving to the digital world, in all aspects, especially communication, it becomes even more important to properly plan processes and implement solutions that will strengthen the enterprise's credibility towards its stakeholders (Osburg, 2019).

There is no need to prove that building customers' trust in a product or service is important for an enterprise's profit (Paliszkiewicz &

Klepacki, 2013). Today, in the era of digital society formation, a crucial role in this matter is played by Internet Communication which allows for establishing and enhancing a good relationship in commercial interactions (Golik Klanac, 2005). Enterprises use different electronic tools to create a positive image of their activity and to gain customers' trustworthiness (Kuczamer-Kłopotowska, 2009). Websites are of key importance for this communication. However, while analyzing the Internet activity of trust-building enterprises from our target group, the focus was additionally placed on their ability to be a part of social media, as well as their transparency and credibility.

Practice and literature suggest many different tools important for building trust among customers. Most of them are implemented via *websites* that attract customers with both enterprise's portfolio and experience (Walaitis et al., 2017). The enterprise's website should be easy to use and have a professional design. A potential user should have no problem finding clear information about the enterprise's profile, its history, short descriptions of staff, and portfolio of available products or services. A reliable enterprise often presents professional accomplishments, certificates, and awards there. Moreover, it may share testimonials provided by business partners and customers' reviews. It is also recommended to make available such elements like address, e-mail address (preferably enterprise-branded e-mail), contact form for users that are not able to send an email during their visit and telephone number to make possible direct contact when more detailed information, complaining, advice, or recommendations needed (Paliszkiewicz & Klepacki, 2013).

Enterprises that are building trust on the web use tools enabling confirmation of their transparency and credibility. In the following part of our chapter, we characterize both areas and identify tools that have proven successful in business practice. At the end of this section, we also discuss the importance of social media in building an enterprise's trust.

Transparency in the business sphere is understood as an enterprise's openness to communicate about its performed activities (Gold & Heikkurinen, 2018). In other words, it is making some enterprise-specific information available to those outside this enterprise (Bushman et al., 2004) or to both external and internal stakeholders (Gold & Heikkurinen, 2018). However, as the authors remark, transparency is not only about sharing information but also means acting transparently. And this is important from the point of view of customers' purchasing preferences. As Foscht, Lin, and Eisingerich note, when an enterprise itself is seen as transparent, customers get more involved in sustainable and responsible consumption themselves (Foscht et al., 2018). This automatically increases positive attitudes toward the enterprise's brand (Bae, 2016). Thus, it becomes an opportunity to build a sustainable competitive advantage based on trust.

As we read in Forbes: "transparent companies share information relating to performance, small business revenue, internal processes, sourcing, pricing, and business values" (Kappel, 2019). According to practitioners (Barker, 2019; Kappel, 2019), the transparent organization should provide:

1. Open communication channels with employees and external audience, using different available messengers, forums, or videoconferences tools; all this to be able to chat, asking questions, on-line meetings or share files, manage workflows, schedule tasks, or maintain discussion board where team members can contribute their ideas or opinions about a certain topic;
2. Digital systems instead of manual ones, to give all stakeholders in supply chain access to expected information in real-time;
3. Clear and honest information on the state of enterprise's affairs (even bad entrepreneurial experiences), employee performance, and opportunities for improvement;
4. Clear information about the prices and wages (optionally).

Credibility means the fact that someone can be believed or trusted (Cambridge Dictionary, 2020). In business reality, corporate credibility is defined as "The extent to which consumers believe that a firm can design and deliver products and services that satisfy customer needs and wants" (Keller, 1998). Thus, main attention is paid to expertise and trustworthiness (Bae, 2016). Credibility is the element of brand judgments. In this meaning, it is considered in three dimensions: perceived expertise, trustworthiness, and likability (Keller, 2013). These three attributes were explained by the author, as follows:

- Brand-perceived expertise entails competencies, innovativeness, and market leadership;
- Brand trustworthiness is seen as dependable and keeping customers' interests in mind;
- Brand likability means fun, interesting, and worth spending time with.

Among the proven techniques of building an enterprise's credibility, professionals specify among other things: Benchmark – comparing own performance against another business considered to be the best in a given industry; Publishing (articles, books, guest post, etc; to be aligned with respected brands; Guaranteeing the service; Celebrity support; Being quoted or interviewed in media articles – acting as an expert; Giving public speeches; Promotion of qualifications, accreditations, and certifications; Sharing expertise through information products, like e-books, audio recordings, podcasts, videos, and webinars (Dale, 2020).

Currently, the most popular distribution channel of information enabling to strengthen both brand's credibility and enterprise's transparency is *Social Media (SM)*. Enterprise's profiles on SM are almost as popular as their websites. Enterprises present their current offer and build their brands there. In the literature, this channel of business communication is well known as a new hybrid construct of the promotion mix (Carraher et al., 2006; Mangold & Faulds, 2009; Mądra-Sawicka et al., 2020). On the one hand, it combines a chance to establish an enterprise's easy dialogue with a wide group of users, and on the other one, it enables customers to talk directly to one another at the same time. Enterprises take advantage of user-generated content (UGC) which makes up the social proof of the offer quality (Herhold, 2019). Global competition forces organizations to position their brands in social media. Competing to be awarded by "Likes" or "Star rating" has become a necessity in e-commerce. It has also become a norm to keep at least one account in social media to offer products or services directly to customers (Faucher, 2018). Thirty-nine percent of Edelman's research population declare that they were unlikely to become emotionally attached to a brand if they were not interacting and communicating with it via social media (Fogel, 2018). Furthermore, quick dissemination of positive market feedback is of big importance, especially in the case of innovative products or services. As shown in Roger's model, shortening the stages of the diffusion process may significantly affect the economic effect of an innovative enterprise (Rogers, 2003; Borowy, 2017).

Methodology

This research was carried out at the turn of August and September 2020 on a sample of 100 enterprises. The target group was selected at a random-quota manner from a population of 447 enterprises, nominated as Positive Impact Enterprises by Kozminski Business Hub, BNP Paribas, Orange, and Samsung Electronics (2020). This particular type of economic activity is conducted by innovative enterprises which combine the pursuit of better economic performance and welfare with the natural environment.

The analyzed organizations represented 10 categories divided into such industries as social activation, construction and interior design, education for sustainable development, cosmetics and cleaning products, protection of biodiversity, responsible fashion, reduction of raw material consumption, health, sustainable tourism, and transport, as well as food. Enterprises from each category were selected randomly for research samples, according to the proportional share of n = 447.

For research purposes, a special tool was developed that allows for the analysis of existing websites. The subject of the analysis was both the websites of enterprises and their profiles on social media. Four subject areas were analyzed, divided into website basic information, transparency, credibility, as well as ability to be a part of social media. We have distinguished 16 key indicators, next divided into 40 detailed data being previously verified.

An important element of the research process was the implementation of pilot research on a 5% sample of start-ups from the n = 447 set, which allowed for improving the research tool.

Findings

Most of the analyzed enterprises, regardless of business activity type, built trust in their brand online by placing offers in social media – 80%. Twice less often through activities that confirm their transparency – 36% or credibility – 32%.

Structurally, taking into account 10 analyzed categories of economic activity, usage of social media by an enterprise was a norm in most categories (6/10) – 79–96% of cases. However, enterprises representing such categories as *Health* or *Reduction of resource consumption* used social media to a much lesser extent – 53% and 61%, respectively (Figure 18.1). It is also worth noting that almost 90% of enterprises that have an online store had an SM account at the same time.

In the group of enterprises that had implemented measures aimed at increasing transparency, those from the category of *Health* and *Construction & Interior furnishings* were dominant – 48% and 47%, respectively. While in enterprises representing such categories as *Cosmetics and cleaning products*, *Food,* or *Responsible fashion*, these

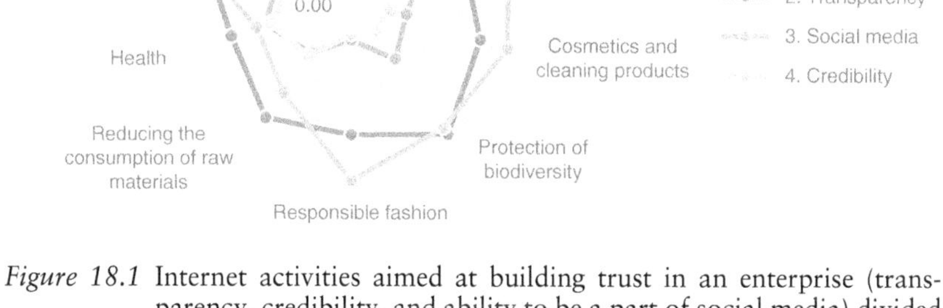

Figure 18.1 Internet activities aimed at building trust in an enterprise (transparency, credibility, and ability to be a part of social media) divided into 10 industry categories. Source: Own elaboration based on empirical data.

Table 18.1 The Areas Examined are Divided into Specific Indicators

Area	*Tool*	*Percent*
Transparency	Portfolio	91%
	Company description	85%
	Team names and surnames	56%
	Team photo/video	48%
	Team role	44%
	Box mail	40%
	Newsletter	34%
	Team Bio	29%
	Blog	27%
	Video	23%
	Current messages / information	23%
	Direct mail / phone number	20%
	FAQ	20%
	Non-financial reports	5%
	Financial results	2%
Credibility	Court Register Number, Tax ID number, Industry Identification Number	63%
	Legal form	57%
	Description of projects	50%
	Business partnerships	36%
	References	28%
	Awards	22%
	Media information	19%
	Famous people / influencers	5%
	Certificates	4%
Social Media	Social Media profile	93%
	Social Media update <= 2M	85%
	Social Media profile > 1	67%

Source: Own study based on empirical data.

activities were implemented much less often: by 31–23% of enterprises (Figure 18.1).

In the group of enterprises that implemented measures aimed at increasing credibility on the Internet, most enterprises belonged to the category of *Health* and *Construction & Interior furnishing* – 45% and 46% respectively. These actions were implemented twice less frequently by enterprises representing the categories of *Responsible fashion, Biodiversity protection* or *Cosmetics and cleaning products*: 20–22% (Figure 18.1.)

The table below summarizes the types of Internet activity of the analyzed enterprises, serving transparency, credibility, or ensured presence in SM (Table 18.1).

To increase transparency, enterprises most often made a portfolio of their products or services, and a description of their activity available on the website – 91% and 85%, respectively. Much less often they publish newsletters – 34%, main staff bios – 29%, or other information/

statements describing the current situation of the enterprise – 23%. Current performance reports were practically not shared 2–5%.

To be credible on the Internet, enterprises most often provide data confirming national business or tax registrations – 63%, information on the legal form of activity – 57%, and descriptions of completed key projects – 50%. They report much less often about business partnerships – 38%, references – 28%, or awards – 22%. They do not use the support of influencers or certificate-based authentication – 5% and 4%, respectively.

Most of the enterprises that used Social Media have more than one profile on different sides – 67%. They usually made updates in the period not exceeding 2 months before our audit – 85% (Table 18.1)

Discussion

The need to build a trustworthy image on the website translates into an enterprise's economic performance. This is confirmed by the conclusions of other researchers (Paliszkiewicz & Klepacki, 2013), as well as statistical data showing the change of society in using new technologies and consumer expectations, which is confirmed by the scale of interest in e-commerce. Data shows that 68% of Poles declare that they use the Internet at least once a week (CBOS, 2020), and 85% of Internet users declare that they have bought something online at least once (CBOS, 2020). This is also confirmed by global data which shows that the average number of online transactions (per person/per year) for Western Europe is 18.4, North America 19, and Easter Europe and Russia 11.9 (KPMG, 2017). These changes in customers' approach are becoming an important argument for the development of Internet communication by enterprises.

Enterprises recognize this necessity and invest in Internet communication and build their image on the website. Looking at the data of the Central Statistical Office in 2020, 71.3% of enterprises had their website, where 67.3% – among small ones, 88.6% – among medium-sized ones, and 92.5% – among large ones (GUS, 2020). However, despite significant changes in this respect, Poland lags behind the EU member states and is below the European average, which in 2018 amounted to 77% of enterprises declaring having a website (Poland 70%) (GUS, 2020). It is all the more significant that 96% of the analyzed enterprises had their own website. It is probably related to the fact that innovative and dynamically developing enterprises consciously build their communication on the website.

When it comes to communication activities in social media, in total, these websites were used by 35.4% of enterprises in Poland, out of which 32.2% were small ones, 45.6% – medium-sized ones, and 67.7% – large ones (GUS, 2019). This percentage is much lower if we take into account, for example, data from the U.S. When it comes to small enterprises, 64% have a website, and 58% of those which have not done it yet so far were planning to create a website in 2018 (Clutch, 2018). Against this background, the enterprises which were analyzed stand out – as much as 93% of them had at least one profile on social media.

In the case of using social media, 32.5% of enterprises declared to do it to create the enterprise's image, 22.7% of enterprises received or responded to comments/comments and questions from customers, and 15.2% to recruit employees and cooperate with business partners (12.3%) (GUS, 2019). The enterprises being analyzed follow similar motives in building their activities on social media. However, the very assumption of a profile is not everything. Systematic communication is of key importance, and in this respect, it was carried out by 85% of enterprises in the analyzed sample.

In 2019, when it comes to on-line sales, 16.5% of enterprises sold online, out of which 14.5% were small enterprises and 21.6% were medium-sized ones (GUS, 2020). In the case of the analyzed start-ups, 51.4% had an online store. It is worth noting that some of the analyzed start-ups did not have an online store, due to the profile of their business activity.

Building trust based on communication on the Internet is a big challenge. Data on customers' confidence in business from the U.S. and U.K. research perspective show that 55% of respondents do not trust enterprises they buy from as much as they used to, 65% do not trust enterprise press releases and 71% do not trust sponsored social media advertisements (HubSpot, 2018). Organizations should include not only paid advertising or press releases in their activities. Among the analyzed organizations, 23% of enterprises published them. It is also important to strengthen communication in other areas that would make its activities and product quality more credible. In the analyzed group of enterprises, only 4% published information on the awarded certificates, 5% on non-financial reports, 22% on awards, and 28% published references. Brand trust is indicated as one of the key factors in building customer loyalty – 94% of respondents say they are likely to be more loyal to a brand that offers complete transparency (Label Insight, 2016). Within the dimension of Internet communication, the enterprise's transparency is built through, for example, access to important data and additional information on management personnel. However, the analyzed organizations do not do well in this respect, 85% had an enterprise description, but only 56% gave the names and surnames of team members, as well as 44% indicated the role of an individual person.

Conclusion

Trust is the foundation of any solid enterprise. Nowadays, in the era of Industry 4.0 and Digital Society, when 50% of purchase transactions take place on-line, entrepreneurs' striving to achieve trust have gained a completely new dimension. Enterprises create their image as trustworthy partners, mainly on the Internet. That is why most, i.e., 70–90% of Polish enterprises (depending on the scale of activity) have their own website. In the case of the analyzed group of enterprises honored with the prestigious title of *Positive Impact Enterprises*, as many as 96% of organizations ran a website and 80% of them had at least one profile on social media. Therefore, the above-mentioned arguments confirm the correctness of the first hypothesis (H1) put forward in the chapter, which says that: "Modern start-ups strive for a market position by building trust on the Internet".

Creating an image of a trustworthy enterprise online requires public disclosure of information confirming credibility and evidence of proceedings in a transparent manner. According to the statements of experts-practitioners cited in the chapter, a transparent organization should provide specific intra- and Internet tools. These include primarily: Open communication via different available messengers, forums or videoconferences tools; digital systems implementation instead of manual ones; clear and honest information on state of enterprise affairs, employee performance and opportunities for improvement; clear information about the prices and wages (optionally). The analyzed start-ups, in order to increase transparency, restrict themselves mostly to share general information about their activities and portfolio of products or services – 85% and 91%, respectively. They publish much less often: Newsletters – 34%, main staff bios – 29%, statements or information describing state of the enterprise affairs – 23%, FAQ or direct e-mail address to choose staff representative – 20%. Current performance reports were practically not shared 2–5%.

Among the proven techniques of building an enterprise's credibility, professionals, in turn, emphasize the importance of benchmark; publishing of articles, books, guest post, etc., to be aligned with respected brands; guaranteeing the service; celebrity support; being quoted or interviewed in media articles – acting as an expert; giving public speeches; promotion of qualifications, accreditations, and certifications; sharing expertise through information products, like e-books, audio recordings, podcasts, videos, and webinars. The analyzed start-ups restrict themselves mostly to share data confirming national business or tax registrations – 63%, information on the legal form of activity – 57%, and descriptions of completed key projects – 50%. They report much less often about business partnerships – 38%, references – 28%, awards – 22%, and media information – 19%. Actually (on websites), they do not use authentication by certificates or the support of influencers – 4% and 5%, respectively.

Therefore, the above arguments only partially document the second hypothesis (H2) put forward in the chapter, which says: "Polish successful start-ups build trust on the Internet, based on credibility and transparency". Although enterprises provide information on the Internet to confirm their credibility and transparency, they do it in a moderate manner and usually limit these activities to the necessary minimum.

The above considerations lead to reflection on the future of Polish start-ups and further research to answer the question of which activities of enterprises related to building trust will bring a measurable economic effect, in conditions of a high level of mutual distrust of market contributors.

The current results already provide some practical tips for entrepreneurs, but there is still no confirmation of which of the above-mentioned activities are more important in the conditions of the Polish economy and those of other countries, comparatively. The presented research results, due to the limited research sample, focus on Polish start-ups. It is a starting point for creating comparative studies about other countries and drawing conclusions that would be consistent from the perspective of the economies of different countries.

References

Bae, M. (2016). *Overcoming scepticism toward cause-related marketing claims: The role of consumers' attributions of company motives and consumers' perceptions of company credibility.* [Doctoral dissertation, Michigan State University]. Retrieved from https://d.lib.msu.edu/etd/3943/datastream/OBJ/view

Barker, S. (2019, Aug. 1). *How to maintain transparency in your business at different levels.* Retrieved from https://www.smartinsights.com/customer-relationship-management/how-to-maintain-transparency-in-your-business-at-different-levels/

Blomqvist, K. (2002). *Partnering in the dynamic environment – the role of trust in asymmetric partnership formation.* [Doctoral dissertation, Lappeenranta University of Technology]. Retrieved from http://urn.fi/URN:ISBN:978-952-214-598-7

Borowy, M. (2017). *Knowledge and innovation transfer from the science sector to the economic environment (on the example of life sciences universities in Poland)* [Transfer wiedzy i innowacji z sektora nauki do otoczenia gospodarczego (na przykładzie uczelni przyrodniczych w Polsce)]. Warsaw, PL: Warsaw University of Life Sciences.

Bushman, R. M., Piotroski, J. D., & Smith, A. J. (2004). What determines corporate transparency? *Willey Online library, Journal of Accounting Research*, 42(2), 207–252.

Cambridge Dictionary. Cambridge University Press 2020. Retrieved from https://dictionary.cambridge.org/dictionary/english/credibility

Carraher, S. M., Parnell, J. A., Carraher, S. C., Carraher, C. E., & Sullivan, S. E. (2006). Customer service, entrepreneurial orientation, and performance: A study in health care organizations in Hong Kong, Italy, New Zealand, the United Kingdom, and the USA. *The Journal of Applied Management & Entrepreneurship*, *11*(4), 33–48.

CBOS (2020, Apr.). *Zaufanie społeczne. [Social trust]*. Retrieved from https://www.cbos.pl/SPISKOM.POL/2020/K_043_20.PDF

Clutch (2018, Jan. 31). Small business websites in 2018. Retrieved from https://clutch.co/website-builders/resources/small-business-websites-2018

Dale, C. (2020 Nov. 20). *10 proven technique to build your credibility*. Retrieved from https://www.marketinghq.com.au/marketing/10-proven-techniques-to-build-your-credibility/

Edelman (2020, Jan. 19). *Edelman trust barometer 2020. Global report*. Retrieved from https://www.edelman.com/sites/g/files/aatuss191/files/2020-01/2020%20Edelman%20Trust%20Barometer%20Global%20Report_LIVE.pdf

Fogel, E. (2018, Sept. 9). *7 Research-backed notes on how brands can build trust on social media*. Retrieved from https://www.socialmediatoday.com/news/7-research-backed-notes-on-how-brands-can-build-trust-on-social-media/531876/

Faucher, K. X. (2018). *Social capital online: Alienation and accumulation (critical digital and social media studies)*. Westminster, UK: University of Westminster Press.

Foscht, T., Lin, Y., & Eisingerich, A. B. (2018). Blinds up or down? The influence of transparency, future orientation, and CSR on sustainable and responsible behaviour. *European Journal of Marketing*, *52*(3/4), 476–498.

Gold, S., & Heikkurinen, P. (2018). Transparency fallacy. Unintended consequences of stakeholder claims on responsibility in supply chains. *Accounting, Auditing & Accountability Journal*, *31*(1), 318–337.

Golik Klanac, N. (2005). *Internet communication in the development of business relationships*. 18th Bled eConference, eIntegration in Action, Bled, Slovenia, June 6–8, 2005, 1–2.

GUS (2020). *Information society in Poland in 2020*. Poland, Warsaw, Szczecin: Statistics Poland, Statistical Office in Szczecin.

GUS (2019). *Information society in Poland. Results of statistical surveys in the years 2015–2019*. Poland, Warsaw, Szczecin: Statistics Poland, Statistical Office in Szczecin.

Harris, R. B. (1993). Relationship marketing: Trust - A foundation for building business. *Manager's Magazine*, *68*(6), 15–17.

Herhold, K. (2019, June 21). *5 ways your business can build trust on social media*. Retrieved from https://startupnation.com/grow-your-business/build-trust-social-media/

HubSpot. (2018, May 9). *The hard truth about acquisition costs (and how your customers can save you)*. Retrieved from https://blog.hubspot.com/service/customer-acquisition-study

Kappel, M. (2019, Apr. 3). *Transparency in business: 5 ways to build trust*. Retrieved from https://www.forbes.com/sites/mikekappel/2019/04/03/transparency-in-business-5-ways-to-build-trust/?sh=7d1e28eb6149

Keller, K. L. (1998). *Strategic brand management*. New Jersey, US: Prentice Hall.

Keller, K. L. (2013). *Strategic brand management. Building, measuring, and managing brand equity* (4th ed.). Essex, UK: Pearson Education Limited.

KPMG, (2017). Online purchase behaviour. Retreived from https://home.kpmg/ru/en/home/insights/2017/03/online-purchase-behavior.html

Kramer, R. M. & Cook, K. S. (Eds.). (2004). *Trust and distrust in organizations*. New York, US: Russell Sage.

Kuczamer-Kłopotowska, S. (2009). Internet as a marketing communication tool *Scientific Journal of Szczecin University. Economic Problems of Services, 559*(42), 548–558.

Label Insight. (2016). *Driving long term trust and loyalty through transparency. Transparency ROI study*. Retrieved from https://www.labelinsight.com/hubfs/2016_Transparency_ROI_Study_Label_Insight.pdf

Luhmann, N. (1979). *Trust and power*. Chichester, UK: Wiley.

Mangold, W. G., & Faulds, D. J. (2009). Social media: The new hybrid element of the promotion mix. *Elsevier Business Horizons*, *52*(4), 357–365.

Mayer, I., Mayer, R. C., Davis, J. H., & Schoorman, F. D. (1995). An Integrative model of organizational trust. *Academy of Management Review*, *20*(3), 709–734.

Mądra-Sawicka, M., Paliszkiewicz, J., & Horm Nord, J. (2020). Determinants of social media usage in business by women: Age and development of the country. *Special Issue Knowledge Management, Trust and Communication in the Era of Social Media, MDPI*, *11*(9), 1–14.

Osburg, T. (2019). Changing relevance of trust in digital worlds. In T. Osburg, & S. Heinecke (Eds.), *Media trust in a digital world communication at crossroads* (pp. 15–35). Cham, CH: Springer.

Paliszkiewicz, J., & Klepacki, B. (2013). *Tools of building customer trust. Management, Knowledge and Learning*, International conference in Zadar, Croatia, 19–21 June 2013, 1287–1294.

Paliszkiewicz, J. (2018). Trust: A multifaceted notion. In B. Kożuch, S. Magala, & J. Paliszkiewicz (Eds.), *Managing public trust* (pp. 9–23). Cham, CH: Palgrave Macmillan.

Putnam, R. D., Leonardi, R., & Nanetti, R. (1993). *Making democracy work: Civic traditions in modern Italy*. Princeton, NJ: Princeton University Press.

Rogers, E. M. (2003). *Diffusion of innovation*. New York, US: Free Press.

Rok, B. (Ed.). (2020). *Positive impact start-ups*. Warsaw, Poland: Kozminski Business Hub. Retrieved from http://raportspw.kozminskihub.com/

Rymsza, A. (2007). *Classic concepts of social capital* [Klasyczne koncepcje kapitału społecznego]. In T. Kaźmierczak, & M. Rymsza (Eds.), *Social capital. Social economy [Kapitał społeczny. Ekonomia społeczna]* (pp. 23–40). Warsaw, Poland: Institute of Public Affairs.

Sztompka, P. (2007). *Trust* [Zaufanie]. Cracow, PL: Znak.

Van Lange, P. A. M., Rockenbach, B., & Yamagishi, T. (2017). Trust. Introduction and trending topics. In P. A. M. Van Lange, B. Rockenbach, & T. Yamagishi (Eds.), *Trust in social dilemmas* (pp. 1–8). New York, US: Oxford University Press.

Walaitis, B. K., Ivankovich, J., & Avdic, A. (2017). *Internet tools in communication development role of small and medium enterprises in Croatia*. 20th International Scientific Conference "Economic and Social Development", Prague, Czech Republic, 27–28 April 2017, 683–692.

19 Trust Building Strategy Among Food Listed Companies in the Digital Economy Era

Magdalena Mądra-Sawicka
Warsaw University of Life Sciences

Introduction

The financial crisis highlighted the role of trust for well-functioning markets and the importance of companies' financial stability (Lins et al., 2017). The financial crisis in 2008–2009 deteriorates trust in corporations, capital markets, and institutions (Lins et al., 2017). Thus, a company that can keep investors' trust and form a stable relationship with stakeholders notice smaller price changes. This parameter was included in the study as a Beta variable that expresses the investor's level of risk assessment. This coefficient shows a particular company's riskiness to the level of risk inherent in the total economy. If the Beta level is lower than one, it shows that investors' risk assessment is the lower company to detailed sector analysis. The level of the Beta impacts the WACC. Thus, it determines companies' value (Schmitt & Neu, 2017) and market attractiveness.

The food industry and food processing companies play a significant role in the economy. This industry plays an important role due to the growing demand for food and its application in various industries like pharmaceuticals, cosmetics, medicine, etc. Food industry firms also contribute to bio-based economy and food safety (Jaworski et al., 2019; Strøm-Andersen, 2020).

Listed companies in financial markets face a fundamental tension for trust. The on-going digital era information process in financial markets gives quick and easy access to information to a wide range of potential investors (Mądra-Sawicka, 2020a). Furthermore, regulatory changes promote financial integration in developed and developing capital markets (Mądra-Sawicka & Paliszkiewicz, 2020). This process brings many benefits like possibilities to use the intention model for company valuation, quick assessment of company capital cost, access to tools used to diversify portfolio risk, and benefits with a risk-sharing strategy (Liu, 2020).

The study aims to analyze trust-building strategies across listed companies based on the food processing companies from the food industry. The chapter reviewed different factors that influence business trust in the financial market. The chapter presents the trust definition review

DOI: 10.4324/9781003165965-19

according to trust relationships with stakeholders' perspectives on the capital market. It shows the historical approach of trust-building strategy due to analyzed factors that reduce asymmetry information. The chapter describes the food processing companies' CSR reporting, audited financial results reporting, the role of company size in trust-building strategy, market recommendations analytics, and dividend strategy used for trust signals. The chapter describes the application of companies' different activities to reduce the variance of the stock price investigated with the Beta coefficient used in the weighted average cost of capital (WACC) methodology.

Trust in Financial Markets

Trust in the capital market could be defined as the belief that a potential trading partner will act honestly (Bottazzi et al., 2016). Another approach defined it as the subjective probability individuals attribute to the possibility of being cheated (Guiso et al., 2008). The definition of "investor trust" relate to investors' perception of the risk and potential losses (Ko, 2017). Trust can be addressed as an expectation that another person (or institution) will perform beneficial actions (Sapienza & Zingales, 2012). Trust is shaped by an individual's experiences and is a factor that affects investors' decisions (Ko, 2017). To conclude, trust is important in the financial market; thus people exchange their money for promises (Guiso et al., 2008). Trust requires investing money in the financial market for promises of capital appreciation or dividends in the future (Kersting et al., 2015). People invest money in their best believe that they will not be defrauded (Hoffman et al., 2009).

In literature, multiple measures are related to trust-based behaviors on the capital market, like experience, market integrity, or financial development. Trust is positively associated with investors' investment experience and the propensity of risk (Kersting et al., 2015). Trust shapes investors' behavior in equity transactions and influences the capital market integration process (Liu, 2020). The on-going financial market integrity process depends on market participants being truthful, open and honest with each other (Tomasic & Akinbami, 2011). Trust is positively related to financial development (Guiso et al., 2008), as investors' protection is a crucial determinant of financial systems development (Mayer, 2008).

In the study, trust is defined as a belief of investors in companies' trustworthiness, which was reflected by a stable price index compared to sector price trends.

Trust Building Strategy Among Listed Companies

The primary strategy for trust increasing includes access to information which is shaped by the existing market asymmetry of information

(Mądra-Sawicka & Paliszkiewicz, 2020). Investors' reliance on trust varies with information credibility, investors' ability to process information, information asymmetry, and market conditions (Guiso et al., 2008; Bottazzi et al., 2016; Jung et al., 2017; Lins et al., 2017). The information asymmetries theory comprises signaling models, agency cost, and the free cash flow hypotheses (Amidu & Abor, 2006). Companies use a signal for demonstrating the effects of their performance as important business mechanisms to communicate information to investors (Chen et al., 2010). Trust-based information sharing strategy implementation produces competitive advantages and reduces uncertainty in business transactions (Wilson, 2000). Investors' trust is a significant managerial concern (Wei & Zhang, 2014); thus trust has a positive and significant effect on stock market participation (Guiso et al., 2008).

The sector, market, and agency risk could be underlined as a key factor of trust-building relations with stakeholders (Das & Teng, 1998; Fiet, 1995). Transparent cooperation with investors involves providing information about competitors' development plans that are not listed on the stock exchange. However, this approach allows for a significant reduction of information asymmetry. Investor trust affects the accounting information revision into the stock price. However, stock prices may never fully incorporate accounting information (Wei & Zhang, 2014). One of this behavior is a strategy of investment decision good information presentation.

Trust in financial markets is dependent on complex laws, regulations, supervisory procedures, institutions, and market practices (Blommestein, 2006). In financial markets, companies demonstrate trustworthiness by accepting regulatory bodies' requirements (Blois & Ryan, 2013). Investors rely in their decision less on trust when the company possesses external certification by reliable institutions, including credit rating agencies (Gul & Goodwin, 2010; Wei & Zhang, 2014). Good reputation among financial analysts and institutional investors gives the ability to attract investors (Mazzola et al., 2006). The role of financial market regulations increased after the financial crisis investors experience. According to Carlin et al., regulations can substitute for trust in capital markets (Carlin et al., 2009). Furthermore, trust developed is different among investor types that are able to accept a varied level of risks (Maxwell & Lévesque, 2014). However, according to Guiso et al., trust is not just a proxy for low-risk aversion (Guiso et al., 2008); its mechanism is more complex.

Financial and Non-financial Information Impacting Investors Trust

A firm's trustworthiness affects investor perception of earnings news, showing the importance of financial information reporting. This information is later used by marker analytics into market recommendations for investors. For example, the investor's underreaction to earnings news is stronger when the firm is perceived as less trustworthy (Jung et al., 2017). Thus, earnings announcements are essential communication channels between a firm and investors (Pevzner et al., 2015). The relation between trust and investor's reactions to earnings announcements depends on ex-ante information asymmetry (Pevzner et al., 2015).

To achieve trust, investors assess companies' financial data's reliability and expected future performance (Strauss, 2018). A trusted source of information will support the company's reputation as a trustworthy unit. In countries with a low trust level, companies have limited demand for equity as they find many difficulties in attracting investors (Guiso et al., 2008). This opportunity has only the biggest companies with long market history. Mostly for these companies, market analytics prepare recommendations for investors.

Social capital matters in economics and finance; thus, deciding to invest in the stock includes the risk and faith (trust) that the data and information are reliable (Statman, 2009). CSR reporting firms implement processes focused on stakeholders' engagement over the long term (Eccles et al., 2014). The belief that CSR activities build social capital and trust is widespread among corporate managers (Lins et al., 2017). High social capital firms are perceived as more trustworthy; investors may place a valuation premium on these firms (Guiso et al., 2008). However, according to Lins et al. CSR activities matter in periods when trust in corporations is in crisis (Lins et al., 2017).

The Weighted Average Cost of Capital (WACC) estimation, as financial data, considers the market conditions in a given period (Mądra-Sawicka, 2020b). The market value of capital reflects capital providers' actual claims and is directly related to the market nature of the cost of capital. The Beta coefficient is used as a risk approached in the cost of capital calculation (Franc-Dąbrowska et al., 2018). In addition, the Beta coefficient is also used to create hedging strategies to hedge the investment portfolio against changes in a given asset's price or for creating portfolio analysis and defining investment risk. Also, the WACC methodology was also used by Vilata et al. in modeling trust argumentation (Villata et al., 2013).

Research Methodology

Research Tool

In the study, stock market data cover stock prices collected for European countries from Thomson Reuters Eikon Databases for the period 2017–2020. The trust of investors in the financial market was measured by the Beta coefficient based on TR methodology. The Beta level is a primary index for the country of the company's primary equity listing. The used Beta factor is calculated for a fiscal year for each company. This coefficient measures how much the stock moves for a given move in the market. It is reflected by the covariance of the security's price movement concerning market price movement. Stock price changes as a measure of trust were also introduced in other studies (Easton & Zmijewski, 1989; Teoh & Wong, 2014; Wei & Zhang, 2014). To present the trust perspective among investors in financial markets, several variables were selected and studied based on a literature review. The Beta dependent variable was investigated according to the following:

- Equity Risk Premium forecasts,
- The rate of return (Return on Equity – ROE and Return on Assets – ROA),
- Size of the company (companies reported total assets, total revenues, and market capitalization),
- CSR reporting data (dummy variable – 1 when the report was published, 0 – no report action),
- Dividend payment (dummy variable – 1 the dividend was paid, 0 – no dividend payment was made),
- Number of analytics recommendations (for each company, several recommendations could be made e.g., for four companies noticed over 30 recommendation of analytics),
- WACC – the cost of capital level, financial market measure.

According to TR definition, Equity Risk Premium forecasts excess equity market return minus the risk-free rate. This calculation includes a long horizon for a particular equity market in a given country, based on the aggregate market valuation combined with a long-term forecast of GDP and inflation. ROA was calculated as a relationship of net financial result to total assets and ROE as a relation of net financial result to share capital. WACC is calculated as an average rate that a company is expected to pay for its debt, equity, and preferred stockholders to finance its assets. Rates of return as an earning perspective in investor trust assessment were also used in other studies (Wei & Zhang, 2014; Brandl, 2021).

Market capitalization represents the value of a company traded on the stock exchange established by a number of shares multiplied by the share price. Total assets and total revenues variables also presented the size of the company; this approach is widely used in other research as control variables (Lee et al., 2008; Wei & Zhang, 2014).

Cost of capital as one of the financial measures that impact the investor's decision and trust level were also induced by Wei and Zhang (2014). The dividend payment variable was prepared based on annualized data. The study does not include the level of dividend but only its payout decision in a particular year. Dividend payout information was used in trust investigation in other research (McNichols & Dravid, 1990; Brav et al., 2005; Coulton & Ruddock, 2009).

Sample

The study investigates companies listed on European stock exchanges. The primary industry is food processing, distinguished according to the TRBC Industry Classification Standard (first stage of sample selection). This group of companies was chosen according to the similar nature of operating activities. On the second stage of sample formation, observations were limited to 4 last years to erase the data gaps. The researched period relates to the available time-series data in Eikon Database – Thomson Reuters (TR). The WACC methodology includes a two-step calculation of equity-based cost on the capital assets pricing model and debt cost. Its valuation is available only for 4 years back. From this part of the calculation, the Beta coefficient was used. The research sample constitutes finally 187 companies (744 observations) in a 4-year study period for 30 countries (country of exchange): Austria (2), Belgium (7), Bosnia and Herzegovina (4), Bulgaria (5), Croatia (13), Cyprus (3), Denmark (1), Finland (4), France (11), Germany (7), Greece (11), Iceland (1), Italy (7), Lithuania (5), Luxembourg (1), Macedonia (3), Netherlands (1), Norway (8), Poland (18), Portugal (1), Republic of Ireland (3), Republic of Serbia (4), Romania (3), Russia (8), Spain (4), Sweden (15), Switzerland (10), and United Kingdom (24). Investigated companies are listed on 47 European capital markets (most entities were listed on London Stock Exchange (24) and Warsaw Stock Exchange/Equities/Main Market (15).

In the investigated sample, 51.9% of observations were related to dividend payment, 19.6% of observation noticed CSR reports access, 1,727 of buying stock on the market recommendation were settle (442 in 2017, 419 in 2018, 436 in 2019, and 430 in 2020).

Methods

The research part includes data analyses of descriptive statistics and Pearson correlation analysis. Pearson correlation was used to infer causal relationships between the Beta coefficient and selected financial and non-financial data. Multiple linear regression analyses were used to test trust investors' attitudes. Regression analysis (backward stepwise method) was used to estimate the model fit. The model formula can be presented as follows:

$$Y = \beta 0 + \beta 1X1 + \beta 2X2 + \cdots + \beta k\, Xk + E$$

where,

Y – dependent variable,
X1, X2, .., Xk – independent variables,
β0 – intercept,
β1, β2, ..., βk – represent the coefficients of independent variables,
E – random error item.

Results

Figure 19.1 allows performing a more thorough analysis of the Beta level across the food processing companies. The 25–75% of observation was located under 1.0. When the beta coefficient is below 1.0, it is called "defensive stock". According to this definition, if the market index loses, the analyzed stock price level will statistically lose less. The situation is similar in the case of an increase in the index price, as the defensive stock price statistically increases also less. The price of the defensive stock

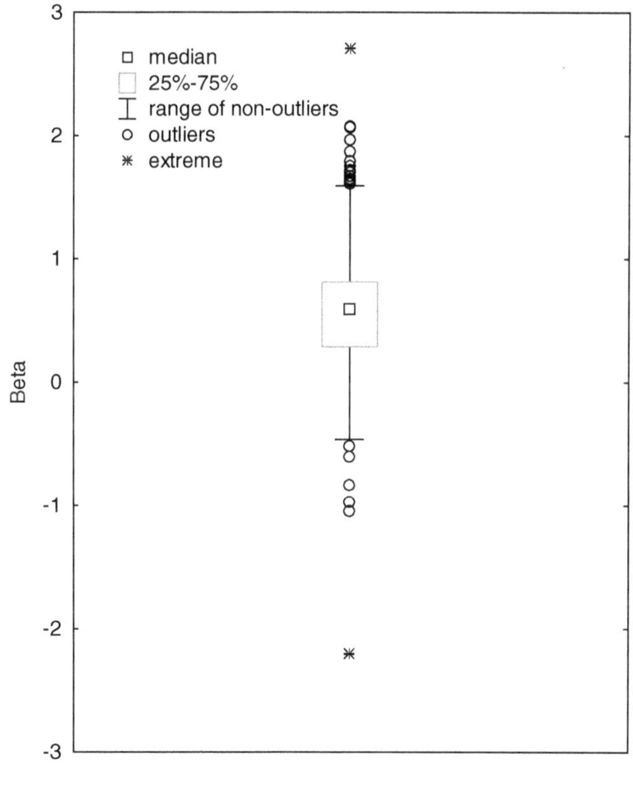

Figure 19.1 Beta variable characteristics. Source: Own elaboration.

Table 19.1 Summary Statistics, Correlation Selected Relations, and Regression Results

Detailed	*Descriptive Statistics*				*Correlation*
	N	*Mean*	*50 th Pctl*	*Coefficient of Variation (%)*	*Beta*
Beta	663	0.58	0.59	80.61	1.0000
Equity Risk Premium (%)	651	5.99	5.96	24.00	0.0355
Weighted Average Cost of Capital (%)	663	4.45	4.22	56.13	0.7984*
Total assets (mln EUR)	719	4 438.42	293.01	419.96	–0.0016
Total revenue (mln EUR)	730	3 265.69	274.65	335.77	–0.0067
Market capitalization (mln EUR)	590	5 606.04	186.84	451.40	0.0061
ROA (%)	700	1.80	3.23	1 493.02	0.0438
ROE (%)	685	4.46	6.73	1 371.81	–0.0460
Dividend payment	744	0.51	1	96.37	–0.2451*
CSR reporting	744	0.16	0	225.94	0.1448*
Market recommendation	744	2.32	0	197.40	0.1359*
Regression model	Beta (Y) = 0.6859 WACC – 0.1814 Dividend payment + $0.0309R^2$ = 70.01%, Adjusted R^2 = 61.09%, F(4,658) = 158.15 p<0.0000; Error std. estimation: 0.34015				

Notes
* values indicate significance at 5%.Source: Own elaboration.

moves "slower" as compared to to the market index's price. It means that more conservative investors will keep this stock in their portfolios for a more extended period until they will be satisfied with their return rates.

Table 19.1 displays the results of descriptive statistics, Pearson correlation, and regression model for selected measures of trust among food processing companies. The Person correlation between the Beta and equity risk premium was insignificant, showing that these two variables capture different dimensions of stock price changes. It found that significant relation with the Beta level was relatively high for WACC (0.7984) and dividend payment, but these relations were weaker (–0.2451). CSR reporting (0.1448) and market recommendations (0.1359) noticed a lower level of correlation with the Beta coefficient, however significant. The size control variables (assets, revenues, market capitalization) did not record significant relations to the Beta variance changes as well as the rate of returns like ROA and ROE. Investigated companies noticed a high level of rate return variation what can influence its relation to the Beta ratio changes.

Regression shows that the Beta coefficient (dependent variable) that reveals the investor's trust decision is impacted by reported WACC level and dividend payment as one way to obtain benefits ($b = 0.6859$ and $p < .001$). The regression result supports the theory of signal and asymmetry of information. The WACC as a predictor of value creation is a market indicator that plays a crucial role in investors' valuation models. On the other hand, companies' dividend payment strategy is being shaped according to investors' expectations, a particular industry, market trends, and companies' profitability. Negative dividend variable impact means that the chances of selling the stock of companies decrease with a stable dividend payout policy implemented by the food processing company. The value ("R-squared" row) represents the proportion of variance in the dependent variable that was explained by our list of independent variables. The estimated multiple regression model predictor for 61% of the dependent variable variance. The regression model was significant for $F(4,658) = 158.15$ $p < 0.001$.

Discussion

According to Liu, trust distance has a negative effect on stock market returns (Liu, 2020). This relation was not confirmed due to the high level of returns variance, which reveals a different level of profitability during the food industry's investigated period. The Beta's ability to explain returns could be unreliable (Lee et al., 2008), and this situation appears in the case of analyzing companies' samples. Furthermore, companies that published CSR reporting disclose a large amount of information to the market and financial data might not be so value-relevant for investors (Jung et al., 2017). However, this situation did not appear in food processing companies listed on the European stock exchange. The information concerning CRS reports was not significantly impacting the price changes. The major focus here could be related to the stage of capital market development that was not directly examined in the study. The regression model also does not include the number of recommendations; thus there was a lot of observation without any analytics information. It is related to the level of particular capital market development and its efficiency with different agencies and institution cooperation.

The significance of the WACC level in the Beta exploration could be explained by its fundamental role in expressing the macroeconomic factors that influence the capital structure determinants (Hussain & Chakraborty, 2010; Simmons-Süer, 2018; Rady et al., 2019).

The Implication to the Theory and Practice

The study's implication to the theory of asymmetry information explains investors' trust in financial data presentations. The importance of signal theory in this aspect is crucial, whereas the most worth investing in are companies that pay dividends. This indicates a significant share of investors expecting income from dividends and not changes in share prices

From the practice perspective, we can observe fast-moving tends to digitalize a wide variety of information quickly. However, financial data are still being used in the first place as a basis for investment decisions in the case of food processing companies. It proves the need to strengthen the importance of the data presented in CSR reports in order to improve investor confidence. Proper and reliable data presentation will create a more trustworthy image of the firm among investors. Institutions evaluating a given companie's financial status also play an important role, as they support building trust in a given market.

Conclusions

Prior research highlighted the positive relations of trust across investors in the financial market. The novelty of study concerns the trust approach based on stock price volatility. The market business trust related to price changes was generally more impacted by financial data publication than CSR reports or analytics recommendations.

The literature review and results expand the need to present more CSR reporting information across investigated food processing companies to strengthen investors' trust relations.

The study results show that food processing companies can increase long-term trust relationships with stakeholders by paying regulatory dividends and keeping the WACC relatively optimal. The other non-financial data did not report such high importance in stock transaction changes on the market, which also expresses practical information usage limitation. It can be concluded that the signal theory based on dividend payout announcement and the discipline in WACC level formation of capital structure impacted investing decision concerning keeping the stock of each company by investors in their portfolio with a belief of future earnings possibilities.

The study contributes to the research literature by providing a basis to explain empirical evidence that investors' trust in financial markets could be highlighted as a long-term investment strategy for a particular stock with confidence that this instrument is trustworthy for future investment. This measure is objective and is not based on "questionnaire answers" concerning trust attitudes in other studies.

The limitation of the study concerns the usage of only one variable with the market price variations. Also, for further studies, the research period should be longer; however, more extended time series were not available for the chosen dependent variable. Also, the study does not include the capital market stage of development and its impact on investors' trust attitudes. Therefore this issue was not added to the presented discussion of the results

The study is based on the processing food industry sample, and further research will be enlarged for the whole food industry sample that will include the U.S. financial markets.

References

Amidu, M., & Abor, J. (2006). Determinants of dividend payout ratios in Ghana. *The Journal of Risk Finance*, *7*(2), 136–145.

Blois, K., & Ryan, A. (2013). Affinity fraud and trust within financial markets. *Journal of Financial Crime*, *20*(2), 186–202.

Blommestein, H. J. (2006). How to restore trust in financial markets? In *Enron and World Finance* (pp. 180–190). London: Palgrave Macmillan.

Bottazzi, L., Rin, M. Da, & Hellmann, T. F. (2016). The importance of trust for investment: Evidence from venture capital. *The Review of Financial Studies*, *29*(9), 2283–2318. Retrieved from http://www.nber.org/papers/w16923

Brandl, B. (2021). Trust relationships in employment relationships: The role of trust for firm profitability. *International Journal of the Economics of Business*, *28*(1), 139–161.

Brav, A., Graham, J., Harvey, C., & Michaely, R. (2005). Payout policy in the 21st century. *Journal of Financial Economics*, *77*(3), 483–527.

Carlin, B. I., Viswanathan, S., & Dorobantu, F. A. (2009). Public trust, the law, and financial investment. *Journal of Financial Economics*, *92*(3), 321–341.

Chen, Y. H., Chien, S. H., Wu, J. J., & Tsai, P. Y. (2010). Impact of signals and experience on trust and trusting behavior. *Cyberpsychology, Behavior, and Social Networking*, *13*(5), 539–546.

Coulton, J. J., & Ruddock, C. (2009). Corporate payout policy in Australia and a test of the life cycle theory. *Assessment*, *51*(March 2010), 381–407.

Das, T. K., & Teng, B. S. (1998). Between trust and control: Developing confidence in partner cooperation in alliances. *Academy of Management Review*, *23*(3), 491–512.

Easton, P. D., & Zmijewski, M. E. (1989). Cross-sectional variation in the stock market response to accounting earnings announcements. *Journal of Accounting and Economics*, *11*(2–3), 117–141.

Eccles, R. G., Ioannis, I., & Serafeim, G. (2014). The impact of corporate sustainability on organizational processes and performance. *Management Science*, *60*(11), 2835–2857.

Fiet, J. O. (1995). Reliance upon informants in the venture capital industry. *Journal of Business Venturing*, *10*(3), 195–223.

Franc-Dąbrowska, J., Mądra-Sawicka, M., & Bereżnicka, J. (2018). Cost of agricultural business equity capital-a theoretical and empirical study for Poland. *Economies*, *6*(3), 37. Retrieved from https://doi.org/10.3390/economies6030037.

Guiso, L., Sapienza, P., & Zingales, L. (2008). Trusting the stock market. *Journal of Finance*, *63*(6), 2557–2600.

Gul, F. A., & Goodwin, J. (2010). Short-term debt maturity structures, credit ratings, and the pricing of audit services. *Accounting Review*, *85*(3), 877–909.
Hoffman, P. T., Postel-Vinay, G., & Rosenthal, J. L. (2009). The role of trust in the long-run development of French financial markets. In K. S. Cook, M. Levi, & R. Hardin (Eds.), *Whom Can We Trust? How Groups, Networks, and Institutions Make Trust Possible* (pp. 249–285). New York: Russell Sage Foundation.
Hussain, T., & Chakraborty, L. (2010). Is the cost of capital an important determinant of market performance of private commercial banks in Bangladesh? *Proceedings of ASBBS*, *17*(1), 390. Retrieved from http://www.blurtit.com/q197532.html
Jaworski, J., Czerwonka, L., & Mądra-Sawicka, M. (2019). Determinants of capital structure: Evidence from Polish food manufacturing industry. *German Journal of Agricultural Economics*, *68*(1), 45–56.
Jung, J., Kang, J., Lim, S. S., & Yoo, C.-Y. (2017). Perceived Firm Trustworthiness and Market Underreaction to Perceived Firm Trustworthiness and Market Underreaction to Earnings News.
Kersting, L. M., Marley, R. N., & Mellon, M. J. (2015). The association between financial literacy and trust in financial markets among novice nonprofessional investors. *Academy of Accounting and Financial Studies Journal*, *19*(3), 201–213.
Ko, K. J. (2017). Economics Note: Investor Confidence, October, 1–7. Retrieved from https://www.sec.gov/files/investor_confidence_noteOct2017.pdf
Lee, C. L., Robinson, J., & Reed, R. (2008). Downside beta and the cross-sectional determinants of listed property trust returns. *Journal of Real Estate Portfolio Management*, *14*(1), 49–62.
Lins, K. V., Servaes, H., & Tamayo, A. (2017). Social capital, trust, and firm performance: the value of corporate social responsibility during the financial crisis. *Journal of Finance*, *72*(4), 1785–1824.
Liu, Y. (2020). The importance of trust distance on stock market correlation: Evidence from emerging economics. *Borsa Istanbul Review*, *20*(1), 37–47.
Mądra-Sawicka, M. (2020a). Differences in the cost of capital: the case of food companies from emerging and developed European economies. *Acta Scientiarum Polonorum. Oeconomia*, *19*(3), 49–56.
Mądra-Sawicka, M. (2020b). Financial management in the big data era. In J. Paliszkiewicz (Ed.), *Management in the era of big data: issues and challenges* (Data Analy, pp. 71–81). CRC Press, Taylor & Francis Group.
Mądra-Sawicka, M., & Paliszkiewicz, J. (2020). Information sharing strategies in the social media era: The perspective of financial performance and CSR in the food industry. *Information*, *11*(10), 463.
Maxwell, A. L., & Lévesque, M. (2014). Trustworthiness: A critical ingredient for entrepreneurs seeking Investors. *Entrepreneurship: Theory and Practice*, *38*(5), 1057–1080.
Mayer, C. (2008). Trust in financial markets. *European Financial Management*, *14*(4), 617–632.
Mazzola, P., Ravasi, D., & Gabbioneta, C. (2006). How to build reputation in financial markets. *Long Range Planning*, *39*(4), 385–407.
McNichols, M., & Dravid, A. (1990). Stock dividends, stock splits, and signaling. *Journal of Finance*, *45*(3), 857–879.

Pevzner, M., Xie, F., & Xin, X. (2015). When firms talk, do investors listen? The role of trust in stock market reactions to corporate earnings announcements. *Journal of Financial Economics*, *117*(1), 190–223.

Rady, A., Meshreki, H., Ismail, A., & Núñez, L. (2019). Variations in valuation methodologies and the cost of capital: Evidence from MENA countries. *Emerging Markets Finance and Trade*, *55*(9), 2106–2123.

Sapienza, P., & Zingales, L. (2012). A trust crisis. *International Review of Finance*, *12*(2), 123–131.

Schmitt, S., & Neu, W. (2017). The beta in the WACC for regulated fixed and mobile telecommunications services: Its role and robust estimation. In *28th European Regional Conference of the International Telecommunications Society (ITS): Competition and Regulation in the Information Age* (pp. 1–21). Passau: International Telecommunications Society.

Simmons-Süer, B. (2018). How relevant is capital structure for aggregate investment? A regime-switching approach. *International Review of Economics and Finance*, *53*, 109–117.

Statman, M. (2009). Social capital in financial markets: trust, but verify. *Journal of Portfolio Management*, *35*(3), 93–102.

Strauss, N. (2018). The role of trust in investor relations: A conceptual framework. *Corporate Communications: An International Journal*, *23*(1), 2–16.

Strøm-Andersen, N. (2020). Innovation and by-product valorization: A comparative analysis of the absorptive capacity of food processing firms. *Journal of Cleaner Production*, *253*(1), 119943.

Teoh, S. H., & Wong, T. J. (2014). Perceived earnings auditor response quality and the coefficient. *The Accounting Review*, *68*(2), 346–366.

Tomasic, R., & Akinbami, F. (2011). The role of trust in maintaining the resilience of financial markets. *Journal of Corporate Law Studies*, *11*(2), 369–394.

Villata, S., Boella, G., Gabbay, D. M., & Van Der Torre, L. (2013). A socio-cognitive model of trust using argumentation theory. *International Journal of Approximate Reasoning*, *54*(4), 541–559.

Wei, C., & Zhang, L. (2014). Trust and certification in financial markets: Evidence from reactions to earnings news. Available at SSRN 10.2139/ssrn.2469034.

Wilson, P. N. (2000). Social capital, trust, and the agribusiness of economics. *Journal of Agricultural and Resource Economics*, *25*(1), 1–13.

20 Building Brand Trust in Managing Relations Between the Company and the Representatives of Generation Z

Anna Korombel and Olga Ławińska
Czestochowa University of Technology

Introduction

Members of Generation Z, i.e., individuals born in 1995 and later, are currently entering the market game (Kamenidou et al., 2019). This group, also referred to as iGen, Gen Z, Centennials, Founders (Dorsey, 2016), makes up around 40% of consumers in the United States, Europe, and BRICS countries, and around 10% in the other countries (Barclays, 2018). This means that Generation Z is a very important partner for today's businesses – it has a huge direct as well as indirect purchasing power by influencing how households spend their money. To avoid losing market share, businesses have to gain an understanding of Gen Zers and make them a part of their business strategy by building long-lasting relationships with them (Barclays, 2018), which are essential for achieving a success in a given market even in the case of the best products and business practices (Leading Insight, 2020). Trust influences business negotiations, buyer–seller relationship, relationship marketing, cross-cultural communication, learning and various types of cooperation, and many more (Paliszkiewicz, 2011). Trust is the most important factor in customer relationship management (Sobel, 2020), and trust building is a long-term process that requires consistent two-way communication, which can be achieved by enterprises with the help of social CRM strategies.

Generation Z's purchasing decisions are more influenced by websites and apps than TV commercials or online banners (Criteo, 2017). This indicates that social media is the proper place for building relationships with Generation Z, and enterprises should turn to them to build communities and initiate customers' engagement, as relationships with a brand community, i.e., customer-brand, customer-product and customer-company relationships, have a positive impact on building brand trust (Habibi et al., 2014). With trust playing an important part in the purchasing process (Powers et al., 2012), knowing whether and how brand communities on social media impact brand trust is crucial to entrepreneurs (Habibi et al., 2014).

DOI: 10.4324/9781003165965-20

The more information an enterprise will gather about the customer, the better it will be able to personalize the form of communication and content of its message. This, in turn, will translate into a better customer experience, building of trust and, ultimately, better sales performance. People who trust an enterprise, brand or product, are likely to become customers or partners of that enterprise. Social media are the place where enterprises should attempt to build relationships with Generation Z. The aim of this chapter is to identify enterprises' social media activities that earn the most trust in brand among Gen Zers, prompting them to make a purchasing decision. The next section presents the theoretical background followed by the conceptual framework and its relational constructs. After detailing the analysis and the results of a quantitative survey, this article presents some implications, research limitations, and possible future research directions.

Literature Review

Ogilvy (1985) defined brand as the intangible sum of a product's attributes including its name, its history, packaging, price, its reputation, and the way it's advertised, whereas brand trust is defined as an average customer's willingness to rely on a brand's capacity to fulfill a specific function (Chaudhuri & Holbrook, 2001). Trust has a heterogeneous, multi-dimensional, and complex nature (Mandal et al., 2020) and is a key driver of attitudes and behaviors exhibited toward the seller's brand and plays an important role in purchasing (Powers et al., 2012). Trust is likely to be a bigger issue when there is information asymmetry and chances of opportunism. Decreasing information asymmetry leads to increased trust. Thus, one way for brands to earn customer trust is by providing them with necessary information about the product and brand (Chiu et al., 2010).

Findings of three studies (Delgado-Ballester & Munuera-Alemán, 2001, 2005; Reast, 2005) demonstrate that credibility and customers' relationships with a brand depend on brand trust. At the same time, Doney and Cannon (1997) note that trust is connected with the brand's acting in the best interest of the customer based on shared goals and values. Thus, beliefs about reliability, safety, and honesty are important aspects of trust (Zehir et al., 2011).

The literature indicates that brand trust leads to brand loyalty or commitment (Moorman et al., 1993; Morgan & Hunt, 1994). Commitment is understood as a permanent desire to maintain a valuable relationship and refers to a permanent wish to continue the relationship with the brand (Erciş et al., 2012). According to Zehir et al. (2011), brand trust has full mediating effects on the relationship between brand communication and brand loyalty, as trust creates highly-valued exchange relationships (Chaudhuri & Holbrook, 2001). Habibi et al. (2014)

found out that consumers' relationships with elements of a brand community (brand, product, company, and other consumers) in the context of social media increase brand trust. Zehir et al. (2011) suggest that brand trust contributes to purchasing loyalty. From the perspective of management, trust is the first step in drawing the consumer to the offer. Trusted brands are bought more often and create more commitment.

Brand communication has a positive impact on brand trust. This finding is supported by Grace and O'Cass (2005) as well as Low and Lamb (2000), among others. Brand communication creates a trust-based platform for relationships between the brand and customer. The quality of services has a positive impact on brand trust, which was confirmed by Parasuraman et al. (1988).

Companies use social media to expand communication with customers, which results in better interaction with them. Customer relationship management is about getting closer to and communicating with customers (Cerchia, 2016). The theory of trust transfer suggests that an individual's trust can be transferred from a trusted source to an unknown target, if a certain connection exists between the two (Doney & Cannon, 1997; Liu et al., 2018). The literature on brand trust reports that customers' trust in brand can be transferred to brand communities (Jung et al., 2014).

Brand community is a geographically unrelated specialized community that is based on an organized set of social relations among brand admirers (Muniz & O'Guinn, 2001). Company-initiated communities of brand admirers established on social media platforms (Laroche et al., 2012) provide companies with a potential tool for developing and maintaining relations between their brands and customers (Muniz & O'Guinn, 2001). There is no doubt that companies that make an intensive use of the possibilities provided by social media to connect with their customers, employees, and other stakeholders achieve better results compared to other companies (Corstjens & Umblijs, 2013). Also, social media have changed purchasing behaviors (Powers et al., 2012). Consequently, there is an increasing need to gain a deep understanding of the circumstances in which brand communities on social media impact the relationships with the brand (Laroche et al., 2012; Liu et al., 2018).

Generation Z is the youngest generation, and at the same time it will make up the largest customer base by 2030 (Euromonitor, 2018). Generations are most often classified based on a cohort's birth year: Silent Generation (1925–1945), Baby Boomers (1946–1960), Generation X (1961–1981), and Generation Y/Millennials (individuals born after 1981) (Brosdahl & Carpenter, 2011). However, there is no consensus in the literature on the exact starting and ending birth years for the individual generations. For the purpose of this study, the authors assume that the term Generation Z refers to the generation of individuals born between 1995 and 2009 (Priporas et al., 2020), (2010 is the first birth year of Generation Alpha (McCrindle, 2014)).

Based on previous research, the most important features characterizing Gen Zers are: financial awareness, openness to the world, lack of professional experience, and technical savviness (Sladek & Grabinger, 2018). Gen Zers are highly educated, technologically savvy, naturally creative, and innovative (Ernst & Young, 2015). They value individual expression and avoid labels, mobilize themselves for a variety of causes, believe profoundly in the efficacy of dialogue to solve conflicts and improve the world, make decisions, and relate to institutions in a highly analytical and pragmatic way (Francis & Hoefel, 2018). This generation will strive to achieve emotional, physical, and financial security (Seibert, 2021). Uncertainty felt by Gen Zers may result largely from the instability of their environment, which is connected with violence, aggression at school, 9/11 events, or coronavirus pandemic (Marshall & Wolanskyj-Spinner, 2020).

Customers representing Generation Z: 1. constitute a significant purchasing power – they spend a lot of money both in online and offline stores; 2. They devote a lot of time to using mobile devices – around 11 hours a week, 3. They like very much to watch online TV shows, movies, and listen to music and podcasts online – they spend around 23 hours a week on such activities, 4. Their purchasing decisions are more impacted by websites and apps than TV commercials or online banners, 5. They often look at products online and then buy them in offline stores (Webrooming, 34%); they also often look at a product in a store and buy it online (Showrooming, 23%), 6. They expect a personalized approach that involves not only personalized ways of communication, but also a personalized communication in the form of advertisement (Criteo, 2017). To Generation Z, which is pragmatic, consumption means access rather than possession; it is an expression of individual identity as well as an ethical issue. Personalization will be replacing mass production (Francis & Hoefel, 2018).

In summary, the existing research on building brand trust by means of social media refers to population as a whole without focusing on Generation Z. The few studies conducted among Gen Zers concentrated around two areas. The first was concerned with factors impacting repurchase intention. For instance, Maziriri et al. (2020) examined the impact of satisfaction with food consumption and restaurant loyalty on repurchase intention and positive word-of-mouth opinions about fast food restaurants in the RSA. The second area of research was concerned with factors driving impulse purchasing. For instance, Djafarova and Bowes (2021) examined which types of marketing tools on Instagram were most effective with respect to Generation Z's impulse purchasing behavior in the fashion industry in Great Britain. However, the literature still lacks evidence verified through a quantitative empirical study that would specify which activities undertaken by enterprises on social media earn the most trust in brand among Gen Zers and induce them to make purchasing decisions. In order to fill this gap, a research problem was defined by formulating the following research questions:

1. Do social media activities undertaken by enterprises earn Generation Z's trust in brand, as confirmed by their decisions to make a purchase?
2. If so, which of the activities undertaken by enterprises on social media encouraged Gen Zers most to make a purchasing decision?
3. Do activities undertaken by enterprises on social media impact Gen Zers differently depending on gender?

With respect to the above-defined research problem, the aim of the paper was indicated, which was to identify those social media activities undertaken by enterprises that earn the most trust in brand among Gen Zers, inducing them to make a purchasing decision.

The following hypotheses were formulated:

H1. Activities undertaken by enterprises on social media impact purchasing decisions of Gen Zers.

H2. Activities undertaken by enterprises on social media impact Gene Zers' purchasing decisions differently depending on gender.

Research Methodology

The study into enterprises' social media activities that earn the most trust in brand among Gen Zers inducing them to make a purchasing decision is part of research conducted by the authors among students of the Management Faculty of Czestochowa University of Technology in 2018 and 2020. Both the studies, which included qualitative and quantitative aspects, used the method of indirect measurement, i.e., survey research, the technique of a survey, and a survey questionnaire as the research tool. For analyzing the research material, descriptive statistics measures were used. Before undertaking the main research, the authors conducted pilot studies in 2018 to identify errors in the survey questionnaire and eliminate them before conducting the main research. The survey research was conducted in 2018 and 2020. The first study was carried out in November and December 2018, whereas the second study was conducted in January 2020. In both the studies, the respondents were students of the Management Faculty of Czestochowa University of Technology. In the 2018 study, 264 students participated, with responses of 223 students qualified for analysis. In the 2020 study, 157 students participated, with responses of 151 students qualified for further research. The research was conducted using the CAWI technique – the online survey questionnaire was available on the platform Webankieta.pl. Both studies used random sampling. The difference in the size of research samples between 2018 and 2020 was due to decreased recruitment of students and decrease in the overall number of students in 2020 compared to 2018. It is also important to stress the high degree of feminization of the group of students qualified for the research, which impacted the gender structure of the respondents. As the respondents were all students, the research group was not diverse in terms of education. Based on the results received from the research, the authors of the research calculated the number and frequency of the respondents' responses to the individual questions on the survey. Statistical methods were used to verify the research hypotheses formulated. Statistical inference was conducted with ex ante significance level at $\alpha = 0.05$. All the analyses were conducted using the software Statistica v.13. The set of variables used in the research was proposed based on critical analysis of the literature (Moroz, 2013; Petrykowska, 2013; Gregor & Kubiak, 2014). There is no consensus in the literature concerning the birth year of the individuals representing Generation Z. The most mentioned year is 1995, which the authors of the paper accepted as the cut-off year in their studies.

Research Findings

Based on the research conducted, the most popular social networking sites among Gen Zers are: Facebook (98.01%), You Tube (94.04%), Instagram (78.15%), Snapchat (63.58%), Pinterest (15.89%), and Twitter (5.96%) (the respondent was allowed to choose more than one answer). In the next step, the authors made an attempt to find out whether, and if so, which, social media activities undertaken by enterprises earn brand trust, translating into Gen Zers making purchasing decisions. Figures 20.1 and 20.2 present proportions for the individual activities.

The research conducted shows that activities undertaken by enterprises on social media impact purchasing decisions of Gen Zers, thus confirming hypothesis H1. The activities with the biggest impact on Gen Zers' purchasing decisions, both in 2018 and 2020, are as follows: *publishing information about promotion* (80.72%; 76.16%), *offering a discount coupon* (77.58%, 69.53%), *presenting an application of a specific product/service* (68.61%, 65.57%), *publishing information about what is new in the offer* (68.16%, 62.25%), and *charity actions* (52.47%, 58.27%).

The respondents who chose the answer "Other, specify" wrote: Answering questions fast, frequently publishing posts and updating data on social media, product placement by influencers, product-related videos. Next, the authors performed statistical analysis and determined the impact of enterprises' social media activities on purchasing decisions depending on gender (Table 20.1).

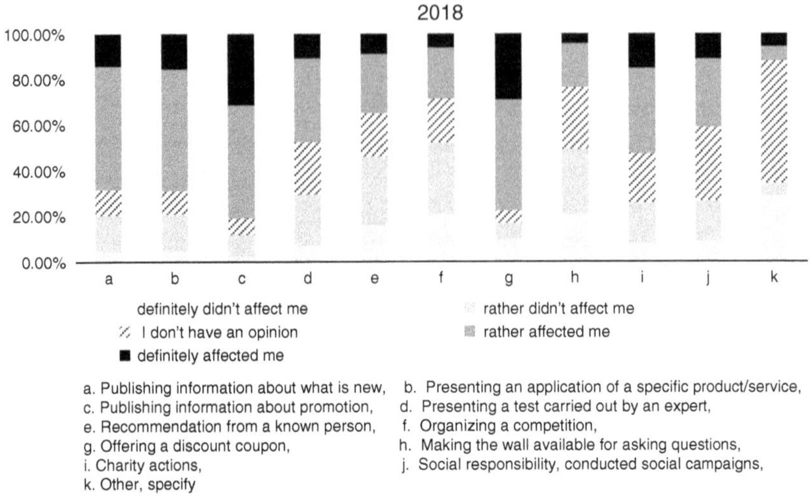

Figure 20.1 Respondents' evaluation of the activities undertaken by enterprises on social media – results of 2018 studies. Source: Own work.

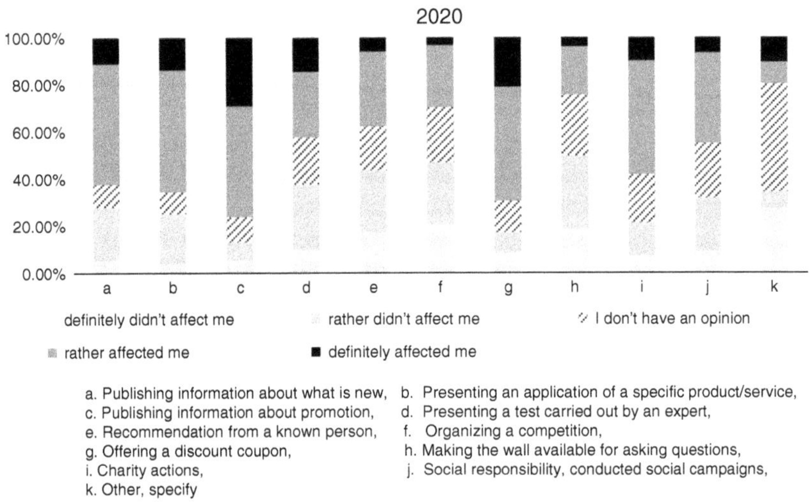

Figure 20.2 Respondents' evaluation of the activities undertaken by enterprises on social media – results of 2020 studies. Source: Own work.

Table 20.1 Mann-Whitney U Test Taking into Account Gender – 2018 and 2020 Study Results

Activities Undertaken by Enterprises on Social Media	*2018*					*2020*				
	Sum of Ranks Female	*Sum of Ranks Male*	*U*	*Z*	*p*	*Sum of Ranks Female*	*Sum of Ranks Male*	*U*	*Z*	*p*
Publishing information about what is new	3681.50	21294.50	2820.50	**–2.44**	**0.01**	9887.50	1588.50	1263.50	1.56	0.12
Presenting an application of a specific product/service	4286.50	20689.50	3425.50	–0.82	0.41	9787.00	1689.00	1364.00	1.05	0.29
Publishing information about promotion	3397.00	21579.00	2536.00	**–3.20**	**0.001**	10009.0	1467.00	1142.00	**2.17**	**0.03**
Presenting a test carried out by an expert	4514.00	20462.00	3653.00	–0.21	0.84	9685.50	1790.50	1465.50	0.55	0.59
Recommendation from a known person	4207.00	20769.00	3346.00	–1.03	0.30	9628.00	1848.00	1523.00	0.26	0.80
Organizing a competition	4413.00	20563.00	3552.00	–0.48	0.63	9715.00	1761.00	1436.00	0.69	0.49
Offering a discount coupon	3716.00	21260.00	2855.00	**–2.35**	**0.02**	9982.50	1493.50	1168.50	**2.03**	**0.04**
Making the wall available for asking questions	4554.50	20421.50	3693.50	–0.10	0.92	9850.00	1626.00	1301.00	1.37	0.17
Charity actions	4554.00	20422.00	3693.00	–0.10	0.92	9930.00	1546.00	1221.00	1.77	0.08
Social responsibility, conducted social campaigns	4307.00	20669.00	3446.00	–0.76	0.45	10140.00	1336.00	1011.00	**2.82**	**0.005**
Other, specify	5079.00	19897.00	3244.00	1.30	0.19	9714.50	1761.50	1436.50	0.69	0.49

Source: Own work.

Table 20.1 Mann-Whitney U test taking into account gender – 2018 and 2020 study results

Based on the data analysis, gender had a significant impact on the differences between the analyzed variables in the following cases:

a. (2018) publishing information about what is new $p = 0.01$, publishing information about promotion $p = 0.001$ and offering a discount coupon $p = 0.02$.
b. (2020) publishing information about promotion $p = 0.03$, offering a discount coupon $p = 0.04$ and social responsibility, conducted social campaigns $p = 0.005$.

In the case of these variables, such activities impacted females' purchasing decisions with a significantly higher strength compared to males. Thus, hypothesis H2 has been confirmed.

At the next stage of the research, the authors made an attempt to identify the most appropriate form of communication with the enterprise via social media according to Gen Zers. The findings showed that the most expected form of communication is Messenger (29.14%), followed by chat with a consultant (21.19%), fanpage (13.25%), redirection to the enterprise's website (11.92%), e-mail (7.95%), LIVE transmission during which a product/service is presented and which provides a chance to express opinions and ask questions online (7.28%), open discussion on the forum (5.30%), and SMS (3.97%) (the respondent was allowed to choose more than one answer).

Discussion

The findings presented in the paper can be selectively compared with concepts and findings from the reviewed literature. The selectivity results from the lack of research findings on the development of trust-based relationships with Gen Zers by enterprises via social media. Djafarova and Bowes (2021) proved that clothing brands' Instagram activities have a strong impact on purchasing behaviors of female Gen Zers, which has a direct influence on impulse purchasing. The authors also suggested that each sex turned to this platform to satisfy different needs; therefore brands should use a different approach to males and females. The impact of gender on Generation Z's purchasing decisions was also confirmed by the findings of the study on the presented group of respondents. Statistical analysis of the collected data has shown that in the analyzed group of respondents selected activities undertaken by companies on social media had significantly larger impact on purchasing decisions of females. However, it is hard to discuss Generation Z gender differentiation specifically in the aspect of trust. Our research has shown that Facebook is the most popular portal among Gen Zers, which is not in line with the research conducted worldwide (Dorsey, 2016; Mintel Group Ltd., 2019).

Accenture Polska along with FashionBiznes.pl conducted a study in Poland in 2019 to analyze consumer behaviors in two age groups: millennials and Generation Z. The aim of the studies was to understand how Generation Z behaves on the Polish market (Accenture, 2019). Generation Z consumers tend to pay more attention to the social stand and responsibility of the companies whose products they buy compared to the older generations. The results of the studies are in line with our findings, as the statistical analysis has shown that socially responsible actions have a stronger impact on females.

In a broader context, the results of the above-mentioned research in Poland can be compared to research findings on young people in Romania (Cerchia, 2016), as both Poland and Romania are post-socialist countries. The research has shown that individuals using social media in Romania are mostly aged 18–34. This age group is specifically targeted by companies with their social media activities, as older people lived most of their lives in Communism and have limited trust in activities conducted via the Internet. The author of the research stressed that most companies use social media to communicate with young customers and do so to increase sales. The conclusions for Romania (Cerchia, 2016) confirm that research into the role of social media in impacting users' purchasing decisions should be concentrated on the youngest customers, including Generation Z, which may lead to increasing brand awareness, gaining popularity among them and winning their trust.

Implications for Theory and Practice

The research conducted by the authors has consequences both for scholars and entrepreneurs/managers. It can provide scholars with new information allowing them to identify factors that impact trust building and, consequently, purchasing decisions made by Gen Zers on social media. Of importance is also the information about gender differences in terms of trust building and impact on purchasing decisions. The research findings can benefit entrepreneurs as well. Social media activities undertaken by entrepreneurs vary in how effectively they impact trust building, and consequently Generation Z's purchasing decisions. Thus, entrepreneurs can use the research findings to invest more financial resources in those activities that are most effective, which will contribute to a more effective capital location. It is also important that enterprises take into account gender-specific behavior differences in trust building and in purchasing decisions, and then identify different communication strategies in order to choose the most effective one, i.e., the strategy that earns trust of both females and males.

Conclusions

The research conducted allowed to achieve the goal, answer the research questions, and confirm the research hypotheses. On the basis of the conducted research it was found that the actions taken by companies in social media influence purchasing decisions of the representatives of generation Z. The activities with the biggest impact on purchasing decisions of representatives of generation Z included: Publication of information about a promotion, offering a discount coupon, explaining the use of a specific product/service, publication of information about new products on offer and charity actions. In the case of the mentioned variables, these activities impacted females' purchasing decisions with a significantly higher strength compared to males. The findings contributed to partially fill the research gap by indicating which actions taken by companies in social media earn the most trust in brand among Gen Zers and contribute most to their purchasing decisions.

The research conducted, which can be regarded as contribution to the existing literature on building trust-based relations with Gen Zers, has certain limitations. Due to the sample size and gender asymmetry, the findings cannot be generalized to entire Generation Z. Future research could not only use a bigger research sample but also a more balanced gender ratio. Moreover, bearing in mind that the use of survey research has some limitations such as, providing only a superficial understanding of the phenomena being studied or a possibility of inaccurate answers given by respondents, the quantitative methods might be supplemented by qualitative ones. Brand trust includes many other factors such as mutual evaluations, feedback, brand experience, etc., which have not been taken into account in the research. The research was conducted in Poland, where enterprises are only learning to build relations with their customers on social media. It also should be mentioned that only one social group, i.e., students, participated in the research. Future research could be conducted in other countries and other social groups to find out whether the same activities undertaken by enterprises on social media earn Generation Z's trust and induce them to make purchasing decisions. Moreover, a more in-depth analysis of enterprises' social media activities could be conducted to identify new activities that can be undertaken on social media and new opportunities they offer. Future research might compare the impact of enterprises' activities on behavior of representatives of different generations on social media.

References

Accenture (2019). Jak kupuje Generacja Z? [How Generation Z shops?]. Retrieved from https://www.accenture.com/_acnmedia/PDF-98/Accenture-raport-2019.pdf#zoom=50

Barclays (2018). Gen Z: Step aside millennials. Retrieved from https://www.investmentbank.barclays.com/our-insights/generation-z.html

Brosdahl, D. J., & Carpenter, J. M. (2011). Shopping orientations of US males: A generational cohort comparison. *Journal of Retailing and Consumer Services*, 6(18), 548–554.

Cerchia, A. E. (2016). Social media – a strategy in developing customer relationship management. *Procedia Economics and Finance*, *39*, 785–790.

Chaudhuri, A., & Holbrook, B. M. (2001). The chain of effects from brand trust and brand affects to brand performance: The role of brand loyalty. *Journal of Marketing*, *65*, 81–93.

Chiu, C. M., Huang, H. Y., & Yen, C. H. (2010). Antecedents of trust in online auctions. *Electronic Commerce Research and Applications*, *9*, 148–159.

Corstjens, M., & Umblijs, A. (2013). The power of evil: The damage of negative social media strongly outweigh positive contributions. *Journal of Advertising Research*, *52*(4), 433–449.

Criteo (2017). Gen Z Report. Retrieved from https://www.criteo.com/wp-content/uploads/2018/05/GenZ-Report.pdf

Delgado-Ballester, E., & Munuera-Alemán, J. L. (2001). Brand trust in the context of consumer loyalty. *European Journal of Marketing*, *35*(11/12), 1238–1258.

Delgado-Ballester, E., & Munuera-Alemán, J. L. (2005). Does brand trust matter to brand equity? *Journal of Product & Brand Management*, *14*(3), 187–196.

Djafarova, E., & Bowes, T. (2021). 'Instagram Made Me Buy It': Generation Z impulse purchases in fashion industry. *Journal of Retailing and Consumer Services*, *59*, 1–9.

Doney, P. M., & Cannon, J. P. (1997). An examination of the nature of trust in buyer-seller relationships. *Journal of Marketing*, *61*(April), 35–51.

Dorsey, J. (2016). iGEN TECH DISRUPTION 2016. National Study on Technology and the generation after millennials. The center for generational kinetics. Retrieved from https://genhq.com/wp-content/uploads/2016/01/iGen-Gen-Z-Tech-Disruption-Research-White-Paper-c-2016-Center-for-Generational-Kinetics.pdf

Erciş, A., Ünal, S., Candan, F. B., & Yıldırım, H. (2012). The effect of brand satisfaction, trust and brand commitment on loyalty and repurchase intentions. *Procedia – Social and Behavioral Sciences*, *58*, 1395–1404.

Ernst & Young (2015). What if the next big disruptor isn't a what but a who? Ernst & Young LLP.

Euromonitor (2018). Generation Z: The next wave of consumers. Retrieved from https://www.euromonitor.com/generation-z-the-next-wave-of-consumers/report Accessed 02 December 2020.

Francis, T., & Hoefel, F. (2018). 'True Gen': Generation Z and its implications for companies. McKinsey&Company. Retrieved from https://www.mckinsey.com/industries/consumer-packaged-goods/our-insights/true-gen-generation-z-and-its-implications-for-companies

Grace, D., & O'Cass, A. (2005). Service branding: Consumer verdicts on service brands. *Journal of Retailing and Consumer Services*, *12*, 125–139.

Gregor, B., & Kubiak, T. (2014). Ocena działań prowadzonych przez firmy w mediach społecznościowych w świetle wyników badań ich użytkowników.

[Evaluation of activities undertaken by companies on social media in the light of the findings of the studies of their users]. *Marketing Instytucji Naukowych i Badawczych*, *4*(14), 3–27.

Habibi, M. R., Laroche, M., & Richard, M.-O. (2014). The roles of brand community and community engagement in building brand trust on social media. *Computers in Human Behavior*, *37*, 152–161.

Jung, N. Y., Kim, S., & Kim, S. (2014). Influence of consumer attitude toward online brand community on revisit intention and brand trust. *Journal of Retailing and Consumer Services*, *21*(4), 581–589.

Kamenidou, I. C., Mamalis, S. A., Pavlidis, S., & Bara, E.-Z. G. (2019). Segmenting the Generation Z Cohort University students based on sustainable food consumption behavior: A preliminary study. *Sustainability*, *11*(3), 837.

Laroche, M., Habibi, M. R., Richard, M.-O., & Sankaranarayanan, R. (2012). The effects of social media based brand communities on brand community markers, value creation practices, brand trust and brand loyalty. *Computers in Human Behavior*, *28*(5), 1755–1767.

Leading Insight. Building business relationships. Retrieved from https://www.leadinginsight.com/business-relationships

Liu, L., Lee, M. K. O., Liu, R., & Chen, J. (2018). Trust transfer in social media brand communities: The role of consumer engagement. *International Journal of Information Management*, *41*, 1–13.

Low, G. S., Lamb, Ch.W. Jr. (2000). The measurement and dimensionality of brand associations. *Journal of Product & Brand Management*, *6*(9), 350–368.

Mandal, K., Otola, I., & Roy, K. (2020). Is trust influencing longer business relationship? An empirical study. In A. Korombel, O. Ławińska, & M. Okręglicka (Eds.), *Proceedings of the 3rd International Conference Contemporary Issues in Theory and Practice of Management* (pp. 189–197). Częstochowa: Politechnika Częstochowska.

Marshall, A. L., & Wolanskyj-Spinner, A. (2020). COVID-19: Challenges and opportunities for educators and Generation Z learners. *Mayo Clinic Proceedings*, *95*(6), 1135–1137.

Maziriri, E. T., Rukuni, T. F., & Chuchu, T. (2020). From selected multi-sensory dimensions to positive word of mouth: Data on what really drives Generation Z consumers to be attached to quick service restaurants in Bloemfontein, South Africa? *Data in Brief*, *32*(106279), 1–8.

McCrindle, M. (2014). *The ABC of XYZ: Understanding the global generations*. Sydney: McCrindle Research Pty Ltd.

Mintel Group Ltd. (2019). Technology Habits of Generation Z – UK – September 2019.

Moorman, Ch., Deshpande, R., & Zaltman, G. (1993). Factors affecting trust in market research relationships. *Journal of Marketing*, *57*, 81–101.

Morgan, M. R., & Hunt, D. S. (1994). The commitment-trust theory of relationships marketing. *Journal of Marketing*, *58*, 20–38.

Moroz, M. (2013). Efekty budowania wizerunku marki poprzez serwisy społecznościowe - badanie opinii internautów pokolenia Y. [Effects of brand image building through social media networks – survey of Generation Y Internet users]. *Studia Ekonomiczne. Zeszyty Naukowe Uniwersytetu Ekonomicznego w Katowicach*, *157*, 123–132.

Muniz, A. M., & O'Guinn, T. C. (2001). Brand community. *Journal of Consumer Research*, *27*(4), 412–432.

Ogilvy, D. (1985). *Ogilvy on advertising*. New York, NY: Vintage Book.

Paliszkiewicz, J. O. (2011). Trust management: Literature review. *Management*, *6*(4), 315–331.

Parasuraman, A., Zeithaml, V. A., & Berry, L. L. (1988). SERVQUAL: A multiple-item scale for measuring consumer perceptions of service quality. *Journal of Retailing*, *64*(1), 12–40.

Petrykowska, J. (2013). Kształtowanie relacji z klientami jako podstawa budowania lojalności. [Customer relationship development as a basis for loyalty building] In A. Wiśniewska (Ed.), *Kształtowanie lojalności konsumenckiej* [Developing customer loyalty] (pp. 6–16). Warszawa: Zeszyty Naukowe, Wyższa Szkoła Promocji.

Powers, T., Advincula, D., Austin, M. S., Graiko, S., & Snyder, J. (2012). Digital and social media in the purchase decision process: A special report from the Advertising Research Foundation. *Journal of Advertising Research*, *52*(4), 479–489.

Priporas, C. V., Stylos, N., & Kamenidou, I. (2020). City image, city brand personality and Generation Z residents' life satisfaction under economic crisis: Predictors of city-related social media engagement. *Journal of Business Research*, *119*, 453–463.

Reast, J. (2005). Brand trust and brand extension acceptance: The relationship. *Journal of Product & Brand Management*, *14*, 4–13.

Seibert, S. A. (2021). Problem-based learning: A strategy to foster Generation Z's critical thinking and perseverance. *Teaching and Learning in Nursing*, 6, 85–88.

Sladek, S., & Grabinger, A. (2018). Gen Z the first generation of the 21st century has arrived! XYZ University. Retrieved from https://www.xyzuniversity.com/wp-content/uploads/2018/08/GenZ_Final-dl1.pdf

Sobel, A. (2020). Client relationship management. From expert for hire to trusted partner. Retrieved from https://andrewsobel.com/client-relationship-management/relationship-management-the-big-picture/

Zehir, C., Sahin, A., Kitapçı, H., & Özsahin, M. (2011). The effects of brand communication and service quality in building brand loyalty through brand trust; the empirical research on global brands. *Procedia Social and Behavioral Sciences*, *24*, 1218–1231.

21 Trust as an Element of Building Brand Relations with Environmental Groups

Agnieszka Werenowska and Ewa Jaska
Warsaw University of Life Sciences (WULS)

Introduction

In the 21st century, trust is one of the most important elements influencing building relationships with environmental groups. Nowadays, the instruments that brands use to form relationships are more accessible and diverse. They can be applied to almost any group of recipients. Digital technologies open up new, previously unknown, and inaccessible opportunities to learn about and meet consumers' needs. World statistics unequivocally show great interest in social media. This phenomenon particularly concerns the generation Z.

The analysis of survey results conducted in the generation Z group showed a regular use of social networking sites such as Facebook, Instagram, and YouTube. The portal that tends to promote products most often is Instagram, where the ads appear when browsing the reports of the profiles followed, as well as during regular scanning of posts with the indication that the post is sponsored. The displayed content is usually tailored to the areas of interest, which makes it easier for the company to reach the potential buyer and creates trust through personalized contact. The aim of the chapter was to present social media as a tool for building trust and managing brand relationships with customers.

The chapter consists of three main sections. In the first, the analysis of the literature on the subject is performed with the introduction of definitions and concepts for the idea of trust. The next one is a presentation of the results of the survey and a discussion related to the topic. The last one covers the conclusions and suggestions related to the conducted research and its limitations.

Literature Review – Defining the Concept of Trust

The subject of trust in literature is taken up by many authors. Each of them draws attention to a different aspect of it. An unequivocal definition of this concept is difficult because it can be classified in various categories (Grudzewski et al., 2009): Disposition, i.e., mental attitude

DOI: 10.4324/9781003165965-21

toward the other party (evaluation, anticipation, expectation), decision, i.e., intention and behavior resulting from entrusting something to the other party. Wereda (2015) defines it as the belief that "the other party shares our values and standards and will also make efforts to act for the benefit of their partner or without causing harm to him". Trust is the probability that "a" worst, they will not knowingly or voluntarily harm you, and at best they will act in your best interest (Gambetta, 1988). Weymouth et al. (2020) also write about trust in the social dimension. Encyclopedically, trusting an object is knowledge or belief that its actions, future condition, or properties will turn out to be in accordance with our wish (mfiles.pl). Trust can also be distinguished by its specific features; for example, Paliszkiewicz (2011) specifies the following: Trust is interpersonal (occurs between specific individuals), trust is voluntary (it results from choice, you cannot force trust in someone), trust involves fear for the honesty of both parties, trust is dynamic and temporary (it develops over time, increases, or is lost) because it is related to action, it is based on experience.

Trust is based on special values, which are observance of legal principles, honesty, and reliability. The problem of trust was a subject of research for scientists as early as the 1960s (Rotter, 1967).

It is worth emphasizing that the original definition of trust referred mainly to interpersonal relationships. Nowadays, attention is paid to trust in the institutional (Wojciechowski, 1962) and technological dimensions. These days, especially the last dimension is the subject of many studies and papers. It was defined in the publications of you (2001), Sztompka (2007), Paliszkiewicz (2013), Lippert and Forman (2006), and Ghanem et al. (2020). The issue of trust in technology is also raised in the works of Ejdys, who formulated the following definition: "Trust in technology is the tendency to rely on technology, resulting from the perceived properties of technology and environmental factors, in the situation of potential risk related to the use of technology, determining intentions regarding the future use of technology. The tendency to rely on technology is primarily due to its functionality, reliability, and support system" (Ejdys, 2017, p. 22).

Materials and Methods

In order to achieve the goal, the method of analyzing the literature on the subject, a diagnostic survey, and scientific observation were used. The source of many conclusions and presented facts were also observations from 2019 to 2020. The research was carried out in two stages. Pilot studies took place at the turn of 2019/2020, and the proper ones in June–July 2020.

The diagnostic survey method enables statistical description and helps to explain some mass phenomena, more important processes occurring

Table 21.1 Research Stages

I	*II*	*III*	*IV*	*V*
Preparation of the survey questionnaire	Testing of the questionnaire among 129 respondents	Verification of the survey questionnaire	Selection of respondents	Conducting research among 278 respondents

Source: Own study.

in large sets on the basis of representative statistical samples (Apanowicz, 2002, p. 70). For the purposes of the research, a questionnaire consisting of 17 questions was used. Most of them were closed questions, and five questions were related to respondent's particulars.

The pilot studies were conducted in an online format. The selection of the research sample was made on the basis of a snowball. The snowball method is a non-random method of selecting respondents for the studied sample. Thanks to the use of this method, it was possible to verify the questionnaire. In the selection of the sample, the non-probability convenience sampling method was used. It should be mentioned that the research was exploratory. In the pilot study 129 respondents participated, 69.8% of whom were women. Among 129 people, 3.9% of respondents did not use social networks. Most of them were representatives of generation Z (80.6%) and 19.4% of generation Y. Most respondents lived in towns with fewer than 10,000 (34.9%) and more than 500,000 inhabitants (34.11%).

The research stages are presented in Table 21.1.

The actual research was carried out in a group of 278 representatives of the generation Z, 97.8% of whom confirmed the fact of using social media.

The research was carried out via an online form. The snowball method was used to select the population. Most of the respondents were women (78.4%). More than half of the respondents (59.7%) completed secondary education, and 37.4% university education. Among them, 74.8% were students and pupils. The respondents lived mainly in cities of more than 500,000 inhabitants (46.8%). The rest were residents of smaller towns (33.8%) and villages (19.4%).

Generation Z grows up and lives in times of dynamic technological development, which results in a number of differences between the generation Z and other generations. In definition, the term generation stands for "all people of a similar age, especially when they have similar experiences, etc." (Bańko, 2007, p. 65). The average generation length is around 20 years. Currently, there are four generations on the market (Hysa, 2016):

- Baby boomers – born between 1945 and 1964, called the generation of demographic explosion and economic boom,
- Generation X – born between 1965 and 1980, grew up in the economic crisis of the 1970s,
- Generation Y – born between 1980 and 1995, commonly known as millennials,
- Generation Z – born after 1995.

The biggest difference between Generation Z and earlier generations is the fact that for the youngest ones, the Internet is an everyday reality, and this also applies to social media. They do not care about stability at work but about escaping from routine (Hysa, 2016).

Members of the Z community feel very comfortable in the virtual environment. They find it very easy to locate and disseminate information found on the Internet, and they strive to find the truth. Generation Z is a generation that has never been before. This young generation significantly exceeds its predecessors in terms of knowledge about the utilization and use of the Internet and mobile devices. The reason for this is in an environment that is completely natural for them. At the same time, it is a generation that cannot function without new technologies (Jaska & Werenowska, 2018).

In this context, it is particularly important to pay attention to the issue of young users' trust in social media (SM). The main aim of the research was to identify those SM that inspire the greatest trust in promotional activities carried out by enterprises and influence the creation of their credible image. Therefore, the respondents were asked for their opinion on whether and how the company should conduct promotional activities in social media in order to build the image of a reliable and trustworthy entity and what a credible and trustworthy advertisement should look like.

Research Results

In order to achieve the survey goals and assumptions defined at the beginning of the research work, the first questions asked were about the use of social media. As many as 97.8% (272) of respondents confirmed that they use SM. A very important element from the point of view of the conducted research was also determining the knowledge of particular SM. The analysis of the pilot studies results shows that there are five most popular portals, namely, Facebook, YouTube, Instagram, Snapchat, and Pinterest. The distribution of responses was very similar in the case of the portals they use most often.

Each respondent could indicate three portals that he uses most often. Facebook was the leader (100%), followed by YouTube (95.97%), and the third place was taken by Instagram (84.68%). Among the portals indicated as frequently used by respondents, there were also: Snapchat

(60.48%), Pinterest (22.58%), Google + (16.94%). The others, namely, Twitter, LinkedIn, Tumblr, Reddit, received less than 10% of responses, the least of which was Tumblr (3.23%).

According to the respondents, promotional activities, including advertising, are also most often noticed on Facebook (42.6%) and Instagram (37.5%). A Mere 19.1% pointed to Youtube and only 0.7% Google+.

In addition to the intensity of social media activities, the credibility of messages addressed to the potential recipient is important because when the effectiveness of this type of activities increases and more durable relationships are created with groups of the environment, an environment of loyal stakeholders is created. In the main research, a question was asked about the credibility of promotional activities on individual social networks and their assessment on a scale of 1 to 5. According to the respondents, the most reliable is Instagram which received 4.01 points on a five-point scale (Figure 21.1). Currently, a lot of marketing campaigns are conducted on this portal in cooperation with influencers, and this is one of the possible reasons why this communication channel is perceived as more credible than the others mentioned. However, it should be noted that promotional activities conducted on Facebook and YouTube also inspire confidence (3.94 points and 3.82 points, respectively). On the other hand, Snapchat turned out to be the least reliable and trustworthy. This may be due to the fact this website is currently used by fewer people compared to the other websites mentioned in this question.

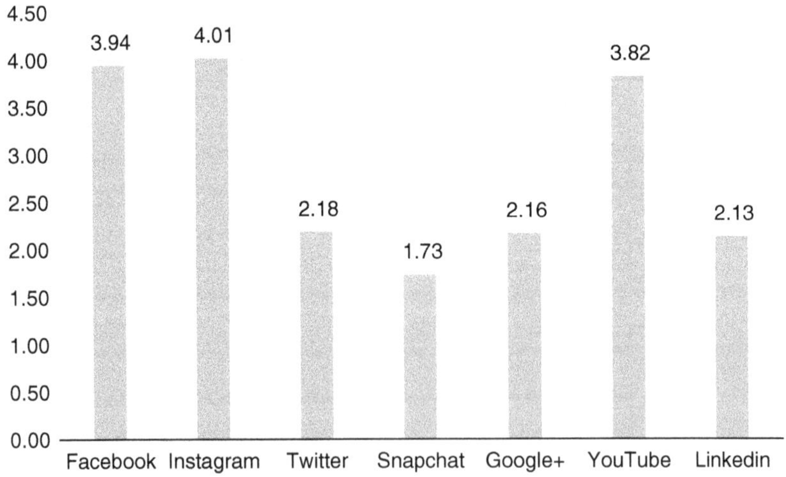

Figure 21.1 Credibility of the company's promotional activities on individual social networks. Source: Own study.

Despite the fact that the respondents, among the goals of using social media, mentioned in the first-place dialogue with friends and obtaining information, they also pointed to the business goal and stated that companies should use social media in promotional activities and building relationships with groups around them. This answer was given by 64.7% of the respondents, and the opposite opinion was given by 7.4% of the respondents. Others were unable to specify their opinion on this matter.

An important issue is the tendency of Internet users to look for information after seeing an advertisement of an unfamiliar brand. It turns out that as many as 75% of respondents look for such information, but only when the advertisement attracts their attention. It is worth noting that social media were mentioned in the first place as sources of obtaining in-depth information, as credible media. Almost every fourth respondent stated that he is not influenced by advertising.

One of the dimensions of credible and trustworthy advertising is its influence on purchasing decisions. According to the survey, almost 60% of respondents indicated that after seeing an advertisement, they sometimes purchase the advertised product. Of course, there are also people who show an attitude of negating advertisements and do not buy advertised products (27.2%). Only a small group of respondents admitted that they often succumb to advertising (4.4%). In the surveyed group, 8.8% did not have an opinion in this regard.

According to the respondents, the advertisement should first of all interest the recipient so that it is perceived as a reliable and trustworthy message. This feature was most often mentioned in the first place on a 5-point scale (4.42 points). The short formula (3.99 points), transparency, and colors (3.93 points) were mentioned in the second and third places. A clear logo was not an important trust-building feature (3.4 points). It was assessed that properly selected music has the smallest impact on creating trust towards the brand (3.27 points).

The respondents were exceptionally unanimous as to the impact of the company's presence in social media on creating the image of a trustworthy company. More than half of the respondents said definitely yes (51.1%), and 45.3% said yes. Such an opinion is more and more often presented in the literature on the subject, and it is noted that today a company's position on the market is very much dependent on how it runs its social media.

The respondents considered the possibility of acquiring customers (73.4%), and thus an increase in sales (59.7%), as the most important result of conducting promotional activities (Figure 21.2). More than half of them considered the increase in the company's recognition and building its credible image and trust with stakeholder groups as a significant result. Banners appearing on social media and on websites were considered the most reliable advertising tool (42.4%). Much fewer indications were for TV advertising (28.1%) and product placement (28.1%).

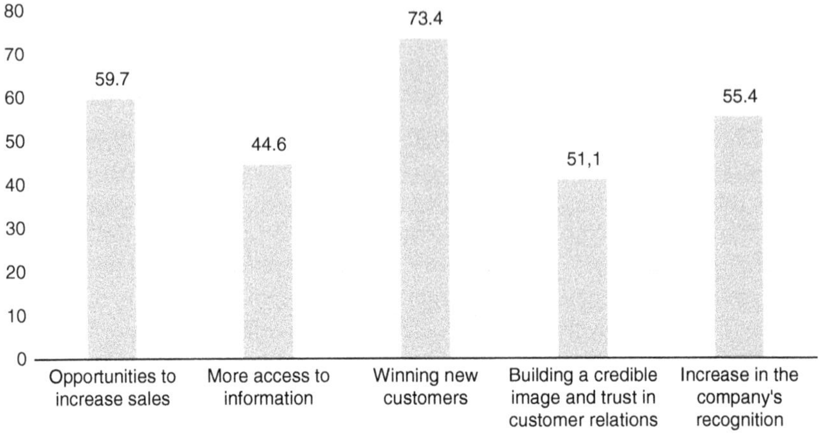

Figure 21.2 The effects of conducting promotional activities by companies in social media [%] *the respondents could choose more than 1 answer. Source: Own study.

Discussion

Nowadays, the presence of brands in virtual space, including in social media, has become a necessity. They are used on very different levels, especially in building relationships with customers. They are popular among the youngest customers who belong to the generation Z.

The development of social media made that today every company that wants to succeed and gain new customers must conduct its information and image policy also in virtual space. Creating a credible space for communicating with target groups has become an indispensable element of entrepreneurial activity. Trust and security in social media are one of the factors influencing the accomplishment of online transactions. The importance of this element is emphasized in the studies of Frąckiewicz (2011), Tongora (2014), Gradzi (2017), and Chmielarz and Parys (2018). Veloutsou (2015), in her research, indicated the strength of a positive relationship with the brand, which mediates between trust, satisfaction, and attitude the brand.

This is the reality of the representatives of generation Z, which is the subject of many scientists' research in order to analyze their behavior in various social situations and, at the same time, to predict it in situations, e.g., making various life decisions. The subject was dealt with, among others, by Lechowicz and Pikuła (2013), Espinoza (2016), Poláková and Klímová (2019), and Magano et al. (2020).

According to statista.com, approximately 50% of the Polish population used social networking sites in January 2020 (Statista, 2020).

Social media websites already have over 3.5 billion of users, which is about 45% of the world's population. The largest group of people using social media are men aged 25 to 34, which accounts for as much as 19%. The average time spent on the websites is 2 hr and 16 min (Digital Report, 2019).

Social media are a source of a lot of information about a potential consumer, e.g., what he is interested in, what genre of music he listens to most often; thanks to that, the offer can be adapted to the scope of his expectations. It is not surprising then that more and more companies are transferring their marketing activities to the Internet and implementing strategies for promoting products through social media. The most popular social networks according to the criterion of active monthly users, active accounts, ads, or unique visitors are (Wearsocial, 2020):

- Facebook – 2,449 million,
- YouTube – 2,000 million,
- WhatsApp – 1,600 million,
- Messenger – 1,300 million,
- Instagram – 1,000 million.

Just a few years ago, a continuous increase in the number of users from the Y and Z generations was observed. In September 2019, there were 18,300,000 FC users in Poland, and in September 2020, there were already 19,950,000 (Users in Poland, 2020). In January 2020, 19 million users of Social Media were recorded in Poland. Their number increased by 1.4 million (+7.8%) from April 2019 to January 2020 (Digital Report, 2020).

There is a decline in Facebook users, especially among young users. More than two billion people use it every month, which is almost a third of the world's population. The data of the Interaktywnie.com report show that only 51% of American teenagers (13–17 years old) declare using this platform, which is a decrease compared to 71% in 2015 (Raport media społecznościowe, 2019).

The Dentsu Aegis Network report (2019) on the Digital Society Index survey shows that in 2019, social media interest among people of the generation Z decreased. It turned out that one-fifth of users in this age group decided to resign from active participation in social media, and one-third loses confidence in them and restricts access to sensitive information. More than half (58%) of the respondents reported the lack of trust in technology companies and the ways in which they utilize users' personal data (Socialpress, 2020).

Conclusions

The conducted survey confirmed the popularity of social media among the representatives of generation Z. The main aim of the research was to identify those SM that inspire the greatest trust in promotional activities carried out by enterprises and contribute to the creation of a credible image. Despite the enormous popularity of Facebook, Instagram is the most trusted portal in promotional campaigns. Promotional activities carried out with the use of this communication channel greatly affect the creation of the image of a reliable entity. According to the respondents, advertising is also an important instrument for creating credibility and building trust, but this type of message should first of all interest the recipient.

In summary, Instagram inspires the greatest trust in promotional activities of companies among the representatives of the generation Z, and this is mainly the result of the fact that currently many marketing campaigns are conducted on this portal in cooperation with influencers, and this is one of the possible reasons why this channel of communication is perceived as more reliable than the others mentioned. The analysis of the research results confirmed that Instagram is perceived as the most credible and trustworthy medium. This is a particularly important practical indication for brands that gather around them stakeholders from the generation Z. Knowledge about the preferred communication channels is key to build trust and relationships with customers.

The results of the conducted research are a valuable source of information for enterprises targeting young stakeholders from the generation Z group. The authors are aware of the limitations of the presented study. One of the most important is the relatively small size of the research group and its limitation to Polish SM users only. The research should be continued in the future and should take into account changes in the use of social media and include representatives of generation Y and other age groups.

References

Apanowicz, J. (2002). *Metodologia ogólna [General methodology]*. Gdynia, PL: Wydawnictwo "BERNARDINUM".

Bańko, M. (2007). *Słownik Języka Polskiego [Polish Language Dictionary]*. Warszawa, PL: Wydawnictwo Naukowe PWN.

Chmielarz, W., & Parys, T. (2018). Wykorzystanie technologii mobilnych w handlu elektronicznym [The use of mobile technology in e-comerce]. *Annales Universitatis Mariae Curie – Skłodowska Lublin – Polonia*, section H, 2, 17–30.

Dentsu Aegis Network Report (2019). Retrieved from DAN-AdSpend-June-2019_Comp.pdf (kc-usercontent.com)

Digital Report (2019). Retrieved from https://wearesocial.com/global-digital-report-2019

Digital Report (2020). Retrieved from https://datareportal.com/reports/digital-2020-poland

Ejdys, J. (2017). Determinanty zaufania do technologii [Determinants of trust in technology]. *Przegląd Organizacji*, *12*, 20–27.

Espinoza, Ch., (2016). *Milenialsi w pracy [Millenniums at work]*. Warszawa, PL: Studio EMKA.

Frąckiewicz E. (2011). Aktywność zakupowa klientów w sieci i jej determinanty [Purchasing activity of customers in the network and its determinants]. *Studies & Proceedings of Polish Association for Knowledge Management*, *51*, 5–16.

Gambetta, D. (1988). Can we trust trust? In D. Gambeta (Ed.), *Trust: making and breaking cooperative relations* (pp. 213–237). Oxford: Basil Blackwell.

Ghanem, M., Elshaer, I., & Shaker, A. (2020). The successful adoption of IS in the tourism public sector: the mediating effect of employees' trust, *Sustainability*, *2*(9), 3877. https://doi.org/10.3390/su12093877.

Gradzi, D. (2017). Bezpieczeństwo płatności elektronicznych jako element cyberbezpieczeństwa państwa – przegląd regulacji prawnych [Security of electronic payments as part of state cyber-security – review of legal regulations]. *Przegląd Bezpieczeństwa Wewnętrznego*, *9*(16), 38–54.

Grudzewski, W. M., Hejduk, I. K., Sankowska, A., & Wańtuchowicz, M. (2009). *Zarządzanie zaufaniem w przedsiębiorstwie [Managing trust in the company]*. Kraków, PL: Oficyna Wolters Kluwer Business.

Hysa, B. (2016). Zarządzanie Różnorodnością Pokoleniową [Managing Generational Diversity] *Zeszyty Naukowe. Organizacja i Zarządzanie*, *97*, 385–398.

Jaska, E., & Werenowska, A. (2018). Chatbots as a new communication tool for enterprises and clients. In M. Podkowińska (ed.), *Communication. Education. Culture*. University of Presov. SL: Pro Communio.

Lechowicz, N., & Pikuła, D. (2013). Determinanty kształtujące nowe pokolenia oraz ich implikacje dla współczesnego świata [Determinants shaping new generations and their implications for the modern world]. *Rynek – Społeczeństwo – Kultura*, *3*(7), 17–23.

Lippert, S. K., & Forman, H. (2006). A supply chain study of technology trust and antecedents to technology Interna-lization consequences. *International Journal of Physical Distribution & Logistics Management*, *36*(4), 271–288.

Magano, J., Silva, C., Figueiredo, C., Vitória, A., Nogueira T., & Pimenta Dinis, M. A. (2020). Generation Z: Fitting project management soft skills competencies—A mixed-method approach. *Education Sciences*, *10*(7), 187.1 0.3390/educsci10070187

Paliszkiewicz, J. (2011). Orientacja na zaufanie w przedsiębiorstwach [Trust orientation in companies]. Retrieved from http://ptzp.org.pl/files/konferencje/kzz/artyk_pdf_2011/082.pdf

Paliszkiewicz, J. (2013). *Zaufanie w zarządzaniu [Trust in management]*. Warszawa, PL: Wydawnictwo Naukowe PWN.

Poláková, P., & Klímová, B. (2019). Mobile technology and Generation Z in the English language classroom—A preliminary study. CALO. *Education Sciences*, *9*(3), 203. https://doi.org/10.3390/educsci9030203

Raport media społecznościowe (2019). Retrieved from https://interaktywnie.com/biznes/artykuly/raporty-interaktywnie-com/raport-media-spolecznosciowe-2019

Rotter, J. B. (1967). A new scale for the measurement of interpersonal trust. *Journal of Personality*, *35*(4), 651–665.

Socialpress (2020). Retrieved from https://socialpress.pl/2020/08/coraz-wiecej-osob-z-pokolenia-z-dezaktywuje-swoje-konta-w-mediach-spolecznosciowych

Statista (2020). Retrieved from https://www.statista.com/statistics/282846/regular-social-networking-usage-penetration-worldwide-by-country/

Sztompka, P. (2007). *Zaufanie. Fundament społeczeństwa [Trust. The foundation of socjety]*. Kraków. PL: Znak

Tongora, E. F. (2014). E-commerce obstacles & security for online payment transaction in Tanzania. *Zeszyty Naukowe Uniwersytetu Szczecińskiego*. Ekonomiczne Problemy Usług, *12*(1), 207–218.

Users in Poland (2020). Retrieved from https://napoleoncat.com/stats/facebook-users-in-poland/2020/09

Wearsocial (2020). Retrieved from https://wearesocial-net.s3.amazonaws.com/uk/wp-content/uploads/sites/2/2020/01/11-Social-Platform-Ranking-%E2%80%93-DataReportal-Digital-2020-Global-Digital-Overview-Slide-95.png

Wereda, W. (2015). Orientacja na zaufanie a budowanie relacji [Trust orientation and relationship building]. *Research Papers of Wrocław University of Economics* (376), 216–232.

Weymouth, R., Hartz-Karp, J., & Marinova, D. (2020). Repairing political trust for practical sustainability. *Sustainability*, *12*(17),7055.

Wojciechowski, M. (1962). Zaufanie instytucjonalne w kontekście ustawowej zasady zaufania jednostki do państwa [Institutional trust in the context of the statutory principle of individual trust in the state]. *Ruch Prawniczy, Ekonomiczny i Socjologiczny*, *74*(2), 5–17.

Veloutsou, C. (2015). Brand evaluation, satisfaction and trust as predictors of brand loyalty: The mediator-moderator effect of brand relationships. *Journal of Consumer Marketing*, *32*(6), 405–421.

Index

For Product Safety Concerns and Information please contact our EU
representative GPSR@taylorandfrancis.com
Taylor & Francis Verlag GmbH, Kaufingerstraße 24, 80331 München, Germany

www.ingramcontent.com/pod-product-compliance
Ingram Content Group UK Ltd.
Pitfield, Milton Keynes, MK11 3LW, UK
UKHW022349190926
475702UK00015B/2196
* 9 7 8 0 3 6 7 7 6 2 1 8 6 *